THE ARCHITECTURE OF
GEORGE PACE

THE ARCHITECTURE OF

GEORGE PACE

CVO MA FSA FR Hist.S FRIBA

1915-75

PETER G. PACE

AA Dipl. ARIBA

B.T. BATSFORD LIMITED · LONDON

ACKNOWLEDGEMENTS:

The author is indebted to:

The Revd Canon F. W. Dillistone, DD, former Dean of Liverpool, Fellow Emeritus of Oriel College, Oxford, Canon Emeritus of Liverpool Cathedral; and the Right Reverend and Right Hon. Lord Coggan of Canterbury and Sissinghurst, former Bishop of Bradford, Archbishop of York, and Archbishop of Canterbury; for early and continued encouragement.

Prof. A. Peter Fawcett BA (Hons) (Arch.), (Manc.) Architect, RIBA, MRIAI, of the Department of Architecture and Planning, the Queen's University of Belfast; Dr Derek Linstrum, Dip. Arch., Ph.D, FSA, RIBA, Radcliffe Reader in Architectural History and Conservation, Director of Conservation Study, Institute of Advanced Architectural Studies, University of York; Dr Pat Nuttgens CBE, MA, Ph.D, Dr Univ., ARIBA, Honorary Professor in the University of York, Past Director Leeds Polytechnic, broadcaster and architectural historian; Prof. Jack Anderson DA (Edin.), FRIAS, MSIAD, RIBA, Partner-Bickerdike, Allen Partners; Prof. Douglass Wise OBE, B.Arch., Dip.TP, RIBA, Director of Institute of Advanced Architectural Studies, University of York; John Hutchinson, FSA, FR Hist.S, FSAI, FSA (Scot.), Architectural Assistant to George Pace and architectural historian; Ronald G. Sims, Dipl. Arch., RIBA, Associate and later Partner to George Pace; and Jane Hatcher BA, M. Phil., Architectural Historian; for help and guidance.

My mother, Mrs I. F. C. Pace, for invaluable encouragement and support; Mrs B. Helps, former secretary to George Pace, for so willingly typing the manuscripts; Fred Spencer, photographer, who graciously endured my interference with his Art, together with R. G. Sims and J. Kershaw for many other fine photographs; the many Deans, Vicars and laymen of the Church of England who kindly opened their buildings and records; the contractors, craftsmen and artists mentioned in the text who contributed testimonials and other valuable first-hand information.

All works illustrated in this book, including drawings, are by George Pace, unless otherwise indicated.

The author gratefully acknowledges generous financial support from:

RIBA Research Award
Sheldon Memorial Trust
Marc Fitch Fund

Book designed by Peter G. Pace in collaboration with B.T. Batsford Ltd.

Front cover illustration: Llandaff Cathedral: the Great Restoration 1949–64

Half-title: St George's Chapel, Windsor Castle, King George VI Memorial Chapel: wooden prototype finial to wrought-iron entrance screen, painted matt black and gilded 1968

1 (*Frontispiece*): Llandaff Cathedral: George Pace on the scaffold during the restoration of the Prichard spire, 7 March 1955

2 (*Title-page*): The family coat of arms granted to George Pace as Commander of the Victorian Order (CVO) for services to Her Majesty The Queen, 1971

© Peter G. Pace 1990

First published 1990

ISBN 0 7134 6273 6

Typeset by Servis Filmsetting Ltd, Manchester

and printed in Great Britain by
Courier International, Tiptree, Essex
for the Publisher
B.T. Batsford Ltd
4 Fitzhardinge Street
London W1H 0AH

CONTENTS

FOREWORD

*The Right Reverend and Right Hon. Lord Coggan
of Canterbury and Sissinghurst*

One of the best-known lines of the poet Rupert Brooke runs: 'Now God be thanked Who has matched us with His hour.' God, it would seem, has a way of doing that frequently in the course of history. He certainly did it in the case of George Pace. The years of his most powerful and influential work covered a period when the Church's understanding of worship and its expression in liturgy were undergoing something of a reformation in Britain and far beyond. Worship, the primary function of the Church, was seen anew to be the offering of the *whole* people of God, not least in its central act of the Eucharist. The 'Parish and People' movement had done much to alert the Church, and the period of 'experimental services' (leading to the publishing of the Alternative Service Book, 1980) saw the natural expression of the new (or renewed) understanding. Greater freedom in worship, symbolized by the bringing of the altar down from the east end of the church to a more central position, demanded new arrangements in the church's building and furnishing. No detail was too small for George Pace's attention and care. The designing of new church buildings gave him welcome opportunity to express his genius. He was God's man for the hour.

This book will give abundant evidence of his skill as architect and aesthete; of his handling of brick and stone and concrete; of his marrying of modern techniques and design to ancient structures sacred and secular. Many more knowledgeable than I have already written about these things; others will do so, for his work will live.

I wish to make the point that his success was due not only to his mastery of his craft and to his technical expertise, but also to the fact that his work proceeded from his own Christian faith and his theological thinking.

When he created the Chapel in the grounds of Scargill House, in the depths of the lovely Yorkshire countryside, he said to a friend that he wanted the Chapel 'to grow out of the ground'. It did so with remarkable intimacy. It is a tribute in stone and wood to a man whose architecture *grew out of the ground* of his own religion, and of his own theological and liturgical knowledge and sensitivity. His church buildings are worshipful because he worshipped.

The quantity of his work is shown in this book; its range is hard to believe. The quality of his work is better experienced than written about.

In All Saints' Church in North Street, York, the city of George Pace's adoption and love, there is a monument to John Etty, the distinguished seventeenth-century York craftsman:

His Art was great, his Industry no less.
What one projected, ye other brought to pass.

The words might equally well have been written about George Pace.

Si monumentum requiris, circumspice – words of another architect, Sir Christopher Wren. His *monumentum* was St Paul's Cathedral. George Pace's *monumentum* can be found in distinctive buildings in many parts of these islands and abroad, and in the memories of a multitude of men and women who were privileged to know him (and I was one of them) and of a smaller number who were proud to be his disciples.

Laus Deo

4

PREFACE

Professor A. Peter Fawcett
BA(Hons) (Arch.), (Manc.), Architect, RIBA,
MRIAI, *The Department of Architecture and
Planning, The Queen's University, Belfast*

The Festival of Britain of 1951 was a watershed in the history of modern architecture in Britain; here at last was a new architecture with a popular face – an architecture for everyman. Unfortunately, in retrospect, the three decades following that event were turbulent years for British architecture: a wholesale rejection of a traditional architectural language inherited from the Arts and Crafts movement (at which the better practitioners excelled), and the adoption of continental modernism in its more brutal forms, produced an architecture for the 1960s which alienated and betrayed a public whose optimism had been fuelled by the Festival and the buildings it spawned. More recently, the reaction to the excesses of the 1960s have not been auspicious; an escape into vernacular forms or into the applied decorative effects of so-called Post-Modernism seem an effete response to the need for an architecture truly representative of the end of the twentieth century.

However, when the traumas of these thirty years are re-assessed, the work of one architect, because of its constancy, will shine out like a beacon. This architect is George Pace. Pace, uniquely for prominent architects of the period, successfully straddled that interface between tradition and modernism in a highly effective distillation of both. He was most certainly the doyen of ecclesiastical architects from the period, his work being on the one hand an extension of Lethaby and Prior, and yet at the same time embracing modernism, a remarkable demonstration that the two traditions were compatible and that fundamentally their aims were common.

Like Lethaby and Prior, Pace showed an immense understanding of materials and building techniques, always the soundest basis of any architectural vocabulary, and this must account for the integrity of his buildings. Unlike the work of many of his contemporaries, his architecture never regresses into mannerism nor, worse still, relies on a thin historicism which has been the plight of so many contemporary ecclesiastical architects. Also like Lethaby and Prior, Pace embraced architecture at all levels; the campanile at Chester and particularly his sadly abortive scheme for Sheffield Cathedral in 1957 are master works of monumental scale but the same care is bestowed on the communion rail or lectern of a minor parish church.

Lethaby and Prior have been mentioned as obvious sources for Pace's architectural vocabulary. Lethaby wrote effectively but built little, and likewise Prior was less than prolific. Pace, however, over a long and significant period in the development of 'modern' architecture in Britain produced a prodigious volume of work from the insertion of new furnishings for medieval churches to new buildings of large scale. All demonstrate immense care, verve, wit and a sensitivity to context. As we approach the end of this century it is these very ingredients of our architecture to which designers are increasingly addressing themselves; Pace's work offers many lessons and these alone are ample justification for a full appraisal of his work.

6

OPPOSITE
5 Chester Cathedral; crossing ceiling decoration 1973 – gilding on red background

6 Sheffield Cathedral; one of many schemes George Pace put forward for the completion of the Cathedral, 1956–61. Ink, charcoal and colour wax crayon, on coarse paper 14 x 19in (35.5 x 48.3cm) undated

Christ College Brecon
Extensions as seen from west
end of ruined Nave.

10

BIOGRAPHICAL INTRODUCTION

The strict, religious, family atmosphere in which George Pace grew up provided a strong base on which he stood solidly for the rest of his life; but as to whether exposure to religion was responsible for his overwhelming desire to become an Ecclesiastical Architect from the age of 11,[1] one can only surmise.

George Gaze Pace was born in Croydon, Surrey on 31 December 1915, the elder son of George Henry Pace (1877–1940) and his wife, Barbara Alice Gaze (1874–1958). The Edwardian era had arrived, but his parents still retained an extreme Victorian moral outlook, and though this must have influenced a great deal of his later thinking, they had no wish to stifle his creative urge; indeed they actively encouraged its development.

George Pace saw architecture as a form of art, and found little to interest him in his father's position of Head Accountant in a shipping firm in the City. His younger brother Norman, on the other hand, chose to follow in his father's footsteps. Instead, George spent much of his boyhood sketching and visiting churches.

Fortunately his father nurtured a significant talent for watercolour painting and encouraged both of his sons to accompany him at weekends on bicycle trips into the Surrey and Kent countryside, where they studied the picturesque regional vernacular buildings and landscape.

He grew to know more of architecture from his uncle, who had worked under Mackintosh, and also from an older cousin who, though interested in ancient buildings, designed many modern Art Deco cinemas. By coincidence, both George Pace and his cousin became Fellows of the Society of Antiquaries on the same day.

After a private education[2] he became articled to a firm of architects, James Ransome and Cootes of London, and attended evening lessons at the Department of Architecture, Regent Street Polytechnic, London. Here a fellow student, William Lockett (whom he was to meet again later at Liverpool)[3] recalls him as a 'quiet thoughtful student and although industrious [he] preferred to let his ideas mature slowly'.

William Lockett also observed that George's interests tended to differ from those of his fellows, for, 'whilst most of the students enthused about Lloyd Wright or Gropius, George was more concerned with the ideas of William Morris, Lethaby and Burges', and he disclosed that

while many of the Polytechnic students hurriedly crossed Regent Street to follow the progress of the new BBC building, George would turn round the

8

8 Unidentified cottage, probably in Surrey or Kent – a typical watercolour by George Pace's father, G. H. Pace – 1911. 7 × 10in (17.8 × 25.4cm)

OPPOSITE
7 Unexecuted design for extensions to Christ's College Chapel, Brecon, 1965. Indian ink and felt-tip – actual size

corner into Margaret Street to study Butterfield's masterpiece.[4]

This interest in unfashionable architects associated with ecclesiastical architecture serves to underline his single-minded pre-occupation with the Church; but there is also evidence to confirm a quiet, deep-seated interest in the principles and aesthetics of the new architecture of the Modern Movement.

His design project work, for example, consistently illustrates a good grasp of modern architecture – indeed, one would have difficulty at this stage in identifying his work as being significantly different from those of his own contemporaries.[5]

In later years we find George Pace admitting to having held a great respect for Gropius, the 'instigator of the New Style', the man 'who determined the character of Modern Architecture', but at the same time he concluded that 'Modern Architecture is not, and cannot be naturally, in the service of the Church,'[6] and throughout his career he sought material from elsewhere for much of his inspiration.

Medieval Gothic architecture was one of the more important of these sources, and his student studies on the subject proved invaluable, both in his later design work and in his conservation work to existing buildings. Over the two year period between 1935 and 1937, in his spare time he

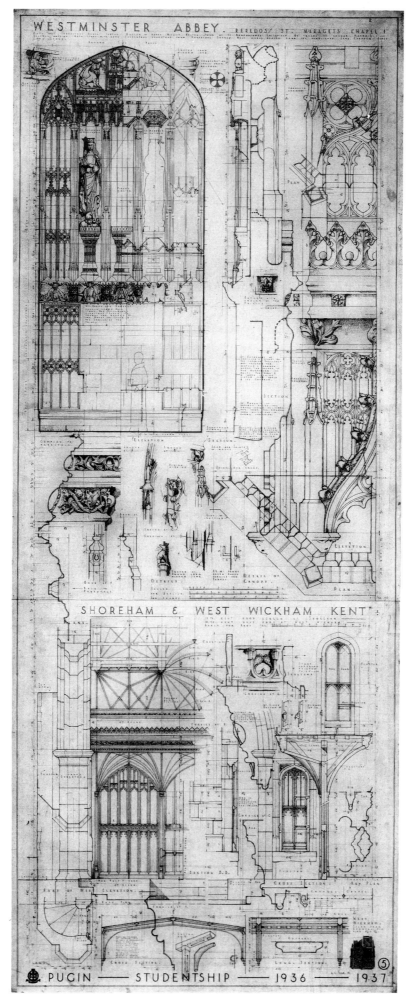

9 *and* **10** The Pugin Studentship drawings, 1936–37. Two from a set of eight measured drawings forming the winning entry

9 Drawing in pencil with part colour wash, 27 × 67in (68.6 × 170.2cm)

10 Drawing in pencil
with part colour wash,
26 × 74in (66 × 188cm)

11

prepared his entry for the Pugin Studentship – a bi-annual competition for the study of Medieval Architecture open to architectural students world-wide. The study took the form of measured drawings (ILLUSTS 9 and 10),[7] a common enough practice in those days as a glance at contemporary Architectural Association sketch books shows.[8]

Pace's drawings range from the roofs, chancel screens and lych-gates of country churches, to a reredos in Westminster Abbey.[9] All display a deep understanding of the principles of Gothic architecture, and an exceptional flair for freehand, pencil draughtsmanship.

His boyhood studies of those churches of Surrey and Kent figure prominently alongside newly discovered churches of Norfolk; he also explored the area in which his mother's family roots lay – Lincolnshire, Northamptonshire and Cambridgeshire.[10] He included Fotheringhay in his travels, where in addition to the wonders of fifteenth-century aisles and a thirteenth-century porch, the 'aesthetic wildness' of the churchyard left an indelible impression on him, for he cites this example in later years[11] when defending 'that special and particularly lovely thing: the English Country Churchyard',[12] observing that 'the wind rippling through the long grass at, say, Fotheringhay or Corcomroes Abbey produces feelings and atmosphere of very special quality and delight'.[13]

Nearby, at Peterborough Cathedral, the repair work to the shattered fan vaults of the New Building, by the consultant architect Leslie Moore (closely related to that 'great but unsung church architect' Temple Lushington Moore),[14] provided a fortuitous opportunity to measure the building from the scaffolding. 'I remember seeing this work in progress,' he recalled many years later when he himself was Consultant Architect to the Cathedral, 'marvelling at the techniques and learning an enormous amount.'[15]

Whether through chance or by intention, the architects' offices in which he worked before qualifying made no specialization in church work. In 1935 he joined Darcy Braddell and H. Deane where he gained experience of a wide variety of buildings, ranging from a Ladies' Club to new housing, and alterations to country houses.[16]

In his card index record of work at this time, a somewhat precocious attitude, no surprise in a confident young student, now surfaces – 'Darcy [Braddell] used to do the designs, but generally I managed to keep the fussiest detail from being perpetrated,' he confides.

In 1938, the year of his finals, he changed office again, this time to the architects Pite, Son and Fairweather, in Carteret Street, London; here he later designed his first church, though not before cutting his teeth on fire stations and a number of hospitals.

As a student, George Pace excelled. In 1934 he won the John Tirantiti prize for design, and in 1937 the Pugin studentship fell to him. In 1938 he became a Robert Mitchell Gold Medallist, and in his sixth year at the Regent Street Polytechnic he won the Bronze Medal.

In 1939, in his final examinations, he gained first place, winning, to his great joy, the RIBA Asphitel prize as the best architectural student in England. This characteristic need to excel in everything remained with him to the point of obsession, throughout his life.

Dedication to work left him little time for leisure, or social activities, and to his surprise – as much as anybody else's – on a rare holiday horse-riding in Norfolk in 1938, he met and fell in love with Ina Florence Catherine Jones (b. 1915), the 23-year-old daughter of a London iron and steel exporter, Harvey Sheridan Jones (1874–1953) and his second wife, Ina Nellie Scott (1880–1930). Within six weeks they had become engaged.

Though their backgrounds differed they proved to be well suited. They shared an interest in architecture, but more importantly his fiancée understood from her own short experience as a ballet dancer the implications of a life of dedication.[17] Without someone willing to accept the inevitable sacrifices and to provide the necessary support, George Pace might well have trodden a very different path.

War time

The early years of the Second World War caused little disruption to George's life. Admittedly, talk of cancelling his final examinations must have been

11 Ina Jones shortly before her engagement to George Pace in 1939

12

12 The restorers of Llandaff Cathedral: *from left to right* – The Rt Revd Glyn Simon, Bishop of Llandaff; George Pace, architect to Llandaff Cathedral; and The Very Revd Eryl S. Thomas, Dean of Llandaff Cathedral; in the Deanery Garden, Llandaff, about 1962

13 Typical 'York' safe from St Cuthbert's Church, Peasholme Green, York; used to illustrate an article in the *Architectural Review*, April 1944

alarming, and he did have to use every ounce of ingenuity to convince the authorities that the construction of Christ Church, Orpington, Kent (1939–40) (ILLUST. 14), designed largely by him whilst working with Pite, Son and Fairweather, should be allowed to continue, his ingenious argument being that the crypt could assume the guise of an air-raid shelter!

Frustration set in when one of the partners – Mr Fairweather – placed severe restraint on this, his first church design, particularly to the interior, to such an extent that he declared sadly:

> I would not have anything further to do with it. The font is based on my sketch. I intended the roofs to be painted in vivid colours. The furniture is not my work.[18]

However, the church is interesting for its display of steeply pointed Gothic arches rising from near floor level. These are not dissimilar to Prior's transverse arches at Roker, 1907, or to those he admired at the west end of Edward Brantwood Maufe's Guildford Cathedral[19] (then under construction close by). Such arches re-appear in his own later work, for example Nether Poppleton Lych-gate (1949) (ILLUST. 15) and Christ Church,

Fulwood, Sheffield (1954) (ILLUST. 71).

This brief, though valuable association with Pite, Son and Fairweather, declined, and by October 1939 he had taken up a full-time teaching appointment at his old seat of learning, The Regent Street Polytechnic, moving as co-teacher of the first year students through to the fourth year students, until his army call-up in 1941. Life then inevitably, and dramatically, changed for him. Now, quite abruptly, came an end of commuting to a polytechnic whose authorities had refused to evacuate; an end to his trips into London – sometimes during the blitz – to meet his fiancée (who worked in a Reserved Occupation with a firm of Lloyds Brokers during the day, and was attached to a nursing unit at night); and an end to home life with parents in Croydon, a town lying dangerously in the path of German bombers.

With what must have been very mixed feelings, but with few illusions, at the age of 25 he enlisted in the ITC – The Queen's Regiment at Guildford. Though he enjoyed the 'roaring about on a motorcycle' as he put it, he derived little excitement from firing blanks on training exercises, preferring to keep his rifle unused and clean, making more time for sketching and writing!

14 Christ Church, Orpington, Kent – begun 1939. Designed largely by George Pace whilst working for the London architects Pite, Son and Fairweather

15 Nether Poppleton, near York; lychgate 1949. Post-war scarcity of materials precluded the use of much wood. The shape was intentionally modelled by George Pace on the adjacent aisled barn

Nothing would have prevented him from fighting for his country, his patriotism being beyond doubt, but the prospect of life in the army did not appeal. Within the limited choice facing him, he saw one place where he could make good use of his knowledge and enthusiasm – The Royal Engineers. From a training course for military Foremen of Works, he found himself in Essex building block-houses and pill-boxes with the 21st Army Tank Brigade, later making a fortuitous move to Lavenham where he was amongst the beloved East Anglian churches of his youth.

By now, in the second year of their engagement, and with the most uncertain of futures confronting them, he and his fiancée determined to marry as soon as the army would allow. After three false starts, on 23 November 1941, George Pace and Ina Jones were married in the bomb-damaged Lady Chapel in the Cathedral of St Saviour, Southwark, London, a frequent meeting place of theirs from earlier years.

Unlike other officers on his course Pace was not posted abroad, but at the end of 1941 he was moved north, first to Ripon on another training course, then to Headquarters Lands Branch Northern Command at York to take up the appointment of Assistant Land Agent Valuer, Northern Command with the rank of Lieutenant. In 1942 he was commissioned by the War Office, and appointed Supervising Architect HQ War Department, Lands Branch, Northern Command. By 1943 his main work consisted of requisitioning and derequisitioning buildings used by the army in the North of England, including large country houses, hospitals, remote farmhouses, and even piers along the coast.[20]

Despite this enormous work load, neither the army nor the war could deflect him from his earlier declared aims, and he found the time to pursue and develop his attitudes and beliefs on church architecture. 'Whenever I had a moment', he admitted, 'I continued to examine and sketch churches. I even wrote a book entitled *The New Churches*[21] which fortunately I never finished. But I cannot be too grateful for the respite which enabled me to think out my attitude to the kind of church which would be needed in the post-war world and the architectural possibilities and solutions which the new churches would offer.'[22]

The New Churches became very important to him and from 1943 to 1945 he spent much time working on several redraftings.

Numerous sketch books survive from this period, filled with careful analyses of all manner of churches, sometimes identifying special regional characteristics or noting features which he believed must have influenced the work of major architects such as Sir Giles Gilbert Scott or Goodhart-Rendel.

16

16 Sketch of a common Yorkshire regional characteristic, found on Halifax Parish Church. Pencil 2 × 6in (5.1 × 15.2cm) 1942

OPPOSITE
17 Pencil sketch of E. S. Prior's St Andrew's Church, Roker, Co. Durham, 1942. 7 × 5in (17.8 × 12.7cm)

OPPOSITE
18 An unusually light-hearted pencil survey of a typical nineteenth-century Surrey 'bedhead' churchyard memorial, drawn in 1941, later used with others to illustrate articles in the *Architectural Review* in 1944 and 1946. 6 × 4in (15.2 × 10.2cm)

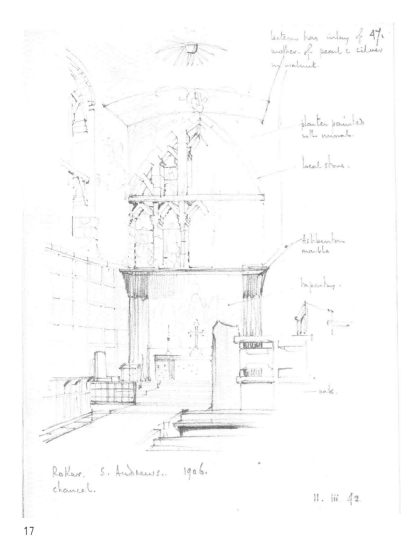

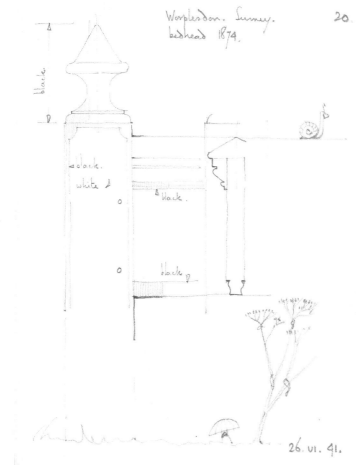

The sketch of the interior of Patrington Church, East Yorkshire in October 1943 suggests, for example, 'The Nave arcade and aisle vaulting appear to have furnished Temple Moore with a model for Sledmere Church.' (*see* ILLUST. 436).

Recognizing his own privileged educational background, he would spare time to write personal letters on behalf of those soldiers in his unit who could not write, and incredibly still found time to produce articles for architectural magazines. One, entitled 'Churchyard Bedhead Embellishments' published by the *Architectural Review* in 1944, involved measuring (with the help of his wife while he was on leave) the vulnerable small wooden memorials placed at the head and foot of graves, known collectively as 'bedheads' (ILLUST. 18). Few now survive. He even managed a lecture to the York Georgian Society in 1943, entitled 'A critical approach to Architectural History'.

The association with the army did not terminate at the end of the war, and, now with the rank of Major, he continued derequisitioning buildings until 1949. During his eight years in the army, he held responsibility at one time or another for some 60,000 buildings.[23] As this work inevitably diminished when buildings were returned to civilian use, he suggested to the army that he used any spare time to develop a small architectural practice. Surprisingly the suggestion was accepted.

Remaining in the North held advantages too, particularly with regard to the quality of family life, where the varied expanses of the Yorkshire countryside seemed to offer so much to a young couple with children. Already by the end of the war a daughter, Jancis Ina (b. 1944) and a son, Nicholas Gaze (b. 1945) had arrived.

His new venture faced one important drawback: would exile from the London architectural world prove a handicap to the development of a national practice, being too far removed from those founded by the eminent Victorian architects he so much admired – Street, Butterfield and Scott? In the event the opposite proved true. York was to provide George Pace with a key to the whole of the ecclesiastical world – in Britain and beyond.

Early practice

In common with many of his fellow architects in the dawn of the post-war era, George Pace started looking for opportunities in the planned reconstruction of Britain; and from his kitchen table in a large rented house in Front Street, Acomb, York, he worked on competition entries for the redevelopment of town centres,[24, 25] and even obtained a commission to design a factory.[26] None of these projects left the drawing board, and he found more success in the field of architectural history.

19

Several of his articles were published, including an important one on the Gothic Revival[27] which drew him to the attention of (Sir) John Summerson, Goodhart-Rendel and (Sir) Nikolaus Pevsner. Further articles on 'bedheads' were supplemented by a number on 'York Gothic Safes', which described the distinctive and varied fronts found on church vestry safes and which were produced by local iron foundries in Regency and Victorian times (ILLUST. 13). Directing National Building Record Work (for which he had volunteered in 1940) led to a thorough acquaintance with the city's medieval churches, York Minster, many Georgian buildings and some nineteenth-century work. He carried out similar studies in Scarborough and Whitby.

The important, sought after, ecclesiastical link came when he approached the Very Revd Eric Milner White (1884–1963), Dean of York Minster (1941–63), whose ambitions, he discovered, included the formation of a Northern Centre of Craftsmen, through which the traditions of the Church and its ancient buildings could be kept alive.[28]

The Dean, with commendable foresight, recognized at once the potential in George Pace, and a close association soon formed. Over the next four years the Dean introduced his 'rising architect'[29] to a number of vicars, resulting in small commissions for new furnishings and fittings in numerous ancient churches scattered about the York Diocese.

The pendant lights at Christ Church, Scarborough (1946) (ILLUST. 20), the new font cover

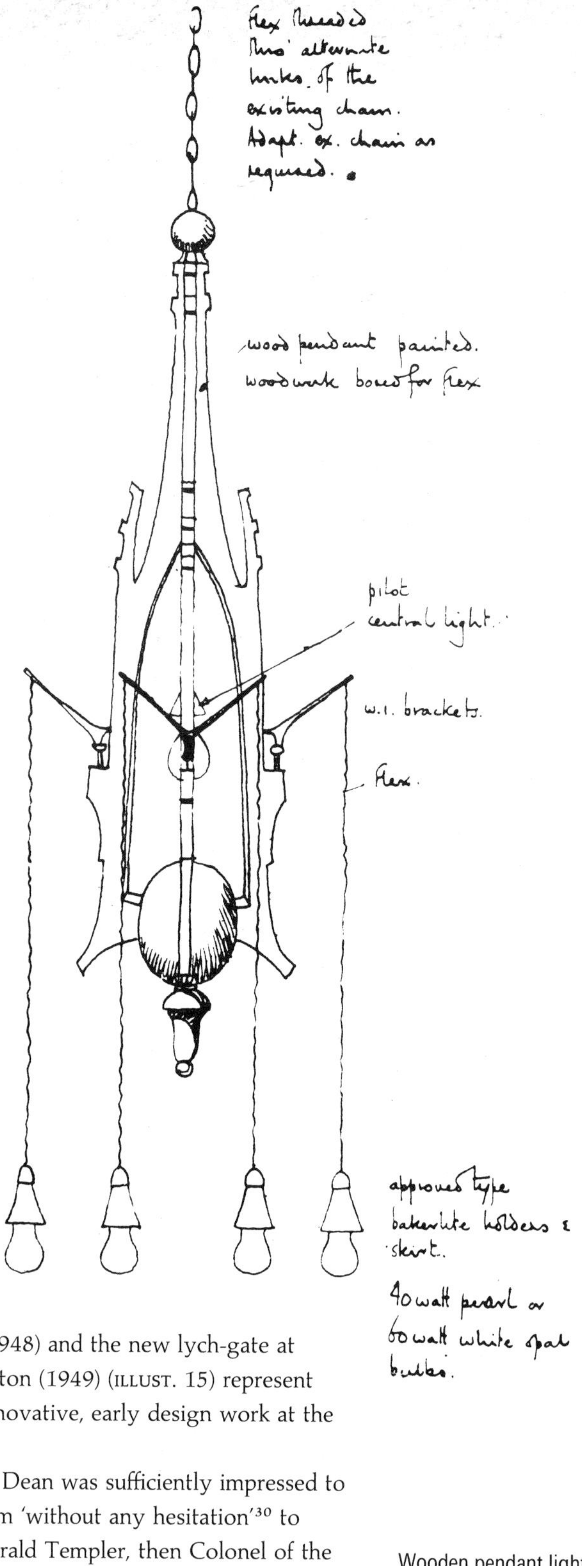

[handwritten notes on drawing:]
Flex threaded thro' alternate links of the existing chain. Adapt. ex. chain as required.

wood pendant painted. woodwork bored for flex

pilot central light

w.i. brackets.

flex.

approved type bakerlite holders & skirt.

40 watt pearl or 60 watt white opal bulbs.

20

at Pickering (1948) and the new lych-gate at Nether Poppleton (1949) (ILLUST. 15) represent some of his innovative, early design work at the time.

In 1948 the Dean was sufficiently impressed to recommend him 'without any hesitation'[30] to General Sir Gerald Templer, then Colonel of the Royal Irish Fusiliers, who having no idea of whom to employ as an architect for a Regimental Chapel in Armagh Cathedral, wrote to the Dean for advice. This gave him his first large commission for integrated furnishings (*see p. 147*) and went some way to prepare him for his next commission – one of his most important, the restoration of Llandaff Cathedral (1949–64) (*see p. 155*).

In 1949 an event occurred which was to have the most profound effect upon George Pace's career – the death of the great ecclesiastical architect, Sir Charles Nicholson (1867–1949). Quite suddenly, numerous churches and several cathedrals across Britain were looking to appoint a

Wooden pendant light fittings

19 Sherburn in Elmet; 'light oak' 1953

20 Christ Church, Scarborough; wood and metal pendant for Nave. Ink drawing, 4 × 8in (10.2 × 20.3cm)

OPPOSITE
21 Rotherham All Saints Parish Church; nave pendant light fittings in light oak, 1957

23

Wrought-iron pendant
light fittings

OPPOSITE
22 Laughton-en-le-
Morthen, 1973

23 Bolton Percy, 1965 –
fittings hung from far side
of arcade rather than arch
centre reduce
interference with the play
of the architecture

25

24 Hatfield, 1968

25 Langton, 1967

24

new architect. With incredible good fortune he
stood ready. Old enough to be taken seriously, and
with the immensely influential patronage of Dean
Milner White now firmly behind him, he could not
have been better poised to fill this vacuum. Of the
seven cathedrals in the offing,[31] George Pace
collected three – Lichfield (1949–75), Llandaff
(1949–75) and later Sheffield (1953–61).

Elevation to such high positions at the 'tender'
age of 34 'both encouraged and humbled' him:

> When I was able once more to tread the earth, I
> discovered I was rather frightened, but activities
> followed thick and fast and there was nothing for it
> but to press on regardless.[32]

Now at last he was granted the opportunity to put
into practice his theories and philosophies on
design and conservation, thought out during the
war. These views were not widely known and to a
certain degree required work and improvement,
particularly at Llandaff, where the concept evolved
of creating a new cathedral from the ashes of what
had been essentially a parish church. Looking back
some years later he saw

How noble, how trusting and tremendously
encouraging these Deans and Chapters have been,
above all Llandaff who have never panicked, and
have, and still do, wait patiently for my mind to
work.[33]

But a decade was to pass before he felt confident
that his theories on church design were sufficiently
formulated, and proved through first-hand
experience, to warrant publicizing.

By the same token, his theories on conservation
and his abhorrence of the 'compulsive repairing
mania', publicized in the 1960s, were all born from
the fruits of his earlier practical work on church
fabric repairs. Lichfield Cathedral provided both his
earliest and one of his largest challenges in
combatting the natural ravages of time on
stonework (unlike Llandaff where the wartime
damage was essentially the result of enemy action).
The 15-year programme of repair began in 1954,
but as a prelude, in 1949 he faced the 'daunting'
task of repairing the great central spire.
Inexperience nearly cost him his life, when on his
first ascent the wind roaring through the lucarne

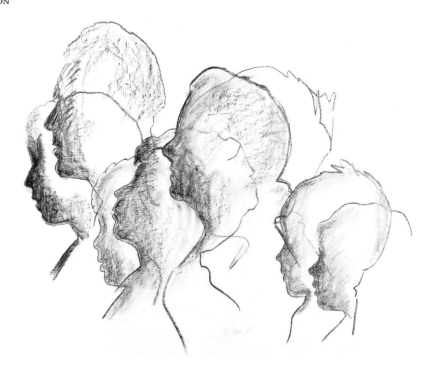

26 The Pace Family, 31 December 1956: shadow silhouettes traced in charcoal by George Pace during his forty-first birthday celebrations. Detail on paper 29 × 24 in (73.7 × 61 cm). From left to right: Jancis, George, Martin, Nicky, Ina, Peter, Gillian

opening almost succeeded in wrenching his grip from the ladder. Having found the 40 feet (12 metres) of apex stonework 'sadly dilapidated and easily rocked by quite gentle pressure from one hand' he descended to find further trouble on the ground: 'there was the BBC all ready to interview the architect, but plainly disconcerted that such a disreputable and juvenile object could be so exalted a personage'.[34] This apparent lack of fear of heights was to stand him in good stead in his later church repair work. Workmen came to realize that no part of their work could be safe from close scrutiny, and this was clearly illustrated for one contractor when he saw 'Mr Pace climb the outside scaffolding to the top of a tower, without the aid of any ladders whatsoever'.[35]

The family increased in size with the birth of another son, Martin Gaze (b. 1949) quickly followed by twins, Gillian Catherine (b. 1950) and Peter Gaze (b. 1950). They now lived in the rather isolated village of Skelton, just north of York. Although his work took him away, sometimes for days on end, George Pace remained a devoted family man. Story-telling to his young children at night-time became a ritual which he seldom neglected, no matter how late he might return.

In 1949 George Pace realized he needed to establish a more stable economic base on which to develop his practice. Dean Milner White, anxious to keep his protégé in Yorkshire, approached the Archdeacon of Sheffield, Leslie Hunter, who in turn offered him the post of Diocesan Surveyor – rather a tedious and time-consuming job, mostly concerned with 'dilapidations' to vicarages; but nevertheless (like his Army job) it provided a bread and butter income – until 1956. With sufficient other work then in hand, he resigned and turned

his full attention to churches.

Increasingly, new commissions arrived as a result of previous works. For example, admiration for the spire apex cross at Lichfield Cathedral resulted in several commissions, including a new chapel to be built in Africa. He explained the story in later years in a talk to the Friends of Lichfield Cathedral:

> Dean Iremonger wanted the new summit cross to be a St Chad's cross. After much thought I evolved a design which made this possible and organised the four little floating crosses, so that they remained anchored in position [ILLUST. 27]. One day the Dean had a visitor, who looking up, was captivated by the cross, and after enquiring the name of the designer, approached me to design the Chapel of the Resurrection, Ibadan University (1951–54), [ILLUST. 279] – the first church building designed to be used by all Christian denominations. From that came the commissions for a school chapel in Lagos (1954), the new Cathedral at Ibadan (1954–65) [ILLUST. 363] and the complex at Keele University (1959–65) [ILLUST. 346]; so the Lichfield summit cross has had far-flung influence.[36]

The publicity surrounding these buildings helped fuel a growing reputation, particularly the Ibadan Chapel (1951–54), described as 'one of the most outstanding churches to be designed since the war by a British Architect'.[37]

In 1954 the family moved once again, this time to a large Victorian terraced house opposite Clifton Green in York, and here George Pace was to spend the rest of his life, working from home and from the office he had by now established at St William's College in the centre of the city.

Within a very few years his area of work had expanded from a few Yorkshire churches, to encompass cathedrals in Ireland, Wales and Staffordshire; and even a chapel in Africa. His appointment as Consultant Architect to Durham Cathedral (1954–75) and Peterborough Cathedral (1956–75) increased his sphere of influence in England, in the North and South respectively: and as word spread of his work at Llandaff Cathedral, a steady development of commissions in southern and mid-Wales also surfaced.

Craftsmen

The expansion of Pace's practice accentuated the existing difficulty in obtaining craftsmen and construction labourers trained in the apprentice tradition. The execution of both his new church building work and his repair work on existing churches required a special knowledge of, and skill in, traditional techniques. He also required the individual touch of the finest craftsmanship in his new furnishings and fittings.[38]

In those days of post-war reconstruction, the face of the British building industry was changing, and the advent of industrialized pre-fabrication and the like seemed set to eclipse the need for the old apprentice craft system, condemning it to obscurity and possible extinction.

By seeking out small local Yorkshire firms still possessing the necessary attributes, and by explaining the techniques required, sometimes to the extent of picking up tools and demonstrating by example, he collected together a nucleus of craftsmen, persuading them to travel with him to distant parts in something of the manner of medieval masons.

In principle, there was nothing new in this, for Sir Ninian Comper (1864–1960) trained and maintained the same body of carvers, painters and embroiderers throughout his 72 years of practice.[39] Similarly, the building firm of Anelay (once of Doncaster), who re-furnished Cantley for Comper in 1894, was persuaded by Walter Brierley (1862–1926) to move entirely to York in 1900 with a promise of work[40] (where they later also did much work for George Pace).

Mr Arthur Gillam, director of a long-established joinery and cabinet-making firm in Sheffield, Yorkshire, recalls his long association with 'Mr Pace':

> . . . I well remember him calling at our office dressed in his army uniform with the insignia removed. He asked if we would be prepared to work for him as he hoped to do a considerable amount of work in the area and beyond.

> . . . There was in this area, in the ecclesiastical field, a strongly held opinion that the best in craftsmanship could only be obtained in London. Mr Pace set out to prove how mistaken was this conception.

27 Lichfield Cathedral: central spire, new summit cross in gunmetal gilt, 1950

27

He gathered around him masons, carpenters, joiners, leadworkers, glass specialists, blacksmiths, silversmiths, sculptors, painters and illuminators into what was called affectionately amongst them 'Pace's Menagerie'. All these tradesmen employed real craftsmen and so work went along and there developed an unofficial friendly association of companies under one inspired leader. He knew what he wanted, was pleased when he got it, but did not hesitate to criticize when he didn't. Always he would listen to and appreciate a contractor's difficulties and be prepared to amend his ideas to overcome such difficulties in the best possible manner.

To depart from his drawings without prior consultation was to call upon one's head near retribution. I well remember an incident concerning a wooden communion table with 'ball feet'. The Bishop objected to the feet and we were asked to remove them, which we perhaps foolishly did. His reaction was – 'I don't care if the Archbishop of Canterbury doesn't like them, put them back.'

23

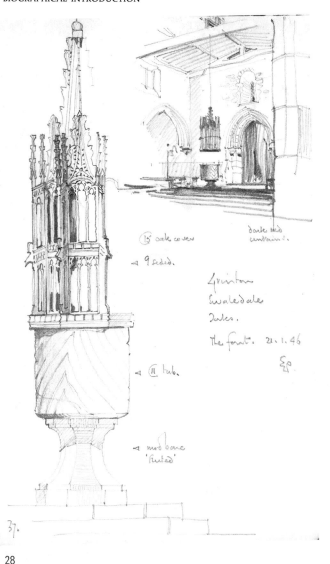

28

29

. . . One fact always stood out above all others. All traders were regarded as 'Partners in a Venture' along with himself. This was illustrated most clearly at the consecration of the church of Fairweather Green, Bradford [1966, ILLUST. 113].

Representatives of all trades, including those who had prepared the site, were lined up in a semi-circle below the chancel steps and were presented, by name and trade, to the then Bishop of Bradford. I have never seen it done but this once in a long working life.[41]

But whilst the Victorian architect generally searched for 'the satisfactory block contractor'[42] – William Butterfield (1814–1900), for example, preferred to use a builder he knew whenever possible, with two-thirds of his 150 buildings executed by a group of about 20 firms[43] – George Pace willingly used good local contractors in other parts of the country, particularly for construction work. It was generally the furnishings and fittings that were made in Yorkshire. On the Llandaff Cathedral rebuilding, for example, William Clarke (whose father and grandfather worked on the Prichard restoration) together with Messrs Hinkins

and Frewin of Newport, were employed as main contractors, though much of the interior joinery and furnishing was the work of Gillams of Sheffield, or Anelays or Houghtons, both of York. Sometimes suitable local contractors just could not be found, particularly in other parts of Wales. Here, the difficulties of working on remote and isolated ancient churches were only overcome by importing Yorkshire firms. Geoffrey Kaye of York, a stonemason, with his apprentices K. Dodsworth and R. Thompson (both of whom were later to found their own firms) carved inscriptions, moved monuments and renewed eroded stonework. Joe Hardgrave of York roofed many a Welsh church. Dowsons of Kirbymoorside, North Yorkshire, made wrought-iron pendant light fittings, gates, crosses and flower vases (transported on the long journeys in the back of the architect's large Humber car). Like that of Walkers of York, whose iron railings may be seen outside the British Museum in London, Dowsons' work for George Pace is evident throughout England – at Windsor, for example, and at Ibadan in Nigeria, where they made the screen gates in the narthex.

Pencil sketches in Swaledale, Yorkshire, NR, 1946:

28 Medieval font in Grinton Church, 5 × 7in (12.7 × 17.8cm)

29 First encounter with Marrick Priory. In his conversion of the building to an adventure centre many years later, the east end shown here remained substantially intact and became a small chapel (*see* ILLUST. 30), 5 × 6in (12.7 × 15.2cm)

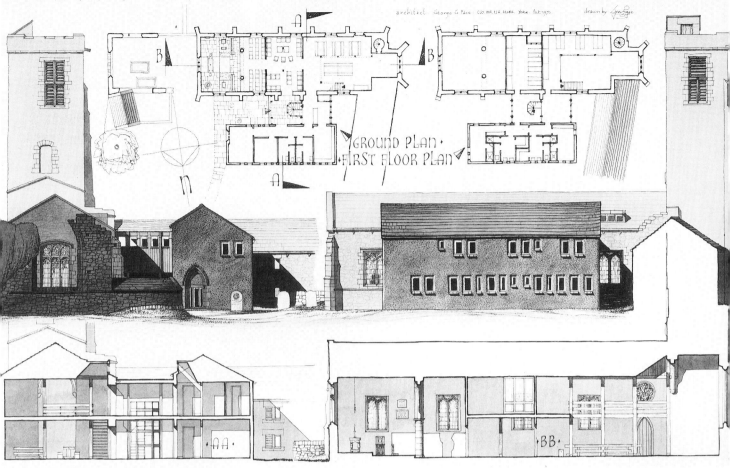

MARRICK PRIORY : SWALEDALE : ADAPTATION AS YOUNG PEOPLE'S ADVENTURE CENTRE

architect: George G Pace: C20 MA FSA FRIBA, York. Oct 1970   drawn by [signature]

·GROUND PLAN·
·FIRST FLOOR PLAN·

·AA·

·BB·

30

31

30 Marrick Priory: conversion to an adventure centre using a modern interpretation of the vernacular language of the Yorkshire Dales. Ink and wash, 23 × 14in (58.4 × 35.6cm), 1970 – exhibited at the Royal Academy Summer Exhibition 1971

31 Disserth, October 1955: typical of the many small Welsh churches George Pace came to admire and cherish, and to which he referred in his article 'Welsh Churches and Chapels – A National Heritage', 1960

Theory and early designs

The surveyorship association with the Sheffield diocese brought George Pace into close contact with influential figures such as Bishop Leslie Hunter and his successor as Archdeacon, the Ven. Douglas Harrison; with the result that proposals for several large Sheffield diocese commissions began to appear on his drawing board, notably the new churches of St Mark's, Broomhall, Sheffield (1950–63) (ILLUST. 335); Intake Church, Doncaster (1954–56) (ILLUST. 75); the completion of Sheffield Cathedral (1955–61) (ILLUST. 325); and St Leonard and St Jude, Doncaster (1957–63) (ILLUSTS 79–81).

Up until this time, the majority of his works comprised new work to or within existing buildings. Now the prospect of designing entirely new, large churches arose, in which his theories for a modern architecture capable of being in the service of the Church would be tested. The Chapel at Ibadan (1951–54) had been a considerable success, but in England the solution would have to be quite different.

Already Pace was convinced that modern technology on its own could not provide the answer. The manner in which he developed his complex theory on church design is examined in detail in the next chapter. Suffice to say here, he

32

emerged. He realized that without using stylistic details, he could capture and distil the essence of the spirit of these older buildings, and in doing so invoke a 'new awareness of spatial relationships and the juxta-position of solid and voids'.[44]

The vernacular barn tradition, for example, is strongly identifiable in his work from its beginnings at Anchorage Lane, Church Centre, Doncaster (1954) (ILLUST. 407); where his conversion of a seventeenth-century barn, built from the stones of a medieval hospice, deliberately accentuates its ancient and vernacular character, creating a small historical and rural oasis, despite pressure from twentieth-century suburban housing which confronts it on all sides. The shape and materials of the new chapel at St Michael's College, Llandaff (1957–59) (ILLUSTS 317–321) strongly evoke the image of the field barns of Swaledale, whilst acknowledging a debt to Le Corbusier.[45] The entirely new Scargill Chapel (1958–61) (ILLUST. 332) in the Yorkshire Dales was widely acclaimed for its sympathetic affinity with local traditional building, whilst achieving a strikingly 'modern' effect.[46]

32 Burton Agnes, north aisle: east window before the new glazing, 1950

had seen a way forward which, whilst combining the very best of modern materials and modern construction, also drew substantially from traditional construction, and the aesthetics of historical styles from the Gothic through to the Renaissance; from vernacular cottages and barns to industrial architecture.

His observations on regional characteristics in buildings, noted in his wartime sketch books and identified later in the magnificent medieval churches of Yorkshire, now under his care, or recorded whilst exploring barns and ruined lead smelting mills during regular family holidays in Swaledale, began to surface in his work.

Within quite a short period his designs so uniquely interpreted and absorbed these characteristics, that his own distinctive style

Writings

With a new confidence founded upon practical achievement, George Pace began to write, leading to a spate of publications appearing in newspapers, learned journals and books over the next five years. He began by promoting a fuller understanding of past architecture in the hope that its relevance to contemporary architectural needs could be better appreciated.

One of his first major articles dwelt on a subject hardly discussed at the time – Victorian

33 Bleddfa, October 1955: typical Welsh vernacular church

33

OPPOSITE
34 Burton Agnes, north aisle: east window, reglazed in 1956. The flamboyant shapes formed by the lead cames intentionally create a completely new secondary tracery order to the stonework

New leaded glazing:

OPPOSITE
35 Leake Tower, west
window, 1962: a
profusion of tulip heads,
mouchettes and the
ogee, reminiscent of the
fourteenth-century
curvilinear period

36

37

36 Adlingfleet: west
window before reglazing

37 Adlingfleet: west
Window reglazed 1952

38 *and* **39** Hatfield,
south-east chapel, south
windows, 1966: an early
example of the shift in
true 'Gothic' tradition,
from curvilinear to fully
fledged perpendicular
forms, which
characterizes much of
George Pace's work from
the middle 1960s

38

39

41

41 St Mary's,
Worsborough: vestry
window glazing, 1967

OPPOSITE
40 St Mary's,
Worsborough: south
porch door in oak with
leaded glazed panels, set
well back to avoid
interference with the
medieval door arch and
so retain a sense of depth
to the opening (note the
incised inscription on the
mid-rail above the
doors); 1966

architecture. During the war he had written on the subject, notably in the *Architectural Review* with 'St Saviour's Leeds and Pusey', alongside an article on Butterfield by (Sir) John Summerson.[47] He liked to refer to those early days 'when the protagonists of Victorian Architecture in the 1930s and 40s were John Summerson, H. Goodhart-Rendel, with me as their very junior disciple', and this interest in and admiration for Victorian architects never left him.

He wrote 'Victorian York' in 1956, which the York and East Yorkshire Architectural Society published in their Year Book,[48] and the people of York, already overwhelmed with a surfeit of medieval architecture and good Georgian buildings must have found this eulogy somewhat disturbing. For example, in referring to the three 'great' schools designed by Brierley in the 1890s he said 'these buildings' spatial relationships, the juxtaposition of solid and void, asymmetrical and symmetrical composition and good brickwork are combined in a prophetic manner . . . Aesthetically these three schools are amongst the most precious of York's heritage of all ages'! 'In the not too distant future', he wrote, 'a Victorian Society may well be necessary to prevent the thoughtless destruction of the outstanding works of that age.'[49]

The long trips he made to Wales left such a profound impression upon him that he was forced to take up his pen in defence of its buildings. The beauty of Yorkshire and its wealth of fine churches had been a revelation to him, but Wales too captivated his imagination. Whilst he travelled the area restoring churches such as Holy Trinity, Newport (1955), or Llantwit Major (1959–61) he came to love and cherish its humble, unknown buildings and recognise their special needs. In 1960 he decided to 'wake the public up' as he believed

neither the Welsh nor the English appreciated these treasures as objects of great national value and he wrote the article 'Welsh Churches and Chapels – a National Heritage',[50] suggesting

> Those with seeing eyes do not need to make a lengthy tour in Wales to be convinced that Welsh churches possess vernacular qualities very different from their English counterparts.

> Wales should be very conscious of the attractiveness of its indigenous churches and the need to appreciate, study and conserve them.

Whilst acknowledging the writings of Tyrell-Green and Fred Crossley, he pointed out that no-one had produced a book on Welsh churches comparable to those written on English churches, in which the photographs of Edwin Smith, the writings of John Betjeman and the drawings of John Piper[51] together had enabled English churches 'to be savoured aesthetically, clear of the obscuring fog of archaeology and ecclesiology'. A book of superlative photographs of Welsh churches and chapels was a crying need, he protested.

> We might expect to see the stark campaniles of Pembrokeshire and the West; the moving simplicity of the interiors of remote one and two cell churches; the spatial complexity of interiors arising out of plan forms almost unknown in England; the many sub-regional groups of tower and bell turret design; the external compositions producing visual and picturesque effects pre-eminently Welsh; the superb Rood Screens of the Border; the subtle relationship between design and materials and the landscape of various geological formations; the assimilation of influences from adjoining countries into definitely Welsh forms; the rude, vital and exciting minor crafts of all ages, in carvings, wall paintings, tombs, headstones and furnishings.

> We might expect to see the white-washed exterior of Llanybri, which would remind us of medieval Danish churches; St Govan's Chapel, overwhelmed by its vast rocks; the stately local Perpendicular of Clynogg Fawr and Llywel; the complex external forms of Rhulen, Llanbardan y Garryg, Llanfrynach and Disserth; the tiny barnlike structure of Llanfihangel-Helygen; the great Jesse at Abergavenny, the tombs of Llantrithyd; the tabernacle work at Llancarfan; the rare Rood figures at Kemeys Inferior and Mochdre. But what we should expect to see is endless.

> Nonconformist Chapels form an important part of the corpus of Welsh ecclesiastical architecture and our imagined book would show simple, unaffected and very moving chapels – Aberayron, Rhydlwyd, Belgelley and Llansadwrnen; those architecturally orthodox – Llanon and Blaenconin; and those that are exotic and architecturally astonishing – Bethesda, Tenby, Aberayron, Kilgelly and Peny-bryn.

42 Durham, Palace Green Library, University College, 1961–6: 'On a highly sensitive site between Cathedral and Castle . . . The Library slots neatly and with distinction into one of the greatest silhouettes of Europe.'[58] Photograph taken shortly after completion with the stonework still retaining its protective thin coat of limewash

42

Consciously distancing himself from the myopia of the pure architectural historian, he warned:

> These buildings which have come down from the past are not museum pieces; they are live buildings serving a living and ever evolving use. Heaven forbid that they should be considered as mere cultural fossils curiously embedded in our midst. Heaven forbid that the kind of petrification which in recent years had laid an unfeeling hand on so many Welsh ruins, should ever overtake its churches and chapels. Harsh as were the attentions of the nineteenth century Ecclesiologists at least they had vitality and their end was to the greater Glory of God. Churches and chapels, especially when old, need constant, loving and highly skilled care to prolong life in their ancient bones and to hand them on to future generations, not only in their present comeliness, but with increased beauty and increased history.

Here were no idle words, and over the years he made a significant contribution to the care and beautification of these buildings, *not* as museums, but 'as live buildings, serving an ever-evolving use'. He treated each church individually, making small or large adjustments as need dictated, using that 'instinct for beauty that enabled him to see in a moment what was needed to beautify a church'.[52] The results are rarely predictable. Often his 'influence appears only as an enhancing of what was already there awaiting his shrewd eye',[53] so that today, one may visit a Welsh church and find at first glance little evidence to show his presence. The restored shingle roof at Cregina (1958), or the restored half-timbered squat belfry tower at Cascob (1965) for example, look untouched and quite natural. But look more carefully and you will find at Cascob a tiny newly leaded glazed window to a typical 'Pace' design hidden away in a slit in the thickness of a wall (1967). At Llanbister you must search the altar to find simple flower vases in copper, bearing small decorative buttress fins (a typical Gothic idiom he used frequently) that when full of flowers might easily be overlooked (1972).

The simple cross surmounting the bell flèche at Llanbadarn Fyndd (1971) is of the twentieth century, but this is only apparent upon close examination.

And then, at other churches, his hand is unmistakable: the new reredos (with Harvey) at Maesmynis (1963–64) draws one to the chancel upon entry from the nave north door, and the new altar frontal, candlesticks and east window combine to produce a jewel in an otherwise puritanical setting.

You cannot miss his decorative colours on the roof timbers at Bronllys (1968–70) in different shades of green; the bright red three bays over the sanctuary resplendent with gilded stars scattered over their surface; and similarly at Llantilio Pertholey (1970–74), the wrought-iron light pendants in matt black contrast with the re-limewashed interior almost to the point of overwhelming one.

Though Pace bestowed the same care and attention upon many greater and more important churches in England, Welsh churches were always to hold a special place in his affections.

His writing in the early 1960s displays a preoccupation with modern Church architecture in an age when new churches were still being built in significant numbers.[54] The timing could not have been better, for when Peter Hammond's book on *Liturgy and Architecture* appeared in 1960, George Pace's articles 'A new approach to Church building'[55] (1958) and 'Modern Church architecture'[56] (1960) were already out and being quoted.[57]

An interest in new church architecture on the part of the clergy in England followed as the spread of The Liturgical Movement gained momentum – much as it had on the Continent before the war, and some of George Pace's buildings began to be illustrated with other examples of pre- and post-war church planning. In Peter Hammond's book,[59] modern continental churches such as Perret's Notre-Dame du Raincy

OPPOSITE
43 Durham University College Library, 1961–66: photograph taken in 1988 shows the rough sawn and rubble Dunhouse stonework now weathering as intended to a mellow brown

44   45   48

(1923), and St Anna Duren by Rudolf Schwarz
(1956), and English churches including Comper's St
Mary's, Wellingborough (1931), Cachemaille-Day's
St Michael and All Angels Wythenshawe (1937)
(ILLUST. 107), were compared with George Pace's
Ibadan (ILLUST. 279), St Leonard's, Doncaster
(ILLUST. 79) and St Mark's, Sheffield (ILLUST.
335).

Encouraged by favourable publicity he now
produced perhaps his most definitive article on
design theory – 'Architecture and architect in the
service of the Church' – which began life as a
paper read at the Liverpool Conference in 1962,
and later in 1964 was published under the
collective title *The Modern Architectural Setting of
the Liturgy*,[60] edited by William Lockett, his student
friend from the Regent Street Polytechnic. Much of
the thinking summarized in the following chapter is
gleaned from this source.

During this period the conservation of existing
churches was not forgotten, with the appearance of
a paper read at the Attingham Park conference in
June 1961, entitled 'Principles and Precepts – the
importance of not spoiling old churches by a
scheme of re-ordering' which surfaced in a book
Making the Building serve the Liturgy, edited by
Gilbert Cope in 1962.[61] George Pace continued to
write throughout his life; indeed his output of
articles and lectures rivalled that of his prolific
design work.

Sense of aesthetic

Though on the one hand George Pace advocated a
thoroughly modern approach to architectural
problems, he also possessed a cautious attitude to
'Modern Architecture' as practised by many of his
contemporaries, recognizing that an enormous
number of their new buildings were completely
insensitive to their environment. In an age where
the office tower block and high-rise flats reigned
supreme, when the renewal of our city centres in
concrete and glass was reaching its zenith, wearing

46

47

44–47 George Pace's book-lined study at home, 18 Clifton Green, York, where he lived from 1954 to 1975 (photograph taken in 1976). Note the Royal Academy drawings above the bookcases

49 Sketch design for Tamworth processional cross, in felt tip, undated, 3 × 6in (7.6 × 15.2cm)

50 Completed design of the Tamworth processional cross, in silver on oak stave, 1967

OPPOSITE
48 George Pace working at his drawing board at home, March 1959, aged 44, on what appears to be a drawing of St Michael's College Chapel, Llandaff (1957–9)

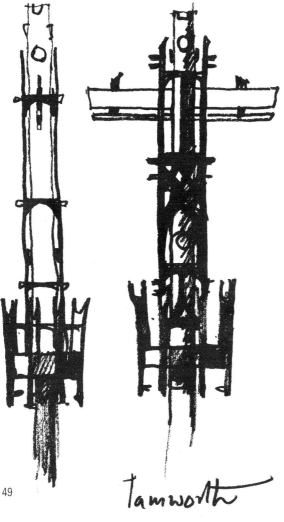

49

Tamworth

50

51

the hat of a general architect rather than an ecclesiastical architect he perceived the need to respect not just the important historic fabric of our towns and cities, but also their sense of scale and their complicated layers of evolution.

To publicize his new understanding of old architecture he produced in 1962 a pioneering study entitled the 'York Aesthetic'[62] which anticipated the development of conservation areas well ahead of its time.[63] He argued that the beauty and charm of York lay not so much in its individual features as in their amalgamation; and that the greatest care should be taken not only to ensure that new buildings in York belong to this age, but also that they are designed so as to integrate into the period buildings that surround them. Propinquity, contrast, high drama, muted drama, set-piece, vulgarity and insipidness were all qualities to be aware of in this townscape, he suggested. 'The York Aesthetic is a very involved quality', he maintained:

> Let us clearly understand that a worship of the past and the joy in ancient building has only a small part to play in understanding the York Aesthetic. If we so desire, and if we properly understand the distilled spirit of the York Aesthetic, we should be able to add to it in our contemporary works.

Pace provided a practical demonstration of this

hypothesis – not in York, but in the equally historic town of Durham, where his new University Library (1961–66) (ILLUST. 43) was successfully inserted into one of the finest views in Europe (now a World Heritage site). The publication of the *York Aesthetic* created considerable interest and the York Civic Trust wholeheartedly endorsed its aims.[64] The High Street Improvement Committee of The Skipton-in-Craven Civic Society was also sufficiently impressed to commission him in 1963 to make recommendations for the improvement and general development of their High Street with an elaborate public exhibition and early exercise in public participation staged in Skipton. Residents disagreed with some of the criticisms and suggestions set forth in his report, but it was generally agreed his attitude was 'fearless, essentially practical and constructive'.[65]

In further studies, notably the 'Llandaff Aesthetic' (1966)[66(1)], and the 'Bishophill: York – Appraisal and Renewal' (1974),[66(2)] he continued to explore his lifelong interest in the relationship of buildings to their surroundings.

51 Liverpool Anglican Cathedral, Chapel of the Holy Spirit: silver altar candlesticks, 1967

OPPOSITE
Sketch designs for the Liverpool Cathedral candlesticks from 1961 onwards:

52 Blue ink, black felt-tip and black Biro, 5 × 7in (12.7 × 17.8cm)

53 Pencil, 4 × 6in (10.2 × 15.2cm)

54 Ipswich processional cross: wrought iron, painted matt black, on oak stave with silver inscription plate, 1967

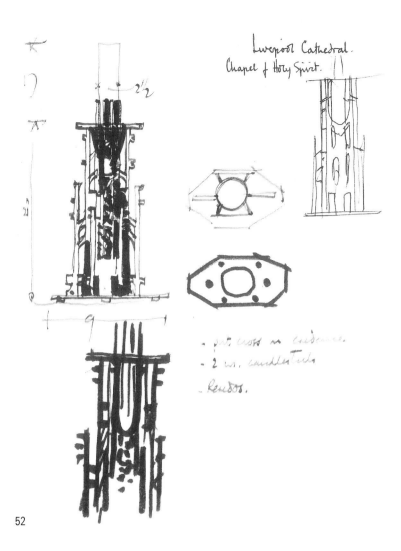

52

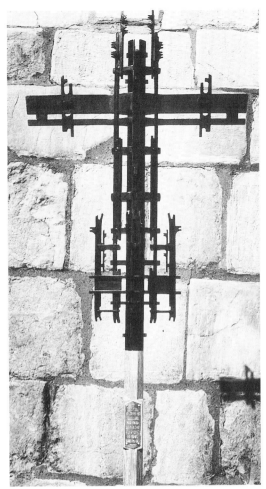

54

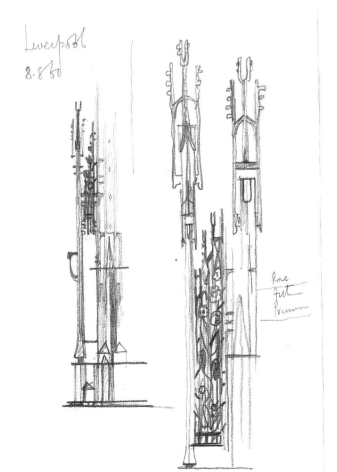

53

Design

The 1960s were fruitful years. Already described as 'one of our leading church architects',[67] George Pace consolidated his position with a huge output of new buildings and furnishings, but they came slowly, as the result of much thought, and in some cases were over a decade in the making. On his *modus operandi* he was adamant. He would not be hurried: 'There should be no time limit in church building,' he once declared, adding: 'The client must not be allowed to insist on a hurried timetable as that could never be compatible with good church building.'[68] One colleague observed:

> His refusal to be hurried on matters of design sometimes brought criticism from his clients, but the fruits of his thoughts in the later finished design nearly always brought the feeling that it was worth waiting for.[69]

A reporter interviewing him in his study for an article on 'North East People'[70] noticed that behind him three drawings for a silver altar cross were draped over the bookshelves. Apparently none of them was yet the right one. 'They suddenly come,' he explained to the reporter; 'you cannot hurry it. You just work at it and go back to it. And suddenly it will be there.'

At any one time several major building designs would be on his drawing board, each consuming

OPPOSITE

55 Branston: view from east end behind new wrought-iron and oak furnishings

56 Branston, rebuilt chancel after fire damage 1964–6: viewed from west end of nave beneath base of the new organ. 'The whole of the East wall is sub-divided into a series of lights related to and interacting upon each other, forming with the stone and oak eastward seats, the barrel-vaulted roof, the stained glass, and the altar table and its furnishings, the focal point of the interior and to which, and in which, every part is integrated to create a whole greater than the sum of its parts'[72]

57 Newport High Altar: silver cross and candlesticks, 1959

enormous amounts of energy and time and often stretching over many years. Design proposals might be frustratingly abandoned or revised to satisfy the changing or conflicting requirements of his clients, who themselves were subject to the vagaries of economics and new liturgical thoughts.

The new church of St Mark's, Sheffield (1950–67) (ILLUST. 335), for example, took 17 years from conception to completion; whilst St Martin-le-Grand, York (1956–68) (ILLUST. 382) took 12 years and Ibadan Cathedral (1954–65) (ILLUST. 363) ran for 11 years. Keele University College Chapel (1959–65) (ILLUST. 347), Holy Redeemer, York (1959–65) (ILLUST. 356) and William Temple Memorial Church, Wythenshawe (1960–66) (ILLUST. 376), each in their turn took six years.

Some churches were completed within just a few years (if the furnishing period, which could extend over a number of years, is excluded) – St Leonard and St Jude, Doncaster (1957–61) (ILLUST. 79), Caer Eithin, Swansea (1961–63) (ILLUST. 411) and St Mark's, Chadderton (1960–63) (ILLUSTS 94 and 98).

Major extension and re-ordering works were generally conceived and carried out more quickly – Bramhall (1958–61) (ILLUST. 74), Branston (1964–66) (ILLUSTS 55 and 56), St John's, Cardiff (1965–68) and Rushmere (1966–68) (ILLUSTS 85 and 86).

At a conference on 'The Architect and the Church' held in 1960, his paper entitled 'A Good Church Building is normally the finished work of a single Designer briefed by the congregation and not closely controlled by the Committee' revealed his techniques for putting ideas across to his clients. These, he explained, often consisted of sketching out preliminary designs in his client's presence and persuading them to make their own model or altar table, thus encouraging them to identify themselves more closely with the development of the project; or as one cynical critic put it, 'helped distract their attention from anything they might not like in the design of the main building they were getting'![72]

What was clear was the extreme difficulty in maintaining a design intact through all the inevitable negotiations with different authorities. Pace admitted, 'it was often hard enough getting the clergy to understand Liturgical matters quite apart from the architectural aspects of church design'.[73] But he showed enormous sensitivity to the problems of the twentieth-century church – changing liturgical fashion being only one of them – and reconciled these by advocating an architecture which, though permanent in itself, would accommodate changing functions.

This aspect of his design approach is revealed more clearly in the proceedings of a seminar on 'Current trends and Personalities in Architecture' held in 1964,[74] where George Pace spoke with

56

Cedric Price, James Stirling and others. One observer noted:

> Whilst Cedric Price builds for an hour or two, then changes everything, not so George Pace, whose lower limit of permanence is 500 years.

But he admitted that in George Pace's flexible approach to the interior of churches, his philosophies 'meet Price's coming round the other way as it were'! For example

> Pace's multi-denominational chapel at Keele University (1958–65) [ILLUST. 348] allows for three simultaneous and mutually exclusive services in separated spaces, or any selected degree of collaboration between them by opening up some rolling screens.[75]

This mixture of ancient traditions, an aesthetic formed from the essence of various distilled characteristics, and an acceptance of modern structures sometimes caused people to fear the unpredictable results of Pace's work. John Kent, Chaplain to the Archbishop of York (later to become Vicar of Selby Abbey) experienced the phenomenon when they met at Bishopthorpe Palace:

> The ceiling of the Chapel was very tatty and Archbishop Garbett wanted it repainting. He suggested a colour, and it looked terrible. I, then his chaplain, suggested another, and it was worse. Dean Milner-White said 'Why not ask George Pace?' He duly came, sat down in the chapel and asked to be left alone. For two hours he looked and thought; after that he knew what he wanted to do. A few days later the painters came. The Archbishop and I were horrified to see appearing spots and wiggles and stripes and chevrons of bright red, blue, green, black, purple and gold. Suddenly, in the end, it fitted together and is magnificent. Later I learned that he had used a traditional medieval pattern. The first experience

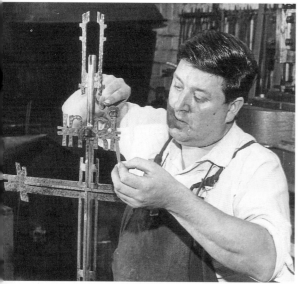

58

was typical: George Pace's work was always deeply considered, I frequently thought he was wrong, and in the end invariably came to admire it.[76]

Reinforcing his argument against a hurried design timetable, George Pace explained that church work was not remunerative: 'No architect designs a church to make money' he said, 'so it doesn't matter how long he takes to do the job'![77] The Dean and Chapter of York recognized this and charged only a low rent on his office premises at St William's College, an action which also reflected their appreciation of the many voluntary duties he carried out as Diocesan Consultant Architect.

The paper he delivered in 1962 on 'Diocesan Advisory Committee Procedure in Theory and Practice'[78] makes clear the financial limitations imposed on church work, and at the same time provides an insight into the type of work load he was obliged to undertake in the designing of even a small piece of furniture or a fitting.

In essence he explains that to do the work properly the architect must be prepared to bear a loss. Even the smallest item of furnishing involves sitting quietly in the church for a long time, considering all possibilities and absorbing its particular atmosphere. Having undertaken a survey and prepared scale drawings, sketch designs are then drawn up for discussion with the Parochial Church Council. After obtaining the statutory permissions, full-sized detail drawings may be started – on a complex furnishing such as a font cover these could take as long to do as a parsonage house:

For the font cover the Architect may be fortunate if he gets Twenty Guineas. For the parsonage house the thought and the one-eighth scale working drawings represent at least half the work and are equivalent to Two hundred and fifty guineas.

Such church furnishings, for reasons beyond the architect's control, could take months, or even years, to reach fruition. Where there were several hundred such furnishings in hand, with fees due only upon completion, the position could well become 'a financial embarrassment'.

Because of his refusal to be hurried on creative matters, he earned the nickname 'Snail's Pace'. Fortunately, the term was not widespread, for it gave an entirely false impression of his personal energy. Few, except his secretaries and architectural staff, were aware of his remarkable ability to dictate constantly for up to three hours, without altering a single sentence (despite telephone interruptions, and sometimes the presence of a cat upon his shoulders!);[79] of his ability to draw considerably faster than the talented assistants around him; and of the 14 hours he usually put into each carefully programmed day, sometimes arranged months in advance.

Work came first. A clergyman's daughter from Sheffield recalls that one of her father's greatest pleasures 'was to have George spend an evening in our house, watching him draw and make sketches of his designs',[80] and he was not beyond inspecting a church at night, with a contractor, by the aid of torchlight.[81]

For all this he still managed to participate in the life of his family, perhaps not as often as he or they would have liked, and yet he generally seemed at ease, and the impression given to clients was one of calm, as the Revd. John Norman, a former Secretary of the York DAC, recalls:

I never ceased to be amazed at the amount of work George Pace got through; or how he kept pace with the demands continually made upon him. He covered a vast amount of ground. He had intense activity. I never knew anyone turn to him in vain. He always could make time, not only for Cathedrals, but for the many town and country churches which he kept in what he used delightfully to call 'his loving care'. And yet the pace at which this ground was covered was unhurried. His work was rooted and grounded in peace.[82]

The practice

George Pace's self-confessed aim, 'to run a nineteenth-century practice in contemporary York',[83] emerged not through any misplaced nostalgia, but from a clear understanding that if the tradition of church architecture as an art form was to be kept alive, then he, like his predecessors, would need specialist architectural assistants responsible to one person and capable of translating designs for lettering, leaded glazing, furnishings, textiles and metalwork into working instructions for his craftsmen.

58 Fabricating an altar cross at W. Dowson's Metalworks, Kirbymoorside, Yorkshire, NR (undated – around 1970)

OPPOSITE
59 St Albans Cathedral, Saints Chapel: the restored Shrine of St Alban used as the centre-piece in the formation of this chapel – pendant lights 1965, stone altar, wrought-iron candlesticks, processional cross and altar rails, 1967

OVER
60 Owston, 1952: nave pendant lights – painted and gilded wood, 'floating in space'[84]

61 Birdsall: nave pendant lights – gilded wood, 1954

The number of staff he employed at St William's College[86] rarely exceeded ten, but the majority remained with the practice throughout its life, each assistant tending to specialize in one or more different fields, so that Pace built up a formidable battery of expertise to draw upon. Only by this means could so much work be undertaken to such high standards at any one time.

As the work of the practice grew, he came to rely more and more upon his principal Assistant Architect and Associate, Ronald G. Sims, not only to supervise the construction of his new buildings and other works; but also, within the overall framework of his control, to contribute significantly with designs for many of the interior fittings and furnishings in his churches throughout the country.

Clients

St William's College may have been the 'office', but the stationery displayed the home address and consequently all the practice's correspondence came to Clifton Green first. Clients also came, Bishops, Deans and vicars arriving on the doorstep, sometimes ready for breakfast. Often the telephone would be ringing with only Mrs Pace left to answer. She spent much of her time calming clients or just guiding them in the right direction.

Clients came from many backgrounds, and though all were united in their association with the Church, they represented an extraordinary mixture of people. A vicar's first contact may have come through a personal introduction from Dean Milner White, or in later years from those Archdeacons and Bishops familiar with George Pace through his work as Consultant Architect to their diocese. As vicars advanced through the ranks of the Church, settling in new and distant parishes, they often took their architect with them. In this manner commissions in various parts of the country could come to him through an association with just one vicar.

The Revd H. Frankham provides a good example: beginning at Middleton, Lancashire, where he commissioned new vestries (1957–60), he then, as co-founder of the Scargill Community (alongside Donald Coggan, at the time Bishop of Bradford), helped commission the Scargill Chapel (1958–61) (ILLUST. 332); and when at Luton, Bedfordshire, initiated the new Church Hall (1967–69) (ILLUST. 82). Finally he appointed George Pace Consultant Architect to Southwark Cathedral, London (1970–75) (ILLUST. 247) where he himself became Provost.

Some 'exalted' appointments resulted from self-publicizing through writings and lectures. The Very Revd Ken Matthews, Dean of St Alban's Cathedral, first met George Pace at the Deans' Conference in Oxford in 1961, and came away so

64 Ronald G. Sims (b. 1926): associate and eventual partner to George Pace (1954–75) and later recognized as his 'Lineal Successor'[87]

St Mark's, Broomhill, Sheffield: New Church 1950–63:

OPPOSITE
62 View from south aisle looking east, 1989. (Altar frontal by others)

63 West End viewed from the nave, 'The quality and workmanship of the masonry and woodwork throughout the building would be hailed as more than adequate were they intended for England's forty-fourth cathedral . . .'.[85] Stained glass: east window by Harry Stammers. West window by John Piper and Patrick Reyntiens

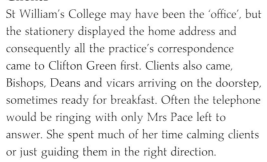

63

impressed with what he heard in his talk entitled 'On Cathedral Architects, their work, qualifications and Duties' that when the chance came to work with him he 'seized' it with both hands.[88] But whilst this appointment to St Alban's Cathedral (1962–73) enabled him to produce some fine works (The Saints Chapel 1967 (ILLUST. 59)) it also led to one of his most difficult experiences at the hands of a Committee Client – in this instance the Cathedral Council – who during the interregnum between Deans questioned his design work, contributing to Pace's decision to resign in 1973. Reacting with typical forcefulness[89] to their accusation that his new nave choir stalls were not understood by visitors to the Cathedral, he replied:

> Of course visitors to the Cathedral do not understand the new stalls, especially if the 'guides' do not explain what the new stalls are and do, and do not expound them with pride and enthusiasm as real twentieth-century works, conceived at the architectural level equivalent of the medieval work in the Cathedral . . . The true use of twentieth-century materials (laminated veneered boards) is something in which to take pride, not to bemoan that the stalls are not like the second-rate nineteenth century permanent choir stalls.[90]

Committees as clients were more often than not a source of frustration to him and he warned that

> no committee can make a work of art, though on the other hand they might easily destroy a work of art during its gestation:

and he once went so far as to say:

41

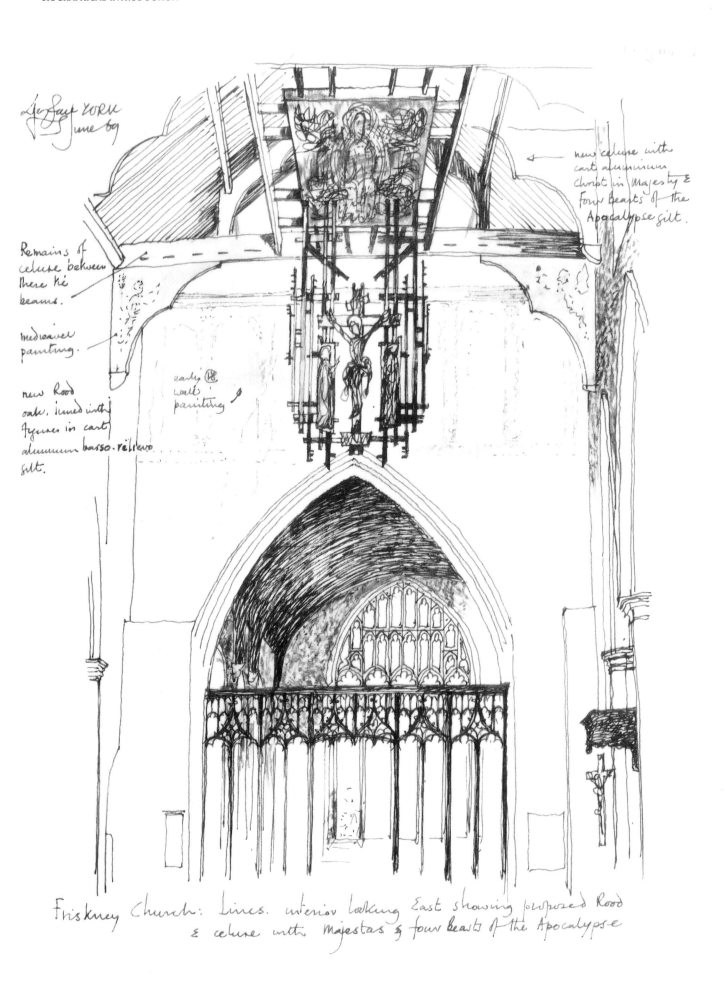

after East YORK
June 69

Remains of
celure between
these tie
beams.

Mediaeval
painting.

new Rood
oak. limed with
figures in cast
aluminium basso-rilievo
gilt.

early 16
wall
painting ?

new celure with
cast aluminium
Christ in Majesty &
four beasts of the
Apocalypse gilt.

Friskney Church: Lincs. interior looking East showing proposed Rood
& celure with Majestas & four beasts of the Apocalypse

It [the Church] must always remember that the collective mind of boards and committees is only the afterglow at least one generation behind the creative thought and work of architects.[91]

The regime of the Church committee, apparently so prevalent today, was not entirely new, as Pace observed in his review of *The Buildings of the Eighteenth Century Church* by Basil Clark,[92] where he said:

The eighteenth-century instructions to architects, the grilling of architects by far from overawed Vestries, the Petition for Faculty and 'fitting up' the church are all described. We find they are not far removed from today's practice.

Reading Mr Clark should be a salutary exercise to those who in the last ten years have 'discovered' the need for Building Committees to give detailed instructions to their architects. There is nothing new under the sun.

However, he was a realist too, and in recognizing committees as a necessary evil, he accepted that they could play an important part in the process of church building, as exemplified in the entry he contributed to the new St Mark's Sheffield Appeal brochure where he suggested:

The Church Architect now finds his client is a committee. But this gives a greater opportunity, for architect and congregation may now go forward together, in enthusiasm to build a church as an Act of Worship. For indeed the church building and liturgical acts performed there express something about christianity which the preacher's word can never give. Such active participation of the 'Lord's Family' is very much bound up in the new Liturgical Movement.[93]

In working with committed Christians in this manner, he saw opportunities to enrich and extend the meaning within his design work, but he never really lost his horror of bureaucracy, and preferred to deal with individuals, be they vicar or Dean, seeing in them a kind of substitute for the now extinct 'municifent donor' of the sort who had provided those 'architectural giants' – Street, Pearson and Butterfield – with so much of their work in Victorian times.[94]

Working with enlightened Deans, and treading carefully with Cathedral Councils, Chapters or Friends, he managed against many odds, in an age of self criticism and doubt, to introduce a significant number of new furnishings and fittings into the greater buildings of the Church. It was also his academic approach to architecture which won him the admiration of the likes of the Very Revd Addleshaw, Dean of Chester – a great academic himself and responsible for books such as *The Architectural Setting of Anglican Worship*.[95] Together they achieved some memorable works at

66 Aston: acolyte candlestick (photographed outside the north door) forming part of the interior reordering, wrought-iron hot dip waxed, 1962–4

OPPOSITE
65 Friskney: proposed rood carried out in slightly modified form, 1973. Drawing in Indian ink on tracing paper, 8 × 10in (20.3 × 25.4cm), 1969

66

Chester Cathedral between 1961 and 1975, particularly the nave choir stalls (1966) (ILLUST. 147), the crossing ceiling (1970) (ILLUST. 5), the High Altar frontal (1973) (ILLUST. 260) and the freestanding Bell House (1968–75) (ILLUST. 389).

Pace's reputation for specialized knowledge and understanding of liturgical matters attracted such eminent churchmen as the Very Revd F. Dillistone, Dean of Liverpool's Anglican Cathedral, who enthusiastically sought his guidance on new liturgical furnishings, in particular a new nave altar and cross (ILLUST. 418). In this instance the Dean had been apprehensive in approaching George Pace: 'I did not think he would take on a Cathedral

67 Windsor Castle – St George's Chapel, King George VI Memorial Chapel, 1967–9: 'The plan shape, windows, mullions, buttresses, parapet and window glazing are all conceived as a mixture of the architectural aesthetics of late medieval ages and modern architecture'.[102] Photograph taken shortly after construction before the new Clipsham stone has begun to weather

68 George Pace's preoccupation with Gothic curvilinear forms extended to the decoration of the family Easter eggs. Here is his own, 1975 (waterproof black ink on boiled cochineal pink background)

68(a) Durham Cathedral – early sketch design for new north vestries. Felt tip on brown envelope. Actual size. Undated, around 1973

like Liverpool – neither ancient or really modern',[96] he confessed later. But then ironically he could hardly have known that not only had George Pace visited the Cathedral as a boy, accompanied by his father (even receiving special permission to view the central tower then under construction), but as early as 1948 he had written in his entry on 'Gothic Architecture' for *Chambers Encyclopaedia*: 'The essence of early twentieth century Gothic is seen in its sublimest form in Scott's Liverpool Cathedral.'[97]

He replied to the Dean's invitation typically, with an answer mixed with joy, pride and humility: 'To have been considered in any degree worthy of becoming Consultant Architect to Liverpool Cathedral [1962–75] will always be to me one of the greatest moments of my life.'[98]

Although in his church repair work he attained an immense practical knowledge of conservation of the fabric of structures, he made few inroads into the secular world. Nevertheless several great Yorkshire country houses did come his way, notably Bramham Park (1957–67) and that eighteenth-century masterpiece, Vanbrugh's Castle Howard (1957–75) (ILLUST. 204). At the latter he formed a 'special relationship'[99] with the owner, George Howard, which lasted throughout their lifetimes. Work began with the restoration of the Temple of the Four Winds (ILLUST. 205) and then moved to the main house (1961–64) which had burnt out in 1940 whilst occupied by a girls' boarding school (ILLUSTS 204 and 206).

There were many other smaller works in the grounds, and a start was made in restoring Hawksmoor's Mausoleum (1968) – a building he often spoke of in terms of awe. Alongside Durham Cathedral he considered this to be one of the 'really great buildings of England.'[100]

Perhaps his greatest client and his greatest honour came with the commission to design the King George VI Memorial Chapel at St George's Chapel, Windsor Castle (1967–69) (ILLUSTS 67 and 393) when 'both the Queen and Queen Elizabeth the Queen Mother took throughout the planning and building a personal interest in every detail of the work.'[101]

He devoted enormous quantities of time and energy to this commission over a two-year period, and to his unfortunate other clients who felt

neglected he would protest, 'The Queen has commanded me to do this work.' But one unsympathetic churchwarden, unmoved, replied to what (with some justification) he took to be a smokescreen, 'I don't see what the Queen has to do with our church!'[103] In 1971 Her Majesty bestowed upon George Pace the honour of Commander of the Victorian Order (CVO) for his work on the Chapel.

The last years

In later years, the stimulus of family holidays on the Continent opened up new avenues of architectural thought for him,[104] particularly in Italy, where he was more fascinated by 'modern' interiors of buildings like the Etruscan Museum in the Villa Guarini, Rome, than by ancient ruins or *palazzi*.

His lifelong interest in regional characteristics never left him, and sketch books from holidays in the 1970s on the Mediterranean island of Gozo are full of studies of stonework details, farming instruments and ancient symbols (ILLUST. 273).

As Dean Addleshaw of Chester noted, 'throughout his life as an architect George Pace was characterized by openness to new ideas'.[105] His new churches of the 1970s – Woolston (1970) (ILLUST. 122), Thornaby on Tees (1970) (ILLUST. 125), James the Deacon, York (1971) and Bransholme Church Centre, Hull (1973) (ILLUSTS 118–120) differed from their earlier counterparts in that less money was available, and that in following the developing new Liturgical Movement approach, no dramatic architectural build-up is evident. Also the age was changing in other respects. The era of the self-build church arrived (Denaby Main 1972)[106] and extensions to ancient churches were beginning to be strongly questioned (Ormskirk 1973).[107]

Those who knew him acknowledge that 'at his death he had not come to the full term of his development.'[108] The Royal Academy drawing of his proposed new vestries at Durham Cathedral (1974) hints at the difficult beginnings of a new phase in its early stages of development. But this was not to be. George Pace died on 23 August 1975, in hospital, after a long and difficult illness. He was 59 years old.

68a

Design

Background

What Pusey's Oxford Movement had been to the nineteenth century, some thought the Liturgical Movement might be to the twentieth century. Peter Hammond defines the Liturgical Movement in his book *Liturgy and Architecture* as 'an attempt to reformulate in terms of contemporary social and cultural patterns the essential function of the Church in the Modern World, being not confined to any one country or denomination'.[109]

Certainly George Pace himself believed the Liturgical Movement to be more than a passing fashion,[110] but he underlined the 'immense importance' of the Movement in this country being grounded on a disciplined study of first principles. Only after the acceptance of, and grounding in, these principles, would roots be sent down in the hearts and lives of clergy and laity, he believed; and so 'only thus will the Liturgical Movement in this country avoid becoming yet another mere fashion in church furnishing'.[112] Without the deep thought on the New Liturgy by the Church there could be no real progress in the development of 'Church Architecture', he maintained; and he emphasized that 'the Church has much to do. It is fatal to leave architects to grope in the dark. It is no part of an architect's work to try to evolve a programme when designing for the Church'.[111]

Particularly he saw:

> Worship is deemed to be pre-eminent, and architecture and the related arts to be its handmaidens . . . for worship appears in its functions as the inspirer and the consumer of architecture.[112]

For him, personal guidance on these matters was to come from amongst the clergy with whom he worked, particularly the Bishops of Wales with whom he remained in close contact during the rebuilding of Llandaff Cathedral. The Bishop of Swansea and Brecon had, in a sermon commemorating George Frederick Bodley, RA, which was preached at the Annual Festival of the Ecclesiological Society in 1957, indicated the kind of programme 'which the Church must give to architects if they are to respond'.[113] The essence of this text ran:

> There is a profound need in times of transition for theologians thinking sacramentally in the modern context, for historians thinking radically, in the sense that they go back to the roots and help us to prune developments and growths that have grown old or are crowding upon and choking out would-be vigorous new growths. We need liturgiologists who see the wholeness of Christian worship as

70

exemplified, for example, supremely in the Eucharist, and enable architects to see their work in terms of this wholeness. In the Eucharist the prayer, the hymn, the creed, the sermon, the standing, kneeling or sitting, the Canon, the Consecration, the Communion, the thanksgiving are all parts which give significance to and derive their significance from the one whole sacramental act, the offering of all to God through Christ. So the architect sees his glass, his sculpture, his seats, his pulpit, his kneelers, his organ, above all his altar and the relations between it and all the other parts of the church as parts which give significance from the one building whose purpose it is to set forth the Glory of God in the one supreme act of Christian worship.[114]

For George Pace it was essential to analyse the principles that needed to be in operation if post-war rebuilding of blitzed churches, and especially the building of new churches, was to be achieved, not only in a twentieth-century manner, but as a fusion of worship and architecture.[115]

70 Scargill, Wharfedale, new chapel 1958–61: interior looking towards the north porch. Fittings in wrought iron and English oak. Structure of laminated timber and local stone hewn from the hillside

OPPOSITE
69 Wythenshawe, Manchester – William Temple Memorial Church, new church 1960–6: view from enclosed chapel looking liturgically east to the high altar. Fittings in wrought iron and English oak. Structure of rolled steel, brick and concrete

Christ Church, Fulwood, Sheffield. Extensions – new chancel and south aisle 1953–5:

OPPOSITE
71 The new chancel: 'Drama from sheer uncluttered surfaces of huge scale'[116]

72 Exterior as built, ink and pencil, 10 × 9in (25.4 × 22.9cm)

72

73 Proposed war memorial, built in modified form, ink 4 × 5in (10.2 × 12.7cm)

south west corner : War Memorial.   73

When he built his first church, the Liturgical Movement was virtually unknown in Britain, but George Pace managed to grasp that the reason for the excellence of so many continental churches built in the 1930s was the outcome of factors which hardly existed in England:

> *a*. the existence for many years of the Liturgical Movement. Of congregations who had grown up within the movement and who naturally demanded that their new churches should give expression to it. The Liturgical Movement was not something applied from without as a desirable theory. It was something living which demanded satisfaction:

and

> *b*. modern architecture had been a living force for many years and was well understood as a living, natural and very positive way of building. Continental architects had been through a strict discipline. They had stripped building to bare bones. They were not using a style, they were not using clichés, they were living and working naturally in a live architecture.[117]

Early experiments on the Continent impressed him, but he found conditions in England were not so conducive to the emergence of a live, modern architecture.

OPPOSITE
74 St Michael's, Bramhall, western extension 1958–61: the existing church of 1910 was 'a decent stone building in the best tradition . . . but made something special by G. G. Pace's West tower . . . inside typical Pace – an undisguised metal ladder to the top'[121]

OPPOSITE
75 All Saints, Intake, Doncaster, new church 1951–6: built upon the foundations of an uncompleted Neo-Romanesque church began in 1939 but reorientated east/west[120]

76

76 Bramhall; interior of tower

77 Intake: view from north-west

78a–c All Saints, Intake, Doncaster: interior 1956 – walls white-painted brickwork, ceiling fibrous plaster in deep blue, later reredos painted panels by Harry Harvey, 1964. Medieval font on new shaft

77

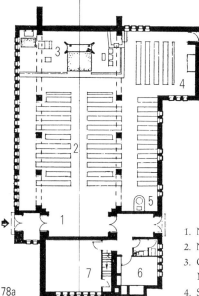

78a

1. Narthex
2. Nave
3. Chancel and N. chapel
4. Side chapel
5. Font
6. Vestry
7. Vestry

78b

78c

George Pace spent much time thinking on these matters and setting down his thoughts in his first book, *The New Churches*, written during the war. This unfinished book formed the basis of another, *Worship and Architecture*, which he added to from 1963 to 1975, though this too remained incomplete. We have therefore to rely on the many papers and articles brought out by him in the early 1960s to understand the background to his principles and precepts on church design, aspects of which he was also to apply to secular design.[118]

In his paper entitled 'Architecture and the Architect in the Service of the Church,' delivered at the Liverpool Conference in September 1962,[119] the thoughts expressed were

> the result of twenty-five years of thinking about modern architecture and its relationship to church building, of having with much travail to evolve my own approach to building new churches, altering and repairing existing churches and designing all kinds of church furniture and fittings. During these years I have had the immense advantage of hearing wisdom from many Bishops, Deans, Priests and Architects.

He went on to suggest that there were three major questions every contemporary architect called upon to build a church should ask himself:

a Is there such a thing as modern architecture, and if so what are the fundamentals?

b Is modern architecture capable of being in the service of the Church? If the answer is no, what does he do about it?

c Why does he want to build a church?

79

St Leonard and St Jude,
Doncaster – new church
1957–63:

79 Exterior under
construction, 1960

80 Plan

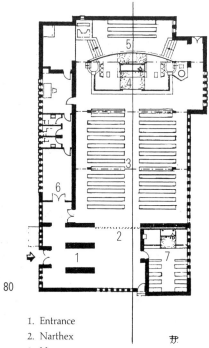

80

1. Entrance
2. Narthex
3. Nave
4. Sanctuary
5. Choir
6. Vestries
7. Chapel

OPPOSITE
81 Interior shortly after
completion: salvaged
furnishings included a
medieval tub font on a
new base, Victorian
pews, and Pugin statues
– all carefully integrated
to become 'part and
parcel of the church as a
whole'. In this church,
George Pace, generally
against obscure
symbolism, conceded the
interior structure of
parabolic arches in
laminated timber were
akin to the ribs of an
upturned boat, 'the Ark of
God' he suggested[122]

ST · MARY'S · CHURCH LUTON

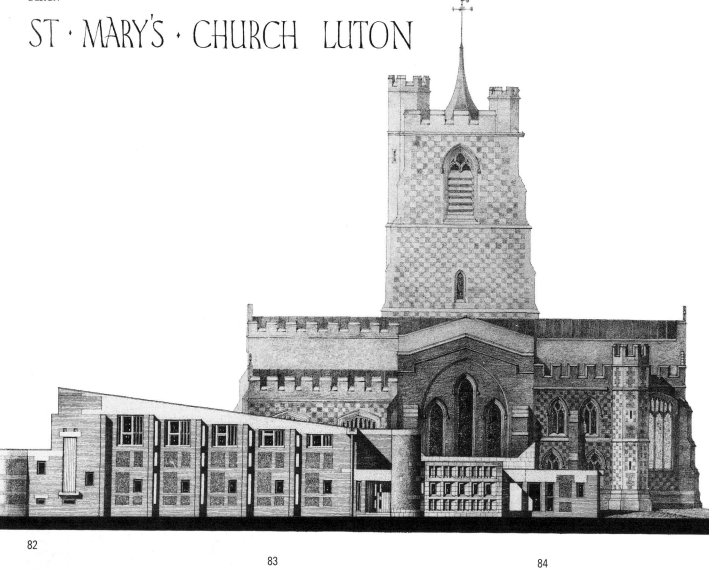

82

83   84

St Mary's, Luton – new vestries and church hall, 1966–69:

82 East elevation abstracted from the drawing exhibited in the Royal Academy Summer Exhibition, 1968. Ink and pencil 33 × 16in (83.8 × 40.6cm), section illustrated 21 × 15in (53.3 × 38.1cm)

83 Link with sacristy: panels in knapped flint with ashlar stone surround to match the church

84 Main entrance and stair turret. 'The design is contemporary but in the spirit of additions made to the church in medieval times and leaves the best of the exterior views intact'[123]

As George Pace expected the Church to question its liturgical roots, so he expected church architects to question the fundamentals of their architecture. They could only do this, he argued, from a sound knowledge of the history of architecture.

Organic culture

He saw the past as holding the key to understanding the future. He believed past organic cultures would form both the model and the inspiration for a new 'living' architecture. It is important to understand George Pace's vision of the past, his preoccupation with organic cultures, and his rejection of 'modern' architecture, in order to see the context of his development of a twentieth-century architecture capable of serving the Church.

What was this organic culture, the culture of the Middle Ages to which he constantly referred? He saw it as a period in human history where growth was slow and steady. It was a time when developments in all departments of life could be absorbed and digested; in stark contrast to the technological materialistic civilization of the twentieth century, where an almost complete severance from the prime realities (or grass roots) of existence removed the essential foundation imperative for the sustenance of an organic culture. In the organic culture of the Middle Ages the whole man could exist. A dynamic architecture flourished capable of satisfying every building need of society – satisfying all naturally and in due degree.

> Gothic architecture was pre-eminently able to give concrete form to the aspirations of the Church. But once again, in due degree, slipper chapel, parish church, collegiate, monastic and cathedral church. There was none of the architectural anarchy which today in an English town might well give as high an architectural emphasis to a public convenience as to a parish church.
>
> Those who designed the buildings and those who wrought upon them were closely related. All worked unselfconsciously within the discipline of the organic culture, happily knowing only the comfort and authority of a closed tradition. All worked as individuals, yet were not guilty of violent individualism.[124]

This aspect of the organic culture, whereby medieval designers and craftsmen neither sought nor gained great personal reputations, appealed to George Pace, for he believed that only by anonymous creation could churches be conceived as 'theological affirmations'.

Though he found interest in knowing which buildings were the work of John Ramsay, and found it instructive to compare the works of Henry

85

86

Rushmere, Suffolk, new extensions 1967–8:

85 New south-east entrance

86 New east end with nave altar, and furnishings

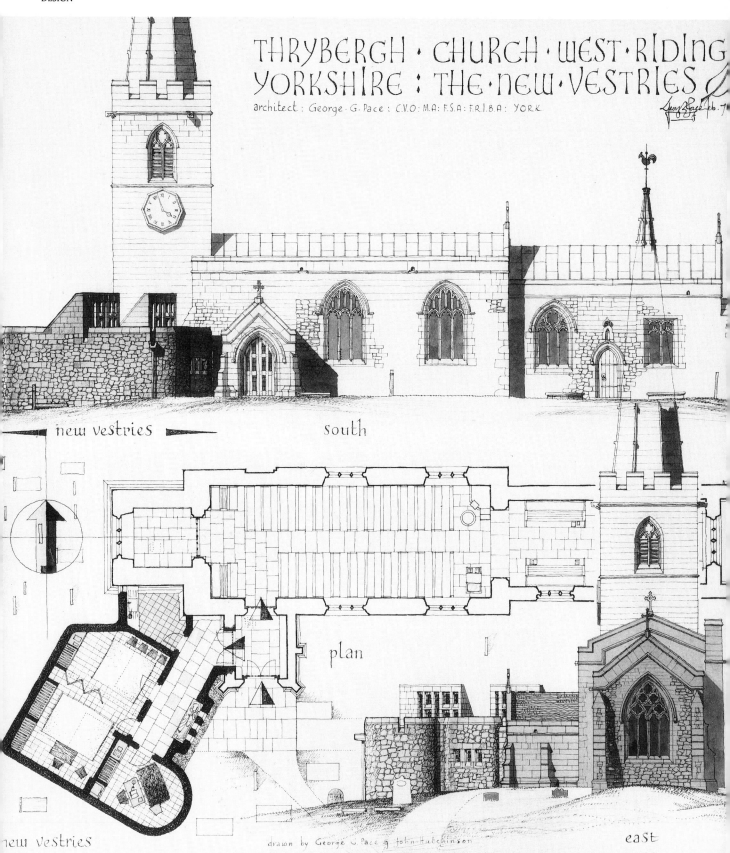

THRYBERGH · CHURCH · WEST · RIDING
YORKSHIRE : THE · NEW · VESTRIES
architect : George · G · Pace : C.V.O : M.A : F.S.A : F.R.I.B.A : YORK

new vestries   south

plan

new vestries   drawn by George G Pace & John Hutchinson   east

87 Drawing exhibited at
the Royal Academy
Summer Exhibition,
1971. Ink and wash
16 × 17in
(40.6 × 43.2cm)

Yevele, William Wynford, John Clyve and John Lewyn, he realized such knowledge was inessential and incidental to the lively appreciation of the nave of Canterbury or King's College Chapel. The great medieval church is beyond human scale, he said, and often quoted: 'This is none other but the House of God, and this is the gate of heaven'. J. N. Comper in his *Of the Atmosphere of a Church* emphasized the same point, and George Pace acknowledged the debt he owed to Comper in formulating many of his own thoughts on church architecture.

He saw the Renaissance as producing a climate hostile to the building of 'theological affirmations' by encouraging the emergence of the architect, sculptor and the painter as individuals. However, he acknowledged that

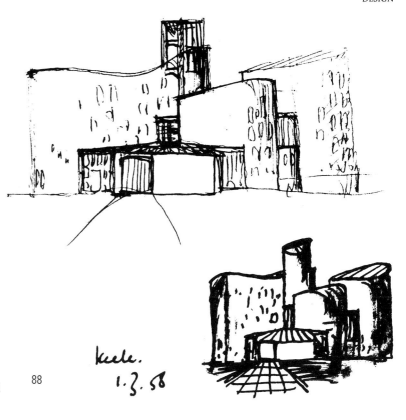

88

> The Architect, the artist, and the craftsman were still enfolded in an organic culture and still worked more or less unselfconsciously within a closed tradition. Growth and development in all departments of life could still be fully absorbed and digested. The whole man could still emerge. Charles II could appoint Wren, then Savilian Professor of Astronomy, as his assistant surveyor. In doing so he was following the traditions of Renaissance humanism which saw no separation of arts from sciences, decreed architecture to be but one department of the intellect, and would see nothing incongruous in making an astronomer into an architect or vice versa.

In this era, he said, one could still appreciate the great buildings of St Paul's Cathedral or St Stephen's Walbrook without knowing the architect: 'In this most important attribute of an organic culture, the English Renaissance and Gothic of the Middle Ages were largely at one'.

But he believed that the vogue of the Grand Tour which followed, and especially the new archaeological interest in the excavations and plunder of ancient Greece and elsewhere in the Near East, gave powerful encouragement to the stirrings of an historical conscience.

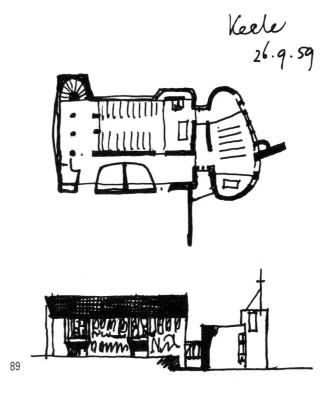

89

More of George Pace's thoughts on the damage caused to creative work through the interference of an historical conscience are expressed in the following chapter, but it is enough here to say that he believed the fashions of the Adam brothers and Wyatt's Classical and Gothique work, although of varying degrees of delightfulness, all indicated a lowering of architectural depth, and were symptomatic of immense and unprecedented changes, which were 'not only slowly but surely destroying organic culture, but creating a total environment in which an organic culture could no longer exist'.

He claimed the Industrial Revolution finally banished organic culture. The new climate

Early sketch designs for Keele University College Chapel:

---

88 Red Biro and blue ink 4 × 4in (10.2 × 10.2cm)

89 Indian ink 4 × 4in (10.2 × 10.2cm)

encouraged, indeed demanded, the emergence of individualism, he said. The closed tradition had vanished, 'and the spiritual gulf which separated the Gothic faith from what was to follow now appeared in all its starkness'.

He saw lack of spiritual faith as the major cause for the demise of architecture. 'It was the world of the spirit, the "interior castle" that was left to decay, while the discoveries of the scientific materialism were pursued'.

In this period of cultural chaos, with the arts exposed to every whim and fancy of rampant individualism, he suggested there was 'a dehumanization in all parts of life and abjuring of God, and even of man', producing conditions having no parallel in history.

With information on past and current theories printed and illustrated in an overwhelming torrent of books and pamphlets, immense strides were made in understanding, recording and disseminating knowledge about the architecture of previous ages. Thus, he said, 'The simple unsophisticated closed tradition vanished. Everybody knew too much about what the past had done in architecture'.

Living creation had died, he claimed – no longer could the manner of building alter as the years pass, by natural changes from within. Not only was there the entirely new phenomenon of technological advance on a vast scale, but it was no longer possible to absorb and digest it. The changes which now followed thick and fast could only be from without and 'the mere titivations of passing fashion'.

This lack of depth was to continue into the twentieth century. Essentially, he maintains, the nineteenth century saw dimly the nightmare world of dehumanization, and most sought escape in the safety of revivals of past Golden Ages. There were exceptions:

Augustus Welby Pugin grasped that all was not well with Revived Gothic, and in his propagandist books – but hardly in his buildings – he pointed a way to salvation.

Several other Victorian architects in letter (and some obscure ones like Thomas Harris even in deed) did likewise, but with little impact, for the devastating logic of Viollet le Duc was denied to the English theorists; they were incapable of, and would certainly have been frightened of, following theories where they inevitably led.

Modern culture

In his consideration of the late nineteenth century and early twentieth century, George Pace was looking for the emergence of a new architecture, one reflecting the new age, as the organic culture of the Middle Ages had reflected its own faith. He

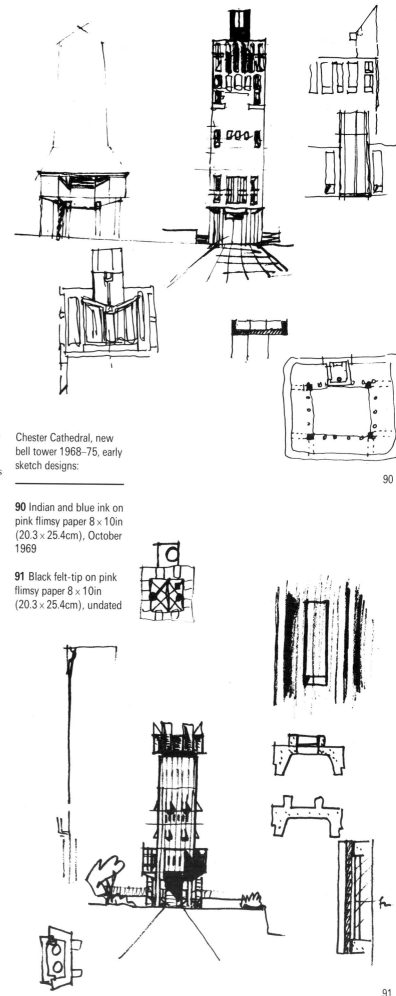

Chester Cathedral, new bell tower 1968–75, early sketch designs:

90 Indian and blue ink on pink flimsy paper 8 × 10in (20.3 × 25.4cm), October 1969

91 Black felt-tip on pink flimsy paper 8 × 10in (20.3 × 25.4cm), undated

90

91

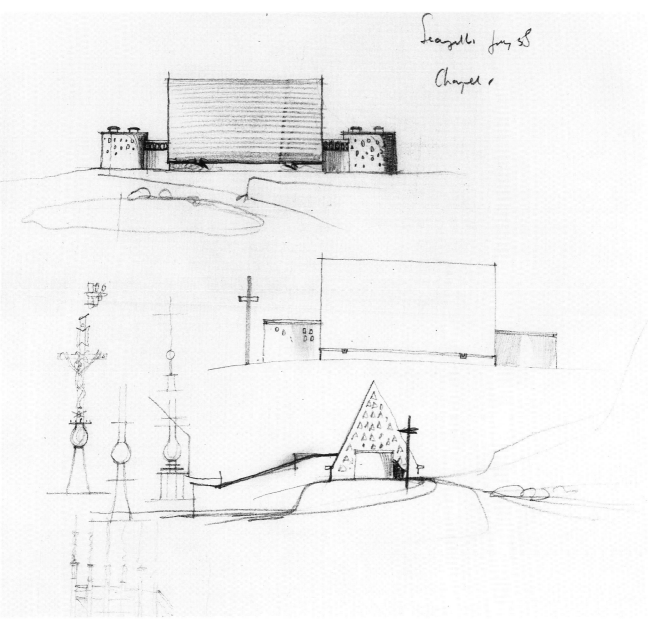

Scargill July 58
Chapel.

92

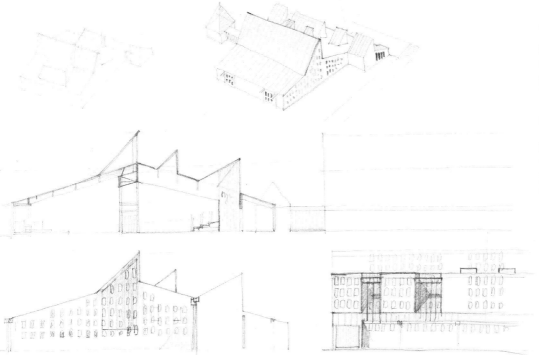

Early sketch designs:

92 Scargill Chapel 1958–61: pencil on tracing paper, July 1958, 12 × 11in (30.5 × 28cm), (cross and candlesticks unidentified)

93 St John's College Chapel, York, 1962–7: pencil on Rowney drawing paper, 8 December 1962, 11 × 9in (28 × 22.9cm)

93

94

found encouraging new styles and new conceptions of spatial relationships emerging, but they were based on materialism, not spiritualism.

Early engineer-architects like Telford, Brunel and Stephenson, and those far removed from the practice of architecture – Joseph Paxton etc. – showed the possibilities in their actual works, unsupported by any pretentious aesthetic theories. Painters such as Manet, Cézanne, Matisse and Braque awoke to possibilities which only eyes newly opened to fresh facets of the external core of aesthetics could comprehend, he suggested:

> The works of early engineer-architects and the painters worked as leaven. New conceptions of the interplay of solid and void, new spatial relationships, new awareness of shape, line and silhouette, of texture and colour began to emerge and to be appreciated. In this the silent, ever-present witness of railways, ships, and machinery of all kinds played a great part. Alongside the scholarly and the eclectic architecture of the nineteenth century there existed a despised but vigorous industrial vernacular. Until recently the importance of this industrial vernacular has been rather overlooked.

This is not to say George Pace brushed aside

nineteenth-century revival architecture. Indeed, he held the works of those great Victorian architects – Butterfield, Street, Scott – in enormous respect, recognizing the creativeness of their work as nineteenth-century first, and revival second, but this aspect of architecture is tied up with a spiritual quality of which more will be said later. For the moment we are to concentrate on George Pace's vision of the emergence of a modern architecture

95

94 St Mark's, Chadderton: new church, 1960–3

St Mark's, Sheffield: new church, 1950–67:

95 South wall

97 North wall: the final derivative of the double mullions and through transomes influence from Yorkshire medieval churches, on George Pace's design work (*see* Sheffield Cathedral, p. 175)

96 William Temple Memorial Church, Wythenshawe: new church 1960–6

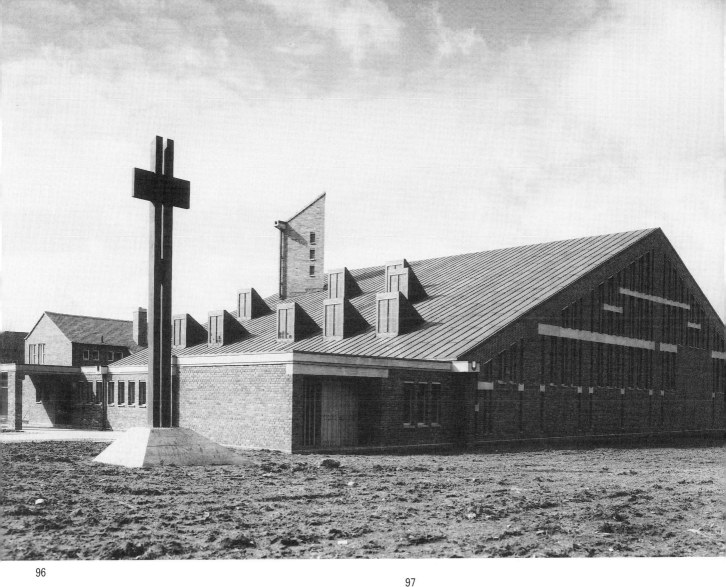

and the question as to whether this could be in the service of the Church.

William Morris, C. A. Voysey and W. R. Lethaby performed vital pioneer work in creating the conditions and climate essential for the general emergence of a modern architecture, George Pace claimed – and here he is in agreement with others such as Nikolaus Pevsner. He admired Art Nouveau, particularly the work of Mackintosh, but he considered the style to be 'a mere passing phase', useful though it was in an age of revolution, as an immediate forerunner of modern architecture. Interestingly he did not see Sir Edwin Lutyens as a well-mannered revivalist, but as someone who

> built with a wit possibly even more highly developed than that of Le Corbusier. He combined his wit with a personal rationale of aesthetics disciplined on a geometrical basis of proportions certainly as awe-inspiring as that of Le Corbusier.

But encouraging as these architectural styles were, for George Pace 'Modern' architecture was represented by the emergence of the 'New Style' (or Modern Movement as it is now known) on the Continent:

RIGHT
98 St Mark's, Chadderton, new church, 1960–3: interior looking east; considered by Pevsner to be 'Almost as raw and wild as Wythenshawe'[125]. (*See* ILLUSTS 94 and 97)

99 Plan of St Mark's, Chadderton

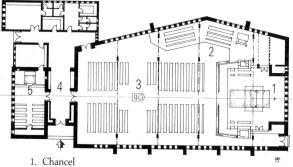

1. Chancel
2. Choir
3. Nave
4. Narthex
5. Chapel   99

In the years immediately preceding the First World War the architecture of reason and functionalism was in full swing in several countries. The underlying basis of the present age as it affects architecture had not only been analysed, but foundations laid by many English architects, artists, and thinkers during the preceding century had enabled certain continental architects, especially Gropius, to create the new architecture and to start proselytizing the world. In Gropius we may see the instigator of the New Style. He determined the character of modern architecture; Dr Pevsner has likened his achievements to the pioneering breakthrough from Romanesque to fully fledged Gothic which the master of the east chapels and ambulatory of St Denis achieved in one supreme white-hot creative act; the root from which all Gothic development of the next eighty years sprang. Against the achievement of Gropius, Gaudi and Sant' Elia appear as freaks, and art nouveau the invention of raving individualists quite properly in revolution against the smug make-believe of the nineteenth century, but without any real understanding of the basis from which the new architecture must spring and the factors it must satisfy.[126]

He mentions the part played by Henri van de Velde, Otto Wagner, Berlage, Behrens, and of the USA architects Louis Sullivan, H. Richardson and Frank Lloyd Wright, but it is the conditions under which this architecture arose, on which he concentrates:

> Modern Architecture has arisen from conditions which have no parallel in history. In its present stage of development it is still part of the dissolution which started some two hundred years ago. During that time civilization has largely abjured God and is well advanced in abjuring Man.

south

west

north

east

UNIVERSITY·OF·KEELE :
THE CHAPELS

101

102

103

101 Durham University College Library 1961–6

Keele University Chapel: 1959–65:

102 From the south west

103 The Roman Catholic south-east apse chapel beyond the raised hydraulic screen

OPPOSITE
100 Design drawing in ink, 1965. 26 × 45in (66 × 114cm)

104

104 Pilgrimage Chapel, Ronchamp, France, 1950–54. Architect – Le Corbusier

105 Ibadan Cathedral, Nigeria, 1954–65. Architect – George G. Pace (project abandoned). Model showing western entrance front (*see also p. 197*)

In recent years there has been rapid growth in dehumanization, the rise of the organizational man and the like manifestations in the social, political and technological fields. The isms and fashions of the last forty years in art are to many baffling phenomena. Not only is apparently serious attention and criticism given to the works of bona fide architects and artists, but the works of lunatics, chimpanzees, the making of pictures by throwing paint or the blind manipulation of bicycle wheels, the production of building by the planned withdrawing of all conscious design and control, are treated with equal seriousness. All this may well be but a manifestation of the dissolution, the chaos of total decay of the past two hundred years, pushed along unconsciously by astute critics climbing on the band-waggon. It seems fairly certain that the choas of total decay, the upsurge of irrationalism and the unhealthy concern, even obsession, with extinction exists, flourishes, and increases because no longer is society able to cope with and keep in subjection these things, having lost faith both in God and itself.

With such admiration for this emergence of a grass-roots, living architecture, founded on first principles, one which produced the early-twentieth-century churches of the liturgical movement on the Continent, one would expect George Pace to be at least in part content, but this is not so.

It is the fundamentals from which modern architecture must spring which George Pace is at odds with, for they run in direct conflict with the requirements of the Church. He saw the aesthetics of buildings such as the model factory at the Werkbund Exhibition, Cologne (1914) produced by Gropius in his 'supreme white-hot creative act' as representing 'faith in social science and rational planning, faith in machines, belief in architecture being a service for all men'. However, this meant

that warm personal relationship between architect and client, as in past organic but craft cultures, has gone for good and that the new conditions require architects to be cold, so as to command impersonal technical processes and anonymous clients, and that there is no place in the present world (and thus in architecture) for mystery and other-worldly speculation.

Here, then, was no place for 'wonder, worship, magic and symbolism', the very ingredients Lethaby saw as the inner heart of an ancient building. The credo of modern architecture – the Gropius flashpoint – is clearly, he said, 'such that modern architecture is not and cannot be naturally in the service of the Church'.

He had noticed that after only a very short period of discipline the reason and functionalism of the Modern Movement came into question. The stern beliefs of the pioneers were found to be hard and straight. 'We are frightened of the logical

outcome of such beliefs.' In Britain works by Wells Coats, Maxwell Fry, Connel Ward and Lucas and Tecton were isolated but brave attempts to use there the developments which were possible on the Continent, but

this country has missed the continent's many years of discipline and the stripping down to the basic modern architecture. We resemble the urgent pianist trying to play Chopin without going through the tedium of the exercise and practice. After World War II, economics and the presence of the second generation of architects from the Schools made sure that the semblance of modern architecture would be the normal approach in this country. But as we see the infantile fashions and clichés which follow one another with bewildering speed, the absence of the tough period of training and discipline has been fatal, the semblance but not the spirit is present.

The nineteenth century saw dimly and sought to escape their nightmare world. We see even clearer and the nightmare is more horrific. They escaped into the safety of revivals of past Golden Ages; we into undisciplined expressionism. Works by Le Corbusier, Ronchamp in particular [ILLUST. 104] in Brazil, in the winning design in the recent competition for Boston City Hall, are really a return to the state of mind which erupted in Art Nouveau. It is little wonder that books on Gaudi pour from the presses. It is little wonder that Expressionist fashions are as ephemeral as those in the rag trade, for once again the dangerous tenet of art for art's sake is in ascendancy.

Contemporary church architecture

The answer to George Pace's first question at the Liverpool Conference – 'Is there such a thing as modern architecture?' – must be 'yes', but the answer to his second question – 'Is modern architecture capable of being in the service of the Church?' – was, quite simply, 'No'. Then what does the architect do about it? This was his next question.

This denial of the credo of modern architecture 'creates great difficulties for the architect striving to work for the Church', but 'it poses a special challenge and opportunity to the Church itself'.

George Pace believed one necessity came above all others – the church architect must be a churchman or believer. At present,

there is a dichotomy between the Church and Architect. Until the end of the eighteenth century the architect and the artist were largely immune from presumption; certainly presumption was exceptional. Then a new philosophy of art began to gain converts in what had become a highly secularized society. The artist was now to be the high priest, 'the dignity of Mankind is now laid into thy hands' (Schiller). Not only is it no longer

106 St Philip, Cosham, Portsmouth, 1936–9. Architect – Sir Ninian Comper

107 St Michael and All Angels, Wythenshawe, Lancashire, 1937. Architect – N. F. Cachemaille-Day

natural for the creator (architect, artist) to submit to the directives of the magician or the priest, but the very foundation of society and faith upon which the natural functions and relationships of priest and creator have always rested, has been destroyed. So far nothing to replace it had grown or been forged.

In the architect as believer, he saw some redemption. Strangely enough it was the Church who challenged this view. In May 1959, representatives from the European countries and the USA met at the Ecumenical Institute of the World Council of Churches and after a week's study produced a 13-point statement. The fifth point of this Bossey Statement suggested that there was no need for the architect of a new church to be a churchman or even a believer. But George Pace declared:

Only if the sole concern is to get a building which is an example of real modern architecture, or the current expressionist escape from modern architecture would this be true. It is not likely to get us very far in bringing modern architecture into the service of the Church, nor is it likely that an architect who is not a churchman or believer will be able to, or want to, discipline himself to take the unpopular but essential standing against the current mumbo-jumbo which envelops architectural publicity at the present time.

'The Church Architect must desire to build a church as an Act of Worship.' In making this statement he not only drew on the experience of his own Christian faith, but cited the lessons which were to be learnt from a study of the more successful English churches of the nineteenth century, where the architects were not only masters of their art, but dedicated churchmen, whose religious beliefs and architectural principles had been deeply thought out and were passionately held. He insisted that

To these men building a church was not just a commission but a way of life and an opportunity of humbly serving God with all their might. When such an architect was linked with a like-minded priest and congregation, the result transcended time and place, and a nineteenth century 'theological affirmation' came into being.

In Augustus Welby Pugin, Gothic architecture was Christian and fused with the enthusiasm of a convert to become his whole being, tempered only by his love of the sea and ships. Studying theology and arguing theology were amongst his recreations . . . Pugin fondly imagined that St Augustine's, Ramsgate was fourteenth-century Kentish Regional newly done, whereas we see it, and savour it, as Pugin through and through, the work of a medieval-Victorian.[127]

The famous Victorian architect George Edmund

107

Street provided another example. Here was a man, intending to take Holy Orders, who had changed his mind and became an architect. George Pace quotes B.F.L. Clarke:[127(a)]

Street was a religious man and believed firmly in the connection between architecture and religion. In his early days he even wished to form a college for instruction in art of which the members should keep a religious rule. He regarded the phases of Gothic architecture as reflections of the spiritual life of the Church. It was Christian architecture and could never be developed except by an essentially Christian intention on the part of the architect as well as on the part of his employers.

In all his designs he aimed at producing churches which could be used. Churches were made for people, not people for churches. A church ought to be free, open, efficiently run, and used by everyone, poor as well as rich, men as well as women. He believed that a town church should not be like a village church, nor should it be an exact copy of an ancient town church. The old plan should be modified.

In the case of George Frederick Bodley we have an Anglo-Catholic as the term was understood in the later nineteenth century. He was a poet and musician, as well as architect, and George Pace considered he brought Gothic to a degree of elegance and refinement which it hardly ever reached even in the Middle Ages; and that he was able to add this new quality because it grew out of the demands of nineteenth-century Anglo-Catholicism, nineteenth-century refined scholarship and the later nineteenth-century version of the historical conscience.

In the twentieth century,

we would find this same utter dedication to the Church in the lives of those architects who have built real churches, twentieth century 'theological affirmations' which though pearls beyond price are not news – Sir Ninian Comper, Dominikus Bohm, Martin Weber, Rudolf Schwarz. The inner life from which the churches of Comper and Schwarz have sprung may be glimpsed in the former's *Of the Atmosphere of a Church* and the latter's *The Church Incarnate: The Sacred Function of Christian Architecture.*

So far we have examined a brief history of English architecture and its relevance to the Church as understood by George Pace. We have noted the special requirements for an architecture in the service of the Church. We know the attributes our church architect must possess. We know the Church is rethinking its liturgy, absorbing the rethought liturgy and arriving at a state where the absorbed liturgy 'demands' to be given appropriate form in the church building.

But we also know we have no living organic culture; the Church is a fringe activity, architecture is purely intellectual and riddled with individualism. How then can modern architecture, in its twentieth-century manifestation, be brought into the service of the Church? George Pace had no doubts – 'it must be done,' he declared. He refused to look backwards to works of the past 'as a legitimate means of solving today's problems of church building' even though

> for new churches it might appear far safer to turn from unregenerate modern architecture and fall back into the safety of revived architectural style. It gives us churches which are readily acceptable and possibly have a superficial appearance of witnessing to the Glory of God. In reality such churches are just an escape and a symbol of defeat. A living Church demands that its churches be living too.[128]

He noted that the 'lifting' of aesthetically pleasant continental solutions in church planning and arrangement was just a waste of time as far as churches for the Church of England are concerned since

> The Anglican positions as laid down in the Articles states that 'the visible Church of Christ is a congregation of faithful men in which the pure word of God is preached and the Sacraments be duly administered'; that is to say, the Anglican position is that there is equal stress on Word and Sacrament. Thus, in addition to the Communion Service, Matins and Evensong, proper provision has to be made for marriages and funerals and many other occasional services. The tendency to dismiss all aspects except the one Sacrament may make liturgical planning very much easier, but it is no answer to the problems of the Church of England.[129]

Above all, he said,

> To design a worth-while church under present

conditions the architect must, in addition to being a master of his profession, hold passionately many principles not at present fashionable or shared by the majority of his brethren, the critics, or the press.

> In an age of social and architectural revolution, the church architect has to work out for himself his own personal approach to the fusion of worship and architecture.[130]

There were a few architects of the twentieth century who had, in George Pace's opinion, worked out churches in which planning and architectural expression were fused, churches which may be said to have played an important part in the evolution of the modern Church. Examples immediately springing to mind were:

> Temple Moore's two churches at Middlesbrough, St Cuthbert and St Columba; and his fine, but unfinished, church of St Margaret, Leeds; together with Mr Cachemaille-Day's St Michael and All Angels, Wythenshawe [ILLUST. 107].[131]

Other churches exhibiting significance in their architectural expression were Randall Well's little church at Kempley; Sir Walter Tapper's St Erkenwald, Southend-on-Sea; and Goodhart-Rendel's St Wilfrid's, Brighton.[132] He agreed Tapper, Comper, Blacking and Travers were capable of creating interiors which were theological affirmations of a very high order, though he admitted too that there were those who said, 'that fine as this work is in itself, it has no relevance in this day and age'. But 'an impartial consideration of an interior such as St Philip's, Cosham, should show that this is too sweeping a denunciation and one which it is hardly decent to make until a modern church of at least equal quality has been built in this country', George Pace quoted,[132(a)] for he considered St Philip's, Cosham (1937) (ILLUST. 106) designed by Sir Ninian Comper to be in all probability the most significant real church built in this country in the 30 years from 1930 to 1960. These and a few other churches akin to them are far nearer to being 'modern churches' than the present eruption of cliché-ridden 'St Liquorice Allsorts', he said. He suggested that, unfortunately,

> in this country there is, as yet, little understanding as to what constitutes a modern church. On all sides we are assailed by pictures of recent English churches which we are told are examples of modern architecture. That these buildings may have an odd look, a dreamland lookout tower, a glass wall which at a touch disappears beneath the floor, and a mosaic of obscure symbolism executed in broken bottles, does not in fact make them modern churches. They are either exhibitions of ecclesiastical art or merely the pedestrian nineteenth-century – production-church dressed up

108 Ibadan Cathedral, 1954–65: a progression of ideas drawn in black ink on 4 × 7in (10.2 × 17.8cm) Basildon Bond writing paper and on the back of an 5 × 3in (12.7 × 7.6cm) envelope (B), between May and July 1959

109 St John's College Chapel, York, 1962–7: sketch design – section exploring forms of main structure in red Biro on 5 × 7in (12.7 × 17.8cm) Basildon Bond writing paper – undated

110 Sheffield Cathedral, 1956–61: sketch designs – sections exploring forms of structure for the new nave in blue ink on detail paper 8 × 7in (20.3 × 17.8cm), an extract from 13 × 15in (33 × 38.1cm) drawing, April 1956

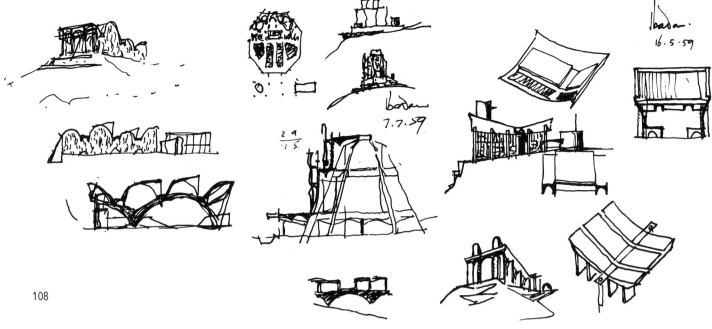

108

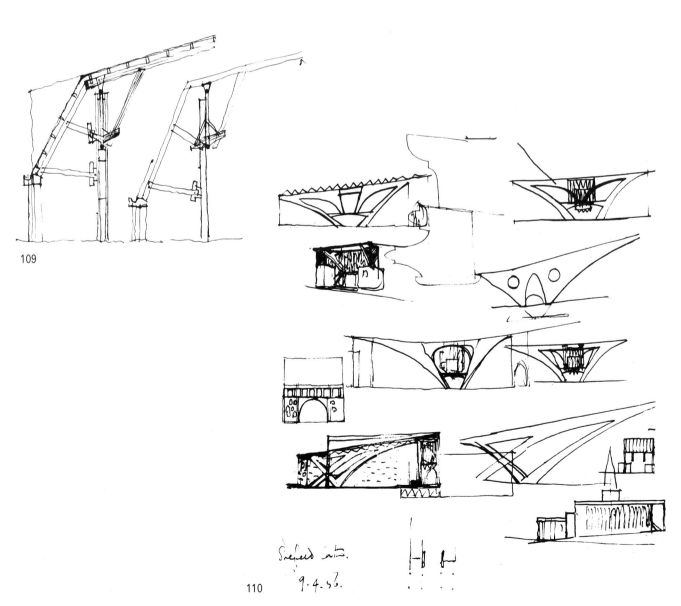

109

110

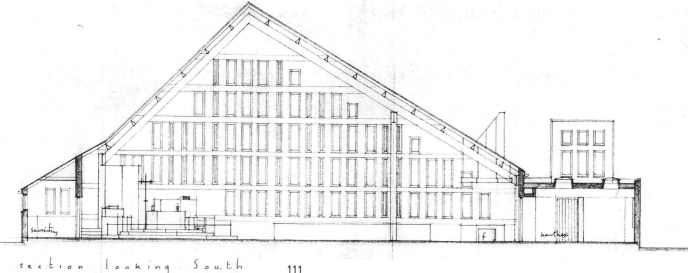

section looking South

111

in clichés 'lifted' from continental churches and illustrated in the architectural glossies.[133]

[Such] modern architecture has perforce little behind it except the intellectual processes of a few outstanding masters and the cacophony of a multitude of fashion-conscious imitators. It is a manifestation of pride of intellect and rampant individualism consciously evolved to satisfy a number of intellectual conceptions, an architecture obsessed with the relationship of buildings to a social or scientific context, to have ceased to be concerned with the Art of Architecture.[134]

The way forward

In spite of all that was happening around him George Pace saw a way forward, one which drew on the strength of the past and on the innovations of the twentieth century. The many strands of thought examined by him in his historical analysis were taken and fused into a wholly new but 'appropriate' approach which might conceivably give form to twentieth-century architecture that could be appropriately used in the service of the Church.

At the risk of repetition it is important to examine these interwoven principles to see how George Pace produced not only a philosophy, but gradually a language of design that evolved slowly during his 30 years of architectural practice.

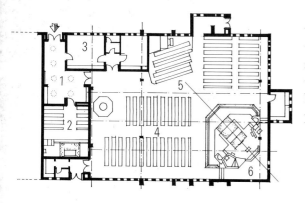

112

Firstly, his preoccupation with 'Organic Culture'. This had developed over a long time, gradually, with changes attributable to grass roots needs resulting from thinking from first principles. The emergence of the New Liturgical Movement of the twentieth century presented an opportunity to follow a similar path, and aligned with this new first principle liturgical thought should be an architecture based on first principles to serve it.

Models from the past were there to substantiate the reality of such architecture. Medieval Gothic, a supreme example of an architecture of first principles, had been the outcome of thinking,

> developed from structural necessities and suggestions, not by addition of ornament to structural forms as some would have it, but by binding structural forms themselves into forms of beauty.[135]

Revivalist Gothic (in the hands of masters such as Butterfield) could also be from first principles as 'an essay in logic, rather than a pastiche of 'cribs' which merely borrows attractive, unexploited features. 'Modern Architecture' by such as Gropius was also an expression from first principles, as a demonstration in 'a faith in science and technology'. George Pace saw an architecture from first principles as essential if it was to be a live expression of contemporary Christian faith.

Organic culture produced designers who worked unselfconsciously within the discipline of a closed tradition, as individuals, yet without violent individualism. The historical conscience destroyed the closed traditions 'forever', but George Pace believed the principle of anonymity should be practised.

> The Architect must be capable of giving his uttermost, yet be able to efface himself, so that the church he builds is to all intents and purposes anonymous in the eye of the beholder. He must be able to resist all desire to use clichés and gimmicks . . . He will be content to feel his way and to work

St Saviour, Fairweather Green, Bradford new church 1966
'The building shows . . . an absence of triviality, an honesty in its use of materials and simplicity – qualities to inspire the work of the church in coming years'[138]

111 Section through an early design, looking south-east. Pencil on tracing paper, 14 × 3in (36 × 8cm)

OPPOSITE
113 Interior looking north east. 'There is no real name for this style. St Saviour's carries the hallmark of the Architect'[137]

112 Ground plan 1963

1. Narthex
2. Chapel
3. Vestries
4. Nave
5. Choir and organ
6. Chancel

114

out, in church after church, his disciplined and deeply thought-out approach. To him, as to Bodley and Comper or Rudolf Schwarz the inevitability of gradualness will be his way.[136]

In addition, he believed the architect would have to

resist the wiles of expressionism and art for art's sake. The contempt of the critics, neglect by the press, the complete absence of star-dust about his head will be his lot, especially if he refuses to 'desert nature and follow criticism' and to hold the belief 'that what matters is not the end-product, the finished church, but the total creative process'.[139]

This suppression of individualism was necessary in order to produce a theological affirmation. Like the designers of the organic culture of the Middle Ages, like the Victorian architects Pugin, Butterfield and Bodley, the church architect of the twentieth century must 'believe in and be moved by a doctrine and liturgy of the Church' and 'must desire to build a church as an Act of Worship'.

In order to do so the twentieth-century architect must use an architecture capable of expressing 'wonder, worship, magic and symbolism'. Without this clear childlike vision, he could not hope to build a church which day and night, whether the Family of God is worshipping or the building is unused, is a constant witness to the Glory of God, and a perpetual act of worship in its mere existence; where 'the beauty of the Vision of God is seen through the witness of men's hands and imagination'. Sadly, though George Pace admired the modern architecture of Gropius for its foundation from first principles, he admitted the church architect of the twentieth century must strive with integrity against many of the first principles of modern architecture because they were in conflict with the faith of the Church. The architect 'must raise "modern architecture" from a mere intellectual relationship of a social or scientific context, to being the art of modern architecture'.

The architect will recognise that a church is the only building of more than human scale, the only building which demands an increase beyond human scale. He will not want to design a church because architects like to be given churches as it gives them opportunities to evolve strange shapes;

In continuing his argument he often quoted an extract from the first volume of *The Ecclesiologist* to show there was nothing new in this: 'fresh from his Mechanics' Institute, his Railway Station, his Socialist Hall, he [the architect] has the presumption and arrogance to attempt a church'.[140]

Citing the church of St Francis, Pampulha;[141] the rebuilt interior of the Franciscan Church, Ulrichgrasse, Cologne; and Le Corbusier's chapel at Ronchamp (ILLUST. 104), he suggested that many different and equally valid approaches to church design are possible within the corpus of modern architecture, and these examples provide a foretaste of what modern architecture in the service of the Church could become. But, he says,

It is perilously close to 'Walt Disneyism' and is an awful warning of what could happen if pride of intellect and the expression of purely personal emotionalism are not disciplined in a re-established union between Church and Architecture.

In 'modern' architecture and technology he did find 'new conceptions of the interplay of solid and void, new spatial relationships, new awareness of shape, line and silhouette, of texture and colour emerging' and saw no reason why one could not borrow from this store (even if the basic principles of its architecture conflicted with his) because historically he saw the tradition of 'pushing forward our awareness of spatial relationship, solids and voids' as being 'always the major aspiration of Western European architecture'. For example he cited the work of Hawksmoor, working at the time of the English Renaissance, when the vestiges of organic culture still remained:

Hawksmoor, especially at St Anne's Limehouse, and the Mausoleum, Castle Howard, occupies a position of special importance to us. We are able to appreciate, in a manner impossible to most of his contemporaries, his genius in advancing the frontiers of architectural experience. We are able to delight in his concern for, and handling of, volumes, the interpenetration of solids in enclosed space, and spatial relationships, disciplined disunity and fragmentation, as part of total architectural conceptions. The exploration of these aesthetic principles is very much part of the best architectural effort of today.

He placed Sir John Soane in the same category, as one who had achieved similar new conceptions, even though still using the language of classical architecture.

George Pace had no wish to copy styles from architectural history in the manner prevalent in the eighteenth and nineteenth centuries. He recognized that the Historical Conscience had played a great part in the destruction of organic culture; but admitted it was hard to escape from this:

114 Yorkshire Dales vernacular: typical seventeenth or eighteenth-century farmhouse near Low Row in Swaledale – an area explored over many years on family holidays

OPPOSITE
Influences — regional characteristics of Yorkshire Gothic:

115 Drax: nave, north clerestory windows, late fifteenth century

116 York Minster: choir, south clerestory, fifteenth century with the double mullions and through transomes (*see* ILLUST. 97)

115

116

It is a force to be reckoned with, fought and dethroned but possibly not utterly destroyed since deep within it there may be attributes which should have a place in the organic culture of the future.

In aspiring to emulate that ancient tradition of pushing forward aesthetic awareness, he saw a solution; for it represented the continuance of an organic approach to culture, one which grew from its past.

> If the architect has sufficient artistic gifts and immense scholarship he may carry further Sir Ninian Comper's 'Unity by Inclusion'. In doing so he may well find that without using stylistic details, either Gothic or Renaissance, he can distil an essence which can be expressed in an entirely new way by invoking our new awareness of spatial relationships and the juxtaposition of solids and voids.[142]

He saw that 'many principles could be learned from ancient buildings which were just as valid today as in the past and which could be, and should be, assimilated in spirit'.

He noted that the ancient churches and the vernacular buildings of the countryside in England and Wales were 'a mine from which those who have the eyes to see can extract very valuable ore, which in turn can be used in creating new alloys'.[143]

Being 'rootless was bad'. He, therefore, endeavoured to abstract from old churches the essence of their characteristics, and to infuse these into a contemporary style to give them a new lease of life.

> In this I was encouraged to know that Le Corbusier not only studies vernacular buildings, but is greatly influenced by them – Ronchamp has immovable roots in peasant building, small Romanesque churches, Greek churches such as Mykonos, Coptic churches, but all digested and given new life in and through Le Corbusier's genius[144] (ILLUST. 104).

This desire to borrow from the past, to evolve an architectural style founded on tradition but enhanced by considerable innovation found expression in the hands of some of the more masterful Victorian and Edwardian architects. Butterfield and Street have been named already, but J. F. Bentley, W. D. Caroe, Basil Champneys, E. S. Prior, W. R. Lethaby, C. F. A. Voysey and Leonard Stokes are others.[145]

There is little doubt George Pace was influenced by these architects,[146,147] and he acknowledged a great admiration for Sir Giles Gilbert Scott. In his article, 'Power Houses of Faith',[148] he says of the new Liverpool Anglican Cathedral:

> Scott had succeeded in doing what his father [George Gilbert Scott II] in all his enormous

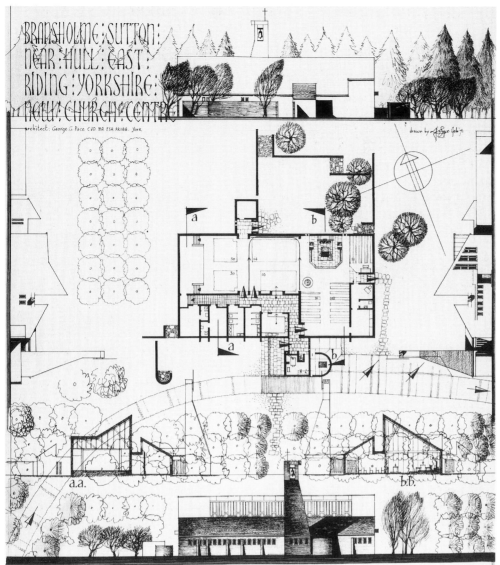

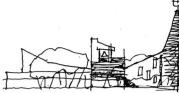

Bransholme. 118

Bransholme, Hull – new church and church centre, 1968–73:

---

117 Royal Academy Drawing, 1971. Ink 16 × 18in (40.6 × 45.7cm)

118 Early sketch design. Ink, 5 × 3in (12.7 × 7.6cm). December 1968

117

119

119 Interior looking north east, before furnishings were in position

practice had never been able to do: he had built a church which had continuity with the best work of the past, but which was at the same time a new thing.

In the same article he moves on to the new Guildford Cathedral, designed by Sir Edward Maufe, which he considered to be

a very personal statement of a rare architectural mind and personality . . . Guildford's roots go back to the English love of good brickwork, which was given architectural grandeur in churches by Butterfield at All Saints Margaret Street; by Edmund Scott's St Bartholomew, Brighton; and by Sir Walter Tapper's St Erkenwald, Southend. Other roots embrace Bodley's St Augustine's, Pendlebury; Temple Moore's Middlesbrough churches of St Cuthbert and St Columba: as well as much good work of the 1920s and 30s in Scandinavia and Germany. Sir Edward Maufe's St Saviour's Acton and especially St Thomas the Apostle, Hanwell; are his own forerunners and experiments for Guildford.

Liverpool and Guildford are not Ronchamp or the cathedral for Brasilia, but basically they are equally legitimate expressions in the twentieth century's

cultural chaos and Liverpool and Guildford in their physical presence will almost certainly have the longer existence.

Working in this tradition, and by encompassing some of the aesthetics of modernism, together with an honest exploration of new materials, George Pace 'successfully straddled that interface between tradition and modernism in a highly effective distillation of both'.[149]

Practicalities

On the practical aspects of building George Pace was convinced that

. . . the need for long life without maintenance; and the quality of ageing gracefully are to be deemed to be major requirements in church design, and to be equated with the Liturgical brief. That this is not an idle or reactionary attitude is fully borne out by the present state of the fabric of many of the 'cheap' churches built between the wars.[150]

More often than not, in the 1950s and '60s, new churches had to be built on a shoestring, but this did not mean that they had to be 'cheap and nasty',

OPPOSITE
New churches:

---

120 Bransholme, Hull, 1968–73

121 Thornaby-on-Tees, 1968–70

122 Woolston, Lancashire, 1968–70

120

121

122

he said. He welcomed the strict economy as an excellent discipline and maintained that, far from limiting him, it 'will be an added inspiration' . . . 'Enforced economy is a patent encourager of real and lasting beauty'.[151]

He possessed a clear understanding of the nature of modern materials as well as traditional ones;[152] and saw the need to choose carefully both the materials and structural systems of his new church building.

> In the past, church buildings produced the opportunities for exciting structural experiment and for that agelong striving in the architecture of the Western world – the mastery of spatial relationships. By and large, structural experiment now takes place in buildings other than churches. It should be remembered that many apparently exciting new structural systems are uneconomic when used in church building, and will not satisfy the demands for long maintenance, free life, and of ageing gracefully. Stern discipline is needed in church building today in the choice of structural systems and materials. The English climate has many endearing qualities, but it is harsh and unkind to building materials. Generally, it will be found that simple structure and first class, well-tried materials are the answer. The simpler the roof the more economic it is likely to be in first cost and future maintenance. Cut up roofs, strange shapes, some types of roof lights not related to the English weather and the material used, and short-life roofing materials all spell future financial headaches. The means of disposing of rainwater, protection against piled up snow and the effects of high winds need much more thought than is usually given. The increasing practice of placing rainwater pipes within the building is to be deprecated. The external use of ferrous metals, unprotected reinforced concrete, and large areas of timber, should be avoided. In churches, reinforced concrete should not be left exposed to the external elements. Some architects, bursting to use current clichés, may feel this unnecessarily cramps their activities, but in church building it is a discipline to be ignored with peril. Timber, properly used, detailed and maintained, could have a part to play in the external cladding of church building, as is demonstrated by its performance in many ancient churches in the Home Counties, East Anglia and the Border. Much greater attention, based on deep knowledge and experience, should be given to the detailing of stonework and brickwork. Many present-day clichés in these materials require detailing which is only applicable to short-life buildings.[153]

Thornaby-on-Tees, new church, 1968–70:

123 Exterior – west face originally designed to accept a church hall extension – a second phase, not undertaken

The creative architect

George Pace believed that architecture in the service of the Church in the twentieth century should be forward looking and creative. He saw his own efforts, and those of the few architects he admired, as producing an 'infant modern architecture. It is still very crude Saxon, and will be generations before it reaches its Perpendicular'.[154] In striving towards this goal the architect would have to face numerous obstructions:

> . . . architects for their experiments need to have opportunities on a very different scale from those needed by painters, sculptors, and the like. They have to have a client who is prepared to bear the cost of the architects' experiments. This presupposes in the client an enlightened interest in new creation in architecture. But it is much easier for a so-called informed opinion on painting and sculpture to be nourished by the spoken or written word, and when it has been nourished, for many reasonably intelligent people to be able to come quietly to an understanding and appreciation of continuing developments in these arts. New creation in architecture is altogether more difficult to explain even to the intelligent. To very few are given the gifts needed before new creations in architecture may be assimilated, understood or appreciated; especially is this so at a time when the historical conscience is so highly developed. The scales have been heavily weighted against the general appreciation of the possibilities in new architectural creation, and architects have had a long battle for the opportunity to experiment and demonstrate their belief in modern architecture.[155]

RIGHT
125 Interior looking west from behind the high altar to baptistry and enclosed chapel behind. Steel frame – matt black. Ceiling – white-faced fibre insulation board with regularly spaced rough-sawn battens over. Altar – limestone block. Hanging cross – stainless steel. Candlesticks – wrought iron. Pews – ash with frames stained matt red. Floor – Granwood cement/fibre tiles to nave and stone paving to sanctuary

124 Plan

1. Chancel
2. Nave
3. Chapel
4. Vicarage
5. Church hall (not built)

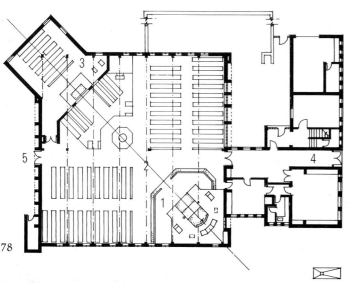

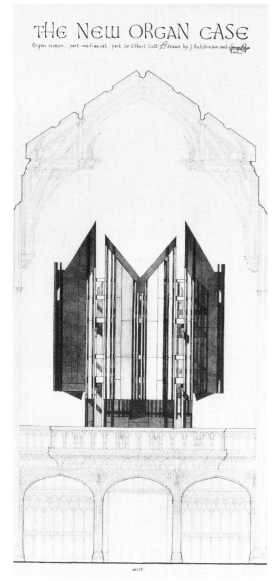

THE NEW ORGAN CASE
Organ screen: part mediaeval, part Sir Gilbert Scott & drawn by J Hutchinson and George Pace

126

The Church must place its trust in the real architect. The financing of new churches is now such an involved matter that a vast bureaucratic machine has arisen. In itself this spells safety first. How can a church conceived in expediency and swaddled in the bands of 'revivals' be built as an act of worship? Further, this earthy approach makes the emergence of real creative architecture next to impossible. Only too often a mere travesty of a 'modern church' gets built. But this wretched building is accepted by the unthinking as a 'modern church' and attracts criticism which brings the possibilities of the real 'modern church' into disrepute. If the Church wants unity with architects, it must give them freedom, it must trust them, and it must be prepared to bear their failures. It must always remember that the collective mind of boards and committees is only the afterglow, at least one generation behind the creative thought and work of architects. It must always be so. Boards and committees can never assist at the moment of creation. The Church, like the nation, has become obsessed with boards and committees

and pretends to find in official bodies wisdom in aesthetic creative matters that no collective mind can ever possess. Let boards and committees carry on with their true function of police activity in curbing the inefficient, the incompetent and the bogus, but let them stand aside (or sit back, perhaps) when the real architect is demonstrating the mastery of his art.[156]

George Pace's interpretation of, and extraction from, mainstream Gothic, classical and vernacular traditions has been described as 'individualistic'[157] and suggests he possessed an acutely rare visual awareness, He found fresh areas for inspiration, previously unmined, particularly in the regional styles he identified in his studies of Yorkshire and Welsh churches. In his design for the completion of Sheffield Cathedral (1955–61) (*pp. 173–7*) he speaks of using a distillation of the regional characteristics found at the churches of Nun Monkton, Bridlington Priory, York Minster, Drax and St Mary's Abbey, York.[158] At Newport Church (1950–55) (ILLUSTS 285–290) and for the Welch Regimental Chapel at Llandaff Cathedral (1956) (ILLUSTS 299–303), churches from the Vale of Monmouth are studied.[159]

At St Michael's College Chapel, Llandaff (1957–59) (ILLUST. 317), regional characteristics from Monmouth Cathedral, Brecon Cathedral, the Yorkshire barns of Swaledale (ILLUST. 114) are all contemplated, together with Le Corbusier's work at Ronchamp (ILLUST. 104), with various strands taken and developed.[160]

Perhaps almost inevitably, George Pace's love and great knowledge of Gothic architecture led to the distillation of a Gothic spirit being . . . 'transmitted in his own vigorous way in his work'.[161]

Dean Addleshaw of Chester Cathedral observed that Pace was steeped in the tradition of the great church architects of the nineteenth century – Gilbert Scott, Bodley and Pearson, and in the twentieth century Giles Scott. Like them, he worked in a Gothic idiom, but 'his work was far removed from what we usually associated with the Gothic architecture of the last century . . . His work was in an idiom peculiar to himself, strange, very personal, at times rather disconcerting'. In drawing a comparison with the seventeenth-century architect, Guarini, an architect who gave his own very personal idiom to the baroque architecture of his day, the Dean argues that George Pace 'stands in much the same relation to twentieth century Gothic: the Guarini of our day'.[162]

The emergence of this style can be seen in the chronological study of his major buildings (*see pp. 145–222*) but perhaps even more so in his furnishings and fittings.

127

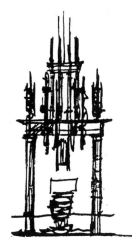

128

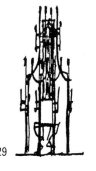

129

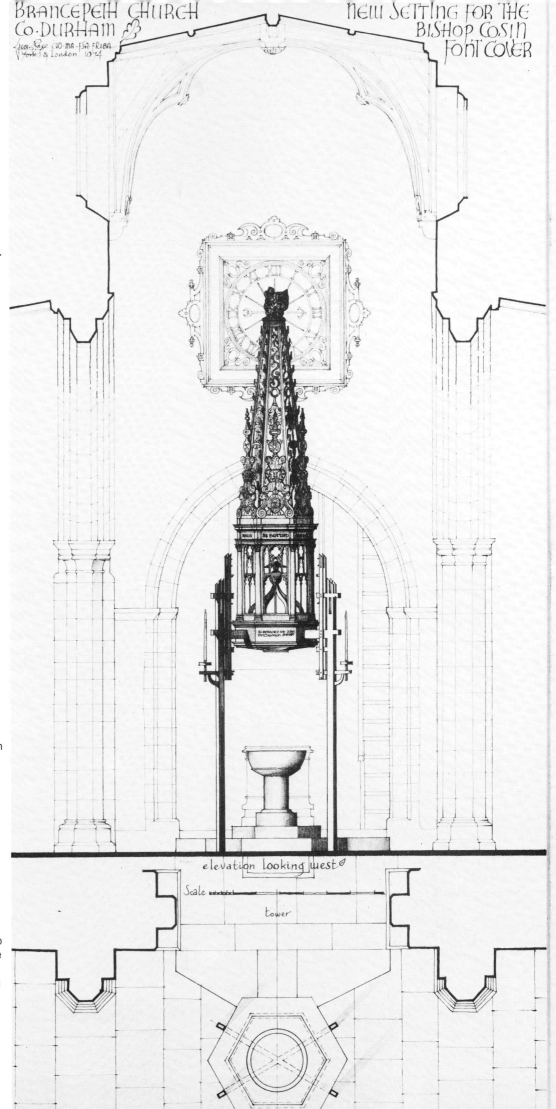

BRANCEPETH CHURCH
Co·DURHAM

Geo. Pace CVO·MA·FSA·FRIBA
York & London   10·74

NEW SETTING FOR THE
BISHOP COSIN
FONT COVER

elevation looking west

Scale

tower

130 Brancepeth, font cover stand: 'There is a similarity in spirit between the wooden spikiness of Bishop Cosin fittings like those at Brancepeth and Sedgefield, and the spikiness of George Pace's metalwork'.[163] Pencil with some ink, 11 × 24in (27 × 61cm), 1974. Drawing exhibited at the Royal Academy Summer Exhibition, 1964. The existing Bishop Cosin font cover is held up permanently on new metal supports to avoid having to move the heavy cover, which had been exerting through its counterbalance hoisting mechanism, severe structural strain on the roof beam above

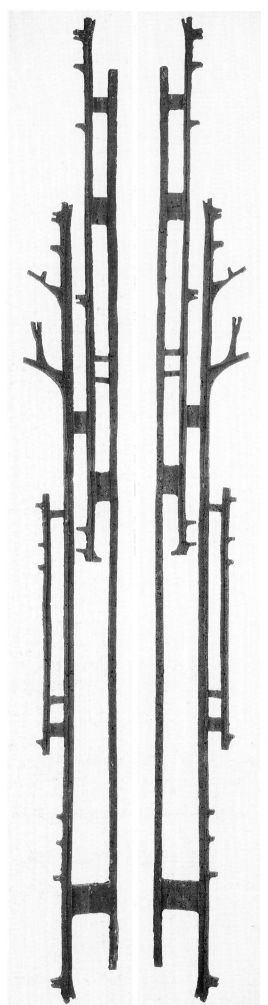

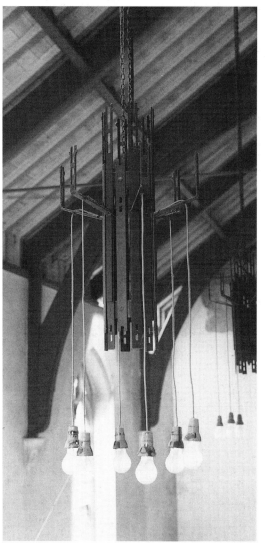

131 39in (99.1cm) high full-size mock-up in cast aluminium (using technique with polystyrene moulds developed by the sculptor Frank Roper) of finials to canopy over archdeacon's stall, Llandaff Cathedral, 1964 (*see* ILLUST. 316)

132

Fittings and furnishings

Interestingly, it is in Pace's designs for new fittings more than in his new buildings, where we find a Gothic presence pared down to a semblance of structural forms, which nevertheless exhibit in themselves an elaborate, decorative quality. 'Gothic in character, but not in form' as Pevsner observes.[164] Upon closer examination the apparent profusion of buttresses, flying buttresses, pinnacles and finials, for example in the light pendants at Birdsall (1954) (ILLUST. 61), the font cover at St Olave's, York (1963) (ILLUST. 196) and the wrought-iron screen at Windsor (1969) (ILLUST. 405) may be seen to result from the repetition of relatively simple forms, miniature structural elements in themselves or, as he himself admitted, 'architectonic forms'. George Pace acknowledged that:

> [whilst] in the past church furniture has largely been designed as miniature replicas of the building style of the time, for the first time in architectural history this is no longer possible. Utterly simple architectonic forms, carried out with superb craftsmanship is one solution – probably the most satisfactory under present conditions.[165]

132 Silsden; wrought-iron pendant lights, 1968. (Roof decoration: trusses deep green, boarding and rafter sides white, rafter soffits red.)

OPPOSITE
133 Helmsley font cover: dark-stained oak with gilding, 1952

131

134

135

136

137

He broke away from

> the peculiarly Anglican approach to designing church furniture started by Bodley and Sedding, written up by Percy Dearmer and so nobly continued by Tapper, Comper, Blacking and Travers . . .[166] [as he held] a sincere belief that Gothic where continuing into the twentieth century needed twentieth century treatment.[167]

In a similar manner to his building designs this twentieth-century treatment developed gradually, through a series of experiments. He began with the use of recognizable classical elements in works such as the priest's stall at Bainton (1948), the screen at Armagh (1950) (ILLUST. 274), the light fittings at Kimberworth (1958) (ILLUST. 134) and the porch at Beverley (1962) (ILLUST. 140). These were concurrent with a period of hybrid classical/Gothic

134 Kimberworth: stained-oak font cover, 1956, later raised permanently on wrought-iron legs, 1972. (Note wooden pendant lights 1952, and roof decoration 1956)

135 Yapham: light-oak font cover with inscription, 1961

136 Scarborough, St Mary's: light-oak font cover with some gilding, 1961

137 Aston: dark-stained oak font cover, 1964

138

OPPOSITE

140 St Mary's, Beverley: south porch in oak with wrought-iron handrail, 1962

141 Pocklington: priest's desk with altar rail, 1952

142 Penistone: priest's desk, 1959; priest's seat, 1963

143 Egglescliffe: priest's desk and inscription, 1971

141   142   143

144 Drawing – ink on cartridge paper with pencil shading 24 × 18in (61 × 45cm), exhibited at the Royal Academy Summer Exhibition, 1972

structures such as the font covers at Helmsley (1952) (ILLUST. 133) and Tinsley (1953) (ILLUST. 197b). Finally he arrived at a style characterized by the vertical element, reminiscent of the Perpendicular style, 'which reinterpreted the Gothic spirit in a purely twentieth century way,'[168] as clearly illustrated in the organ screen at Holy Trinity, Micklegate (1965) (ILLUST. 165), Chester Cathedral nave choir stalls (1966) (ILLUST. 147), Ipswich processional cross (1967) (ILLUST. 54) and the screen gates at Windsor (1969) (ILLUST. 405).

Another solution to the problems of producing 'worthwhile church furnishings'[169] lay, he suggested, in bringing into collaboration sculptors, painters and workers in stained glass and precious metals. 'But', he warned, 'unless the Architect has absolute control the result will be aesthetic chaos and the churches will merely become exhibitions of ecclesiastical art'.[170]

144

ST GEORGE'S CHAPEL : WINDSOR CASTLE
MOVEABLE SCREENS & CANON'S STALLS IN THE NAVE ∅ ∅

plan   section   front elevation   side   section

Designed by George G. Pace, C.V.O., M.A., F.S.A., F.R.I.B.A., Architect ∅ drawn by John Hutchinson ∅

145

145 Chester Cathedral: new nave choir stalls, and beyond the new stalls for Bishop and Suffragan Bishop incorporating seventeenth and nineteenth-century woodwork, 1966

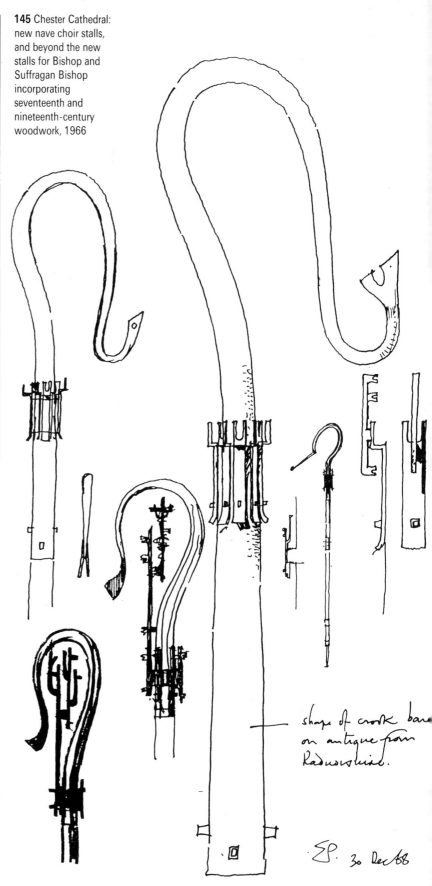

shape of crook based on antique from Radnorshire.

ξP. 30 Dec 68

146 A composite of sketch designs made during 1968 for a crosier for the Bishop of Monmouth (drawings slightly reduced, black ink on white paper)

Under present conditions, he maintained, to be successful a church must be the creation of one mind, with the artists employed working towards the goal set by the architect, so that all the parts integrate and the resultant church is 'architecturally greater than the mere sum of the parts'. However, he acknowledged,

> this places the architect in a position which, if he is not highly disciplined, could lead him to take up the arrogant position all too often assumed by architects of secular buildings. The disciplined church architect knows only too well that he can never do well enough: he will always fall short of the goal.[171]

He had little time for any artist exhibiting rampant individualism and he issued a warning, quoting a passage by the Reverend E. C. E. Bourne:

> If the Church needs the artist, so too does the artist need the Church. A Work of Art is indeed the expression of a unique imaginative experience, but the experience is part of the artist's whole personality, and this in its turn depends on his contact with his fellows. Great art is in the truest sense of the word 'catholic'; that is, it exists not as an isolated event, but as part of a whole. Art which lays all the emphasis on the things in which an artist differs from his fellows will never achieve greatness. It is only within a community integrated by a common purpose and a common allegiance that the artist can escape from the cramping limitations of his own individuality.[172]

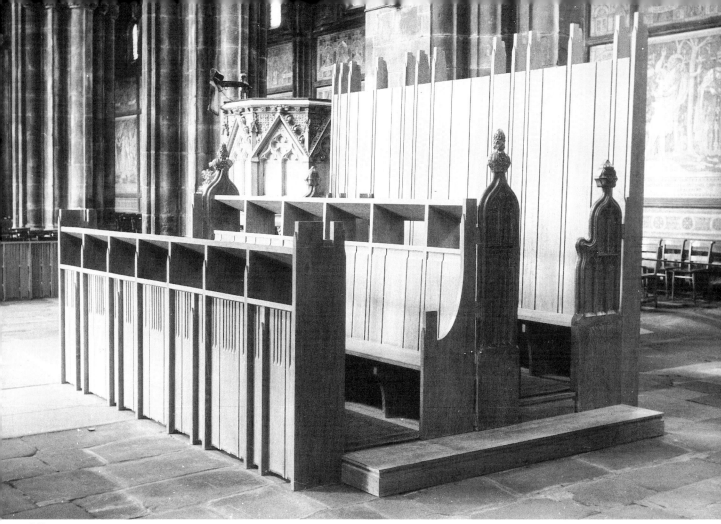

147

147 Chester Cathedral: new lay clerks' and choristers' stalls incorporating Victorian (1846) woodwork, in limed oak, 1966

148 Coity: east face of kneeler rail. Stained oak, 1953

Wakefield Cathedral Bishop's Throne, 1974:

149 Sketch design – ink, 1973, 2 × 3in (5.1 × 7.6cm) selected from several on 8 × 10in (20.3 × 25.4cm) page

150 The completed throne in light oak set on the south side of the choir

150

148

149

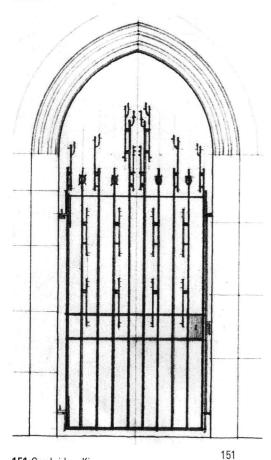

151 Cambridge, Kings College Chapel: proposed wrought-iron gate to doorway between chapels 11 and 12, 1967

151

Hatfield – addition to Welch Monument:

152 Sketch designs in ink, 7 × 8in (17.8 × 20.3cm) 1969

153 Completed work in polished limestone with incised lettering to both sections painted red, 1971. Approx. size 12 × 30in (61 × 76.2cm). (*See* ILLUST. 39 for an eighteenth-century solution to extend a monument)

153

Happily he forged lasting associations with a number of artists, sculptors and craftsmen, in particular Sir Jacob Epstein (*see* The Majestas, Llandaff Cathedral, ILLUST. 306); John Piper with Patrick Reyntiens (*see* St Mark's, Sheffield, stained glass, ILLUSTS 62 and 63); Frank Roper (*see* the gilded aluminium reredos at St Martin le Grand, York, ILLUST. 257); Harry Harvey (*see* the painted panel reredos, Intake Church, Doncaster, ILLUST. 78b); and Harry Stammers (*see* Majestas, St Michael's College Chapel, Llandaff reredos, ILLUST. 322).

But in the tradition of church furnishing set by such ecclesiastical architects as Butterfield, Pearson and Comper, George Pace conceived much of the furnishings and fittings for his churches himself – as the aesthetic expression of the liturgical plan and the architectural ordering of the interior.

Whether designing new work for ancient or Victorian churches, the design would be offered 'as a theological affirmation . . . true to its age and yet not to be in violent collision with earlier work.'[173]

Tracery

George Pace's quest to find new means of expression and beauty led him into many different fields. His conscious development of a Gothic art form to new levels may be seen most clearly in his tracery designs for window glazing and painted panels.

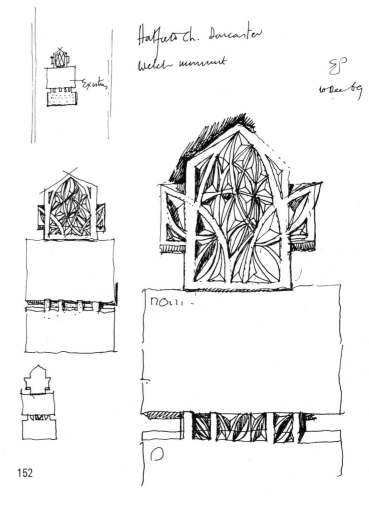

152

The mouchettes and dagger shapes so familiar in the fourteenth century's flamboyant and flowing stonework tracery are found in his early examples of reglazed heads to ancient church windows. These often replaced uninspired and dilapidated Victorian diamond-patterned, tinted, obscure glazing which had borne little or no relationship to the windows into which it was set. Using a mixture of clear rectangular-shaped glass quarries in the lower part of the window, with complicated traceried heads formed in the lead cames, he brought a new dimension to many windows, creating through the lead came tracery a secondary order to the stonework tracery. Typical examples are seen at Burton Agnes Church (1956) (ILLUST. 34) (where salvaged sixteenth-century glass has also been carefully integrated); and Leake Church (1962) (ILLUST. 35).

By the middle 1960s the sudden introduction of closely spaced alternate thick and thin verticals, joined in the head at differing levels by broken horizontals, heralded a move in true Gothic tradition from the Decorated to the Perpendicular style.[174] This can be seen in Hatfield south-east chapel (1966) (ILLUSTS 38 and 39); East Rounton chancel (1965) (ILLUST. 236); St Martin le Grand, York (1968) (ILLUST. 154); or Tamworth south aisle, west window (1969) (ILLUST. 241). The roots of these designs may lie in the fifteenth century, but in their abstract, almost De Stijl 'Mondrian' form, the effect is pure twentieth-century.[175]

155

New window tracery:

157 Sheffield Cathedral: proposed west window illustrated in the 1957 Appeal Brochure

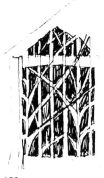

158

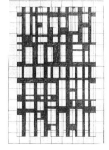

160a

158 and **9** Sheffield St Mark's: chancel east window – early sketch designs – blue ink on detail paper, extract from 12 × 7in (30.5 × 17.8cm) drawing, January 1960. And the final design completed 1963. *See interior* ILLUSTS **63** and **340**; where the squarish nature of the tracery section, reminiscent of Prior's window at Roker (ILLUST. **17**), is more evident

159

Tracery patterns:

Tracery patterns:

155 Tadcaster: tracery in screen by the architects Bromet and Thorman, *c.* 1900 (*compare with* ILLUST. 402)

156 Market Weighton reredos panel: gilding on red background, 1965

156

160

160 St Olave's, York: profile of bracket to organ-case, 1953. Compare with ILLUST. 224

160a St George's Chapel, Windsor: nave kneeler. Full size detail drawing 13 × 9in (33 × 23cm), 1969

OPPOSITE
161 St Olave's, York: new organ-case at east end of north aisle. Painted deep green with soffit to cornice and angular support in red, 1953

161

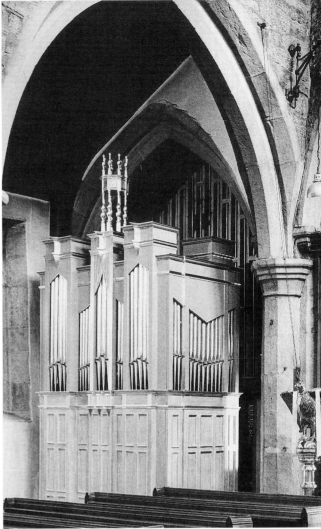

162a

162b

162a Bingley: postif organ at east end of north aisle. Base limed oak, upper portion pine, painted pale blue and gilded. Note screen to choir organ in stained oak and stainless steel vertical rods, 1959

162b Bradfield: north aisle organ screen. Limed oak with upper secondary verticals painted-front face light green, sides very pale red, 1972

Designs for new traceried stonework in windows is rarer. Perhaps the most striking example may be seen in the east and west windows of St Mark's Church, Broomhill, Sheffield (early 1960s), which Pevsner describes as 'wild tracery'[176] (ILLUSTS 158 and 159). Pevsner sees George Pace's innovative designs as forming part of a tradition, noting for example that the windows of St Michael's, Tettenhall ('courageously' designed by Bernard Miller in 'totally unmedieval form' —) are 'halfway between Lethaby and Mr Pace'![177]

Generally George Pace relied on simple, rectangular window openings, but achieved special effects by grouping them closely together (*see* Intake Church, Doncaster, 1956, ILLUST. 75) or, as became more common in later years, placing windows of differing width and length at differing levels, irregularly spaced (*see* Keele University Chapel 1965, ILLUSTS 100 and 346). Unfortunately Pevsner found little affinity with these window formations, seeing those at Keele merely as 'windows in the odd rhythm Mr Pace likes'.[178]

The traceried patterns formed on many painted ceilings or reredos panels are much more complicated, using interlacing differing orders in a variety of bright colours. The forms take further

the work of the architects Bromet and Thorman of Tadcaster near York, whose amazing traceried panels in local churches George Pace admired so much (ILLUST. 155). The patterns traced by the ribs of medieval vaulting are followed but are barely recognizable, as the free flowing lines take on abstract naturalistic qualities in a progression of crossing ceilings. This can be seen, for example, at St Mary's, Beverley (1962) (ILLUST. 3); leading to St Saviour's, Leeds (1965); King George VI Memorial Chapel, Windsor (1969) (ILLUST. 404); Chester Cathedral (1970) (ILLUST. 5); and Southwark Cathedral (1974); and similarly on the reredos panels of Market Weighton (1965) (ILLUST. 156); or St Oswald's Chapel, Peterborough Cathedral (1967) (ILLUST. 234).

Organ screens and cases

His remarkable capacity for invention is demonstrated in organ case screens where George Pace solved a problem without precedent. Mr Buchanan, Director of Walker Organs, explains that George Pace's achievement was to impose a radical solution posed by the appearance of old organs by cutting the 'Gordian knot'.

163

164

The façades of organs became steadily more and more utilitarian throughout the nineteenth century, until finally they were nothing more than a row of pipes with posts at either end and panels below. The façade pipes usually had mouth lines that followed the tops of the pipes and almost always had enormous over length. This practice continued well into the 1950s and 60s.

After the War a new organ in this country was a rarity. Blitzed churches provided a fund of available old, once good organs, all with the same tedious sort of appearance. Architects and Organ Builders wrestled with squeezing or elongating these old façades into new spaces with patently ridiculous results, especially when the façade pipes were put in different order. Even when new façades were provided nobody seemed capable of breaking out of the standard arrangements.

Organ screens:

163 Keele University College Chapel Ink on tracing paper, 8 × 7in (20.3 × 17.8cm) 1966

164 York, St Helen's: new organ-case. Dark green with red highlights. 'Restful and self-effacing',[180] 1959

OPPOSITE
165 Holy Trinity, York: 'A typical Pace, light wood with his closely set verticals – Gothic in character, but not in form'.[179] Limed oak, 1965

166

The idea of a proper organ case during these times was as remote as a new organ – more so in fact. In any event, the squat dimensions of most English organs contradicted the vertical principles of good case design.

George Pace saw a splendid and obvious solution. He rejected the idea of front pipes entirely. That is not itself novel, Leeds Parish Church is a famous example of the pipeless façade, but the idea of placing a screen in front of an existing façade, or of an organ with its previous façade removed, was new, practical, economical and artistic.

. . . The problem of presenting old material as new was solved at a stroke by screens which let the sound out freely, but prevented the eye from viewing the unedifying insides.[181]

This technique is used early on at Newport (1955) (ILLUST. 289) and Llandaff Cathedral (1957) (ILLUST. 307), and undergoes various transitional stages, for example St Helen's, York (1959) (ILLUST. 164), before emerging at Lastingham (1963) (ILLUST. 435) and finally appearing in a very refined form at Holy Trinity, York (1965), (ILLUST. 165). This refined form was then frequently used elsewhere, for example Branston (1968) (ILLUST. 168), or Spalding (1971) (ILLUST. 425).

But opportunities for raising the art of pipe façades did occur from time to time, particularly in the early and later years, for example Pocklington (1950), St Olave's, York (1953) (ILLUST. 161); Oxford (1969) (ILLUST. 386); Clifton, Nottinghamshire (1969) (ILLUST. 166); and Standish (1970).

166 Clifton, Nottinghamshire: new organ – framework and panels in limed oak with inset panels in red and black, 1969. Note the asymmetrical balance of the diagonal thick and thin members, spaced alternately

167 Penistone: western organ 1975 (bearing a family likeness to the organ at Standish 1970) – on furnishings, *see* ILLUST. 142

167

OPPOSITE
168 Branston new organ-case: screenwork painted very pale green, inverted pyramid, vaulting deep red with marbling effect in gilt, 1968

OPPOSITE
169 Llandaff Cathedral: Welch Regimental Chapel Battle Honours. Full sized by the architect and carved by Geoffrey Kaye of York, 1958

Lettering

Memorials within the church or in the churchyard were embraced with equal seriousness – the development of George Pace's lettering is an art worthy of study in itself. Stylistically he developed an alphabet derived from classical Roman, which he continually adapted and rethought. Frank Roper, sculptor, describes George Pace's early lettering in the Welch Regimental Memorial Chapel at Llandaff Cathedral (1958) (ILLUST. 169).

> One of the first lessons for the sculptor and architect to learn with regard to letter-cutting is that a block of stone is a vastly different proposition to a page in a book. Frequently the stone is part of a building, when the panel of lettering must be considered in relation to the architecture. Even if the stone is free standing, as in a tombstone, one should respect its mass and try to preserve its unity. If we refer to Roman inscriptions, it will be seen that often legibility was sacrificed in the cause of preserving an 'all over' pattern of lettering. Words were split between lines, letters overlaid and spaces between words were almost non-existent.
>
> The new Battle Honours panels in the Welch Regiment Chapel are delightfully determined to drive this lesson home.
>
> At first glance one is apt to find them very interesting, but rather experimental. On a second visit one realizes that these are panels of stone with surface decoration, but the stones have a structural function and the decoration is an essential part of the whole Chapel. The unity of the stones has been preserved and a pleasing pattern achieved inspite of the horrible problem presented by lines of widely varying length. How easy it would have been to have used inch-high letters and marked out each line from the centre, but how disastrous would have been the effect on the architecture.

170

171

170 *and* **171** Goathland: headstone memorial to McLane 1965, also carved by Kaye. The symbols relate to the Revd McLane's work as a priest. The lettering designed as a sculptural form in three planes was believed to have been unique at that time[182]

To the Memory of
MICHAEL GUY PERCIVAL
11th BARON MIDDLETON
Knight of the Garter ⌀ Military Cross
⌀ Indian Cavalry ⌀ Served
1887-1970 1914-1918 ⌀ 1939-1945
Chancellor of Hull University
Lord Lieutenant of the East Riding

172

173

His friends remember
before GOD
CAREY FREDERICK
KNYVETT
Bishop of Selby 1941-1962
and Rector of this Parish
1941-1958

172 Birdsall: wall memorial in blue slate with incised letters gilded, approx. 40 × 33in (101.6 × 83.8cm). Placed below the garter banner hung from specially designed wrought-iron brackets, 1972

173 Bolton Percy: wall memorial in green/grey slate with incised chalice gilded and lettering painted in red, 1971. Approx. 18 × 12in (45.7 × 30.5cm)

174 Wakefield Cathedral: brass-plated inscription on Bishop's Throne, 1974, approx 4 × 5in (10.2 × 12.7cm)

175

176

178

180

180 Campsall: wall plaque in green slate with incised chalice gilded and all incised lettering and other motifs in red, 1969, approx. 15 × 26in (38.1 × 66cm)

177

179

175 Tinsley: wall plaque, brass engraved, 1960, approx. 6 × 9in (15.2 × 22.9cm)

179 Lichfield Cathedral: incised ledger in grey slate, early 1960s, approx. 24 × 39in (61 × 99.1cm)

181 Kirby Sigston: east window with stained glass inscription, 1958

176 Thormanby Chancel: south window with stained glass inscription, 1952

181

177 Egglescliffe: silver inscription plate on priest's seat, 1971

178 Hatfield: wall plaque – wood painted dark green with lettering gilded, 1968, approx. 5 × 7in (12.7 × 17.8cm)

One is very conscious of the almost eternal quality of stone when looking at Roman inscriptions. Immediate legibility is not a first essential, as is the case with a paper-backed book whose function is to convey a message and then to be put aside. It is right that such names as Mons and Gallipoli should be engraved in stone and it is necessary that the stone should be allowed to retain its integrity and dignity.

The Regiment Chapel is one of the most successful pieces of ecclesiastical architecture in the Principality. It contains a host of challenging detail. We are fortunate that the Battle Honours panels were designed by the same hand and that they are equally stimulating.[183]

The technique of overlapping letters or placing them at differing levels has historical precedents, but his later experiments in three dimensions were, he believed 'unique'.[184]

The first example is found on a headstone at Goathland Church (1965) (ILLUST. 170) where the lettering overlaps and is raised plane upon plane, with the relationship between solid and void creating complicated rhythms. The final flowering of this style occurs in the memorial to Dean Alington in the Galilee Chapel of Durham Cathedral (1970) (ILLUSTS 183 and 186). This memorial is, in effect, an altarpiece, consisting of a wall inscription in Latin from the Venerable Bede with an English translation below, executed in gilded, individual, cast aluminium letters set on limed oak. In his book on *Lettering in Architecture*, Alan Bartram sees this lettering as 'not strictly architectural, but relevant as illustrating a freedom of approach worth discussing'. Unfortunately he is unable to comprehend the relationship of the letters to their oak base, finding this 'elusive', and has reservations on the letter forms, finding them sometimes a little weak. But, he says,

> . . . as so often, the breadth and imagination of concept overrides these points. The sculptural conception of freestanding, floating letters, often superimposing each other; the irregularity of size, of placing and the overlapping of ascenders; the gilded, concave section; the whole idea of a rich, glittering, overall pattern against the sombre wall in this simple Norman chapel is admirable and has lessons for us. Executed in 1970 as a memorial, it suits the situation most fittingly.[185]

183

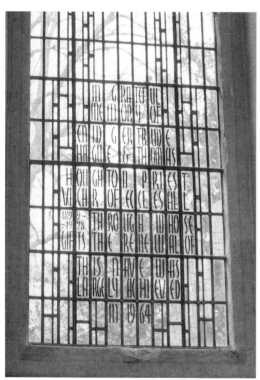

182

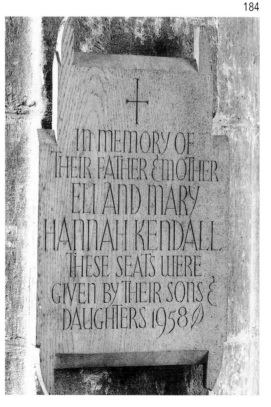

184

185

182 Ecclesall: new nave window glazing with stained glass inscription, 1964

184 Campsall: oak plaque, 1959

185 St Matthew's, Dewsbury: south chapel memorial screen in incised oak, 1953

ABOVE AND OPPOSITE **183** *and* **186** Durham Cathedral: Galilee Chapel, Dean Alington Memorial – cast aluminum letters, gilded and set in an oak framework, 1970

Textiles

In his textile designs, Pace felt a freedom rarely experienced in building construction. Quoting Sir Henry Wotton's definition of architecture – 'firmness, commodity and delight', he confessed he paid more attention to 'delight', as 'firmness and commodity seemed less important in vestments.'[186] He clearly enjoyed himself with works such as his altar frontal at Peterborough Cathedral for St Kyneburgha's Chapel (1973), where

> the design has abstract pattern and vague overtones interlaced with Saxon ornament. It uses gold and silver cords and braid, lurex and wild silk in cherry and summer-sky blue with silver leather. It is an example of beautiful and strangely moving design carried out in wonderful needlework'.[187]

The early altar frontals also owe much to the Gothic spirit (see Llandaff Cathedral, Regimental Chapel, 1956, ILLUST. 189), but modern art, like modern architecture, had its part to play. In his vestment design for St Albans Cathedral (1967) (ILLUSTS 194 and 195) he admits to the strong influence of Matisse:

> The patterns on the chasubles designed by Henri Matisse for the Chapel of Rosary at Vence was a

187 Padgate: detail of cope with fish design, 1963

188a *and* **b** Llandaff Cathedral: cope for use in penitential seasons. Blue background with pattern in gold, green, red and black, 1962

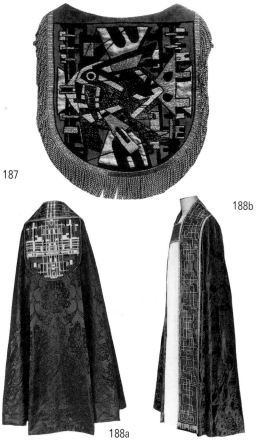

187

188a

188b

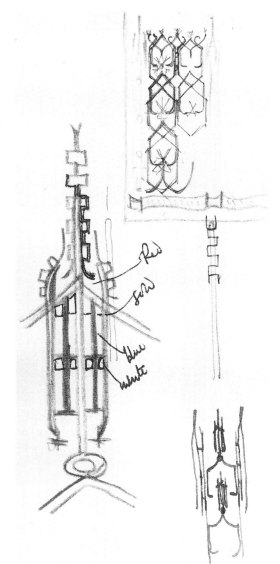

189

190

Llandaff Cathedral – Welch Regimental Chapel altar frontal, 1956

189 sketch design, 7 × 8in (17.8 × 20.3cm), in blue ink, pencil, brown crayon and red Biro, undated

190 Detail of finished frontal. Deep-blue backcloth with decorative pattern formed in white cord, with edge of flower petals picked out in red

OPPOSITE
York, St Olave's – High Mass vestments, 1973:

191 Priest's chasuble. The oak reredos behind has been stripped, bleached, limed, and figures gilded solid. The ceiling above decorated in many colours together with introduction of gilded stars, 1963

192 Priest's chasuble

193 Sub-deacon's dalmatic

OVER
194 *and* **195** St Alban's Cathedral; High Mass set, 1967: priest's chasuble illustrated; which forms a part of the set, including deacon's chasuble, and sub-deacon's chasuble

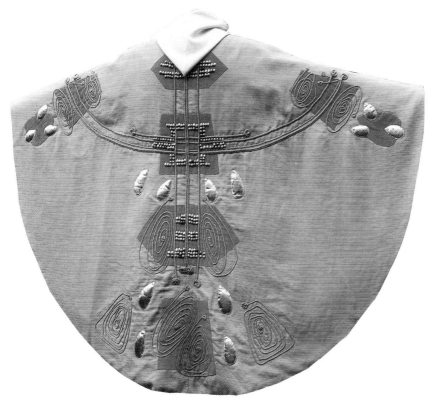

seminal event, opening avenues for aesthetic exploration, the existence of which had previously not been realized. The new vestments for the [St Albans] Cathedral may be deemed to be a distant shoot from the Vence tree.

It is the intention that the patterns and the interplay of the areas of colour in these vestments should be enjoyed for themselves; be seen in lively juxta-position with the whole interior of the Cathedral and its furnishings; emphasize the hierarchical role played by the Celebrant, Deacon and Sub-Deacon when the Family, in its different orders, is present at the Eucharist and to stress the glory and other-worldliness of the stupendous event being enacted in their midst.

In the new vestments the chasuble has been cut on full lines and the dalmatic and the tunicle follow an ancient type which enables their appearance to approach that of an alb, thus having a closer visual relationship with the chasuble. The patterns on the Cathedral's new vestments have been designed to be easily and naturally achieved within the stitchery techniques and the nature of the materials used. But in addition those who wish for symbolism will find it in the patterns.

The symbolism on the front of the chasuble, dalmatic and the tunicle stresses the hierarchical relationship of Celebrant, Deacon and Sub-Deacon. On each vestment near the top is a cross. There is nothing more on the tunicle. The dalmatic has a circular dot on the centre line and near the bottom of the material. This is formed of an endless cord and may be deemed to be representing the whole of mankind as well as eternity. On the chasuble the circular dot is surrounded by an outer circle – mankind enfolded in the all-embracing love of God. The chasuble has additional patterns but these have no symbolic meaning.

On the back of the vestments – that is, the side mostly seen by the congregation all have on the centre line at the top the St Albans Cross. The hierarchical inter-relationship of the three ministers is heavily stressed. Each has a large oval of colour on the centre line near the bottom of the fabric. The dalmatic and the chasuble have two half-moon shapes placed symmetrically about the centre line and the chasuble two additional half-moon shapes, similarly disposed, but nearer the St Albans cross. The back of the vestments are decorated with abstracted patterns, all related, the simplest version on the tunicle and the most elaborate on the chasuble.[188]

By keeping the symbolism at a deliberately low level, George Pace hoped to avoid 'the futility of wanton obscurantism . . . which merely emphasizes that the artist has remained high and lifted up in his intellectual might, and has not humbled himself'.[189]

197a Pollington: oak pendant light fitting 1951

197b Tinsley: font cover, oak with gilding, 1953

197c St George's Chapel, Windsor: design for kneeler, April 1969, full size detail in felt-tip on graph paper 13 × 9in (33 × 23cm). Drawing used to form instructions to embroiderers with limited choice of colours allowed, to retain some individuality

OPPOSITE
196 York, St Olave's, font cover: oak with gilded metal finials, 1963

197b

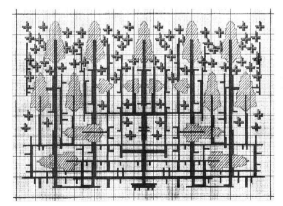

197c

CONSERVATION

Attitudes

In his approach to the conservation of churches and cathedrals, George Pace never lost sight of their function as 'Living Buildings'. By their very existence, he argued, whether by day or by night, whether in use or not, they are acts of worship. In them, he said, 'the family of God in the city and in the diocese may worship, and in them the individual may worship. At all times there is the great corporate devotion to the *Opus Dei*.'[192]

He saw worship and liturgy as ever-evolving and declared that the church and cathedral should never be looked upon merely as ancient or national monuments. The ethos of both new work and repair work on existing churches must continue in the tradition of a live architecture, he believed. The architect had to have inborn creative talents of a high order, not only for new works, but because every repair to a church or cathedral 'involves an aesthetic judement'. This, he said,

> . . . is one of the fundamental differences between the conservation work on buildings with a transcendent Living Use, and the mere technical petrification of a National Monument.[193]

In order to encourage the development of an attitude to conservation which might allow churches and cathedrals to serve their true function in the second half of the twentieth century, George Pace evolved a 'Theory and Philosophy of Conservation'.

Much of his unfinished book *Worship and Architecture* expounds upon 'attitudes', and he collated further material for another book entitled '*Attitudes to Conservation*';[194] but both titles remained in draft form. Fortunately the central theme to his arguments is encompassed within a paper 'The Theory and Philosophy of Conservation' which he read to the Annual Conference of Diocesan Advisory Committees at York in July 1969 and which later in the same year he expanded on and included within his 'Evidence' submitted to the Church Assembly Places of Worship Commission.[195]

This paper stressed the need for the Church ('not merely a committee or council of the Church, and certainly not any society or organization') to come to a common mind on the principles surrounding attitudes. To do this, he said, it was of prime importance to have in mind a clear background of the changing approaches to repairs and conservation work which were in vogue from time to time since the Middle Ages. But the Church was not to concern itself with detail; that was for architects.

St Michael's, Spurriergate, York: restoration 1965–69. George Pace's efforts to retain the special atmosphere of a city church 'which has a different atmosphere from a parish church'[190] prompted Pevsner to suggest that here was the most beautiful of any York church thanks in no small measure to the restoration undertaken since 1965'[191]

OPPOSITE
198 Nave, looking east. The crucifix is formed from an adapted candlestick from Llandaff Cathedral and an antique ivory figure of Christ

199 Detail of the work on the eighteenth-century reredos. Fred Parker of Bellerby's stripped the three blank painted panels to reveal the Lord's Prayer, the Ten Commandments and the Creed and restored the lettering. November 1969

199

Similarly, he pronounced, architects, art historians and lay preservation and amenity enthusiasts were not equipped to make pronouncements on the principles vital to the Church. It was for architects to translate the principles into appropriate conservation principles, and he advised, in a familiar and recurrent theme, that:

> It is not unreasonable to expect that such conservation principles will be very different from those advocated by the State and conservation, archaeological societies and museum curators.

The historical conscience

The English 'Historical Conscience' (a term coined and much used by George Pace) i.e. that phenomenon which emerged from a fascination with classical antiquity in the seventeenth and eighteenth centuries, and later encouraged the varied revivals of the nineteenth century, has immense influence in the twentieth century, he claimed, playing a conspicuous part in the general attitude towards conservation. He saw this Historical Conscience as an attitude of mind arising from the conditions which brought about the demise of organic culture. We have already seen in

201

Major fabric repair:

OPPOSITE
200 Tamworth: west tower, August 1973

201 Lichfield Cathedral: central spire, September 1949

202 Cadeby: replacement bellcote-oak framework and Westmorland slates, 1956

203 Llandaff Cathedral: upper courses of the Prichard Spire removed after war damage, sorted on the nave floor prior to their refixing, March 1955 (*see* ILLUST. 294)

202

203

the earlier chapter on design how George Pace perceived some possible attributes in the historical conscience which 'should have a place in the organic culture of the future', but in the main he believed the historical conscience to be dangerous to the Church and an influence which 'should be vigorously combatted'.

Illustrating his argument, he pointed out:

> As far as we know Conservation in our present day esoteric sense was unknown in the ancient and medieval worlds. Lethaby has written: 'Great epochs of art were times of adventure and discovery. History and criticism are our form of originality.'[196]

Looking closely at the medieval period – in a time of 'a great organic culture', he explains further:

> We know that today's appreciation of spatial relationships and kinetic views were not necessarily appreciated, or given the importance which has been attached to them since the mid-eighteenth century. Vistas in cathedrals; the octagon at Ely when first built, and until 1770, was cut off at floor level by the pulpitum and the enclosed quire and its stalls which run its full width east and west. In addition there were the solid screens and reredoses of the many altars, which divided the aisles and quire proper, into small enclosed compartments.
>
> We may reasonably assume that medieval clients

109

204

and architects had no interest in or understanding
or appreciation of, the colour and texture of
materials or the patina of age, in the sense which
has been evolved during the past 150 years. To the
medieval architect oak was a goodly material, often
easily to hand. If used for anything other than the
strictly utilitarian it would be gessoed, painted and
gilded. Similarly, with alabaster. Great painted
ceilings such as Peterborough nave [ILLUST. 212]
were constantly being touched-up and partially repainted to keep them in prime condition, not as
works of art, but as part of the total physical
setting and apparatus of worship – 'This is none
other but the House of God and this is the Gate of
Heaven'; and the touching-up or re-painting was
done in the manner current at the time of doing.
There was no pretence at recapturing the earlier
manner. (It is also interesting to note that in the
eighteenth century this ceiling was again touched-
up; the work is eighteenth century, not mock-
medieval. The Historical Conscience and the
Exhibit Complex had not been thought of and their
enervating hand was not present to prevent these
lively works being done to the Glory of God or to

204 Castle Howard: the
south front after the fire
of 1940. There was no
question but to undertake
the most accurate
reconstruction of the
building's fabric. On the
other hand the
individualistic painting
on the ceiling to the
dome was only recreated
in spirit[197]

205 Castle Howard:
Temple of the Four
Winds; exterior after
restoration, 1958

205

206

206 Castle Howard: the south front after restoration, 1962. The reconstruction of the dome in association with Mr Trenwith Wills

involved an early use of photogrammetry.[198] George Pace completed the remainder of the extensive work to the house between 1957–65

207 Castle Howard: Temple of the Four Winds; repairing the floor using marble from the war-damaged reredos of St Paul's Cathedral, October 1958[200]

207

destroy the integrity of the craftsman doing them).[199]

George Pace delighted in pointing out that when structural defects occurred and collapse or fire wrought havoc on a medieval cathedral, the opportunity was seized to create new and nobler works or to introduce structural corrections conceived at the highest aesthetic level and all of course in the architectural manner current at that stage of the organic culture.[201] 'It is traditional to be modern' was one of his constant catch phrases.[202]

Archaeological correctness and the amateur

In the later half of the eighteenth century and in the first half of the nineteenth century, the discovery of the 'picturesque' coupled with the Romantic Vision resulted in eclecticism becoming absolute. Detailed studies of medieval remains were now undertaken, with clients and architects

208

209

wanting their Gothic to be 'correct'. George Pace saw the emergence of 'the amateur in knowing about architecture' becoming fully fledged,[203] and noted:

Since the eighteenth century amateur archaeologists, architects, ecclesiologists have flourished. In a country addicted to literary rather than graphic and aesthetic values and with almost no widespread appreciation of the fundamentals of architectural values, the power wielded by the amateur, the preservation society and the like has been, and is, immense. On the whole this curious condition has been beneficial, especially in the 100 years or so which were given over to Revivals, whilst live architecture and live arts were dormant. It still serves a useful purpose today, in making it necessary for architects and artists to fight for their live works. But it should also be remembered that the amateurs are always one and a half to two generations behind the leading architects and that in live architecture there is no place for amateurs. John Ruskin in his attempts to understand architecture and to pontificate to the educated and cultured, is the awful warning, especially in this country where to be able to write well or talk divertingly about architecture is to be given public recognition; presumably because the real understanding of architecture is so difficult.

Glibly expressed theories in a literary or beguiling form are then substituted for architecture as the mother art. The words of Basil Champneys are valuable:

It is easier for a discursive age to criticize than to invent, to produce formula than design; and criticism is apt to flourish when artistic impulse languishes. For Art lives in the absence of self-consciousness and the best work has always been done without taking thought. Moreover, the elements of which art mainly consists are delicate and minute, and are apt to evade the coarse machinery of words.[204]

In the later half of the nineteenth century, up until the 1920s, the Gothic Revival had in many hands become merely an archaeological essay in which lifeless correctness was the aim, George Pace claimed; noting that this enabled the amateur to keep up his end. In his scathing attack on amateurs he illustrated this point, providing the example of Beresford Hope, architectural critic, who,

when confronted by a work of real architecture by possibly the greatest architect of the nineteenth century [Butterfield][205] could miss all the essentials as they were beyond the amateur, but [in his ignorance] he could still say about All Saints,

208 *and* **209**
Peterborough Cathedral – new statue of Bishop Grossetete in Clipsham stone, 5ft 3in (1m 60cm) high. One of a series of 12 representing the benefactors of the cathedral completed between 1958–66 by Alan Durst. 'His approach to sculpture for churches is very much in the spirit of the Fletton church carvings; which are considered to have had such a marked influence on the thirteenth century sculptors on Peterborough West Front and yet Alan Durst's work could not have been done in any age other than the present'[206]

210

211

Peterborough Cathedral:

210 The west front before cleaning in 1958

211 Cleaning with water in 1974[207]

212 The nave, hanging rood, gilded figure and lettering on matt-red wooden cross, 1975 (sculptor: F Roper)

Margaret Street: 'The practised eye of 1861 cannot fail to regret that the clerestory should stand sheer upon the arcade'.

George Pace also observed that, side by side with archaeological correctness,

disturbing and very important events were taking place, some of which may now be seen to be the first stirring of the philosophical and intellectual basis from which Modern Architecture has evolved.[209]

He cites the publication of Pugin's *Contrasts* and his other books, of the publications of the Ecclesiological Society, especially the *Transactions*, together with works by Viollet le Duc, John Ruskin, Sir Gilbert Scott and George Edmund Street. Because of these doctrines, which the Ecclesiologists laid down with such fervour and authority, 'most architects were soon pummelled into restoring churches to the perfect period – mid-Decorated, denuding churches of later, real Gothic works, and almost all post-Reformation work'.

But George Pace does admit to an admiration for some of this work on a certain level:

Of course, much that was done, in self-assurance by the great nineteenth century architects, to

cathedrals and churches, is now being appreciated for its excellence. It should always be remembered the great debt owed to Sir Gilbert Scott for saving so many of the cathedrals and greater churches from collapse. He was a marvellous and very courageous structural restorer. Where a Cathedral has been through his hands the architect of that cathedral today has few structural worries. And Scott did all this without the fuss and publicity which today accompanies the doing of less dramatic works at many of our cathedrals today. They were giants in the land in those days.

In spite of all their self-assurance, the great Victorian architects were caught between two worlds – the organic culture which could no longer grow, and the new culture, whatever it would be, which might evolve from the entirely new and unique conditions. 'They were trying to hold together incompatible opposites and they worried because they failed'. (Humphrey House, 1948.[209])

Moral attributes and the quality of age

Two new elements had now been introduced to architecture, by such as Pugin and Ruskin – namely, moral attributes, and the quality of age. Thus, argued George Pace:

> The Historical Conscience was now fully fledged. Architecture as the Mistress Art has suffered, and still suffers, from the introduction of these attitudes, attitudes which have nothing to do with real architecture. But they are attitudes easily grasped by amateurs and by a public addicted to literary, rather than graphic values, and thus have exerted, and still do exert, great power and sanction.[210]

Age in buildings had taken on a special importance. No criterion remotely like this had ever previously existed, he said. To him, the worship of age had nothing to do with architectural worth;[211] or, indeed, any deeply based appreciation of the profundities of architecture. He illustrated this point by exclaiming:

> . . . the sheer architectural qualities of the Anglican Cathedral, Liverpool; the two Middlesbrough churches of St Cuthbert and St Columba and G. F. Bodley's late-phase churches, are probably greater than those in the Spanish cathedrals and late English medieval churches which inspired them. Architects having the necessary qualities of perception are able to see this, but since these buildings are not old, nobody else is either able to see this architectural superiority, or would dare to say they did so. Scott's Liverpool Cathedral, Temple Moore's and Bodley's churches do get eulogies, but these are based on qualities other than purely architectural.[212]

But George Pace did admit to there being good qualities in the Historical Conscience, qualities even to be 'admired and thankfully received'. He referred to the 'new dimension in appreciation of churches as fine old buildings'.

He sought to protect the antiquities of the churches in his care, and to preserve the charm of patina, texture and colour wherever possible. Towards these ends he actively supported the Society for the Protection of Ancient Buildings, who, in their turn, sought his guidance and consulted him on matters requiring specialized technical advice, though on matters of principle they were not always in agreement. For example, he drew the line on the Historical Conscience when its 'undesirable and very potent qualities were likely to undermine the essential purposes and use of churches and indeed the whole ethos of churches for the Church'.[213]

213

214

213 *and* **214** Branston: reconstruction of fire-damaged nave roof in oak, March 1965

Current approaches and experts

Predicting the potential dangers from this literary legacy of the past, he issued a warning to the Church and advocated ways of avoiding them. The approach to the repairing of war damage to cathedrals and churches and post-war liturgical re-ordering had side-stepped the real issues:

> . . . to make very careful re-creations of what has been destroyed, for example
>
> > – London City churches;
> > – Great Yarmouth parish church;
> > – St James, Grimsby.
>
> Nowhere in the world could such work have been done to such a high standard, but it is really all make-belief and underlines the great hold which the amateur, the literary and the archaeological understanding of architecture has and the dangers of the Historical Conscience.[214]

In the years between the First and Second World Wars,[215] and up to the 1960s, George Pace saw the historical conscience growing stronger, spawning specialists whose views he found particularly ominous:

> The international get-together on Conservation and many of the projects of UNESCO are particularly dangerous because of the narrow specialization of those involved and the utter surrender to the Historical Conscience, The Exhibit Complex and The Compulsive Repairing Mania. Unless the danger is realized European cathedrals and churches could become by AD2100, well maintained museums, exhibiting works of art on organised tourist routes.[216]

As examples, two English cathedrals

> . . . which shall be nameless, now contain conserved wall paintings and paintings on a wood reredos where the restoration work has been carried out by Experts in Conservation. The result, considered as museum exhibits, is excellent. The result is, however, quite deficient in aesthetic impact and content, and there is none of the self-discipline and self-effacement essential in everything associated with the House of God. These paintings now exalt man being clever, and put man's cleverness on show as in a museum.[217]

The tendency to have committees of experts is growing, he remarked; and warned,

> This is one of the most dangerous and insidious attacks which misplaced love and knowledge can make on our ancient churches.[218]

He criticized the Council for the Care of Churches for setting up a Conservation Committee. 'The composition would be excellent for the Victoria and Albert Museum, or the British Museum or Hampton Court Palace – but for the House of God!' It was essential, he insisted, that control of these matters was given to an architect of stature, who is able to make sure

> . . . that everything which is done, is necessary, is technically sound, is aesthetically satisfactory and that the end product of all the work which it is desirable to do properly, integrates with every other part of the building and its setting.

215

215 Branston: nave roof nearing completion

Compulsive repairing mania

'The manifestation of the Historical Conscience is also responsible for the current Compulsive Repairing Mania,' George Pace claimed. This 'disease' effects itself in the following ways:

> *a* the desire to repair, wash, clean, conserve to an inordinate degree;
>
> *b* a pathological love of 'tidiness';

216

216 Branston: new bosses in the reconstructed nave roof. 'The designs exploit the possibilities of simple chisel-cut chipwork, incised lines and piercing, coupled with the light catching qualities of solid gilding'[219], April 1965

218

219

OPPOSITE
217 Adlingfleet: restoration and reordering 1952–6. interior looking west with new ebonized cross and candlesticks on new Laudian altar frontal. The box pews in this 'delightfully Cotmanesque interior create special character they . . . allow the eye to roam freely about the upper parts of a church, but at pew and floor level the eye is channelled into the gangways and charmed by the succession of rectangular cells seen in sharp perspective'.[220] Work included rebuilding the box pews, painting their exterior in matt dark red and their inside a matt pearly grey. The whole of the walls and stonework were limewashed. The chancel floor was repaved in York stone flags, and a new permanent nave altar with cross and candlesticks, installed together with new light pendants, Note the ancient bell preserved at the west end and the nave ceiling lining

218 Aberedw: fabric repairs in early 1950s. Note the simple but effective side scaffold to nave roof

219 Holme-on-Spalding-Moor: restoration of west tower, 1962. The new stonework showing up almost white against the earlier original stonework, prior to weathering

220 Adlingfleet: plan-reordering (drawn in ink, undated)

c a feeling that furniture, fittings, paintings, stained glass, etc. should be protected, conserved, re-arranged, displayed: as though Exhibition items in a museum;

d that we are all failing in our duty if large sums are not being spent upon repairs; and there is continuous conservation activity in progress on churches and their contents;

e the confusion of 'activity' for 'action';

f with the treatment, repair and renewal of stonework, not only is much unnecessary work being done at unnecessary cost, but original work is being destroyed in the process, dubious repair techniques are being employed and a completely misleading climate of urgency and nightmare cost is being built-up. The time scale for most stonework repairs should be three to four generations — 90 to 120 years — not five years, not ten, not even twenty years;

g too much worrying about structural movement, without proper understanding of what happens in ancient structures, coupled with too many flying from their responsibilities and hiding behind the over careful calculations and over simplification of the special structural ethos of old buildings by engineers. Many works at great cost and sometimes of unnecessary magnitude have been thrust upon the Church in recent years because of this approach;

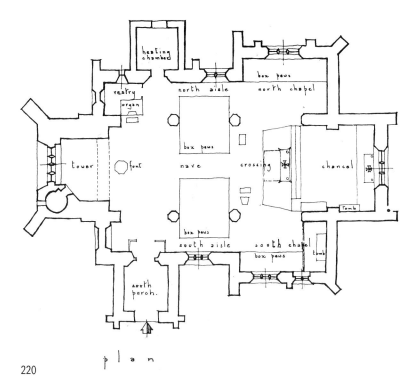

220

h pressure by action groups for conservation of wall paintings, tombs, bells, organs, stained glass and the like, allowed to be mounted, often outside the control of the architect, and involving unwise time-tabling, unsatisfactory techniques and no total aesthetic control;

i proposals for setting up a 'National Centre for Conservation;[221]

It is this kind of approach which leads to proposals such as those for tomb robbing and placing the objects thus obtained on Exhibition (e.g., Archbishop Walter de Grey, York Minster).[222]

It was essential, he believed, that these matters were considered much more carefully, not by specialists, but by dedicated church architects, people who possessed the necessary attributes to view work on church buildings as a whole, over a long time-span.

Qualities of the church architect

Pace suggested that both the church architect and the cathedral architect must possess certain special attributes in order to be adequate to face the two basic tasks which would confront him or her, namely – *(a)* to conserve, preserve and cherish what exists; and *(b)* to create new works as and when these become necessary. A number of both attitudes of mind and innate skills were essential, and these he summarized as follows, not necessarily in any order of priority:

a To be an Architect in every sense of the word – a first degree creator;

b To possess a very comprehensive understanding and extensive knowledge of the history of English Architecture, one which recognises regional characteristics, understands structure, materials and techniques of the past. The need for constant reading and research not to be underestimated;

c To possess extensive knowledge of all the subjects embraced by the term Ecclesiology with further reading and research to be constantly undertaken;

d To have at least normal competence in all requirements for architectural practice;

e To possess extensive knowledge and experience in all the techniques of repair and conservation, not only of building fabrics of all dates, but of all fittings, furnishings, monuments, glass, plate, bells, organ, etc., and the will to continue research and study for life;[223]

f To have the character to make decisions and to accept responsibility. It is essential that architects working for the Church should be under the discipline which is founded in the personal financial responsibility for his advice and work, which the architect in private practice has to bear. This places

221

221 St Hilda's, Shiregreen, Sheffield, by Leslie T. Moore: (eighteenth-century organ-case from St James) – interior before 1952 alteration

222 Bramhall Parish Church: north organ-case and choir stalls before alteration

OPPOSITE
223 St Hilda's, Shiregreen, Sheffield: interior with alterations to chancel screen, organ loft and organ-case, and the introduction of pews, 1952

OPPOSITE
224 Bramhall Parish Church: north organ-case and choir stalls after alteration, 1960

222

223

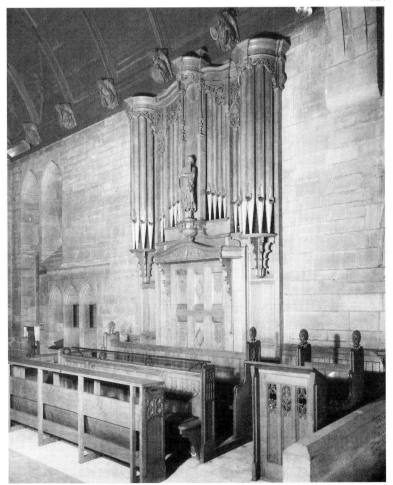

224

him in a very different position from his salaried brother (against whom the ultimate sanction is merely dismissal) and is one of the character forming conditions;

g To be willing to become utterly involved with every aspect of each project, to cherish each church as a father with his child, and not to count the cost of doing so. Emoluments are of the least importance in the work of the Church Architect. If the matter of emoluments is over stressed it is liable to upset the subtle balance needed to bring out the special characteristics of the true Church and the true Cathedral Consultant Architect. The Vicar, the Dean and all members of the Chapter, the Chapter Clerk, and the Cathedral Organist are all subject to holy poverty; so should the architect be, and if a person is not prepared to be subject to this important self denial then he will not possess one of the most important characteristics necessary;

h To possess the desire and the capacity for self discipline, so as to be able to give the uttermost of talent to the task, yet efface himself into anonymity. To be able to understand and enter fully into the life and aspirations of contractors, craftsmen, artists, specialists – and to be able to control and direct their activities towards a pre-ordained end, without stifling them as individuals; so that at the completion of a project the result is greater than the mere sum of the parts; and conveys and has a sense of the Holy;

i He must believe in, and be moved by, the doctrine and liturgy of the Church. This is not a revival of the nineteenth century doctrine that only morally good architects produce aesthetically good churches. But it does mean that unless the architect is heart and soul within the Church he will be unable to find himself in the right state to produce new work which is a 'theological affirmation'.

To be a dedicated churchman provides the foundation on which, alone under present conditions, self-effacing integrity can be achieved and this is one of the most important attributes in a church architect.[224]

Viewing the disturbing climate prevalent in schools of architecture in his day (i.e. during the 1960s and '70s) he suggested that in considering the training of church architects, Reynolds's *Discourses* might well be borne in mind:

There is one precept . . . in which I shall only be opposed by the vain, the ignorant and the idle. I am not afraid that I shall repeat it too often. You must have no dependence on your own genius. If you have great talents, industry will improve them; if you have but moderate abilities, industry will supply their deficiencies. Nothing is desired to well directed labour; nothing is obtained without it;

The purpose of this discourse, and, indeed of most of my other discourses, is to caution you against

BELOW AND OPPOSITE
St Mary's, Beverley:
Canon Tardrew's
memorial screen to
north-east Chapel,
incorporating medieval
woodwork, 'nicely reset
in a G. G. Pace
context'225, 1968

225 Office drawing in
pencil (by J. H.
Hutchinson)

OPPOSITE
226 Screen seen from the
south west

225

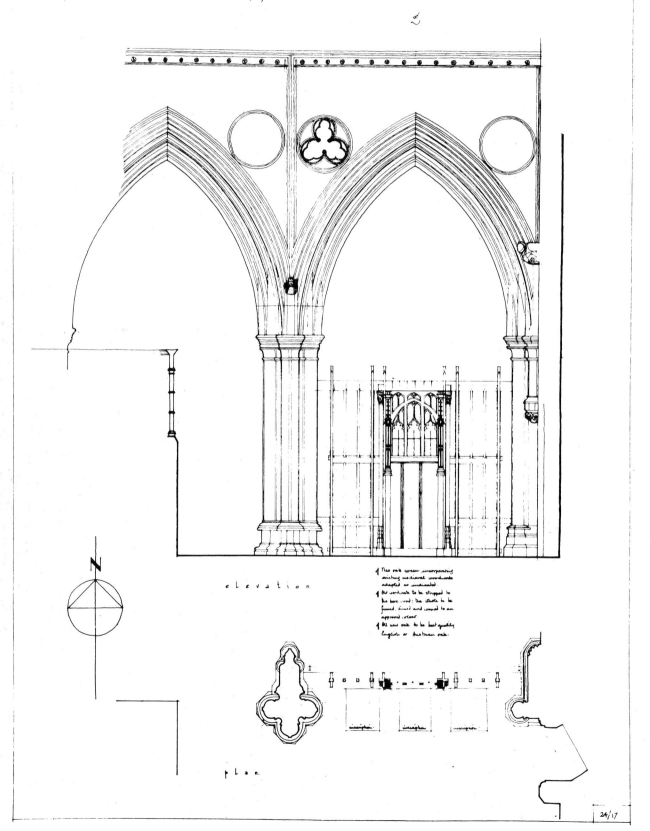

ST MARY'S CHURCH, BEVERLEY.

½" scale drawing of E bay of N. arcade of the choir.

George G. Pace. AA. FSA FRIBA. chartered architect. York. May 1967

drwg. 43
OJ66255

elevation

plan.

the false opinion, but too prevalent amongst artists, of the imaginary power of native genius, and its sufficiency in great works. This opinion . . . almost always produces either a vain confidence or a sluggish despair, both equally fatal to all proficiency.[226]

Cathedrals

Cathedrals were a different matter and required special arrangements over and above those for parish churches. In dealing with cathedrals 'one is dealing with the greatest works of man', George Pace believed.

> [The architect's] tasks should be to control every aspect of the work needed to maintain the cathedral fabric and all aesthetic and technical matters connected with the Close and the buildings of the Close and, of course, all additions, alterations, improvements and new works to the cathedral and its surroundings. It is also necessary that the organisation worked out between a particular Dean and Chapter and a Consultant Architect should allow for constant exchange of views between the two with either side able to raise any matter which they may deem to be of importance.[227]

George Pace regarded cathedrals as the finest creations of architecture, and working on them to be 'the noblest of all undertakings that could fall to an architect'. To him, work for a cathedral, and indeed any church, 'was an act of prayer to be approached with awe and reverence'.[228]

He once said of his work at Durham Cathedral:

> Every work I undertake, not only at Durham but at other cathedrals, always has for me a period of total terror. Will I be inspired with the answer? Can I possibly achieve something which will be sufficiently disciplined to naturally and unselfconsciously integrate with the work of the Masters who over a thousand years have exercised their genius on these buildings? When I seem to be slow and hesitant in designing new work – and I am sometimes reprimanded for this – it is because I must have time to be as sure as I possibly can that I have given of my uttermost and yet have done my best to erase mere personal individualism.[229]

He believed that as there could only be at any one time a very few architects, not only born with the necessary aesthetic gifts, but capable of mastering all the technical matters, cathedrals should be encouraged to appoint a consultant architect 'for a long period, probably his lifetime'. To allow the architect to enter fully into the *Opus Dei*, cathedrals should recognise his status as similar to the Chapter Clerk, providing him with a stall in the Cathedral Quire and ensuring that when he took office this should be done at a solemn service.[231]

There were safeguards to ensure that the

227

227a

227(a) Conisbrough: oak plaque on north wall

227 Conisbrough: formation of War Memorial Chapel with new window and furnishings, 1957: 'Much of its charm lies in its simplicity. White walls render the light, and simple furnishings give space and dignity. The few choice things – an ancient and lovely crucifix and candlesticks; a Persian mat of rich harmonious design; an altar of solid and noble build; a modern desk married in happy blend to a chair where age and use have set a mellowness that could not otherwise have been created; an altar slab that has gathered the devotions of our forefathers in an age long past, and now adorned with simple coverings and a cushion and service book of rich quality – these things speak of a partnership of art and heart that must surely invoke the true spirit of worship'[230]

228 Newport (Holy Trinity): psalms board in oak, 1958

229 Bingley: south chapel reordering: new oak altar, wrought-iron altar rails, cross and candlesticks; frontal, window glazing, stone paving to floor, 1964

230 Askern: chancel reordering: new altar rails in wrought iron and oak, 1958

231 Baldersby: new altar rails in this William Butterfield Church, wrought iron and oak, 1968

cathedral architect could be verbally restrained or criticized, outside the cathedral; and on the whole George Pace considered the primary safeguard – The Cathedrals Advisory Committee (CAC) – to be a body which 'has done excellent work'.

> Its strength and value lie in its members being 'intelligent amateurs' and able to bring sound common sense to bear on cathedral problems. The great disadvantage is that whilst Cathedral Architects cannot regard the CAC other than with benevolent encouragement, others imagine that the CAC is able to be the ultimate voice in all matters concerning cathedrals and their contents. Only Cathedral Architects have the inborn gifts, the experience and the professional authority to deal with every aspect of cathedral fabrics, new works, furniture and fittings. The 'inspired amateur' organization of the CAC is the perfect vehicle for gently handling the reins; keeping the options open, allowing cathedrals freedom for experiment, freedom to make mistakes; all essential in living buildings, used by the living Church and above all continuing Acts of Worship in their very existence.[232]

He used a quotation from Sir John Rothenstein to elaborate on the problems confronting us in the twentieth century:

> In ages when the arts were rooted in traditions not only could the potentialities of a prevailing way of seeing be realized to the utmost, but likewise those of every innovation. For an orderly tradition provides the most favourable setting for fruitful evolution. The potentialities of every innovation can be assessed with relative ease against a relatively stable background, whereas in an almost traditionless time such as the present it is difficult even for the most perceptive artists to distinguish between an innovation that offers fruitful possibilities and some ingenious novelty made for innovation's sake, and destined therefore to sterility.[233]

To make this judgement 'is one of the duties of the Cathedral Architect,' George Pace maintained. 'No Committee can do it' . . .

> . . . nobody can enter in the creative part of an architect's personality. Nobody attempts to do so with painters, musicians and authors: sculptors suffer from it a little, but the poor architect's life can be made a misery by it and to no purpose, except to destroy any vital germ there may be in his work.[235]

He saw clearly that:

> Church Architects must be able to function in full integrity if they are to carry out their tasks. Particularly must they be able 'to make honest mistakes' in re-ordering and new works. Much of the interest we find in cathedrals and churches is due to such 'honest mistakes' in periods of Organic

229

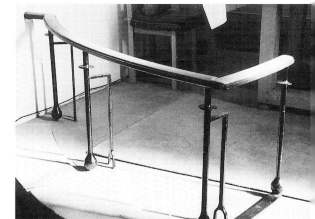

230

231

232

Culture and particularly those of the architectural giants of the nineteenth century.

External control

Interference, particularly through State control or local authority regulation held a peculiar horror for George Pace.

In quoting Osbert Lancaster from *The Future of the Past*, he showed his distaste for any form of involvement in church work in an uncontrolled manner by the State, statutory authorities, or specialized experts – 'for it is a far, far better thing for the House of God to fall into the hands of the infidel than to pass into the keeping of an Office of Works'.[236]

233

He believed the danger of controlling architecture and the arts (and those who offer these skills to the service of the Church) merely to turn churches and cathedrals into a National Monument concept, needed to be thought out at grass roots level. He asked the question:

> Is the Church being pressured into adopting attitudes and organizations, particularly as regards its existing buildings, which are not only against the best interests of those buildings as the high water mark of human architectural achievement, but, of greater importance, against the best interests of the Church?[237]

To George Pace, the Church 'exists to be an agent for liberating individuals and communities to discover in themselves the transforming power of God',[238] and this preoccupation with the petrification of its fabric or the 'Death Wish' could, he believed, only lead to its destruction.

'Christianity cannot be made to fit into a ready-made system of thought, making alterations to suit the customer,' he said, quoting Bishop Barry. The attempt by the Church to be seen to be reforming in the face of an attack by the secular world, to present itself as a body entirely acceptable to atheists, represented the thin end of the wedge in lowering of standards and of weakness, he suggested.

If this weakness in bowing to external pressures continued, particularly in the form of acceding to State interference, then, he forecast,

> . . . for one generation it might be possible for the church to accept State interference in the maintenance of its buildings and still make sure that churches and cathedrals did not fall to the level of National Monuments, in which the Church as a tenant is allowed to camp out on sufferance; but after two or three generations which knew not Joseph, the Death Wish will have been consummated.[239]

Much influenced by Sir Ninian Comper's pronouncements, George Pace believed a very important part of church life was dependent on the background and atmosphere provided by churches and cathedrals – the *Ecclesia Spiritualis* as he termed it.[240] He could not believe that officials or departments, no matter how well intentioned, were capable of comprehending the ways in which these very special and delicate attributes were created and distilled. Churches as acts of worship by their very existence would disappear quickly if maintained by the State, he suggested. Abroad he found evidence to substantiate these theories, and after several holidays spent visiting numerous French cathedrals he declared:

> Only the shell of a mere National Monument

Llandaff Cathedral: St Illtud's Chapel, 1958:

232 The new triptych holding the salvaged Rossetti panels representing the Seed of David, new altar frontal, kneelers, pews, floor paving and inscription

233 Memorial Screen to 53rd (Welsh) Infantry Division separating the St Illtud's Chapel in the base of the Jasper Tower from the nave north aisle. Softwood, ebonized and gilded, bearing a family likeness to the screen at Armagh Cathedral (*see* ILLUST. 274)

234 Peterborough Cathedral: decoration to reredos panel in St Oswald's Chapel, purple/ red on gilt, 1972

OPPOSITE
235 Sprotborough: proposed reordering of the chancel. Ink on tracing paper, 9 × 10in (22.9 × 25.4cm), 1974

Sprotborough Ch
WR. Yorkshire
chancel looking
East.

J. E. Pace
Aug 74

proposed re-ordering of chancel : new dossal curtain : new cornice : Rood aluminium gilt : reduced height of altar : specially designed new frontal : new carpet : wrought iron flower stand : existing candlesticks reused : new cushions & kneelers : new glazing in east window-plain & jewels of stained glass : new lighting : conservation of monuments : redecoration including colour in east bay of roof.

235

236

238 Brodsworth: churchyard war memorial cross, 1964. Based on other crosses in the churchyard exhibiting regional characteristics

remains . . . This is not imagination or prophetic forecasting. It is fact which in a short tour can be seen and felt – even smelt.[241]

He saw that today's instant culture and tourism could bring about the destruction of the very objects and special qualities that so many are encouraged to visit and savour.

Some churches and cathedrals are already under siege and are being destroyed as Houses of God to become mere show places, he argued; and he accused the Church of being oblivious to what was

237

239 Adlingfleet: east window before reglazing

happening, encouraging its self-destruction – another instance of the 'Death Wish'. 'In Italy', he said, 'tourists are made aware that churches are the House of God, and as a result they are.'[242]

In his defence of English churches and cathedrals as living buildings he said:

> . . . the petrification of the type all too often adopted by the Ancient Monuments Department of the Ministry of Works on the buildings and ruins in its care, or the approach to cathedral and church maintenance by the State in, say, France or Denmark, have no place in the maintenance of English cathedral and church. There is no doubt that aesthetically and technically no country is ahead of England in the care of its great churches. This is mostly due to the great tradition of humble service which has inspired cathedral and church architects in this country during the past century, to their self-discipline which has kept in check their aesthetic and technical approach and to the scarcity of money. It cannot be too greatly emphasized that the scarcity of money and the immense missionary and ecumenical possibilities which surround the raising of restoration funds are tremendous safeguards against the fate which has overtaken so many continental cathedrals and are bulwarks against the growth of the National Monument or the museum-conception of the cathedral.

Again, in his 'Evidence' to the Church Assembly Places of Worship Commission in 1969, George Pace expounds at length on this important area in the care of cathedrals and parish churches.

It was essential, he argued, for the well-being of the Church, to safeguard the interior of churches and cathedrals at the highest aesthetic level, to make sure that central government and local authorities should have no control over their interiors. The sole control of the interior of parish churches and others should remain within Faculty jurisdiction and the associated controls exercised by the Diocesan Advisory Committees (DAC) and the Council for the Care of Churches (CCC); and with controls for cathedrals exercised by the Deans and Chapters and the Cathedrals Advisory Committee (CAC).

But even though he acknowledged that bodies such as the Council for the Care of Churches 'does excellent work', he also noted that

> 'recently, there appears to be a tendency [for the CCC] to become involved with Government Departments, and to set up sub-committees composed of Art Historians, Archaeologists, Curators of Museums and Directors of Art Galleries. On occasions it may be desirable to canvas the wisdom of such experts, but the position should never arise when committees composed of such experts, or individual experts, should be placed in a position when they are able to express aesthetic views, or have any control on

236 East Rounton: new leaded glazing in nineteenth-century window replacing obscure diamond-pane glass, 1965

237 St John's Ousebridge, York: window glazing, 1954

240 Tamworth; south aisle, west window reglazed, 1972

242 Holme-on-Spalding-Moor: eighteenth-century crown glass. The minutest pieces saved and releaded thereby introducing new lead cames to bring about a new abstract quality, the importance of the glass overriding any respect for former symmetry in the original lead came pattern, 1960

241 Adlingfleet: east window after reglazing, 1952

aesthetic matters. There are great dangers for the Church in these tendencies.[243]

He found it impossible to contemplate any direct action or responsibility by the State for the fabrics and contents of churches and cathedrals. The techniques and aesthetics of conservation within the ethos demanded by the Church for its buildings are, he said, 'outside the scope of any bureaucratic organization'. Not that this had always been so, he acknowledged, remembering the great architectural achievements of the Royal Master Masons in medieval England, but this took place when organic culture was flourishing, and now there was 'no resemblance between the Ministry of Public Buildings and Works [MPBW], Historic Buildings Council [HBC] and the like and the medieval Royal Masons'.[244]

With today's bureaucratic organizations, he believed, indecisions, procrastinations and hypocrisy were inevitable. Administrators prepare carefully balanced schemes to adjust to the frequent changes of policy, he declared, so that 'all is second rate and without integrity when compared with the organizations of the Church'. He did not place the integrity and interest of the Ministry's professional staff in question, but pointed out the organization of Civil Service departments is inevitably such that architects with the very rare inborn gifts and other attributes previously mentioned would not be attracted to bureaucratic conditions, and even if they were, the bureaucratic conditions would either smother the fragile gifts and attributes or lead to an explosion when the vital personalities came into collision with administrators: 'Bureaucracy cannot provide the conditions needed by architects working on cathedrals and churches – nothing less than being part of the *Opus Dei* of a Cathedral is sufficient'.[245]

In particular he found that the conservation work carried out by the Ministry was careful, technically good, expensive but 'aesthetically utterly uninspired'. He believed that the Church and church architects had nothing to learn from the Ministry's activities.

Worse still, who was to control the State if it was allowed to interfere? He voiced his worries:

If the Church were to permit such Authorities to have any control over the insides of Cathedrals and Churches, or on the outside other than at present, who would control these Authorities, whose record is suspect, and in any event cannot be compared with the excellent record of the Church. It is cathedrals and churches which need to be protected from the maw of secular authorities and certain Societies and Individuals.[246]

Grant aid to the Church should be indirect, and completely separated from the technical and

242

aesthetic aspects of conservation to church and cathedral fabrics, he believed, suggesting this could be done by awarding annual grants towards the cost of maintaining churches and cathedrals of all denominations to a central body – 'The Ecclesiastical Buildings Grant Commission', who would be solely concerned with holding the annual grant and dispensing it to parochial church councils (PCCs) and Cathedral Chapters of the Church of England, and the equivalent bodies of other denominations. Even this body would have no concern with the technicalities or aesthetics of conservation. Applications for grants would be made by PCCs or Chapters accompanied by a certificate approving all technical and aesthetic aspects issued by the DAC or CAC as appropriate. Money for the Grant Fund might fittingly be raised by a tax on tourism.[247]

Re-ordering

George Pace understood any interior re-ordering of our churches and cathedrals – as a demonstration of living faith – was seriously at risk, due to the impact of the historical conscience, the compulsive repairing mania, and the pressures exerted by preservation societies, art historians and the like. He declared that the aesthetic standard of most re-ordering of churches already carried out had been seriously and adversely affected by such interference; stating that in this country it would be difficult to find 20 schemes of comparable aesthetic value to those of the Continent or in Mexico.[248]

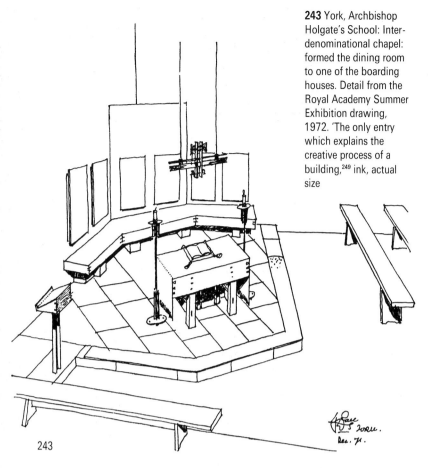

243

243 York, Archbishop Holgate's School: Inter-denominational chapel: formed the dining room to one of the boarding houses. Detail from the Royal Academy Summer Exhibition drawing, 1972. 'The only entry which explains the creative process of a building,[249] ink, actual size

He suggested the current itch to re-order should be resisted with self-discipline, and only after long periods of study and trial could such work be determined as essential. Very often, he warned, 'it may be expected that the studies will make it clear No Re-ordering is needed'.

'It is very difficult to resolve the tension between a proper respect for existing architecture and the bonding of the historical conscience', he admitted, even though the tradition of re-ordering of English churches was well established. He explained:

Our ancient churches show the scars of much re-ordering. The desire to be up to date, one-upmanship, the multiplication of altars, the possession of a holy relic, the cultus of the invocation of Saints, the founding of chantries, the rise of the Guilds, the increasing popularity of preaching, the making good of damage caused by the ravages of time and the elements, re-building after collapse, storm, fire and pillage, meant constant Re-ordering and Recasting, throughout the Middle Ages. More Re-ordering followed the putting down of many medieval practices and pendulum swinging in the reigns of Edward VI and Mary. Further Re-orderings were needed to provide the architectural setting for Anglican Worship. Much of this was largely undone by the Re-orderings to provide the architectural setting for the Theological and Liturgical Revival (the Oxford Movement) as laid down in all its architectural minutia by the Cambridge Movement. But there is no end to Re-ordering; further adjustments were

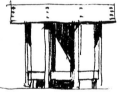

243(a) Ely Cathedral: sketch design for the crossing altar table. Felt-tip on pink copy paper, 3 × 2in (7.7 × 5cm), 1970

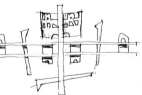

243(b) Durham University, St Mary's College: sketch design for hanging cross, ink on paper 3 × 2in (7.7 × 5cm), 1965

RIGHT
244 Oxford, Wycliffe Hall Chapel: reordering, 1962–3: oak pews stripped and limed, new altar with cross and candlesticks, new priest's desk, new wrought-iron light shades and new leaded clear glazing to north wall windows

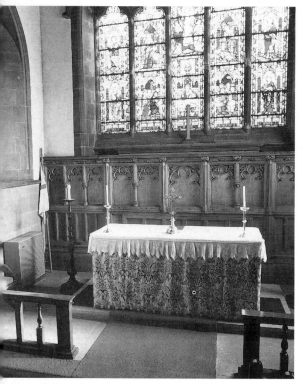

245

246

needed for the fleeting Fashions which then
followed thick and fast from 1890 to 1930.

George Pace saw the historical, technical,
economic, aesthetic and liturgical aspects of reordering and improving existing churches as being
'very involved', and advocated a slow approach.
He worried at the rise of much 'special pleading
and propaganda by various bodies, organizations,
and groups, advocating particular approaches to
these problems' and as a result, in the 1960s he
warned that

> . . . much unnecessary and undesirable re-ordering
> is being done to churches up and down the
> land . . . It seems desirable that the Church should
> give guidance on the Liturgical Goals and that this
> matter of prime importance should not be left to
> pressure groups, special pleaders and bodies
> engaged in pseudo-research. Once Goals have been
> established, parishes and their architects will be
> able to work on a firm foundation.[250]

In reviewing a book on the eighteenth-century
church, he notes,

> It is interesting to read of the alterations and
> eviscerations which the nineteenth century
> performed on the churches of the eighteenth
> century. It is also a warning to those who may feel
> that the received ecclesiology of the 1960s is
> definitive.

Where re-ordering was found to be necessary,
George Pace noticed through experience, that
amongst the churches in which it was more difficult
to do this were

> . . . those designed in the later part of the
> nineteenth century and early part of the twentieth
> century to provide the most carefully worked-out
> solution, practically and aesthetically to the
> Theological Aspirations of the period – i.e.
> churches by G. F. Bodley, Temple Moore, Sir
> Ninian Comper [see ILLUST. 106]

and he suggested a lesson could be learnt from too
rigid an approach to re-ordering. As far as he could
judge,

> . . . the Liturgical Movement is not a party matter,
> not an historical looking backwards as were the
> earlier movements in the century which gave rise
> to 'British Museum Religion', the 'back to Baroque'
> of the Society of SS Peter and Paul and the sterile
> scholarship of the Alcuin Club.

But at the same time he did believe that the
Liturgical Movement was not understood, and that
it was not ready for a means of expression:

> In this country the deep understanding and a desire
> to participate in the Liturgical Movement is as yet
> not widespread amongst the faithful in the
> congregations. A new attitude to worship is

245 Tinsley: chancel
reordering, 1952: paving,
frontal, forward altar,
standard candlesticks,
altar rails

246 Bilborough; chancel
reordering, 1970:
Victorian reredos from St
Sampson's, York, set
freestanding on new
stone plinth with oak
presidents seat below. An
ancient *mensa* set
between new stone
edges on new block
plinth, paving, carpet,
and gilded wrought-iron
hanging cross

OPPOSITE
247 Southwark
Cathedral: Harvard
Chapel reordering 1974.
Pugin tabernacle on new
stone base, oak and
wrought-iron furnishings,
glazed screen with cast
aluminium facings, carpet

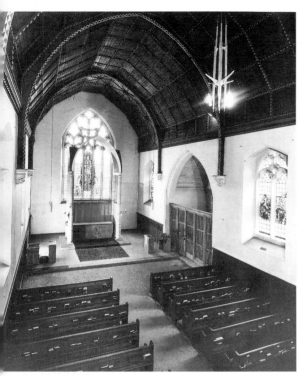

248

249

. . . it unlikely that there will be but one expression of the Liturgical Movement and thus even more unlikely that there will be but one architectural solution. It is to be hoped that in the Church of England we shall look in vain for a directive such as the Archdiocese of Cologne or the Roman Catholic Diocese of Superior in the USA have issued. The genius of the Church of England for comprehensiveness in doctrine is emphasized in Dr Ramsay's 'From Gore to Temple'; comprehensiveness in worship is emphasized in the Commentary to the Experimental Liturgy – The Modern liturgical movement, amongst many achievements, had led to a more flexible approach to the building and furnishing of churches. The instructions about the ordering of the service are brief, therefore, and inclusive rather than exclusive in tone and direction. Thus, the placing of the altar table, the use of lights, the position of the celebrant should not be governed by rule, but may be determined largely by local custom. The vexed question of the celebrant's uniform is best dealt with similarly. Christian tradition in these matters is too rich and manifold to be restricted by fashion and preference (or prejudice), whether it be 'simple primitive', 'fully Catholic', 'soundly Evangelical' or 'what my people like'. The 'ecumenical movement' of the past fifty years has greatly increased our understanding of Christian worship, both in theory and practice, and through this influence we can enrich our traditions without cheapening them.[253]

George Pace saw that each church must be individually studied and the architect must try to reach a reasonably satisfactory compromise in meeting current liturgical demands, preserving what is historically valuable and producing a result which is aesthetically acceptable.

A great many of George Pace's new furnishings in old churches came as the result of the requirements of re-ordering. Forward altars, housling benches, new altar rails, new priest's desks, the moving and re-positioning of choir stalls and chancel screens, and numerous other works were involved. Always he would strive to retain the integrity of the building, to preserve and cherish its older furnishings, incorporating many within new settings or providing a new lease of life by adapting them. In particular, he championed the retention of box pews. In his article in the *Fourteenth Report of the Central Council for the Care of Churches* entitled 'A plea for Box Pews in Modern Adaptations'[254] he discusses the problem of the likelihood of children disappearing from sight because of the height of the box pews. He had, he said, solved this problem at Great Houghton by simply (but ingeniously) raising the floor level inside the pews, thereby retaining the original woodwork.[255]

In the 1950s and 1960s, re-ordering was sometimes seen as the only way to revive the

without doubt coming, but until the clergy have had an opportunity of teaching their congregations and the congregations have had time to absorb the teaching and it has become part of their worshipping life, there will be no deep demand for liturgical planning in new churches or for the Re-ordering of old churches. Until such a demand does exist the architect cannot give any really worthwhile concrete expression to the Liturgical Movement in the architecture of new churches, or in the even more difficult architectural problems that arise in the Re-ordering of existing churches.[257]

In considering the eventual form of re-ordering he thought

248 York, St John's College Chapel: reordering 1954–6. Forward altar with Comper-like ciborium over 'more openly Gothic than his later works'[252]

249 Llancarfan, south Chapel: new stone altar and reredos with painted panels by Harry Harvey; oak kneeler paving and carpet, 1964

OPPOSITE
250 Loughborough Parish Church: proposed reordering: nave altar and associated furnishings. Ink on tracing paper, 7 × 8in (17.8 × 20.3cm), 1963

oughborough looking east

George Pace Nov. 63

Loughborough looking   west   GeoPace Nov. 63

251 Loughborough: nave
looking west with
proposals for new organ-
case on north and south
sides, together with new
wrought-iron pendant
light fittings. Ink on
tracing paper, 7 × 8in
(17.8 × 20.3cm), 1963

252

253

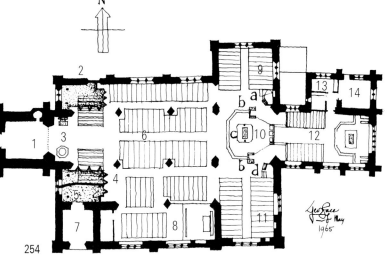

254

255

1. Tower
2. North organ and choir stalls
3. Font and organ console
4. South organ and choir stalls
5. New inner south porch
6. Nave
7. South porch
8. Burton Chapel
9. North transept
10. Nave altar
11. South transept
12. Re-arranged chancel
13. New vestries in old organ chamber
14. Existing choir vestry
   (a) Pulpit
   (b) Priest stall
   (c) Nave altar
   (d) Lectern

Typical reordering,
Loughborough 1965:

252 Interior looking east,
and proposed reordering,
1965

253 The east end as
reordered by Sir George
Gilbert Scott, 1862

254 Plan showing the
1965 proposed
modifications

255 Interior with
eighteenth-century
furnishings before
Victorian alterations

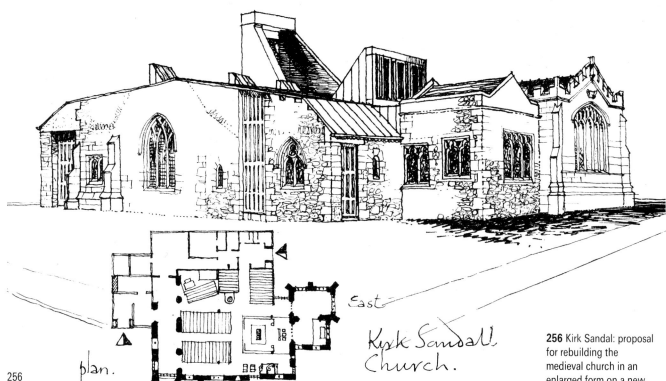

plan.

256

Kirk Sandall Church.

East

George Pace of York

256 Kirk Sandal: proposal for rebuilding the medieval church in an enlarged form on a new site, 1969. Ink on tracing paper, 7 × 4in (17.8 × 10.2cm). 'The Royal Fine Arts Commission thinks removal and re-erection of the old chancel acceptable. Some members doubted whether incorporation of sections of the old wall was justified . . .',[259] Drawings were exhibited at the Royal Academy Summer Exhibition, 1968

community's lost interest, and lost faith. In a representative example the Vicar of Loughborough, Canon R. Jones, in describing George Pace's work, illustrates what could be achieved – (see ILLUSTS 250–255).

> Sixteen years ago (1959) I took over a dull, heavy and tasteless church here – and in many ways a dying church. I am sure that it was his inspired work in designing and re-ordering the building which gave a setting for worship which from the first moment of its use brought life to our church family and began a period of growth. This change in 'shape' which he understood so completely and carried through so carefully – and with such tact in dealing with lay people suspicious of new ideas – is I am convinced far more important than the changes in language which have loomed so large lately . . .[256]

Always George Pace was guided by an instinct to beautify the church, to raise his work to the level of an art form, for 'religious art is essentially an encounter with Christ', he believed.[257]

At all times he was conscious that:

> The Church and Church Architects in dealing with the Re-ordering of existing churches under the influence of the Liturgical Movement, should be concerned with the inevitability of gradualness.[258]

Redundant churches

With certain churches, complex problems over their future use, well beyond the solution of simple re-ordering, force their closure. Much work was done on the problems of these redundant churches in the 1950s and 60s, with legislation passed and various Central Diocesan Committees set up. George Pace saw 'dangers for the Church in all this . . . far too much repair and conservation work is likely to be done to the churches selected to be maintained', he forecast, with the result that:

> The type of conservation is likely to be the 'MPBW Ancient Monument' type which not only means too much will be spent, too much done, but the techniques will be petrification and museum-type exhibition, not the much higher aesthetical level and much more technically difficult Church Repairing Standards. The superb conservation techniques which have been evolved by the best Church Architects over the past 100 years, and which are self-effacing, economic, technically sound, aesthetically satisfactory are likely to be lost. This would be a tragedy.

He recognized that harsh economic fact may make State maintenance of certain redundant churches inevitable, but suggested:

OPPOSITE
257 York, St Martin le Grand; reconstructed fire-damaged interior looking west. Note the 'very original and wholly successful'[260] new organ, and the opening in the transept wall for viewing the reset medieval glass depicting the life of St Martin. The painted ceiling takes further the techniques used by Street and Bodley, 1968

258 St Mary's, Clifton, Nottingham: chancel ceiling decoration 1969: note the tracery pattern to the rafter soffits

259 Nether Poppleton, York: reordering and decoration 1972, rood 1960

OPPOSITE
260 Chester Cathedral: high altar frontal, 1973 – detail showing the scallop shells of St James and the gridiron of St Lawrence

261

261 Chester Cathedral: high altar frontal, 1973

. . . it would be a grave error to imagine that this is a development to be encouraged or welcomed. The latter-day agnostic William Morrises will find that the qualities – the numinousness – and the visual delights, not to mention the subtle smells, they love to find in churches, will have departed; leaving in their stead coldly petrified national monuments, admission two shillings and sixpence.

In some instances he recognized conditions could make it desirable to move a church from one site and re-erect it on another, 'where it starts a new lease of life as a living church', noting that on such occasions 'Archaeology or art history should take a second place'.

He saw the giving of new life to parts of churches on new sites as part of a long tradition in the Church:

in the past examples abound of highly regarded parts of churches, chiefly fonts and doorways, being re-used in rebuilt churches, rebuilt in a grand, and even ostentatious manner. This type of re-use seems 'sentimental' rather than economic. The desire for economy or family pride may have played a greater part in the incorporation in parish churches of structural parts and furnishings and fittings salvaged from conventual churches after the Dissolution. It is usually considered that in 1542 at Llanidloes the five-bay thirteenth century north arcade and the fifteenth century hammer beam nave roof were salvaged from Abbeycwmhir. The nave, clerestory, perpends and statues at Drax (ILLUST. 115) can hardly have been designed for their present position and most probably originally formed part of the nearby Augustinian Priory. Two exceptionally fine fifteenth century Ripon School stall ends are re-used at Leake Church. At Wensley the magnificent fifteenth century Scrope parclose screen from Easby Abbey was re-used with

interesting Jacobean additions to form a family pew. At Welwick a very elaborate late fifteenth century tomb has been built into the south wall in a very random (but aesthetically exciting) manner. Tradition asserts that the tomb came from Burstall Priory. At Llancarfan the superb fifteenth century tabernacle work behind the High Altar incorporated into a softwood frame of eighteenth century date, may well be choir stall canopies from Llandaff Cathedral. Examples could be extended almost indefinitely. Many churches have pulpits, organs and fonts cast out by richer neighbours in the nineteenth century. Furniture made available by the demolition of redundant churches is now usually found a new home in another church under Faculty conditions.[261]

In his own work, salvaged artefacts from ancient and Victorian churches were often deliberately sought and incorporated in his new buildings or existing churches under his care: Pugin statues at St Leonard and St Jude, Doncaster (ILLUST. 81); Pugin altar at Campsall; Pugin tabernacle in the Harvard

262 Lichfield Cathedral: lay-vicar's choral stall hanging. Deep-blue background with design pattern in silver cord with silver and gold leather horizontal bands, and dots in bright red, 1973

262

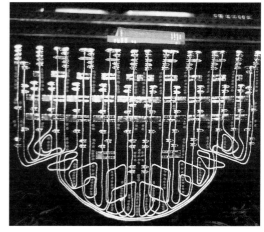

263

Chapel at Southwark Cathedral (ILLUST. 247); medieval fonts at Intake, Doncaster and James the Deacon, York; Pre-Raphaelite statutes, Rossetti reredos and Prichard choir stall-heads at Llandaff Cathedral (ILLUSTS 232 and 316); Victorian pews at the new churches of St Mark's, Sheffield, (ILLUST. 340), Chadderton, Lancs (ILLUST. 98), and Fairweather Green, Bradford (ILLUST. 113); medieval stained glass at St Martin le Grand, York (ILLUST. 154) and Durham Cathedral; eighteenth-century Spanish statue purchased for St Olave's, York; seventeenth-century Spanish wrought-iron lectern at Durham Cathedral; medieval alabaster carving purchased and set in Selby Abbey Memorial Chapel; antique chair and ancient stone altar table, Conisborough Memorial Chapel (ILLUST. 227); medieval woodwork in Tardrew screen, St Mary's, Beverley (ILLUST. 226); medieval effigy, Thryberg (ILLUST. 87); medieval tracery and stones set in Treeton extension; re-positioning of chancel screens at Monmouth and Bronllys; Bodley stalls at St Michael's College Chapel, Llandaff (ILLUST. 323); all examples chosen at random.

But throughout the ages not only were mere parts or artefacts from churches moved, there were examples of the moving and re-erection of complete churches which included: St Mary's, Tadcaster, Yorkshire; St Werburgh's, Bristol; St Paul's, Stockton; St Peter's at Arches, Milton; and of particular interest, the Victorian church at St Andrew's, Wells Street, London.

George Pace posed the question that in such a moving:

a has the church lost the character given by its original designer? and *b* has the transference been worthwhile?

The answer to the first question depends on how much the church may have been altered in its rebuilding, but whatever, 'it could be said the character is altered rather than lost'. Possibly there would be room for architectural improvement. How much, if at all, the fittings and monuments of the interior have lost or changed their character would 'remain a question of opinion'.

The second question – whether it would be worthwhile – 'the answer depends on how much one thinks it is worthwhile to conserve in some degree the artistic efforts of an earlier generation'.[265]

George Pace carried out the rebuilding of major sections of the medieval church of St Mary, Bishophill Senior, York (ILLUST. 355) during the years 1959 to 1965. This was not so much the re-

264

263 Llandaff Cathedral: John Wood's eighteenth-century classical 'Italian Temple' church built within the ruined medieval nave, and demolished by Prichard in the 1869 restoration. George Pace looked for evidence of the Temple, intending to include any in his twentieth-century reconstruction of Llandaff Cathedral (1949–64)[262]

264 Barn near East Witton, Wensleydale, Yorkshire, NR: displaying windows and quatrefoil stonework, probably brought from nearby Coverham or Jerveaulx Abbeys after the Dissolution, with the intention of forming a chapel[263]

265

266

267

265, 266 *and*
267 Pontefract, All
Saints: following
tradition – 'Each age
working to its taste'.[264]
The new extension
within the ruined
medieval nave, 1967

erection of an old church on a new site, but rather a twentieth-century church in which much ancient work had been incorporated. At Kirk Sandal Church he put forward a similar proposal in 1969 (ILLUST. 256) though this was never carried out.

The creation of a church of architectural worth using the whole or parts of other churches must not be prevented 'through over-emphasis on architecture, art history and archaeology' he stressed; 'such approaches may well be of surpassing interest to future generations'.[266]

Technical aspects

On technical aspects of conservation work, George Pace possessed a clear understanding of the nature of traditional materials and techniques. He rarely sought to engage specialists, preferring to attract and use good general contractors or local craftsmen in his work. He thought little of the proliferation of 'special craftsmen' in all sorts of conservation techniques, often techniques, he pointed out, 'which are not at all difficult' or are

> better done naturally by a builder under the architect's direction. This tendency to wrap-up essentially simple things and pretend they are elaborate, difficult and special, is a typical development of today's society. [see ref. 207 and ILLUST. 211)

Quite early on in the days of the practice he found it possible to interest younger craftsmen in restoration techniques, provided that he explained the principles and actually demonstrated the methods. 'Not once, but several times', he said,

I have been able to interest and train young bricklayers in the proper method of pointing ancient walls by spending a day on the church and actually showing them how to do the work. I have found the same to be true with young carpenters and joiners when I have explained and demonstrated the conservation methods of repairs on roofs attacked by beetle. In small towns and rural areas I have been amazed at the interest and pride which the old established builder still has in the parish church. These firms are still suitable for ordinary restorations provided the architect is prepared to explain what is being done, why it is done in that way and to be an enthusiast on the job himself.[267]

One small firm of stonemasons – Ebor Stone of York – worked exclusively on his churches, travelling throughout Britain. Though he could call upon them and many other masons to do his work, it was not unknown for him to carve lettering himself – for example, the inscription on the foundation stone at the new Holy Redeemer Church, York, was the work of his hand.

One of his great strengths lay in his ability to understand the practical difficulties encountered by craftsmen, and his willingness to listen, and if necessary alter his point of view. Lt Commander McGinnes, Clerk of Works at Durham Cathedral for 14 years, expands on this point:

From the beginning I sensed the dedication of the Architect for the Cathedral. Nothing was too great or too small if it was for the good of the Cathedral: as much care and attention was given to the

139

268

269

269 Llandaff Cathedral: the pulpitum, 1956. The hand and mechanical tooling of the shuttered concrete took three months to achieve a fine enough texture to harmonize with the limestone of the cathedral. Obtaining the correct colour, again necessary in order to harmonize with the natural stone, involved much research with a special mix finally devised by the architect, the consulting engineers, Ove Arup and Partners, together with the Cement and Concrete Association.[272] *See* ILLUST. 306

smallest detail as to the largest project. Time did not matter to George Pace when he was working for the Cathedral. He was a good listener and was man enough to see the other man's point of view and on occasions alter his own to suit. One of his main assets was understanding, and the Yard staff respected him as a man and admired him as an architect. As in the architectural field lots of designs are peculiar to that particular architect and are liked or disliked, similarly some of George Pace's designs are not liked, but the actual construction of all his work is *par excellence*. He always knew what he wanted, and in his mind's eye the finished article was there, and he made sure the architectural end was perfect. He always made it his business personally to show his appreciation to the Yard staff for their work.[268]

Also at Durham, the Dean, the Very Revd John Wild, records the results of George Pace's approach:

> Outside the Cathedral, in the College, the work of conservation and repair was so well done under his direction that you would hardly notice that the whole of the Prior's Kitchen and the south wall of the Prior's Chapel in the Deanery, for instance, had been thoroughly restored. The technique of pointing and repairing ancient stonework which he developed and taught to the Cathedral craftsmen was as near perfection as you could get.[269]

At Lichfield Cathedral

> . . . the workmen keenly looked forward to George Pace's visits. They respected his gifts as an architect/designer, and also gave him their warm regard as a man.[270]

In his turn, George Pace rarely forgot his debt to his craftsmen, and, for example, at Lichfield on the occasion of his Silver Jubilee as Architect, in the midst of acknowledging the help given to him by two Bishops and three Deans, he made mention of the masons and carpenters – and 'Leslie, the foreman, undefeated by any problem.'[271]

From time to time he found proposals were made for the setting up of Diocesan Church Repairing Works Organizations, usually suggested as an extension of a Cathedral Works Staff. He thought little of this:

> Fortunately, no such proposal has got off the ground. Such an organization would never be viable economically, would have, to a greater degree than usual, all the economic and technical objections to all Directly Employed Works Organizations; would soon destroy the local love and identification each parish has with its church; above all, it would be the death blow of the magnificent Conservation Ethos evolved by the Church and Church Architects during the past hundred years. It would open the floodgates to bureaucracy, and in two generations, the repairing of churches would have sunk to the level now found in buildings maintained by Local Authorities and MPBW.[273]

He encountered the impossibility of obtaining certain materials, the production of which had absolutely ceased – magnesian limestone for example (since the 1980s now fortunately being quarried again), from which many of the finest South and West Yorkshire churches are built. His technique of building up eroded pockets in this lime stonework using sandstone slate slips bedded in lime mortar proved to be an excellent substitute, being surprisingly indistinguishable aesthetically, and surviving the technical problems of the stones interacting chemically with each other, as an inspection of the work some 40 years later will reveal (ILLUST. 268).

Here, with these simple techniques of repair, he was at one with SPAB and took careful note of the writings of A. R. Powys, Charles Canning Winmill and Alban Caroe.

The number of firms competent to carry out conservation work to churches and cathedrals and the numbers of craftsmen having the necessary skills and experience in conservation work were limited in George Pace's time, much as is the case today. This placed a limit to the amount of conservation work possible in any one year. George Pace recognized this factor as being of greater significance than lack of money. It underlined the importance of proper programming, the selection of priorities, especially the time scale for stonework; and above all, he said,

> . . . for sternly resisting the unfounded and unimportant urges of The Compulsive Repairing Mania.[274]

OPPOSITE
270 Red House Chapel, Moor Monkton: working conservation drawing showing east window tracery, 1971. Ink on tracing paper, actual size

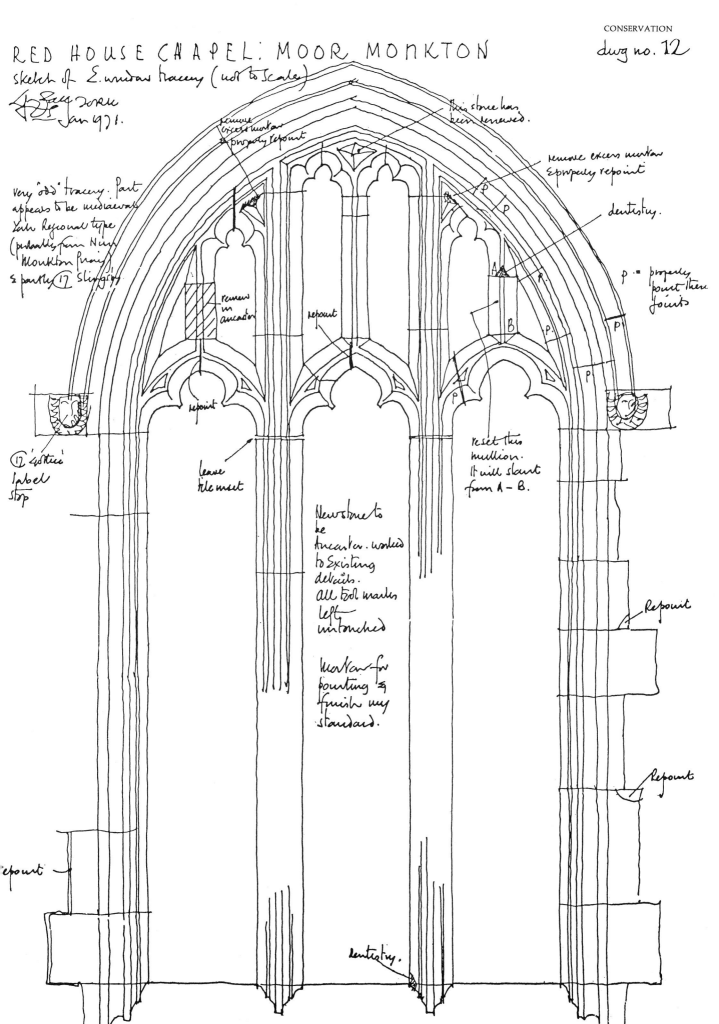

RED HOUSE CHAPEL: MOOR MONKTON

sketch of E. window tracery (not to scale)

[signature]
Jan 1971.

very "odd" tracery. Part
appears to be mediaeval
late Regional type
(probably from New
Monkton Priory
& partly 17 Slingsby)

remove
excess mortar
& properly repoint

this stone has
been renewed.

remove excess mortar
& properly repoint

dentistry.

P = properly
point these
joints

renew
in Ancaster

repoint

(17) 'gothic'
label
stop

repoint

leave
the inset

reset this
mullion.
It will slant
from A – B.

New stone to
be
Ancaster. worked
to Existing
details.
All Tool marks
left
untouched

Mortar for
pointing &
finish my
standard.

Repoint

Repoint

repoint

dentistry.

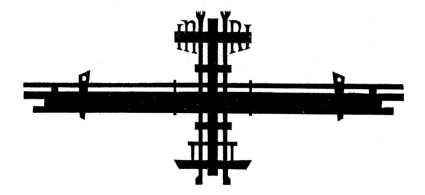

SUMMARY

As an architect, George Pace was 'detached, very much so, from the shibboleth of the modern architectural and cultural establishment and the outlook of its planners and conservationists'.[275] He moved little in architectural circles and during his lifetime was largely unknown to the general public.[276] But he stood in the great tradition of church architecture, believing in, and moved by the doctrine and liturgy of the Church, designing buildings and their fittings to be 'a constant witness to the Glory of God', and 'an act of worship in themselves'.[277]

He was no Revivalist, for he wished to serve a living Church with an architecture representative of its time, and looked beyond the rationalist 'Modern Movement Architecture' of the time, to an architecture capable of expressing wonder, worship, magic and symbolism; to push forward, in the Western European tradition, our awareness of spatial relationships, solids and voids. In this, his unique sense of aesthetics played a fundamental part.

Unavoidably, he held passionately many principles not fashionable with the majority of his brethren, as he set about developing and proselytizing a philosophy and language of architecture which drew inspiration from ancient buildings, distilling the essence of their characteristics, and assimilating their spirit into contemporary style. Combining his scholarly knowledge of the history of architecture and traditional building techniques, he slowly forged his own unique style, reinterpreting the Gothic spirit in a purely twentieth-century manner!

In doing so, George Pace recoiled from what he saw as the aims of contemporary architects – 'the pursuit of excitement based on sensations, on tone colour, on the dream images of the sub-conscious, on shock and disturbance and titillation, and novelty'; and instead sought to retain 'the perception of the age-old natural order of things,' in the approach to his art.

He believed:

the one great unifying theme of the Art of, say, Beethoven, Shakespeare or Tolstoy was that it was above all rooted in obedience to the external moral and natural order, in the perception of those simple, unchanging truths which are at the root of all human wisdom.

For all their artistic originality, the patterns these artists traced were 'essentially moral patterns of a deeply conservative kind'. He looked to base his art upon exalted symbols of the broadest moral sense, to follow a path where 'the relationship of man towards art is religion'.[278]

On the other hand, he did not believe that explicit morals in architecture (such as those held in the doctrines of the Ecclesiological Society or John Ruskin, which pummelled architects into restoring churches to the perfect Gothic period) were relevant to architecture; indeed, he declared, they 'could completely obscure what real architecture is and what real architects do'.[279] He believed the lack of organic culture in contemporary society to be a fundamental problem to the development of architecture, particularly as 'the type of culture we do have is utterly divorced from humanity';[280] and he strove throughout his life to discover evidence of the roots from which a new organic culture could grow; to nurture and develop any such fragile beginning for the enrichment of human life.

Fiercely independent, he saw the architect as a first degree creator;[281] and had little patience for

271 Wyberton: sanctuary reordering – hanging cross, wrought-iron painted matt black

those who held up architectural history and the aura of age as an unassailable defence against placing creative work within our medieval or Victorian churches.

Such an attitude is not to be confused with lack of respect, or a rejection of architectural history; indeed whenever the opportunity arose to save ancient parts this would be taken, as his work in new and old churches demonstrates. Such was his awareness he championed the retention and conservation of much which fell outside the range of public taste at the time – the Victorian choir screen by Sir Gilbert Scott at Lichfield Cathedral being one supreme example.[282] Of the pulpit in the same Cathedral he said – 'Not all love the pulpit, but they will learn to do so'.[283]

As a conservationist he believed the Church had always been able to inspire architects to work for it at the highest level, in a sense of vocation, something State money and administration could not replace. He saw the 'loving, humble, disciplined, economic, lively and aesthetically based Conservation' which dedicated architects practise on behalf of the Church, as contrasting most favourably with the 'arrogant, heavy-handed, impersonal, loveless Museum and Archaeological-exhibit basis which is unavoidable in the repair work of an official body'.[284] To him church buildings were represented 'not as mere pieces of fabric but rather as the means whereby the worship of God might be deepened, and enriched'.[285]

Over a period of 28 years George Pace attained the post of consultant architect to nine cathedrals, to six dioceses and to numerous trusts and societies. He built some 30 new churches and carried out new works and restorations to well over 700 parish churches.

Although his designs were not considered to be 'advanced' his work was sufficiently detached and controversial to earn him recognition in 1974 as an 'esoteric cult figure',[286] a title he secretly rather enjoyed. Above all, he saw his life's work lasting into the next century, where he hoped 'future generations may view my works in a kindly light'.

Sometimes he might appear 'idiosyncratic, positive and critical and could give the impression of arrogance', but as Dr Patrick Nuttgens perceived,

Those who knew him well recognised that beneath the dry acerbity lay a fundamental humility based upon his profound respect for the great architecture of the world, and for the life and meaning of the Church. He had a natural authority derived from his long acquaintance with the art and craft of building which enabled him to work slowly and carefully and see his contribution as part of the continuity of a tradition stretching into the past and the future. His new work was characterized by a highly personal approach to design, by clear understanding of the nature of modern materials as well as traditional ones, and by uncompromising forms generated by his own analysis of a building's function. He combined this rigorous intellectual approach with an unusual sensitivity to the scale and character of old buildings. He thus made additions which were unmistakenly his own and wholly of their period while enriching and extending the original meaning of the building.[288]

His clients were impressed with their discovery of 'the spiritual depth and sensitivity to which his work was an expression',[289] and were struck by his 'unusual ability to speak on things both architectural and theological', and 'his even more unusual ability to relate the two fields'.[290] Of his new chapel at Scargill (ILLUST. 332) Patrick Marsh, Warden of Scargill House, said, 'in designing for us such a lovely building [he] has in a very real sense helped many people to find a new reality in their Christian faith'.[291]

His mind was open to so many interests in relation to his subject that there was always something new and stimulating in his conversation. The Revd W. Field remembers those occasions, 'when . . . we would start discussing the problem in hand, and then drift onto Art'.[292]

He could be endlessly patient if it was for the good of his churches,[293] and would often give all his attention to the smallest of enquiries. Henry Stapleton, one-time curate of St Olave's, York and now Dean of Carlisle, found '. . . he was unstinting in his time and he spent hours in sorting out problems that appeared superficially simple, but in fact were highly complex'.[294]

His manner and attitude to life, made a deep impression amongst those with whom he worked. Bill Lockett, Canon Theologian at Liverpool, who knew him over many years from student days observed:

> To his friends George had a Franciscan attitude to life — warm, generous with his time to people, uncomplicated, a lover of natural and beautiful things and always with a look of joy. Yet one knew that he was, beneath this Franciscan simplicity, an intellectual. In a moment he could turn to detailed practicalities drawing on a wealth of knowledge and experience. Behind the joy were the manifold cares of one of the most remarkable architectural practices. Few could match his practice which included so many of our important buildings supervised by him personally. Many people have wondered over the years how he was able to do it. He was a tremendous example of dedication to a task, yet which did not detach him from people and life.[295]

Canon Cecil Rhodes saw him as one of a small band of persons,

> . . . who stand out in being splendid in their person and splendid in their ability, whose friendship and whose meeting them was always a joy and

273 Gozo, Malta; regional characteristics, noted in a holiday sketchbook, ink, 8 × 7in (20.3 × 17.8), 1973

encouragement. In one way or another they seemed to have laid hold of the things which matter. They have all been essentially humble men and women.[296]

Stained-glass artist Patrick Reyntiens, found that in working with George Pace

> one had above all, a sense of being invited by a distinguished and subtle and sensitive mind and heart to co-operate in a genre of architecture and decoration which was of a quality that is almost nowadays non-existent.[297]

Many who came into contact with him felt 'privileged' to know him,[298] suggesting 'we are all better people for George's existence.[299] As John Piper remarked so poignantly,

> . . . he was a great man, and the effect of his sensibility and scholarship will live on. We are all grateful for his life and influence.[300]

SELECTED WORKS

ARMAGH CATHEDRAL:
The Royal Irish Fusiliers Regimental Chapel
1948–50

OPPOSITE
274 Archbishop D'Arcy memorial screen dividing the chapel from the choir

275 Plan

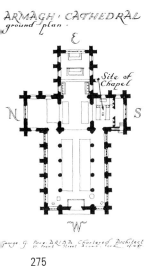

275

276 Chapel seen from south aisle, 1950

277 Memorial-book casket carved in Armagh marble

This commission presented George Pace with his first opportunity to furnish a chapel within the confines of a large building.

Before the Liturgical Movement made the westward facing position at the altar acceptable, George Pace regularly used a dossal curtain and screen to form the eastern setting for the altar, and ones similar to that illustrated here may be seen at Kildale (1948), St Martin's, Birmingham (1956), St Gregory's Chapel, Durham Cathedral (1957), and St Mary's, Rawmarsh (1959).

The remaining furnishings are clustered around the altar, with the outer face of the seating panelled to form an enclosure but 'so low as not to affect the fine feeling of loftiness apparent in the south transept'.[301] On the panelling are carved some 2000 letters of the Battle Honours, all initially drawn out full size by the architect. His centrally placed memorial book casket is carved from Armagh marble, and interestingly exhibits little of the classical influence found in his other furnishings. In contrast, the great 'Spanish' screen dividing the chapel from the choir owes something to Comper's 'Unity by Inclusion' period and represents the first of a series, with notable examples found at St Illtud's Chapel, Llandaff

276

Cathedral (1958) (ILLUST. 233), and the two parclose screens to St George's Chapel, Sheffield Cathedral (1959).

George Pace used his craftsmen in York for the joinery work and such was the interest in his revival of lost techniques, such as gilding by the tip and cushion method, that the furnishings were exhibited locally before their export.[302]

278 The gates erected later in 1955, tentatively explore a number of distinctive techniques which came to characterize George Pace's later wrought-iron design work

278

277

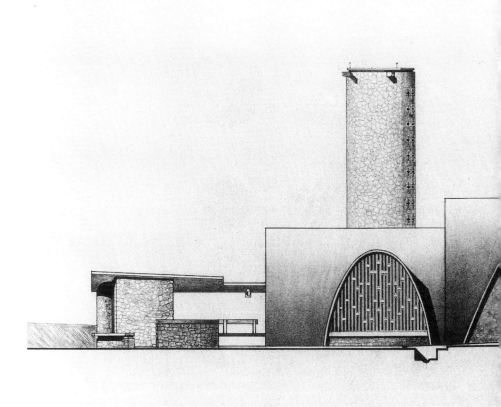

279

280

IBADAN UNIVERSITY COLLEGE CHAPEL
Nigeria, Africa
1951–54

ABOVE
279 East elevation – detail from an early design. Drawing in pencil on cartridge paper, 28 × 20in (71 × 51cm). Detail 28 × 10in (71 × 25.4cm), undated

Ibadan Chapel was conceived at a time when an optimistic mood towards new church building accompanied an equally radical reassessment of the Church's role:

> Instead of clinging to an ascendancy that no longer exists, the loveliest modern churches on the continent and a very few in this country, are marked by the austerity and humility of modest proportions, raw concrete and unrendered stone. Some like Rainer Senn's chapels at Pontarlier and outside Nice, or George Pace's University Chapel at Ibadan, actually recall a tent or shelter. Such buildings seem to express a kind of repentance – a repentance that is with the world.[303]

This new search for identity by the Church brought with it the Liturgical Movement and also a quest for unity amongst differing denominations.[304]

Ibadan is more than a structural expression of the favoured image of 'radiant poverty';[305] it is also designed as a 'Chapel of Unity' to be used by the many denominations joined together under the Christian Council of Nigeria; and, as such, may be seen as an early experiment in ecumenical architecture.

The building bears an interesting likeness to the Church of St Francis Pampulha by Oscar Niemeyer

OPPOSITE
280 Interior view of east end, ink, charcoal and coloured pastel, 16 × 10in (40.6 × 25.4cm), undated

1. Tower, vestry and bell
2. Font
3. Narthex
4. Stairs to gallery
5. Nave
6. Seats for Ministers
7. Lectern/pulpit
8. Altar table
9. Liturgical seats
10. Credence
11. Stage door
12. Transepts (as extended 1961)
13. Vestry
14. Gallery over

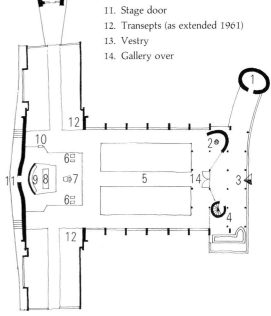

281 Plan (drawn by G. Pace to illustrate his article on shared church buildings in *Church Building Magazine*, No. 27, April 1969)

282 View from north
west: built in concrete
and stone calculated to
resist the extremes of a
tropical climate and
ravages of insect life, the
structure is restrained,
enabling local unskilled
labour to be employed
under the supervision of
an Italian contractor
working for Maxwell Fry
on the main university
building programme

close by. Note entrance
sculpture in Iroko wood
of the Resurrection by
Nigerian sculptor Ben
Enwonwu[306]

(1942) who had, George Pace noted, successfully combined reinforced concrete with traditional Brazilian wall pictures made of glazed tiles.[307]

Ibadan too 'uses twentieth century technology in a forceful contemporary manner', but, as Udo Kultermann, architectural critic notes, it also manages to retain a local identity and a sense of place:

> the African climate which dictates so much of the structural design also suffuses it with an essentially African character, in spite of the elegance of smooth, concrete parabolas and the formality of a traditional cruciform plan.[308]

The cruciform plan intentionally lacks the head or chancel, and thereby provides the means to cope with the ecumenical role of the building. The altar is brought forward, visible from nave and both transepts, and set on a platform to preserve a liturgical area that remains intact at all the services of all the Christian denominations using the Chapel.

The altar is free-standing with three sides available for different forms of celebration and the platform also serves the needs of religious drama. Transepts are planned to be extended if further seating becomes necessary.

George Pace spent some weeks studying at first hand the uncleared second-growth jungle site and worked out a vast landscaping scheme centred round the Chapel, comprising a 700 feet (213 metres) long grove of Cassarine trees planted in the shape of an immense cross, to be visible from civil air routes. The remainder of the site, under grass, was to be maintained in some areas by frequent close mowing and in others areas by scything at less frequent intervals 'the varying textures and lengths so related in a vast abstract pattern'.[309]

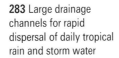
283

284

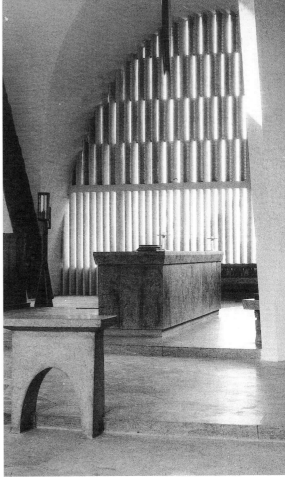

283 Large drainage channels for rapid dispersal of daily tropical rain and storm water

284 Altar in blue Horton stone from Banbury, England, set on a dais in which the symbols of the four evangelists are formed with inlaid crushed seashells. Priest's desk and lamp in Iroko hardwood, and behind, the north transept wall – open to the wind

OPPOSITE
285 Brown Horton stone font and oak cover, seen from the south porch with the new simplified nave arcade also visible

286 exterior, south elevation

287 Chancel, east window recreated and treated as a reredos, filled with stained glass by Harry Stammers depicting the *Te Deum*, designed in close collaboration with the architect. Freestanding altar in brown Horton stone. Floor in red Wilderness stone. Pendant light fittings in oak

288 Font at west end of south aisle in the traditional position at the point of entry

289 Organ screen in painted and gilded pine at the west end of the north aisle and new barrel-vault ceiling, and pews

290 South porch, new oak inner door

HOLY TRINITY CHRISTCHURCH, NEWPORT
Reconstruction
1955–8

For re-building this church, which had been damaged by fire in 1949, George Pace saw two possibilities: to keep the tower and build on to it an entirely new and contemporary church (for example St Mark's, Sheffield 1950–67, *pp. 181–6*) or to build a church incorporating the little-damaged parts of the old church and using these in a design which whilst creative, had an affinity with the previous church. He advised the latter option, and thus the course followed after the 1877 fire was repeated.[310]

The fire destroyed the roofs and furnishings and had so 'severely calcined the stonework of the piers, arches and window tracery, that demolition of these parts was unavoidable'. Reconstruction repeated those features which gave a highly individual character to the interior, but the detail is simplified, particularly in the arcade, and the atmosphere heightened by the altered proportions so that 'The Spirit of the local medieval regional type remains'. Some items were reconstructed faithfully, for example the tracery of the west window of the nave and the east window of the chancel, which in each case was of a high order aesthetically; whilst other windows filled with more pretentious tracery were simplified. New forms were experimented with in the south chapel, where the multiple barrel-vaulted plaster ceiling formed the prototype for the roof of the Welch Regiment Chapel at Llandaff Cathedral (1956, ILLUST. 302).

287

The arrangement of the interior provides an early example of Liturgical Movement planning, for 'the design revolves around the high altar'. Free-standing, this allows the priest to assume a westward facing position during Holy Communion. The Victorian preference for a choir in the chancel in the style of the great cathedrals is not repeated, but the chancel is cleared and the choir returned to the usual medieval position at the west end of the church to form a trained part of the congregation and reinforce the sense of the Family of God at worship.

289

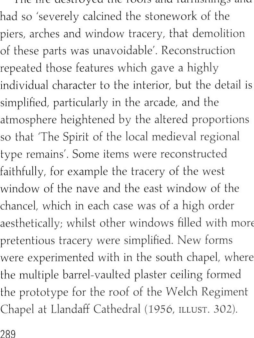

290

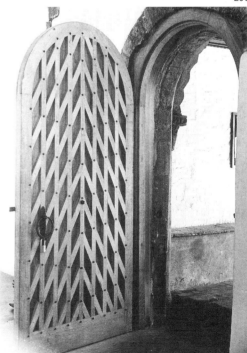

LLANDAFF CATHEDRAL
A.D. 427-1964

Restoration & repair after War Damage & New Works 1949-1964
drawn by the architect: George Pace MA FSA FRIBA York

292

LLANDAFF CATHEDRAL
The great restoration
1949–64

292 The Royal Academy drawing exhibited at the Summer Exhibition, 1965, showing the restoration together with new works – the pulpitum and the Welch Regimental Chapel, ink on cartridge, 36 × 22in (91.44 × 55.9cm), 1964

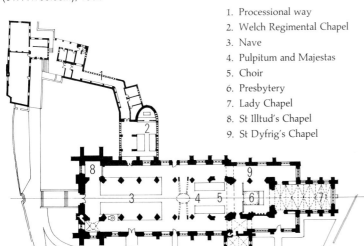

1. Processional way
2. Welch Regimental Chapel
3. Nave
4. Pulpitum and Majestas
5. Choir
6. Presbytery
7. Lady Chapel
8. St Illtud's Chapel
9. St Dyfrig's Chapel

293

OPPOSITE
291 The pulpitum viewed from the north aisle together with the new

pulpit, light fittings and organ-gallery screen in view

293 Plan of the cathedral as completed by 1965

The rebuilding of the war-devastated Llandaff Cathedral was, for George Pace, his most influential commission. Virtually unknown, but backed by Dean Milner-White,[311] he was entrusted with this great task when the Dean and Chapter appointed him architect in 1949, following the death of their previous architect, Sir Charles Nicholson, who had already made a tentative start on the work.

In this, George Pace's first major work, were tested his theories on church architecture, thought out during the war. Here, too, were born the basic foundations of his own creative style. This work would have a profound influence on the development of his work in later years.

His first task on starting a creative work of such magnitude was to decide upon the goal towards which all his efforts must be directed. This he summarized as being 'the creation of a cathedral, the mother church of a great Diocese, a building which by day and night constantly shows forth the Glory of God.'[312]

His approach crystallized into four principles:

a Where ancient work and the work of Prichard's nineteenth century restoration is capable of being repaired, this is done with tender care;

b Where new work is required to make good destroyed parts or to provide for new needs the work is frankly of the twentieth century, but designed so as to integrate itself with the Cathedral. This approach is truly traditional in a building of great age, upon which many generations in the past have naturally expressed themselves in the architecture of their own age;

155

294

295

296

294 Llandaff Cathedral devastated by a land mine during the Second World War, 1941

295 The ruined nave

296 Prichard's 'open' roof destroyed

c Everying in the building and its fittings and furnishings is designed or controlled by the Architect so that all play their appointed parts in the creation of a Cathedral which is greater than the mere sum of its parts;

d Every part to be a Work of Art in itself, but to lose itself in the whole so that the Cathedral is not a mere collection of Works of Art, as in a museum or art gallery. The aim has been to create a Cathedral which is a complete offering to God in which every individual has given of his uttermost, yet has utterly effaced himself.[313]

Until 1949 George Pace knew the Cathedral only from books. His first visit, described in a later address to the Friends, led to him forming a great respect for the building:

I was overwhelmed with the scale and majesty of the Nave arcades. No illustration I had seen had done the arcade even faint justice. Some of the untouched medieval caps I found to be exquisite beyond words. The west front, particularly internally, impressed me, even after the surfeit of magnificence of thirteenth century work which surrounds me in Yorkshire. Prichard's south west tower and spire exceeded my expectations and I had no idea he had so much other good work in Llandaff. The Lady Chapel interior reminded me of the Chapel of the Holy Spirit at Sheffield Cathedral [ILLUST. 328ff.], the Chapel here being the obvious source of Sir Charles Nicholson's inspiration[314]

Past criticism suggested Llandaff to be an

overgrown Parish Church which save for the two western towers had no special features, and was interesting only by reason of the excellent proportion of all its parts.[315]

Though George Pace agreed the general arrangement of the interior was 'akin to a parish church' he had the vision to realize the structure had the attributes of a cathedral, 'I found I did not share in the criticism that Llandaff is merely a large, plain and somewhat uninteresting Parish Church, . . . I did not feel in the least moved to bewail the unbroken ridge line, the lack of transept or the

non-existence of a central tower'.[316]

The Prichard western tower was, he believed, a major monument of the Gothic Revival, and most certainly brought cathedral qualities to the previously undistinguished exterior, *but* much more was needed.

He determined his prime resolve was 'to instil into the new edifice something of the impressive Cathedral atmosphere of St David's,[317] and his interpretation of the solution to these needs was positive and irreversible, but this took 11 long years to achieve, to the mixed accompaniment of admiration and hostility. The local paper – the *Western Mail* – took up the cause to defend this new architect from across the border. 'He has the skill' they said, and

He was able to share the vision of the Dean and Chapter and since 1949 has proved to have the courage and stamina to carry through the immense demands made of him. He has lived through difficult days – days when he came under fire from clergy and laymen alike . . .

297

To get scale and a feeling of distance and remoteness, it was essential that the ceiling should be in small regular panels, but, as both clerestory walls bow outwards to a considerable and irregular extent, it was difficult to achieve this. A study of the general form and the arrangement of the panels nearest to the clerestory walls, will disclose the solution adopted. The ceiling is of Yang wood.[324]

The new level of the nave ceiling meant the presbytery arch had to be lowered. The new arch follows the design by Sir Charles Nicholson, and wherever possible the stones from Prichard's arch were re-used. The lowering of the arch was an operation of some magnitude, which was not without its 'exciting and anxious moments'.[325]

Whilst the nave and the Prichard tower were being restored, a start on the new Welch Regiment Chapel was made. Donated by the Regiment as their private chapel to honour the war dead, the work became a major addition to the Cathedral.

In an address to the Friends of the Cathedral, George Pace outlined his ideas:

I have given much anxious thought to the problems involved. In siting the Chapel it is essential to avoid interrupting the long low lines and general austerity of the exterior, of marking the base of Jasper Tudor's tower, and of spoiling the subtle relationships which exist between the West Front and the Prebendal House. It is also of major importance that the Regimental Chapel should be part and parcel of the interior of the Cathedral. To satisfy these somewhat diverse demands I have suggested that the Chapel is placed at right angles to the North Aisle of the Nave and is approached from the Cathedral under the cill of the window immediately east of the Norman doorway. The three-light reticulated window above the proposed new entrance would remain, but would be unglazed. There would be a passage on the west side of the Chapel forming a kind of aisle and leading from the north door to the new Vestries which in turn would link up with the east end of the Prebendal House. This scheme should allow of the creation of many subtle spatial relationships between the Cathedral, the Prebendal House and the new buildings, and form in effect a miniature Close.[326]

This concept was followed through essentially unaltered, so that, when the building of the Chapel and its associated link was completed in 1950, Pace declared his ambition was nearing its goal in that 'all views of the Cathedral from the north-east, north-west and south-west now disclose complex compositions of a Cathedral character'.[327]

In the process a major creative work had been born – the Welch Regimental Chapel – a significant work in its own right. Here, the Dean and Chapter suggested,

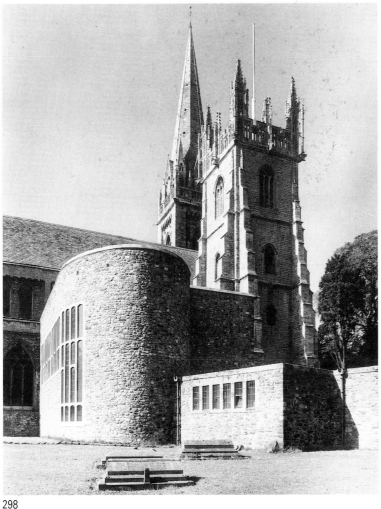

298

298 The new Welch Regimental Chapel and processional way constructed of rounded river stone, mixed with blue pennant rubble stone, forming part of the cathedral 'close'

. . . But Pace pressed on. He was not prepared to allow Llandaff to deteriorate into an undistinguished Parish Church. The interior atmosphere had to be exact. In it there must be awe as well as reverence.[318]

One of the first difficult decisions concerned the nave roof. Sir Charles Nicholson had felt that the nave should have a richly decorated wood ceiling at the level of the original ceiling, as shown by the construction at the base of the inner face of the west gable.[319]

George Pace was most enthusiastic for this conception.[320] In his own research on the building he too noted that Browne Willis records the nave was formerly 'ceiled with painted wainscot'.[321] Prichard, in Pace's opinion, had in the 1869 restoration provided 'an uninspired open timber roof'. As this roof was almost totally destroyed by the war-time land-mine explosion, the opportunity could be taken to give the nave a panelled ceiling at the level of the fifteenth-century ceiling to 'bring back to the nave its inherent dignity'.[322]

George Pace used Nicholson's drawings as the basis for his final design, though he had to make a few adjustments 'to bring it into relationship with my ideas of the interior as a whole.[323]

Here he explains some of the difficulties:

OPPOSITE
297 The new nave ceiling in Sapele, Opele and Yang wood calculated to resist the ravages of death-watch beetle, reconstructed at the level of the fifteenth-century ceiling

299

the Architect has managed to convey a sense of spaciousness and perspective in a building occupying a comparatively small space. This he has achieved by providing large areas of unencumbered floor space, but much more so by the important part played by natural and artificial lighting and by the ceiling, which is formed by a series of longitudinal barrel vaults, creating an illusion of length and height.

Atmosphere is achieved by the use of two traditional principles – first, he has so arranged entry that the full view of the chapel only gradually unfolds as each pier and arch allows more and more exciting glimpses of the whole. Secondly, the windows admitting the natural light are deeply recessed, so that when facing the altar the glazing cannot be seen, and the light takes on a special quality and creates 'atmosphere'.[328]

George Pace saw that the design of the interior of the chapel 'arose inevitably from its plan', but the techniques used for perspective and spatial effects which play 'such a very important part' drew inspiration from the architectural past. In particular the 'form and finish of the piers and arches are an extension of a medieval local Regional type to be found in Llantwit Major and other churches of the Vale of Glamorgan.[329] Distilling the essence of the spirit of ancient buildings and infusing this into contemporary style grew from this period, and became a hallmark of George Pace's work. As Sir Ninian Comper says in *Of the Atmosphere of a Church*: 'Knowledge of tradition is the first requisite for the creation of atmosphere in a church'.

Christ Church, Newport (*p. 153*) provided the test bed for some of the work here, but the windows are totally new. The technique of straining the light to produce 'atmosphere' preoccupied George Pace throughout his life, and he invariably makes reference to this in all his new church work.

300

301

The new Welch Regimental Chapel 1956:

299 Viewed from the west at night

300 Western aisle and entrance to the processional way

301 A window bay in the west wall using Doulting stone and rough-cast plaster. The medieval panels of stained glass were presented by the Regiment and are placed above the Roll of Honour

Returning to the nave, work now began on the 'most important new work in the Cathedral' – the pulpitum, traditionally a stone screen provided to shut off the choir from the nave. The architect gave various addresses to the Dean and Chapter and the Friends to explain the purpose of a pulpitum in a modern Cathedral[330] and in so doing he provided an insight into the manner in which he evolved the final form and the use he had of his collaborators, including Sir Jacob Epstein.

He explained that in medieval days Llandaff Cathedral had a pulpitum in the third bay westwards from the entrance to the presbytery. This pulpitum and the stalls existed at least to the date of Browne Willis' survey in the eighteenth century. When Prichard restored the Cathedral, he did not provide a pulpitum or any marked subdivision in the length of the Cathedral, except for the blocking of the lower part of the Bishop Urban arch by the reredos containing the Rossetti paintings. 'To my mind this was a major fault, and therein lies the criticism that the interior of Llandaff was rather like a large Parish Church', he said.

He looked to other examples of pulpitum design both in England and on the Continent assessing their unique role and how they might be translated for Llandaff;[331] but he hastened to say, 'I do not intend to reproduce any of these at Llandaff, or even a glorious Irish stew of them all'; for he proposed to produce a structure of the twentieth century.

At Halberstadt he noted of the stone pulpitum which carries a rood that its Renaissance design dwells comfortably in the fourteenth-century

302

303

302 The interior as seen on entry

303 Sanctuary furnishings: cross, candlesticks (*see* ILLUST 419), altar rails and altar frontal (*see* ILLUSTS 189 *and* 190, all designed by the architect

304

305

Gothic church, thus substantiating his claim, 'it is traditional to be modern', and each age should build using a live architecture, 'each age working to its taste'.[332] With Nuremberg Cathedral he noted the spatial effect gained from having a highly ornate composition hanging from the roof. He drew attention to the effect of distance given to the roof of Manchester Cathedral choir and the increased mystery created by the fifteenth-century screen and nineteenth-century organ case set between the choir and nave. He showed the Friends an eighteenth-century print of Gloucester Cathedral's stone pulpitum with 'its proper sized organ', noting 'most Cathedral organs or choir screens have been enlarged thus ruining the internal effect as a whole and bringing the Pulpitum into undeserved disrepute'.

He knew there would be great difficulties at Llandaff, principally because, 'for present day use Llandaff is too small a building to have a solid Pulpitum . . . The whole must be used as a single unit; a Nave altar is impracticable', and he had to 'evolve an entirely new conception of a pulpitum'. This took several years to do. The solution arrived after nearly four years of experiment, including the making of models and full-size plywood mock-ups in the Cathedral.

He designed the pulpitum, to satisfy the following factors:

a To leave the west-east vista open at floor level, as the Cathedral had also to be used as a parish church;

b To enable the Norman arch to be seen, and if possible suitably framed, when entering by the west door;

c To provide a definite 'block' in the west-east vista at a height of 25 feet (7.6 metres) from the floor level;

d The block to be interesting in shape in itself and so designed as to heighten the spatial relationships of the interior;

e For practical and acoustic reasons the block to house the Echo organ;

f The block to be a theological affirmation in the sense of medieval architectural design rather than a purely intellectual approach to architecture;

g The whole of the modern equivalent of a pulpitum to be a vital work of art of today.

Upon completion of his pulpitum and other work in the nave in 1957, he proclaimed:

The interior has now been designed as a Cathedral. In this the new nave ceiling, the subordinate ceilings of the Aisles, the lowering of the Presbytery Arch, the Presbytery roof soaring far higher than any other roof, the unblocking of the

The Nave Pulpitum:

---

304 An early scheme

305 Full sized mock-up in plywood, 1953. The final solution emerged after four long years of deliberation

OPPOSITE
306 The nave pulpitum, 1957: intended to break up the vista from the west door, the pulpitum houses the positif organ and carries Sir Jacob Epstein's Majestas in unpolished aluminium. The 68 teak Pre-Raphaelite figures salvaged from Prichard's choir stalls are gilded and arranged in niches gathered round the figure of Christ as a 'Witness to the power of his risen life'[333]

308 View from the Lady Chapel. A progression of twelfth, nineteenth and twentieth-century arches

308

309 Font, carved by Alan Durst, 1952, in Hoptonwood stone. The carvings depict the fall and redemption of man. The dove is the emblem of the Holy Spirit of Baptism. Standard candlesticks in wrought iron by the architect

OPPOSITE
307 The organ-case in the choir viewed from the south aisle, before completion of the choir stalls

Then Pace said, 'Well, there is one man who would be exactly the man and that is Epstein; but I suppose you wouldn't have him?'

Now, as it happened, I had made a special point of seeing all Epstein's great religious works and had been profoundly impressed by them. So I answered at once – 'Of course I would, but surely he would never come down to a place like this.'

'We will write at once' was the reply 'and see what happens'. We did and Epstein replied saying that this was the greatest thing he had been asked to do and that he was sure it would result in a great Act of Faith.

Epstein came down and was inspired by the majesty and solemnity of the thirteenth century nave. The arch and the organ case were set up in wood for the Chapter to see [ILLUST. 305]; two workmen stood one above the other to give an idea of scale; and the Chapter gave its blessing to the scheme.

Attention has naturally been concentrated upon the Majestas, but its true significance is that it is part of a whole, a part of a composition comprising arch and organ and light and shadow, and gilded figures of saints and angels, and that composition part of a plan, a plan which embraces the whole cathedral, and owes its original to the mind, the architectural genius, the profound religious sense of G. G. Pace.

Bishop Urban Arch, the revised floor levels and the view into the Lady Chapel, all have their parts to play; but by themselves these would not produce a Cathedral Atmosphere. On entering the Cathedral the eye must be prevented from seeing all at a glance. The way to the High Altar must be veiled, vista must open upon vista; from the moment of entry the journey to the High Altar should be subtly designed stages. In producing these conditions a Pulpitum has a great part to play.

Another factor which played an enormous part in the conception of the pulpitum was the Majestas, the great rood figure of Christ. The then Dean, the Very Revd Glyn Simon, describes his early thoughts on the matter:

Continually in our minds was the thought of a Rood, but with Christ not defeated but reigning. We felt very much the need to break the line of the nave and the choir . . . we tried more than one scheme – a sort of classical organ screen [ILLUST 304] was put before the Chapter at one stage, but no-one liked it much and it came to nothing.

One evening, looking down on the cathedral from the path leading up to the Green above, I said – 'I am sure that we must have a Rood there, but who is to carve it?'

'There is no-one alive' Pace replied 'who can do the kind of Rood I have in mind'. We discussed two or three names, and silence ensued.

309

OPPOSITE

310 The choir and chapter stalls, 1964. Those parts of Prichard's nineteenth-century stalls capable of repair were carefully integrated within the new design

311 The presbytery: high altar with medieval German crucifix and seventeenth-century Italian altar and standard candlesticks specially purchased. New altar rails in wrought iron and oak. In the window above the Sanctuary arch is stained glass by John Piper, executed by Patrick Reyntiens on the theme 'Supper at Emmaus'. The view through to the Lady Chapel was specially created to provide an unbroken east/west vista through the cathedral at eye level. Just visible is the medieval reredos decorated in bright colours and adorned with bronze reliefs of Welsh flowers by Frank Roper.[38] The roof survives from the Prichard restoration, but is given colour with rafter soffits red, sides in grey, and panels between in blue

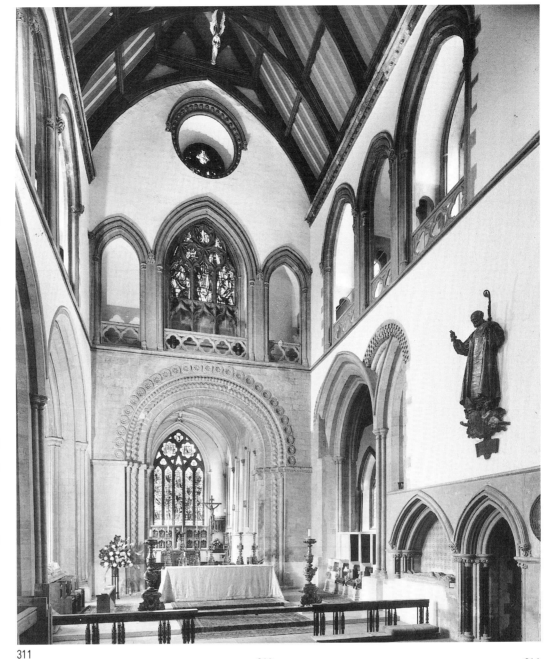

311

313

314

312 Detail of the high altar rails

313 New aumbry, St Dyfrig's Chapel

314 Detail of exterior metalwork to new south doors set on limed oak

It is worth reflecting that in this great achievement both sculptor and architect are men whose native genius was shaped and developed by hard training and grinding study of their craft; theirs is no easily won Triumph.[334]

George Pace was very much aware of the harm of individualist expression unbalancing the work of others. In his notes, which formed the basis of a radio broadcast in 1957, he confirmed these fears:

In the range of human creative activity the building of cathedrals has been the crown of Man's endeavour. It is a task which was easier to bring to success in an Age of Faith and when Organic Cultures flourished. Neither is present today and this raises immense difficulties, for the creation of a cathedral is not merely an intellectual exercise, or an aesthetic experience, but rather it is an Act of Worship. In trying to achieve this today the Architect and all those he has called to help him, have worked under a very strict discipline, which has demanded that all give themselves utterly to the work and yet utterly efface themselves. There has been no place for the individualistic and no room for the art exhibit or the museum piece. All those — sculptors, stained glass artists, silversmiths, embroiderers — chosen by the architect to be the extension of his head and hands, have gladly accepted this discipline. Thus there is a chance that the newly created Llandaff may in some slight degree be a Theological Affirmation in the sense in which a medieval cathedral is.[335]

From time to time he succeeded in finding excellent pieces of medieval or later work for the Cathedral to buy, but he remarked 'it would be unfortunate to turn the Cathedral into a museum and thus at the same time I am gradually bringing together contemporary works'. These included the font by Alan Durst, the Majestas by Sir Jacob Epstein, stained glass by John Piper and sculpture by Frank Roper, and he acknowledged 'I cannot hope to express adequately my indebtedness to these artists for the part they have played in helping me with the scheme'.[336]

Other major works of art — the Prichard reredos and the Rossetti panels — posed serious difficulties:

Prichard's reredos and sedilia of Caen stone are notable monuments to the technical skill of nineteenth century Gothic Revival carvers. I have thought much on the problem of what to do with the Reredos and the Rossetti panels.

He explained to the Friends at a meeting:

I am convinced they must not go back to their original position in the Great Norman Arch. Some people, including myself, hold that the works of the nineteenth century should not be lightly undone, but in this instance, there are overwhelming reasons for doing so, since the

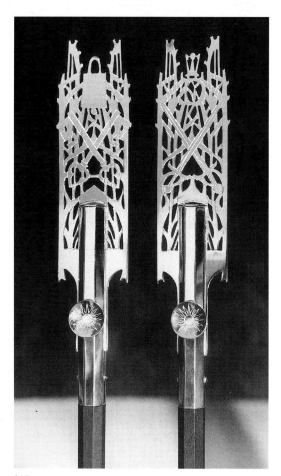

315

whole effect of the interior is at stake. Rossetti himself was so dissatisfied with the placing of his panels that he 'wanted to get busy with a tar brush'.[337]

The eventual solution adopted is seen in St Illtud's Chapel (ILLUST. 232).[338]

The major part of the restoration was completed in 1960, with a Thanksgiving Service celebrated in the presence of Her Majesty the Queen.

In his sermon, the Bishop, the Rt Revd Glyn Simon (instigator of the work as Dean, and later succeeded by the Very Revd Eryl S. Thomas who courageously and with similar skill and foresight steered the works to their successful conclusion) preached some harsh words, perhaps too harsh for the occasion: 'A great church was a dangerous thing to build. It could so easily minister to human pride and ambition, and become a substitute for true religion . . . Aesthetic fashions change. A future generation would find the work distasteful'.[339]

Some challenged this view, asking 'Is it mortal arrogance to believe that here is something which will survive fashion?'[340]

The full restoration of Llandaff took some 14 years. During this time many other important works were begun and completed as the practice expanded rapidly. Some made distinct references to the work at Llandaff, but a significant number explored new ground.

OPPOSITE
316 Canopy over the archdeacon's stall. Though some of Prichard's work was incorporated, a new approach is apparent in the introduction of cast aluminium finials displaying Gothic characteristics far removed from the earlier classical references of the pulpit (ILLUST. 291) or St Illtud's screen (ILLUST. 233)

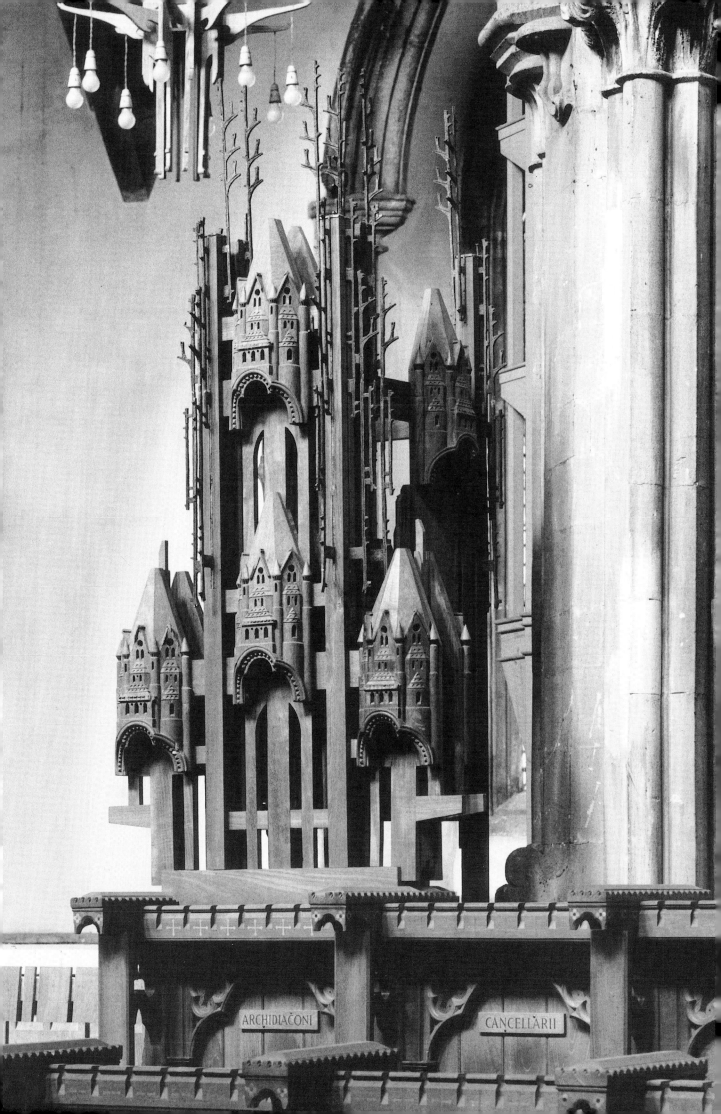

317

318

319

168

ST MICHAEL'S COLLEGE CHAPEL
Llandaff
1957–59

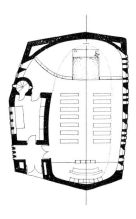

OPPOSITE
317 The freestanding chapel is positioned at the focal point of the College quadrangle and built in blue pennant rubble stone with much ironstaining

OPPOSITE
318 *and* **319** North wall: 'There are no windows in the East or West walls, but in the North walls there are 58 and in the South 20. They are set out irregularly and although of only two stock sizes the impression is of infinite variety'[345]

320 Plan

321 Spiral stair enclosure to organ gallery

A German air raid destroyed the original Chapel to the Theological College. The commission given to George Pace called not merely for the design of a new building, but for help in identifying the liturgical base upon which it should be founded.

The result was a building regarded by him at the time as one of his best works.[341]

Like the Welch Regimental Chapel at Llandaff Cathedral, it specifically attempts to create atmosphere, and although borrowing much from local traditions both from Wales and Yorkshire, owes as much to the twentieth-century chapel of Notre Dame de Haut, Ronchamp, France, by Le Corbusier (ILLUST. 104).[342] Acknowledging his debt to Le Corbusier, George Pace said 'at the low level open to me, I tried to do something similar at St Michael's'.[343]

In his design report he said:

Modern architecture has, as yet, little grammar capable of expressing profound emotion or creating 'atmosphere'. Both these are essential in a church. The Church is thus able to demand of the architects that they shall take modern techniques and dedicate and enrich them until they approach the high level required in a church. What a great adventure and responsibility and what better place for one such experiment than the chapel in the heart of a Theological College from which go out the Priests of the next generation. It is traditional for the Church to lead in great architectural experiments.

It is against this background that this Chapel has been conceived. The supposed lopsidedness which some seem to have found does not exist. The building in plan, section and elevation is a plastic, a sculptural conception. Construction and techniques and the new orientation of aesthetics allow and enrich this. The free plan shape and the rounded angles permit the rubble stone to be used in a traditional way, which, whilst enriching the form and texture of the exterior allows of the omission of dressed stone at the angles and this brings about a very considerable saving of cost. In construction the roof follows a very simple form – king post trusses, purlins and rafters, but the fitting of such a roof over a free plan shape gives the appearance new and exciting possibilities.

The fluid or sculptural conception of the Chapel means that it is not designed on the 'bay' or unit principle of planning, which was a necessity in Gothic and Renaissance times owing to the limited structural systems then possible. In this Chapel the walls are an enclosing skin and to emphasize this

the windows have been arranged in a free pattern. It will be noted that the fenestration is more formal when there are various small units behind the wall and freer where there is a vast fluid void. The fenestration also solves two other requirements – economy of cost and special quality of natural lighting in the interior. Economy is satisfied by the frames of the openings being formed of pre-cast stone which allows them to be the permanent centering of the openings and also removes the need to work the rubble stone of the walling. Only two sizes of windows are used and thus only two moulds are necessary for making them; in use a sense of continuity is introduced into the abstract pattern by the repetition of similar units. The internal light comes through glass which is set near the outer face of the wall and is thus invisible to the worshipper when facing the altar. Some windows have splayed jambs and some not which again refines the natural lighting. 'All these

321

323

aesthetic "tricks" are traditional, and well tried examples of these principles may be seen in the choir at Brecon Cathedral, at Llantwit Major and a host of other ancient churches in Wales.'

The walls and ceiling of the Chapel form one, flowing, sculptural, enfolding entity, emphasized by making these parts white and the floor and seating dark. It is the Majesty hanging above the altar which provides 'a great jewelled splash of colour in the heart of this white and black ecclesiastical cave'. Indeed 'The fullness of the interior and its spatial relationships is only fully revealed with the Majesty in position'.

This consists of a beardless Christ in Majesty surrounded by the four beasts of the Apocalypse made of glass, sheet copper, copper and aluminium strips, lead cames and wood, much of it gilded. A new technique was evolved by the artist, Harry Stammers, and the architect working together on the design. It is intended to dominate the interior of the Chapel, yet the technique which has been evolved assures that it will not overwhelm the interior.

With the exception of various fittings carefully incorporated from the old (bombed) Chapel – the noble Bodley Altar and two decorated stalls – all the furnishings and fittings were designed by the architect.

This Chapel in a very real sense is a product of the twentieth century, yet in its fundamentals it is more closely linked with tradition than a Revival Church because the traditions in it are alive.[346]

Many regarded the building as 'innovative' and 'breaking with tradition'[347] but others recognized the more lasting qualities of a 'rugged Celtic strength'[348] and a 'timelessness which strongly marks Mr G. G. Pace's buildings'.[349]

324

324 Proposed west
entrance to nave: doors
in stainless steel, a
material synonymous
with Sheffield – ink on
coarse paper, 13 × 15in
(33 × 38.1cm), undated

OPPOSITE
325 Model showing new
nave and entrances, June
1959

326 Plan from the 1957
appeal brochure

325

THE COMPLETION OF
SHEFFIELD CATHEDRAL
1956–61

To George Pace 'the first and supreme aim of a
Cathedral is by its own beauty, to give continuous
witness to the things unseen and eternal',[350] and he
approached the momentous task of completing
Sheffield Cathedral with similar dedication and
enthusiasm afforded to Llandaff Cathedral. Indeed,
over six years some 25 schemes were submitted,
requiring such devotion that a number of other
major commissions had to be declined during this
period.[351] Tragically, none of the schemes came to
fruition, but the exercise was an important one in
George Pace's architectural development,
particularly in his window designs and in his
explorations with numerous innovative major
structural systems. He faced a complex problem
from the start, inheriting the unfinished remains of
an early extension scheme built to the designs of
Sir Charles Nicholson between 1919 and 1936.

Extensions.
New portion already built.
Old portion remaining.

326

327 Interior of new nave
looking eastward. Ink
and charcoal with
coloured crayon on
coarse paper, 15 × 18in
(38.1 × 45.7cm), undated
but about 1958

328

328 Model showing the
new north wall and
Nicholson's earlier chapel
of the Holy Spirit, 1959

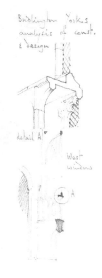

329 Regional
characteristics noted in a
sketch book, 1942: pencil
detail 2 × 7in
(5.1 × 17.8cm), providing
inspiration for the design
of the north wall

Like Llandaff Cathedral, Sheffield started as a
parish church and when in 1914 it became the
cathedral of the new diocese an attempt was made
by Sir Charles Nicholson to lift the building's
status; principally by altering the whole axis of the
church from east/west to north/south. A
complicated Gothic Revival design was begun, but
by the architect's death in 1948 only the
foundation work to the new nave (replacing the
nineteenth-century one), part of the south quire
aisle, and the Chapel of the Holy Spirit were
complete.

George Pace knew that mounting costs
prohibited the completion of 'this magnificent
conception' of Revival Gothic, and he made it clear
that he considered the climate for cathedral
building in 1957 'is very different from that in
1938 . . .'.[352]

> This is not merely financial all prevailing though
> that may be. There is now a much wider
> understanding of the basis of modern architecture
> in the Service of the Church, and with that
> understanding a desire that the Nave and Quire of
> the new Cathedral shall be a Theological
> Affirmation, expressed in the Living Architecture of
> this century.

But his hands were partially tied, for he recognized
that as the new architect, he

> must pay proper homage to the ancient portions
> and the recent outworks. He is bound to respect
> the great axis laid down by Sir Charles Nicholson.
> He has only two and a half external walls to play
> with. The levels and heights of his new parts are
> largely determined for him . . . But within this
> framework something tremendously vital is
> possible.[353]

His scheme allowed for a new nave, seating 800
people, with the quire so arranged as to serve the
double use as a parish church and cathedral of the
diocese.

As the natural light for the interior had of
necessity to come mostly from the liturgical north
side, this wall was designed as a continuous
window; and here we find a monumental
innovative work using a number of historical
precedents combined to produce something
entirely new.

In evolving this window pattern and structure,
he explains:

> the architect has drawn freely on Yorkshire
> Regional motifs of medieval and later date – the

175

THE COMPLETION

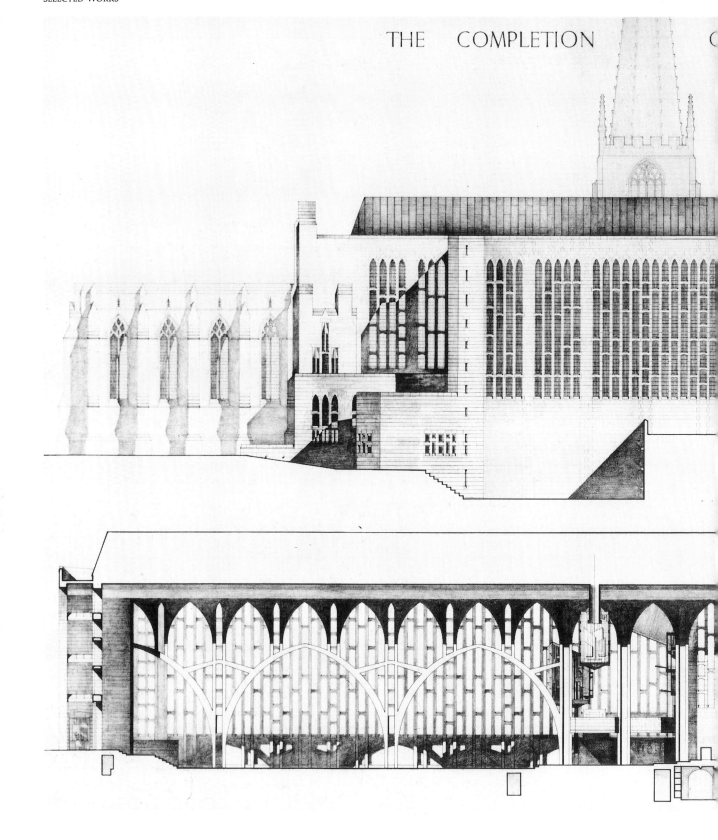

double mullions and through transome heads echo in spirit York Minster, Beverley Minster and Bridlington Priory; the continuous alternating pattern, Nun Monkton church and the stone technique itself, the window ranges in wool workers houses in the West Riding.[354]

Despite a promising start, with a design solution quickly reached and the Appeal brochure launched all within two years, matters became bogged down with a long series of changes required by the

Provost and Cathedral Council – which, George Pace noted wearily, 'necessitated far reaching alterations in the initial working drawings, added to which the need to re-use existing foundations and partially constructed heating ducts produced acute problems'.[355]

Costs had always been a major factor on this project, but however clever the designs had been at reducing expenditure (the rate per cubic foot being calculated by the Quantity Surveyors to be

330 Drawing exhibited at the Royal Academy Summer Exhibition, 1962, pencil with some ink, 50 × 27in (127 × 68.6cm) – the last of many schemes (*see also* ILLUST. 110)

FIELD CATHEDRAL

almost one-third of comparative schemes),[356] the monumental scale of the work, coupled with the rise in building costs, resulted in the final estimate being almost double the Appeal Budget.

Deciding it would not be fair to ask the public to contribute more, the Cathedral Council once again abandoned its plans, and called up an entirely new brief. The solution adopted reversed the Nicholson and Pace axis back to an east/west one.

George Pace believed such action would merely 'produce a larger Parish Church, never a Cathedral'.[357] Unable to approve architecturally and liturgically of such proposals, he resigned, and the work was completed by others to an entirely different design in 1963.[358]

331 Interior facing
liturgically east. Main
supports to roof structure
in laminated timber. Altar
in oak, pews in ash

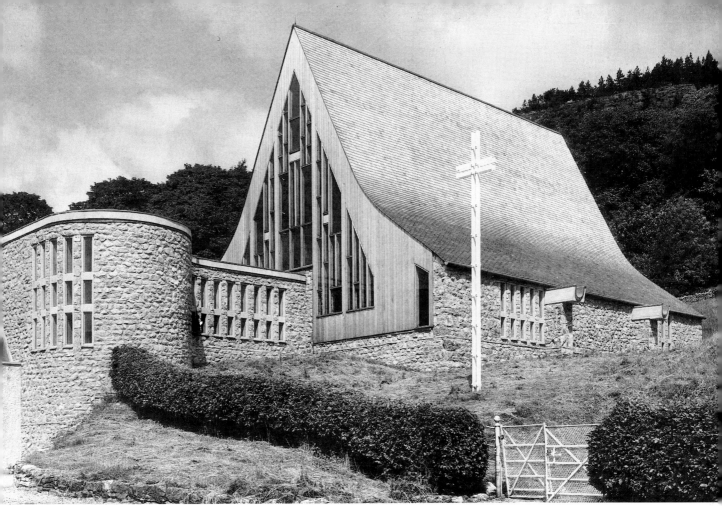

332

332 Exterior, showing enclosed linkway leading from the main house

333 Ground floor plan

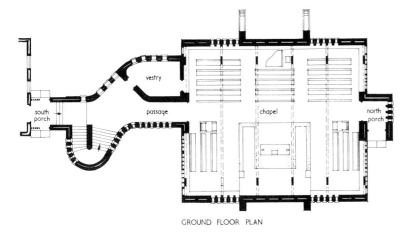

GROUND FLOOR PLAN

333

SCARGILL CHAPEL
Wharfedale
1958–61

A dedicated group of Anglicans from Manchester bought Scargill House to found a religious holiday and conference centre. A chapel was planned almost straight away.

Initially the brief called for a design capable of being built by the people of Scargill House,[359] a factor which must have partially influenced the simple 'cruck design' of mostly roof and very little wall. In the event, it was found that self-building would probably take too many years to complete and the task was given to a local builder. However, the stone was, in part at least, hewn by student working parties staying at Scargill.[360]

Earlier acquaintance with the Yorkshire Dales, and a profound respect for the local vernacular prepared Pace for the delicate task of building a chapel inspiring in itself, but at one with its surroundings. Natural materials which would weather in a few years to a silver-grey – local limestone and red-cedar shingles – were chosen for its construction.

There is neither pulpit nor lectern. Nor is there any stained glass 'and I hope there never will be' Mr Pace commented, 'for I want the chapel to appear to grow out of the dale'.[361]

PROPOSED · CHURCH · OF · ST · MARK'S · BROOMHILL · interior
looking east..... George G. Pace F.R.I.B.A. F.S.A. Chartered Architect. Skelton · York. 1950.

334 Interior of scheme I, with Comper-like ciborium (*see* ILLUST. 106). The Tree of Jesse on the east wall was to have been in mosaic, 'strong enough to withstand Sheffield grime'.[362] Ink, charcoal, and coloured crayon on coarse paper, 11 × 15in (27.9 × 38.1cm), June 1950

335

ST MARK'S CHURCH
Broomhill, Sheffield
1950–67

335 Exterior view of Scheme I, ink, charcoal, coloured crayon, on coarse paper, 16 × 13in (40.6 × 33cm), 1950

336 The Morning Chapel, Scheme I, ink, 6 × 9in (15.2 × 22.9cm), 1951

336

The original St Mark's dating from 1868 perished with all its fittings in a fire caused by incendiary bombs dropped on the night of 12 December 1940. The tower and spire, the south porch and some walls up to plinth level, were found to be repairable and were intended to be incorporated in the new church as a memorial and a link between the first and second St Mark's.

The first of three fully worked out designs for the new church was completed in 1951. The then Archdeacon of Sheffield, the Ven. Douglas Harrison, wrote of that first design:

> it is unmistakably twentieth century while remaining Gothic in feeling; it is unmistakably a church and not a conference hall masquerading as a place of divine worship. It has scale; the height which gives it dignity; the great windows which, though they will hardly be seen internally, will fill the church with light, and the simplicity which is the achievement of genius.[363]

After further study, a larger church was planned, particularly as there arose the possibility of raising a considerable fund locally to augment the expected amount of war-damage compensation.[364]

The second scheme explored, on an immense scale, a new structural support system comprising two enormous reinforced concrete arms cantilevering out spectacularly, not dissimilar to the structures encountered in the early plans for the completion of Sheffield Cathedral (ILLUST. 110).

This proved of such interest the scheme went on show with other modern church designs in an exhibition that travelled the country for two years.[365] At the Royal Academy Summer Exhibition in 1958 the critics remarked:

> George G. Pace has contributed one of the most striking models in the architectural section. It is of the new hexagonal St Mark's Church at Sheffield, the new main building of which is cleverly integrated with the old tower. Amongst its most interesting features are the windows, long or short, but always narrow and grouped together in a style reminiscent of the Perpendicular, but completely, creatively new.[366]

But it was found impossible to raise the whole of the large additional sum needed to finance this scheme, and it had to be abandoned. The third and final scheme was built by 1963 with a plan very similar to scheme 2, but the architectural treatment simplified and the cubic content reduced by approximately half.[367] Further work to the interior fittings continued up until 1967.

In his report[368] which later became embodied as a guide to the new church, George Pace made it quite clear there 'were no fashionable gimmicks. It will not attract crowds of the curious. It will not be "news". It is hoped that it will be a simple church, simply designed, which can be used now and, without difficulty, can evolve in use in the years to come.'

The plan complies with the requirements of the new Liturgical Movement – freestanding altar, large areas of communion rail, and unrestricted sight of the liturgical areas from all 300 seats.

The plan of the church proper is an irregular hexagon. The choir is placed close to the organ on the north side, an acoustically convenient place from where its members can fulfil their function of leading the worship of the people 'yet avoids the risk of their intervening between the people and the altar which is the focal point of liturgical worship'.[369]

337

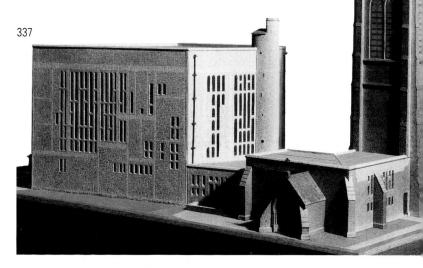

338

337 Exterior Scheme II, 1958 (model)

338 Interior Scheme II, looking liturgically east (model). Compare this structure with that proposed for Sheffield Cathedral (ILLUST. 110)

OPPOSITE
339 Exterior of Scheme III, as built 1961–3, ink on tracing paper, 10 × 12in (25.4 × 30.5cm), 1961 – plan superimposed by author

OVER
340 Interior looking east following full completion of furnishings and organ in 1967

A large narthex, dual-purpose dividable meeting rooms, kitchen, cloakrooms *et al* make up the rest of the building complex to create a headquarters to the benefit of the whole community, where social activities are combined with formal worship.

The structure is of reinforced concrete, but no concrete is exposed to the elements. The walls are hollow – the outer face rubble stone and the inner brick plastered. The main roof is carried on Queen-post trusses (investigation showed that such trusses were the most natural and economic form for this church)[370] and covered with thick, rough, random slates.

The whole of the east wall is pierced, with openings arranged in a special pattern to emphasize the high altar and to give visual correction and unity to the irregular hexagonal plan-form and the distribution of the liturgical furniture. The stained glass is by Harry Stammers and illustrates the *Te Deum*.

The other stained glass is in the west window of the narthex. Designed by John Piper and made by Patrick Reyntiens, it is an abstract. 'Those who wish to find a subject in it may see the Holy Spirit at work in the world of today.'

The exterior of the new parts

is of extreme simplicity and directness and not only emphasises the 'primitive' state in which both Church and Architecture find themselves today, but permits its architect to be anonymous and self-effacing and to make sure that all grows old gracefully and without expensive maintenance.

The interior, whilst being simple, is more involved than the exterior. An attempt has been made to evolve subtle play with spatial relationships, variations in the degree and quality of natural and artificial light, progressions through spaces and volumes of varying size, richness and emotional impact.

St. Mark's Church, Sheffield
from the North-east
George G. Pace MA. F.S.A. F.R.I.B.A. York : Oct. 61.

341

342

343

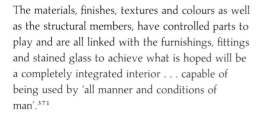

The materials, finishes, textures and colours as well
as the structural members, have controlled parts to
play and are all linked with the furnishings, fittings
and stained glass to achieve what is hoped will be
a completely integrated interior . . . capable of
being used by 'all manner and conditions of
man'.[371]

St Mark's was a milestone in Pace's architecture
and

demonstrates Pace's position at that interface
between traditional English Pragmatism and the
already established convention of modernism. The
exterior owes in its expression and detailing
everything to Lethaby and Prior whilst the interior,
with its huge uncluttered areas of smooth plaster
and wilful, almost Expressionist tracery patterns, is
overtly modern.[372]

After the dedication, Judith Scott, Secretary of the
Cathedral's Advisory Committee, wrote:

The quality and workmanship of the masonry and
woodwork throughout the building would be
hailed as more than adequate were they intended
for England's forty-fourth Cathedral; the masons
and carpenters especially have done their work
magnificently under Mr Pace's direction and one
hopes that this will be a showpiece which craft
apprentices will be brought to see from all over
Yorkshire. There are unlikely to be many new
Anglican churches built to such a standard as that
achieved by St Mark's, Broomhill, Sheffield in the
future, and some may have doubts as to whether, if
we had the money, we could ever again spend it all
on one church with an easy conscience. Yet is it
good to rejoice over the incidence of a deep
pastoral concern and over the care and thought
which have been put into the planning of this
church where the quality of design and
workmanship sing their own veritable
Benedicite.[373]

344

341 View from the south
west

342 North wall

343 North wall detail

344 North-west corner

OPPOSITE
345 The Nave seen from
the narthex entry

UNIVERSITY OF KEELE
The Chapel
1959–65

OPPOSITE
346 Exterior of the liturgical east end with separate chapel towers 'which however don't mark the entrance as Medieval buildings have taught us to expect'[374]. Blue engineering brick and stone surrounds the windows

347 Exterior seen from the south west

In May 1959 representatives of ten European countries and the USA met at The Ecumenical Institute of the World Council of Churches: and after a week's study of the problems of contemporary church building, hammered out a 13-point statement on architecture in relationship to the needs of the Church. Essentially the conclusion was:

> If we prune away the habits and patterns which represent unessential differences between the churches, if we provide buildings which meet the purpose of the Christian Community in today's world, we may find that in tomorrow's world we will indeed be a truer Christian Community broad enough to encompass the differences which should and will remain.[375]

George Pace was asked to provide a building based upon these precepts to serve the various denominations of the student population at Keele University.

Precedents already existed for the joint use of church buildings by different and divided parts of the Christian Church, particularly in Switzerland, Germany and the USA, but he thought these buildings generally showed little awareness of the liturgical possibilities inherent in inter-denominational use, and could more justifiably be said to be orientated towards ecumenical goals than to have achieved a full union.[376]

He saw that ultimately, the effect of the Ecumenical Movement on worship and church building 'may well be revolutionary'. More than anything he saw the need for buildings capable of keeping options open,

> within which organic development could take place without the great cost of structural alterations or

347

causing violent aesthetic disruption to a carefully wrought interior.

> The shared church should be a simple, disciplined envelope, non-directional and without built-up drama . . . capable of infinite re-arrangement and re-ordering . . . Architecture in capital letters should be non-existent. Good building is what is needed.[377]

Such a new venture demanded a new brief thought out from first principles. The first design consisted of three separate chapels, linked together by porches and exhibition spaces so as to form one building (ILLUSTS 88 and 89), very much on the lines of the University Chapel at Waltham, Massachusetts, but this was quickly modified, until in 1960, 'the integration of the whole conception became clearer'[378] and the first version of the design was evolved, whereby each congregation was to be afforded the use of separate sections of the building at appropriate times.

The final plan adopted allowed for a large Chapel, seating 400 with a centrally placed altar table. By lowering a screen wall behind this, the Chapel is divided into a main chapel and a small chapel, the latter seating about 60. This small chapel is available for use by any of the denominations. There are two apsidal spaces at the east end of the small chapel, and one is for the use

348 Plan at ground level. Drawing in ink by George Pace, used to illustrate his article on shared churches,[375] 1969 (*see also* Royal Academy drawing, ILLUST. 100)

1. Choir and staff
2. Console
3. Main seating aisle
4. Seats
5. Pulpit
6. Main altar
7. Hydraulic screen
8. Secondary seating area
9. Lectern
10. Free Churches chapel
11. Bell tower
12. Roman Catholic chapel
13. Confessional
14. Roman Catholic vestry and oratory
15. Up to gallery, library and quiet room
16. Cloaks
17. Vestries
18. Exhibition areas: gallery over
19. Entrance porch
20. Up to gallery and organ

348

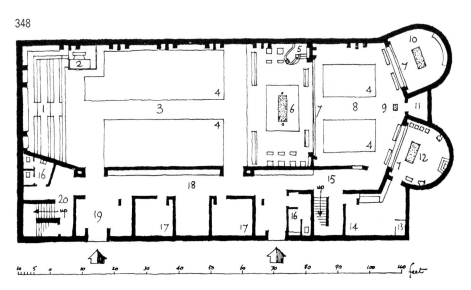

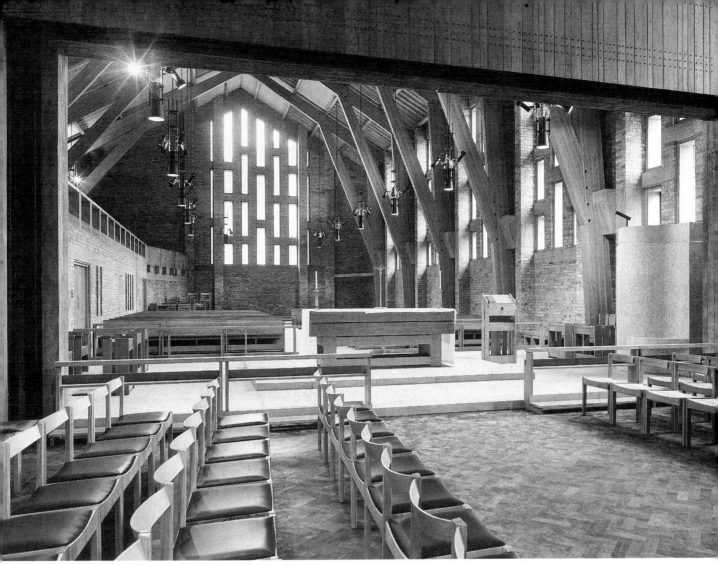

350

351

350 Nave as seen from secondary seating area with dividing hydraulic screen raised. As the site is liable to subsidence due to coal mining, the structure of the chapel incorporated a number of safeguards, the most noticeable being the wide vertical and horizontal movement joints which occur at intervals, and in effect cut up the building into small units, which may move more or less independently of each other[379]

OPPOSITE
349 Interior, north wall

351 Pulpit in concrete

of the Roman Catholic Church for its Reservation of the Blessed Sacrament; the other by Anglicans and Non-Conformists. The screen walls can be lowered to seal off both these spaces (ILLUST. 103).

In this way neither the main chapel nor the small chapel is reserved exclusively for any one denomination; yet arrangements are made to suit the requirements of each denomination. The main chapel may be used for inter-denomination workshops such as the weekly college service.

The exterior of the Chapel has been 'designed to be austere, highly disciplined and timeless'.

The interior is designed as a religious space and has not been given too definite a structural direction – 'Every endeavour has been made to produce an interior which has something of the character of the numinous, and to do this by the simplest and most direct means'.[380]

Certainly Keele proved to be a departure from the design aims of the Llandaff Welch Regimental Chapel and St Michael's College Chapel where atmosphere and drama were so important. Scargill Chapel (ILLUST. 331) had already led the way to this change to some extent, so that Keele represents an interesting staging post between the naturalness of Scargill and the industrial face of Wythenshawe (p. 205).

352

353

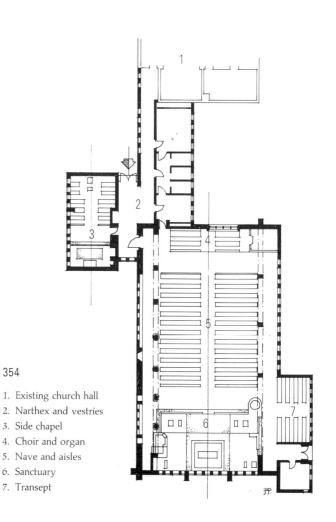

354

1. Existing church hall
2. Narthex and vestries
3. Side chapel
4. Choir and organ
5. Nave and aisles
6. Sanctuary
7. Transept

THE CHURCH OF THE HOLY REDEEMER
Acomb, York
1959–65

352 From the south east

353 Detail of south wall

354 Ground plan

The expansion of suburban housing estates in the 1960s increased the problem of city churches becoming isolated from the main centres of population. The York Diocese studied the feasibility of moving churches to new positions where the demands for a church were greater; and St Mary Bishophill Senior, one of York's oldest churches, was selected for the pilot scheme.[381]

The project was not without opposition, and local parishioners at Bishophill protested at the proposed 'destruction' of their ancient church.[382] In defence the vicar explained, 'We intend to restore St Mary's not in a place where it is not needed, and where few visitors to York would ever see it, not for some secondary purpose such as a museum of archaeology, or as an institute for this or that, but for the purpose for which it was originally built and consecrated, namely to be a House of God in a populous parish'.[383] The vicar and PCC offered to withdraw the application for its demolition and re-building 'if those who wished to see it restored would foot the bill . . . No offers were forthcoming'.[384]

Finding the right solution for integrating large elements of a medieval church into a new building relating to the principles of the Liturgical Movement, produced difficulties to be expected in a 'pioneer project';[385] in all 22 schemes were devised. George Pace explains his brief:

> The request that as much as possible of the ancient church of St Mary Bishophill the Elder, York, should be re-used in a church designed in a twentieth century manner presented a challenge, especially as the strictest economy was also enjoined by the very small amount available for the building of this church. (The average cost of a new parish church is £45,000. The church of The Holy Redeemer, Acomb, has cost approximately £32,000).[386]

> The building to have an expectation life of 500 years. The design to be of the 1960s, but at the same time to be vital and ageless.

> All these requirements have resulted in a simple, highly disciplined building more in the spirit of the small vernacular medieval church than the architectural exhibitionism of the great majority of nineteenth century and twentieth century churches.[387]

Pevsner calls Holy Redeemer

a masterpiece – Mr Pace has a way of blending old and new like no other architect today. He took most of what could be taken when St Mary

355 St Mary, Bishophill Senior, around 1810, parts of which were used to build the new church

356 Holy Redeemer as completed in 1965. Seen from the south west

355

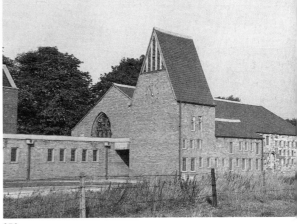

356

Bishophill Senior was demolished and built with it and around it a modern church. The south side tells the story at once: typical Pace windows, vertically oblong of all kinds of length, and two lancets and a small round, arched doorway of c. 1200 in a wall built largely of medieval masonry. This is separated from the building of 1938 (Church Hall) by a projecting chapel for weekday services and a tower with a sharply pitched roof. In the porch is another late twelfth century doorway with chamfered arches and one shaft each side. Enter, and you are in a wide nave with two narrow aisles, the left with an arcade of white brick piers with concrete bands tying them in with the wall, but the right with an arcade, partly of c. 1200 with round piers from Bishophill. The west window with geometrical tracery is Victorian. The altar end has an iron cross and set in its middle, a Saxon stone with a carved figure with very thick hair. Another Saxon stone, with interlace, is built into the pulpit and there are many others built into the south interior work, including one fragment of a hogsback.[388]

Examples of re-using ancient sections of old churches in new buildings, or indeed re-building

359 Pulpit and early-
English arcade with
south aisle beyond

360 South aisle, The
'light straining through'[391]
to achieve atmosphere

old churches elsewhere are found in medieval,
Victorian and Edwardian times; (*see pp. 137–39*), but
as Gerald Randall observes:

> whereas virtually every architect before 1939 and
> some afterwards would have built a gothic church
> in this situation to harmonise with the old
> materials, Pace achieved a radically different and
> perhaps more satisfactory harmony by juxtaposing
> the medieval with the uncompromising Modern.[389]

Liturgically, 'the grouping together of altar, font,
pulpit, lectern, prayer desk, etc . . . is intended to
show that the ministry of both the word and the
sacraments are of equal importance, and all take
place in view of the people, who themselves are
participants in them all'.[390]

OPPOSITE
357 The interior looking
east. Ceiling of fibrous
plaster, pews ash

358 The chancel with
Saxon stones re-used in
lectern and cross

361

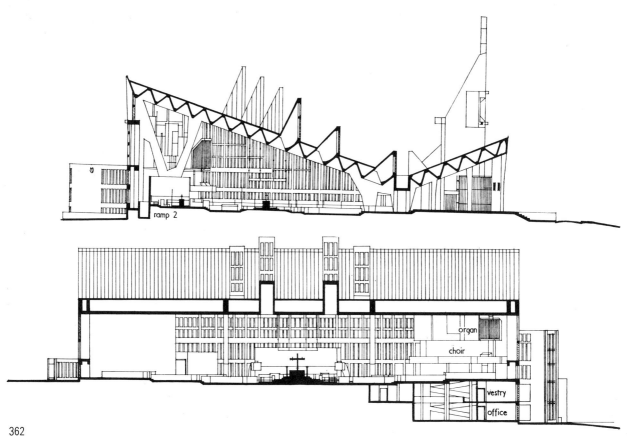

ramp 2

organ

choir

vestry

office

362

196

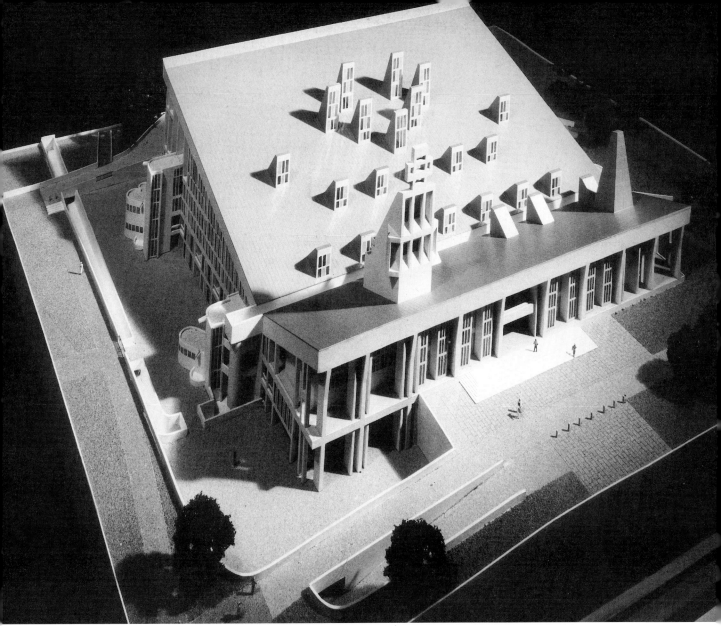

363

IBADAN CATHEDRAL
Nigeria
1954–65

In the present stage of the church and liturgy and
of society and architecture, it is questionable if a
Cathedral in the normal historical and aesthetic
sense now attached to the word is conceivable
within the discipline of the undiluted credo of
modern architecture.

George Pace saw the task before the architect
asked to design a cathedral in the 1950s and 1960s
as 'impossibly difficult' and he went on to observe:

He cannot but fall for the purely individualistic or
the Romantic. The Cathedral Architect's difficulties
should always be borne in mind when attempts are
made to evaluate a new cathedral. The dichotomy
present in most activities in the world today may
be said to reach its zenith in cathedral building. It is
a sobering thought that under present conditions
the cathedrals at Liverpool, Guildford, Coventry,

Brasilia and Ibadan are all equally legitimate
solutions. Pity the Cathedral Architect in his
difficulties; envy him the chance that is his.[392]

Pace believed passionately that 'the designing of a
cathedral is the highest, the most difficult and the
most rewarding task an architect can be given'. He
admired the architecture of Scott's Liverpool
Anglican Cathedral and Maufe's Guildford
Cathedral, believing these buildings were proof of
an ability to create cathedrals in this century.
   In his article, 'Modern Power Houses of
Faith',[393] he says

The architects have risen to the occasion, and have
created buildings which are not only real cathedrals
but cathedrals which could not have been
conceived other than by twentieth century minds.

197

This may not be self-evident at present –
superficial critics cannot really see these buildings
for their Gothic detail – but it will become clearer
with the passing years.

He acknowledged that designing a cathedral today
must of necessity be an individualistic and personal
task, compared with the anonymity which was the
natural order under the closed traditions of the
Middle Ages.[394]

The designing of Ibadan Cathedral took five
years, with several major schemes developed
before the final solution arrived. Such a variety of
schemes was necessitated by the tendency of the
authorities to sell the site without warning and
select another, with scant regard for design work
already achieved.

The first and most spectacular site was on a hill
poised above the city of Ibadan, one of the largest
native cities in Africa at that time. In his *New
Architecture in Africa*[396] Udo Kultermann describes
this scheme:

> The grandiose, volumetric style, based on plastic
> cube forms, clearly derived from the old religious
> clay edifices in the African tradition. Mighty
> symbolic forms are linked, in their similar or even
> identical shape, into a single complex in which full
> account has been taken both of light and shade, of
> curved and straight elements of man and his
> surroundings. [ILLUST. 108]

The final scheme, a design of 'spectacular
originality'[397] which would have produced 'a
seminal great building',[398] was worked out in great
detail before the whole project had to be
completely abandoned due to problems
encountered in the raising of sufficient finance
(despite its predicted cost as being half that of the
Roman Catholic Cathedral of Christ the King, then
being built in Liverpool, yet possessing the same
seating capacity).[399]

The Cathedral was to have been built of
reinforced concrete, much of it pre-cast. As at the
University Chapel of Ibadan climatic conditions
had to be taken into account, as the enormous
central valley gutter to take torrential rain from the
aluminium roof testifies. 'It will be a building
without walls in the recognised sense of the word,
for the sides will be wholly composed of glass or
louvres for continuous ventilation',[400] George Pace
explained. But he made little reference in his
writings to the external aesthetic of his design,
perhaps because much of it speaks for itself, being
an obvious extension of his by now established
style, exaggerated in parts through the dictates of
climatic conditions, drawing inspiration from
contemporary works in the same manner as
Ronchamp had influenced St Michael's College
Chapel (*see p. 161*) yet all synthesized within a

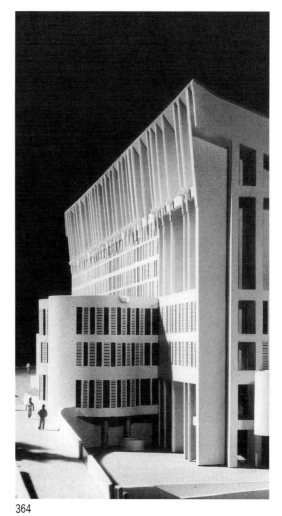

364

Gothic spirit on a scale hitherto unexplored.

The interior liturgical arrangement eschews the
traditional plan of a cathedral, and wholeheartedly
endorses the requirements dictated by the liturgical
movement, for a central altar with seats radiating
out, providing clear unobstructed views for 2000
people. By placing the seating on three distinct
levels, the areas may be divided into small blocks
improving sight lines and breaking up the vast
congregation to introduce a 'friendly, family
feeling'.[401]

364 Model of final
scheme showing east
face with lower chapels

OPPOSITE
365 Main floor plan

366 Model, east face

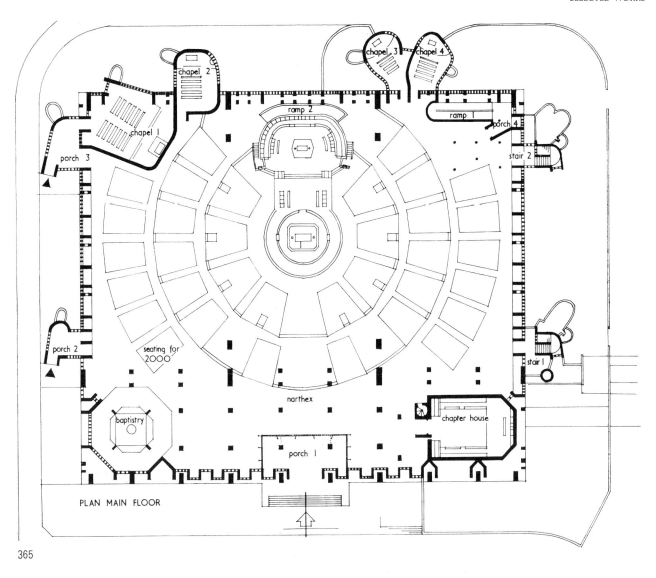

chapel 3 chapel 4

chapel 2

ramp 2

ramp 1

porch 4

chapel 1

stair 2

porch 3

porch 2

seating for
2000

stair 1

narthex

baptistry

chapter house

porch 1

PLAN MAIN FLOOR

365

366

UNIVERSITY OF DURHAM
Palace Green Library
1961–66

Durham is one of the great experiences of Europe to the eyes of those who appreciate architecture. The group of the Cathedral, Castle and Monastery on the rock can only be compared to Avignon and Prague . . . as if it were a vision of Caspar David Friedrich or Schinkel.[402]

Within this great view, standing between the Cathedral and the Castle, the University proposed to erect a new college library. They chose George Pace, the Consultant Architect to Durham Cathedral, to prepare the design. 'This must have presented one of the most intimidating challenges in the whole of the country,' the Civic Trust surmised. 'It did', George Pace replied.[403]

George Pace's solution demonstrates his determination to 'design a building which not only dwells happily in the midst of the great view, but becomes a disciplined, yet positive part of the view'.[404] In his 'nice, bloody-minded drawing'[405] of the proposal exhibited at the RA, a reviewer noted:

> he takes infinite pains to ensure that what he has in mind is right as he sees it, not for George Pace, not for the sake of an argument, not to indicate a method, but for Durham. Perhaps it is not truly functional, but was it functionalism or the environment and the spirit which inspired Bede?[406]

In his design report on the building, George Pace wrote:

> The new library has been worked out to be an organic solution of all the problems, both technical and aesthetic, whilst the building is expressed in the architectural terms of today, the exterior as a whole, and in particular in some of its detail, is in the spirit of a number of local regional architectural characteristics, in particular the silhouette, the relationships of the parts, the type of roofing, the grouping of projections, penthouses, ventilation shafts, and the like, together with the basic idea behind the arrangement of mullion and transomes. The roof of the Prior's Kitchen and the silhouette

368 Drawing exhibited at the Royal Academy Summer Exhibition, ink on cartridge paper, 39 × 23in (99.1 × 58.4cm), 1963. The Library was built under a protective polythene envelope which on removal 'revealed an immaculate building – probably the best on the peninsula since the Cathedral made the first intrusion into the skyline nearly 900 years ago'[412]

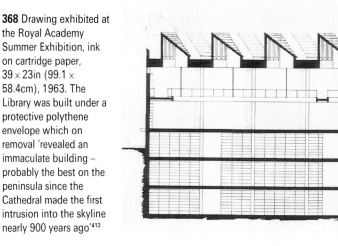

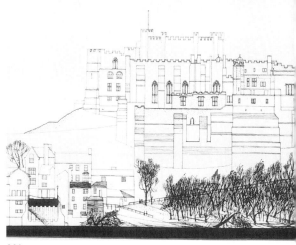

368

of the Castle, the chimney stacks of The Deanery and the now demolished great gateway of the Castle, are some of the local motifs from which the spirit has been distilled.[407]

This 'inspired insertion between two of the most famous pieces of historical architecture in the country'[408] was praised from all directions as a totally modern statement, and yet pays a subtle tribute to its surroundings. He has undoubtedly achieved a tour-de-force,[409] wrote one critic. Another saw the Library in even more exalted terms: 'This is one of the most brilliant examples of Modern Buildings in old surroundings', proclaimed Dr Nuttgens at a conference on New Buildings in Historic Areas.[410] The Civic Trust, in presenting their award, joined in: 'It is a delight to know that we can boast of architects capable of handling such problems with such confidence and sensitivity'.[411]

As the applause died down, a complaint over the height of the building led to the discovery that

367

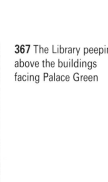

367 The Library peeping above the buildings facing Palace Green

LIBRARY :   Architect : George G Pace : Consulting Engineers : Oscar Faber and Partners   drawn by George Pace

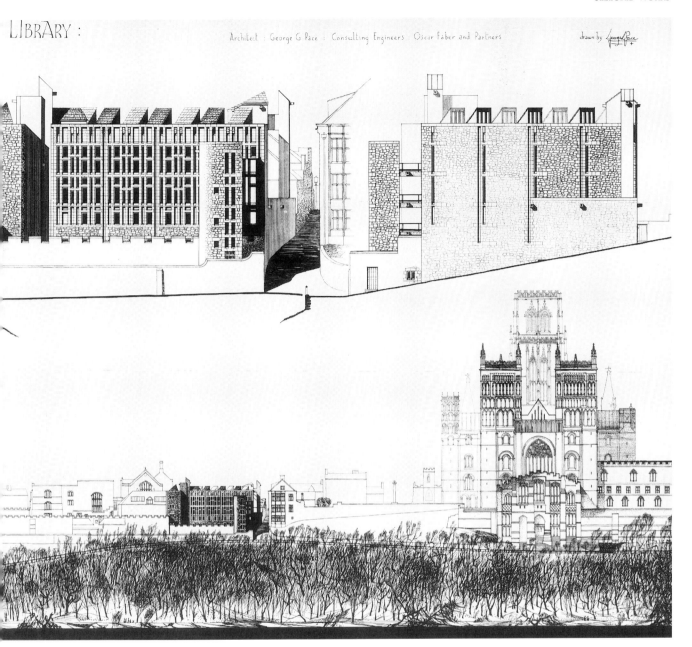

369

369 Approach from The
Gorge

371

OPPOSITE
370 View from the north west

371 The interior looking west showing Reading Room and galleries with seating for 185. The book stacks in the lower floors hold 200,000 volumes

372 South face, fronting the ginnel to Palace Green

373 View from south west

the equivalent of one additional storey on the lift tower was 'violating the sacred skyline',[413] without planning permission. Once again the building came into the public limelight, with sides quickly drawing up, for or against alteration. 'No-one claims it ruins the view, but it has started to intrude',[414] one opponent complained half-heartedly. Only the Royal Fine Arts Commission remained unperturbed, secure in the knowledge that the building had been publicly accepted as a masterpiece.[415] But justice had to be seen to be done. 'Off with its head they cried', and as a compromise the top six feet of water-tank housing and ventilation shaft were removed. Fortunately this was a very minor alteration, but sufficient for some to lament, 'Without Planners' approval the people of Durham were given a masterpiece. That they themselves should have allowed it to be emasculated in the name of planning is unforgivable . . .'.[416]

Today, with its initial external protective coat of limewash weathered away as intended,[417] the colour of the stonework blends happily with that of its neighbours and, largely obscured by trees, the building must be deliberately sought out by those who wish to view it (*also see* ILLUSTS 42 and 43).

373

WILLIAM TEMPLE MEMORIAL CHURCH
Wythenshawe, Manchester
1960–66

OPPOSITE
374 *and* **375** The exterior and interior of an early scheme (ink and charcoal on coarse paper – undated). Compare with completed building ILLUST. 96

376 Looking liturgically east towards the high altar

377 Ground floor-plan as built

The design of this 'revolutionary church'[419] resulted from two years of collaboration between the vicar, the parochial church council and the architect, during which time they worked out from first principles the liturgical arrangement of the church. At the time the resultant plan was believed to be unique.[420]

George Pace suggests in his report:

> The internal and external architectural treatment arises naturally from the liturgical plan and the structural system. To build this very large church for the money available it was necessary to devise a simple and economic structural system.[421]

The first sketch designs had been exhibited at a special parish supper for 400 people in 1961, specifically to gauge the reaction of the parish. Comments received suggested 'many felt such a revolutionary design is necessary to bring people into the church',[422] though not all agreed.

Like most of George Pace's work, there is a reference to the traditions of the past – the free-standing altar with the Bishop's Throne behind it is modelled on the first ancient Christian churches of AD400.[423] However, the plan was unusual in that the axis is set diagonally across a rectangle, with the seating arranged (typically, using nineteenth-century pews rescued from a demolished church) in two blocks, one holding 300 people, the other 200, set at right angles to each other, and both facing a

376

corner-placed altar. An enclosed chapel with the choir in front occupies the opposite corner. When the congregation is small, using only one block of pews, the bulk of the enclosed chapel helps to screen the emptiness of the rest of the church.[424]

Externally the elevational treatment has been seen as 'unnecessarily brutal'[425] with the appearance of 'a sort of workshop for worship, very difficult to understand as architecture, if indeed, a work such as this needs a rational approach'.[426]

Pevsner complains that the building 'accepts restlessness with fervour and in its interior drives it to extremes.[427] He found it difficult to 'appreciate for worship so aggressive a building', admitting 'it is a matter of personal character whether one can accept this radicalism at all, or for churches, but whatever the emotional reaction no-one can deny Mr Pace's courage and that of his clients'.

Gerald Randal, on the other hand, sees in Pace's design a continuation of the spirit of Prior: 'The use of concrete and brick . . . and Ruskinian honesty of construction which makes a feature of the rolled steel beams and girders of the interior', produces a building 'as uncompromising in its day as, say, Roker (ILLUST. 17) was in the first decade of the century'.[428]

377

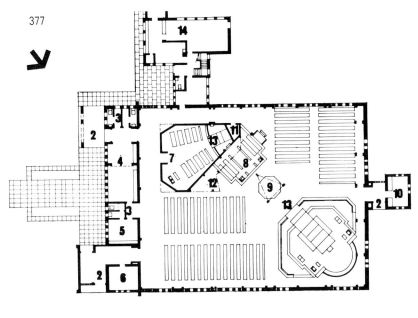

1.	Cross	8.	Choir
2.	Porch	9.	Font
3.	W.C.	10.	Sacristy
4.	Vestry/meeting room	11.	Bell tower
5.	Priests' vestry	12.	Organ
6.	Parish office	13.	Altar
7.	Enclosed chapel	14.	Parsonage

OPPOSITE
378 Interior looking west from behind the oak altar and wrought-iron fittings towards the enclosed chapel (*see* ILLUST. 69 for interior of chapel looking east)

379 Nave roof: with its Ruskinian honesty the roof structure of standardized industrial rolled-steel joists takes George Pace's work closer to the machine aesthetic. The engineer in George Pace delighted in the simplicity of the system where additional strength may be achieved at any required position merely by infilling the perforations[429]

379

380

380 Chancel furnishings: the care taken over the designing of every item of furnishing together with quality of craftsmanship dispels the superficial impression of an industrial shed

St. Martin le Grand York
the Courtyard from North

Tower

ST MARTIN
LE GRAND
York
1956–68

382 St Martin's, considered to be 'one of the handsomest of York churches'[430] seen here in an eighteenth-century print. Destroyed in 1942, the church stood as a ruin for many years

382

OPPOSITE
381 An early scheme put forward in 1957 which surprisingly remained intact throughout the long rebuilding period (1961–8). On the left, the recreated west window in new transept tower; in the centre the fire-calcinated remains of the nave piers, and to the rear the courtyard is enclosed by a new building 'rightly self-effacing'[431], ink and charcoal on coarse paper, 9 × 13in (22.9 × 33cm), 1957

Severely damaged in the Second World War, this church was partially re-built 'ingeniously and attractively'[432] by creating a Chapel of Ease and Shrine of Remembrance in the old south aisle with the remainder of the church left open to the air within an enclosed courtyard.

Before the raid, the important medieval stained glass, depicting the life of St Martin of Tours and set in what had been one of the largest west windows in a parish church, had been carefully removed and so survived intact, unlike the stonework of the window which was destroyed. In a rare departure from his normal approach of making good destroyed parts of churches in a

twentieth-century manner George Pace decided the window stonework should be faithfully re-created in order that the stained glass could be re-set in its original form. To accommodate the 30-foot (nine metres) high window within the new reduced church, a four-sided transeptal tower was designed, to stand directly opposite the south door, in full view of every visitor entering the church; and this 'became the pivot around which the whole of the new work revolved'.[433]

On the church as a whole, the architect decided his policy:

a That the tower and the south aisle were of such architectural importance in themselves and as part of the City, that their restoration by the best conservation techniques was essential, and that when so restored they must be incorporated naturally into the scheme as a whole;

b That the re-building scheme must allow for the natural incorporation of the repaired font cover, clock and Admiral;

c That the fragmentary medieval glass originally in the south aisle windows would be re-arranged where aesthetics and scholarship made this necessary, and would be re-fixed in windows in the south aisle;

d That the tracery of the great west window would be recreated so as to hold the original glass intact;

e That the works covered by *a–d* would be conservation in the highest sense;

f That new parts should dwell happily with the conserved parts, but should be twentieth century in basic conception, even though the detail might not convey that message to the superficial critic. The new work would also be designed to increase the architectural qualities of the original parts retained.[434]

383

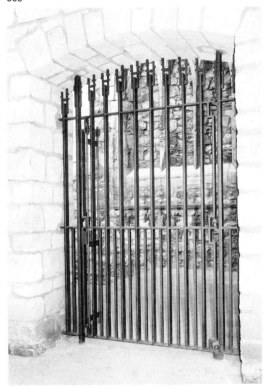

383 The new wrought-iron gate to the courtyard

384

The re-building took seven years. To those who asked why it had taken so long George Pace replied, unmoved:

> There were difficulties in construction, but we also wanted a very high standard of finish and no work has been hurried. It has been the most exciting project of its size that I have undertaken. This is because we have enough money and we have not had to skimp on anything. We have also had first-class craftsmen doing the work.[436]

The interior is a 'delight'; colourful; almost all the fittings designed by the architect, with comfortable, traditional references abandoned only in the glass organ-case 'designed to be seen through rather than seen',[437] (*see* ILLUST. 257).

This work of 'High Art', this 'Jewel' in the heart of York,[438] is embellished with works by artists familiar to George Pace: the gilded aluminium reredos depicting the Last Supper by Frank Roper (alas considered too avant garde and relegated to the west end), and the stained glass to the east window by Harry Stammers, depicting the burning of the church in fiery reds and yellows. Both contribute powerfully to the interior which is one of George Pace's most perfect (*see also* ILLUSTS 154 and 257).

384 The east end as completed, with the new entrance, through to the 'Nave' courtyard in place of the east window. The Admiral's Clock was re-hung close to its original position

RIGHT
385 The reconstructed interior looking east. (*See also* COLOUR ILLUST. 257, *and* ILLUST. 154)

NEW COLLEGE CHAPEL, OXFORD
The new organ-case
1967–69

(In collaboration with Grant, Diegens and Bradbeer, Ltd)

OPPOSITE
386 The new organ astride the adapted J. O. Scott screen

Designing a twentieth-century organ-case to be free-standing in the midst of a great medieval chapel became, in the words of George Pace, 'a daunting task in which there are few open options'.[439] He continues:

> At the start an unavoidable decision had to be taken – should the case by Gilbert Scott's son, J. O. Scott, be kept? In its prime this case was not one of the family's major designs. It had been harshly used, altered and adapted in the past by organ builders, but no matter how further adapted it could never have been made to enclose satisfactorily the magnificent new organ interior of advanced design. In the process of further adaptation the Scott case would have become a distressing aesthetic mongrel. Regretfully, the Scott case had to go; but the metal screenwork is now incorporated in the organ at Exeter College Chapel and many of the pinnacles have been used to increase the aesthetic impact of the Scott balustrade on the west side of the New College organ screen. It may be said that Gilbert Scott's fine organ screen stalls and chapel roof are now seen to better advantage than in the past . . .

387 Looking west

All the technical requirements of this very special organ[440] – the separate sound box units, their size and positioning; the necessity of the steel frame of organic trunk and branch form; the arrangement of visible pipes; the access for maintenance; the position of the Ruckpositiv, the Chamade and the Cymblstern and, above all, discipline imposed by tracker action in an organ of this type and size, have been gladly accepted by the architect.[441] In designing the new case the architect's task has been to give a little push here and a little prod there, sharpening the silhouettes, increasing the controlled aesthetic fragmentation and kinetic viewing and intensifying the total impact of sound and sight, by the choice of materials, colour, texture and finish. In this breathtaking array of polished pure tin pipes on the east front, the plate glass shutters, the natural aluminium channels, the polyester resin with aluminium finish, the limed oak and the painted colours, all play their inter-related parts.

389 Sketch design for tracery panel on soffit of the ruckpositiv, executed in aluminium leaf on black; ink on paper, 3 × 4in (7.5 × 10cm), 10 May 1969

George Pace aimed to produce a 'highly disciplined architectural sculpture', which might be assimilated unselfconsciously, as 'a timeless design in the sense the fourteenth, eighteenth and nineteenth century work in the chapel is timeless and naturally integrated'[442] (*see also* ILLUST. 126).

388 View from the narthex of the organ rear, painted green and red, with centre section in limed oak and wings clad in panels with polyester resin and aluminium finish

387

388

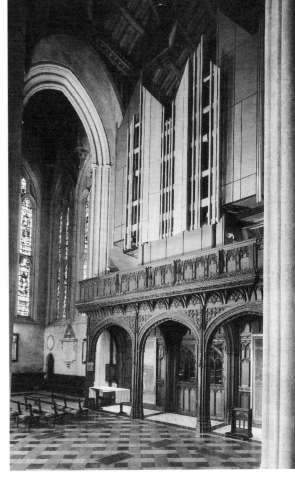

CHESTER CATHEDRAL: THE NEW BELL HOUSE

Architect : George G Pace. MA F.S.A. F.R.I.B.A. York

drawn by : J Hutchinson and George Pace

city wall

chester cathedral
bell-house from Walls.

chester cathedral
bell house from the East

CHESTER CATHEDRAL
The New Bell House
1968–75

OPPOSITE
390 Drawing exhibited at the Royal Academy Summer Exhibition, 1969. Main drawing ink on cartridge paper, with inset dyeline prints from ink on tracing paper – 17 × 24in (43.2 × 61cm)

The erection of a free-standing Bell House, the first to be built by a cathedral since the fifteenth century[443] came about at Chester after studies showed bell-ringing in the central tower could not be continued.

The central tower, poised delicately over the crossing, had never been designed for that most English of traditions – change bell-ringing.[444] Sir Gilbert Scott compounded the problem in his restoration of the tower by his insertion of the eighteenth-century bell frame at a very high level. The layout and position of the ringing chamber meant ringing was 'far from perfect',[445] but more importantly movements in the tower had caused all bell-ringing to stop for safety's sake, in 1963, and 'even with completion of the necessary repairs the potential structural damage to the tower and the Cathedral as a whole could not be overcome'.[446]

The solution to this problem lay in the reviving of an ancient tradition, which stemmed from Saxon and Romanesque times, when bells were hung in a tower or campanile, known in England as a bell house, set apart from the main building.[447] Here lay a safer and more economic answer to the question of retaining them in the central tower.[448]

The Dean suggested that George Pace should accompany him on a tour of Welsh border bell houses prior to attempting a design, but he declined, preferring 'not to be affected by preconceptions'.[449]

George Pace was faced with a complex problem, as he explains in a later report:

> Whilst there was nothing new in a free-standing bell house, there are very few modern examples of free-standing towers designed for change ringing. There are few difficulties in the structural design of a free-standing tower to carry bells hung dead for chiming or for playing as a carillion. With thirteen bells hung for change-ringing and with the maximum movement in the structure and bell frame not to exceed $\frac{1}{32}$ of an inch, very careful investigation of many thousands of different stress combinations has been essential. In this a computer has played a part. The very special stress problems and the need to work out a very simple and economic structural system required collaboration at all stages of the development of the design between the architect and the engineer, Ove Arup and Partners.[450]

The proposed close proximity of the new bell-house to an outstanding medieval cathedral added to an already difficult problem. An enormous number of preliminary sketch designs were made (*e.g.* ILLUSTS 90 and 91) with the external form undergoing a process of radical change over a long

392

period of assessment, until at last the solution emerged and the architect declared 'though the design of the bell house has been worked out from first principles, and with no preconceived ideas of the form and shape, the result bears a family likeness to the timber bell houses of many ancient churches'.[451]

The Dean agreed enthusiastically, suggesting 'the bell house will be no stranger to the border, for its design recalls in a modern idiom the regional characteristics of the border's bell houses, particularly those at Pembridge and Yarpole'.[452]

Others were not so impressed, and comments ranging from 'farm silo' to 'moon rocket' resounded in the press.[453] Representations were made by local bodies against the 'rather feeble design for a more adventurous approach representative of its times',[454] even though the design had earlier been exhibted at the Royal Academy and approved by the Royal Fine Arts Commission. These protests came to naught, and the bell-house proceeded on traditional lines.

The materials chosen – a base of red sandstone, and sides protected with small rough Westmorland slate cladding – were all materials already used in the important buildings of Chester.[455] Allowing for 'his own brand of eclectic detailing', George Pace had created 'a highly functional building', which could stand 'by its very simplicity and form with proper authority in its important historical setting without any recourse to historical pastiche'.[456]

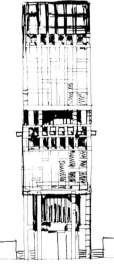

391 Early sketch design – ink on tracing paper, 5 × 12in (12.5 × 31cm), December 1969 (*see also* p. 58)

392 The completed structure clad in Westmorland slate rather than the softer wooden shingles originally proposed

rth quire aisle ·

'GEORGE·VI'

· Key plan ·

drawn by ~George~G~Pace~
feb

· CHAPEL · OF · ST · GEORGE ·   · WINDSOR · CASTLE ·
·HE · KING · GEORGE · VI · CHAPEL   Architects: Paul Paget & George G. Pace ·

KING GEORGE VI MEMORIAL CHAPEL

St George's Chapel, Windsor Castle
1967–69

(In collaboration with Paul Paget, of Seely and Paget, Surveyors to St George's Chapel)

394

394 Model in card, showing the relationship of the new Memorial Chapel to the north side[457]

The full story of the research and development on this tiny chapel is instructive of George Pace's methodical, meticulous, and creative approach to design. Altogether some five schemes were prepared over a two-year period. The essence of the design reports on these schemes is reproduced below, at some length:[458]

> The [new] Chapel is tiny. Seen against the architectural splendours of the Great Chapel, it may appear deceptively simple and to have been easily achieved. This is not so.
>
> For the past hundred and fifty years, the almost complete erosion of the conditions which from time immemorial have brought forth and nourished organic cultures, has made impossible a natural unselfconscious approach when adding new work to historic buildings. During times of organic culture the works of various ages automatically integrated with each other – in, say, the fourteenth century nave at Beverley Minster, the re-used eleventh century font carries an eighteenth century baroque cover by Nicholas Hawksmoor and all is harmony, interest and delight. In their new works at cathedrals the great nineteenth century architects, for all their apparent self-assurance, were inwardly prone to anxiety and worry. 'They were not complacent compromisers. They were trying to hold together incompatible opposites and they worried because they failed'; and this was before the development of the Historic Conscience and the Compulsive Repairing Phobia had reached the powerful and embarrassing positions they hold today. In the earlier years of this century, bereft of the apparent self-assurance of a Sir Gilbert Scott, new works at cathedrals tended to become more and more eviscerated and were only saved from the contemptible by the inborn creative qualities of the architects, which unpropitious conditions could not completely stifle. Within this context the excellence of Sir Robert Lorimer's Thistle Chapel, St Giles, Edinburgh; and Sir Charles Nicholson's Lady Chapel at Norwich, immediately spring to mind. However, nothing like Antoni Gaudi's proposals for the interior of Palma Cathedral had yet been attempted in this country. In post-World War II times some brave and successful attempts have been made to relate and mould the philosophy of modern architecture so that new works, true to the credo of twentieth century architecture, may integrate, to a fair degree, with older buildings which have been conceived within the closed tradition of organic cultures.

OPPOSITE
393 Drawing exhibited at the Royal Academy Summer Exhibition, 1968, ink on cartridge paper, approx. 25 × 36in (58.4 × 91.5cm)

> It is against this background that the architects [Pace and Paget] have had to approach the immensely difficult and very challenging task of building the first structural addition to St George's Chapel since 1504, and to design, within the aesthetic of the twentieth century, something to stand beside a building which architecturally is one of the most magnificent of the final flowering of English Gothic . . .
>
> In its plan St George's Chapel is almost symmetrical. The symmetry is broken on the south side by the tiny Oliver King chantry chapel and on the north side by the omission of a semi-octagonal chapel-tower at the north east corner. When the Lady Chapel was reconstructed on behalf of Henry VII, special provisions were made in the design to keep the new building symmetrically about the main axis of the Great Chapel and to avoid blocking its east window.
>
> The notes which follow, outline the thinking on which the architects' solution of the King George VI Chapel is founded. Before the final integration of every aspect of the problem was evolved, three detailed feasibility studies had been prepared, together with hundreds of sketches, some thirty of which had been developed in detail to scale. Models were made of three schemes. A fourth scheme had snags which were pinpointed in helpful criticism by the Royal Fine Arts Commission and the welcome personal encouragement of Lord Crawford of Balcarres. The fifth and final scheme was then evolved. Because of the peculiarities of the site it is very difficult to show graphically the design as a whole; the cut-away axonometric projection exhibited in the Summer Exhibition of the Royal Academy 1968 [ILLUST. 393] tries to overcome this. Over two hundred working drawings were prepared for the actual building and furnishing of the Chapel.
>
> The main conditions to be incorporated in the design of the Chapel were:
>
> *a* The site to be in the angle between the east wall of the Rutland Chapel and the north wall of the north quire aisle and thus to occupy on the north side of St George's Chapel a position similar to the Oliver King chantry on the south side;

b The Mortuary Chapel to have in its floor a ledger stone of black marble with bold lettering; the whole a contemporary version of the ledger stone of King Henry VI;

c Space to be included for two incised inscriptions and two bronze bas-reliefs, one being a replica of that of King George VI in Sandringham Church by Sir William Reid Dick;

d The Liturgical Chapel to be furnished with a stone altar and credence shelf and two candlesticks;

e The access to be from the north quire aisle, integrated naturally into the fine wall arcading, and arranged so that good views of the ledger stone and the Chapel are obtained from the aisle;

f The smallest possible interference with the existing building, and the windows of the Rutland Chapel and north quire aisle to be unobscured;

g The aesthetic approach to the design to be of this century and inspired by the spirit of late Gothic where this may be deemed to be complimentary.

The Architects considered there was little to be learnt from the way in which the Oliver King chantry is connected with, and approached from, the south quire aisle. They felt that full regard must be paid to the important aesthetic part played in the total impact of the aisles of the Chapel by the stone seats and wall arcading, and the excellent manner in which the doorways have been worked into the arcade.

Some of the fundamentals of modern architecture may be compared with those of late Gothic. Other fundamentals of modern architecture which it seems appropriate to use in the design of the new Chapel are:

    (i) Controlled aesthetic fragmentation of parts;
    (ii) Organic flow of time and movement;
    (iii) Control of the qualities of natural and artificial light to create atmosphere;
    (iv) Ever changing aesthetic impact (kinetic viewing) inside and outside as the user or viewer moves.

They were deeply influenced by the superb integration of every part of the design of the Porch of Honour (especially the sharp poignancy of the vaulting) and by the vaulting in various parts of the Chapel, the cloisters of Gloucester, the Sacristy, Prague Cathedral, the aisles, St Mary, Danzig and the tomb canopy of Archbishop Bowett, York.

In this late medieval vaulting they saw aesthetically the complete integration of rib, pattern and cell, and structurally the ultimate joining of rib and cell into elements worked on the same stone. Some of the vaults studied are illustrated on diagrams included with these notes [ILLUST. 396].

They had the greatest regard to the aesthetics of late medieval design as exemplified in three great

Windows links between main supports & bay & oriel window

Oxford Christ Church: Great Gate
1525-29   John Lebons & Henry Redman designers.

Henry VIIs Chapel
Westminster Abbey   1503-19
Robert Vertue & William Vertue (?) de

Windsor Castle: King Henry VII To
as drawn by F. Mackenzie. 1809.
plan oriel windows.
1498 - 1500. Robert Janyns. junior designer

Windsor Castle: Queen Elizabeth
Gallery. as drawn by F. Mackenzie
plan oriel windows.

ground flow plan.

Thornbury Castle. oriel windows
1511 - 22. Robert Janyns. Junior
(designer ?).

first flow plan.

395

Design influences – sketches and diagrams used to illustrate the design reports:

395 Window variations, ink on tracing paper, 8 × 10in (20.3 × 25.4cm)

396 Danzig St Mary's, south-aisle vault 1484–1502, ink on tracing paper, 3 × 4in (7.6 × 10.2cm)

396

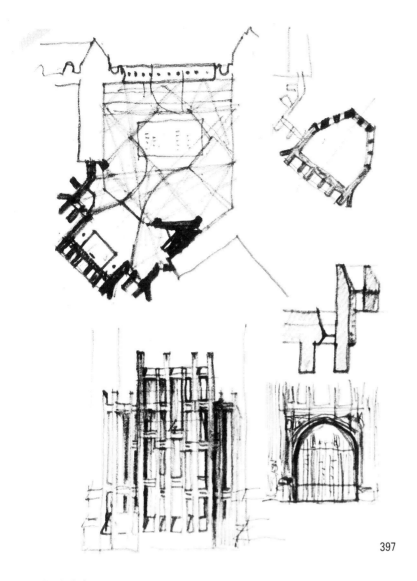

397

Early sketch designs:

397 Felt-tip on writing paper, 5 × 7in (12.7 × 17.8cm), undated

398 Felt-tip on pink flimsy paper, 7 × 7in (17.8 × 17.8cm), 1967

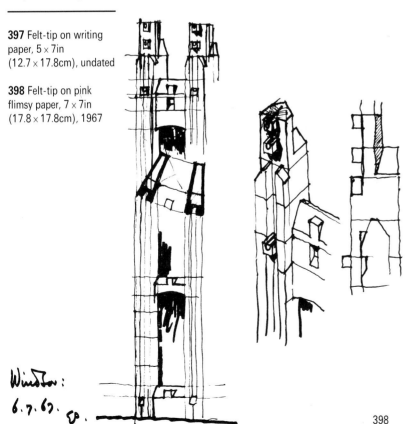

Windsor:
6.7.67. SP.

398

Chapels – St George's, Windsor Castle; King's College, Cambridge and Henry VII's Westminster – that is: the complete integration of all parts; exciting construction handled with assurance and sophisticated self-discipline; the small scale of the mouldings and details; the relationship between solid and void; the control of movement, penetration, continuous recession and the dissolution of the wall. It is considered that all these aesthetic principles should be fundamental in the design of the new Chapel.

They were also very conscious of the use of windows linking main structural elements as seen in buildings designed by Robert and William Vertue and Robert Janyns. English late Gothic design contains many interesting experiments with walling and window treatments, linked between main structural elements, and in bay and oriel windows. Some of these which have been particularly studied for the new Chapel are illustrated on the attached diagram [ILLUST. 395]. Those not illustrated included the late Gothic and early Renaissance interest in bay and oriel windows such as occurred at Nonsuch Palace and many Elizabethan and Jacobean great houses.

The plan shape of the new Chapel, the windows, the mullions, the buttresses, the parapet, and the window glazing are all conceived as a mixture of the architectural aesthetics of late medieval ages and modern architecture.

The King George VI Memorial Chapel is in two parts: the inner Mortuary Chapel and the outer Liturgical Chapel. The entrance is from the north quire aisle through a four-centred arch designed to leave undisturbed the cusped heads and the cornice of the original arcade and to integrate into the magnificent architectural conception and detail of the bay design of the quire. The entrance is guarded by a wrought iron screen and gates (ILLUST. 405 and back cover) in conception of the twentieth century, but able to dwell happily with the many examples of medieval ironwork for which St George's is famed especially that around the Edward IV tomb by John Tresilian and the hearse around the tomb of Charles, Earl of Worcester being outstanding in design and technique. The screen and gates for the Memorial Chapel echo the aesthetic of the new Chapel and in the three-part counterpoint, coupled with the enforced spatial and kinetic viewing, attempt to follow the medieval example but with a design approach and detail which could only be of this century.

Steps lead down into the Mortuary Chapel, and . . . beyond the Mortuary Chapel is the Liturgical Chapel, arranged so as to be symmetrical about the axis running from the centre of the entrance archway through the centre of the opening on the north side of the Mortuary Chapel; the position is determined by the relationship of the great buttresses of the main Chapel and thus the Liturgical Chapel is on a twist, which heightens the

399

400

internal spatial relationships and enables the free-standing stone altar to be seen from the quire aisle. Since the small intricately designed Liturgical Chapel is outside the embrace of the buttresses of the main Chapel, it can be much higher than the Mortuary Chapel. Externally the Liturgical Chapel appears as a free-standing jewel-like shrine, nestling between the great buttresses. The greater height permits of a clerestory on the south side, and this, coupled with the windows set in deep splays in the many angled walls, allows natural light to be strained through the abstract patterns of the stained glass, designed and made by John Piper and Patrick Reyntiens. The ceiling of the Liturgical Chapel, out of sight until the Chapel is entered, is decorated with a twentieth century interpretation of flowing tracery patterns, in white, black and gold leaf. The proposals for exciting vaulted ceilings in both Chapels unfortunately foundered on the rock of cost.

. . . These new vaults would have represented an entirely new form, with the basic pattern an organic growth linking the enforced shapes of the Mortuary Chapel and the Liturgical Chapel. Constructed of pre-formed blocks in various shapes and with sharply sunk splays and affixed to the concrete slab of the roof, the basic organic pattern of the ceiling would have been formed by the hollows extending the full depth between the pendant blocks. Thus instead of ribs there would be 'fragmented' hollows. The soffit of the roof slab where exposed by the hollows would have been covered with gold mosaic. The fillets on the edge of the pendant blocks to be gilded to emphasise the second order counter-point running through the pattern. The sunk splays of the pendant block would have reflected light to varying degrees and, thus, the effect would change with the position of the viewer. Such a ceiling as described may be deemed to carry a stage further the medieval and Coadestone vaults of St George's Chapel. When Alfred Gilbert was designing the Duke of Clarence tomb for the chapel he said – 'I am determined to treat the whole work in such a way that its general appearance should be that of Gothic yet devoid of the slightest evidence of imitation'. In the new Chapel a somewhat similar attempt was to have been made with the vaulting.

399 Fabricating the candlestick in magnesium bronze

400 The components of one candlestick

401 Interior – the main contractor, Mowlem, took full-sized templates to set out the Clipsham ashlar stonework. Floor in snake polished Purbeck freestone. Stained glass by John Piper, executed by Patrick Reyntiens

401

402 Plan of proposed stone-vault ceiling, ink on tracing paper, 23 × 11in (58.4 × 27.9cm), 1967

403 Detail of proposed vault, ink on tracing paper, 7 × 7in (17.8 × 17.8cm)

404 Ceiling as completed with painted tracery patterns – main ribs white, secondary tracery black on gold background

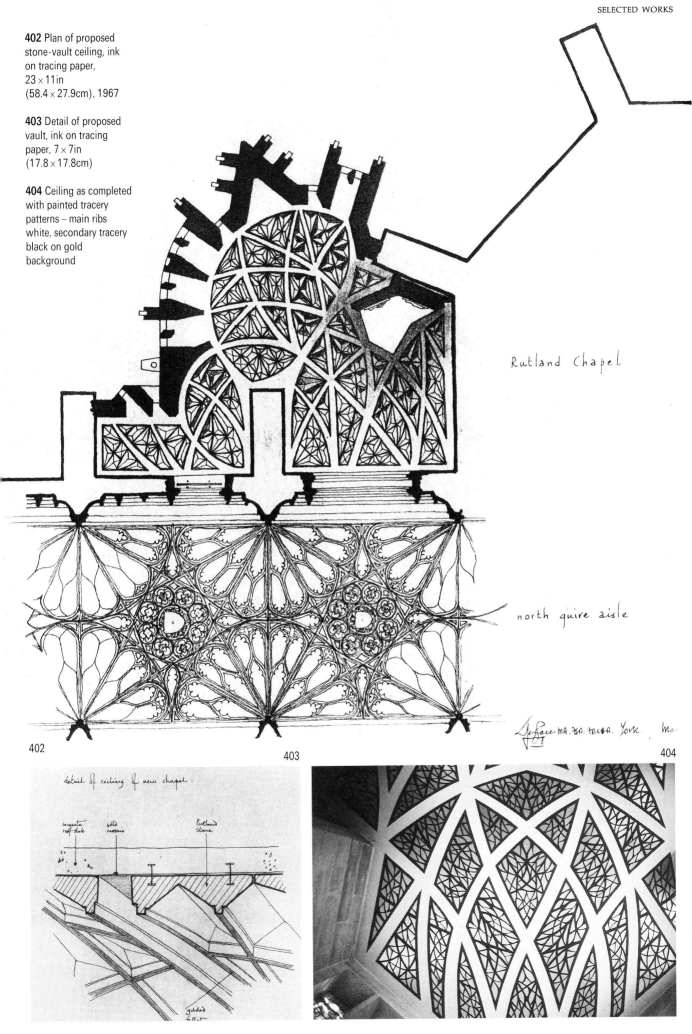

Rutland Chapel

north quire aisle

402

403

404

221

LIST OF ALL WORKS

406

407

St Edmund's, Anchorage Lane, Doncaster: formation of church and youth centre from an existing barn, 1954:

ARCHITECTURAL WORKS 1946-75

Note: All buildings, unless otherwise indicated are ecclesiastical buildings of the Church of England, or the Church of Wales. In large towns and cities, churches are identified by their dedication; elsewhere they may generally be assumed to be the parish church in a small village. Counties referred to are those in existence up until 1975, with later boundary changes ignored. (In Yorkshire the Ridings are delineated ER, NR and WR) Dates are added where possible, and generally refer to the final certification of work. Some undated works may have been abandoned, though drawings will have been prepared. In the interest of brevity only items of design are identified individually. All repair works, whether large or small scale, are included within the term 'fabric repairs'.

A

Abbeycwmhir, Radnorshire
fabric repairs 1963

Aberdare, Glamorgan (St Elvan)
west door 1957
hymn board 1961
decorations 1961

Aberedw, Radnorshire
electrical installation 1954
fabric repairs

Aberford, Yorkshire, WR
Fawcett memorial 1950

Acaster Malbis, Yorkshire, WR
inscription to seat 1968
heating installation 1968
decoration 1973

Addiscombe, Surrey (St Mary)
fabric repairs 1970/71
reordering 1972
notice board
corona/lighting
altar rail
kneelers

Adlingfleet, Yorkshire, WR
fabric repairs 1954–60
south porch doors, 1955
reordering 1956: paving, decorations, adaption of box pews, altar, cross, candlesticks, frontal, missal cushion
lighting fittings 1956
credence 1961
window glazing (south aisle 1962)
heating installation 1968

Adwick le Street, Yorkshire, WR
fabric repairs 1962, 67 (incl. new reconstruction and conservation of nave roof)
electrical installation 1967
kneeler benches 1969

Airmyn, Yorkshire, WR
fabric repairs – restoration stage I 1955
electrical installation
memorial to – R. Turner
                 – M. Mowthorpe

Alice (Cape Province) Chapel, South Africa
furnishings – abandoned 1963

Alkborough, Lincolnshire
tabernacle, south chapel 1964
heating 1967
electrical installation

Allerton, Liverpool, Lancashire (All Hallows)
electrical installation – abandoned
proposed reordering – abandoned

Alwalton, Northamptonshire
fabric repairs 1963–6
south porch doors 1962
electrical lighting 1964
south transept window 1964
reordering sanctuary: altar rails 1965
Perkins memorial 1970
pulpit 1971
south chancel door

Ambleside, Westmorland
fabric repairs 1949

Appleton le Moors, Yorkshire, NR
lighting 1962 (adaption)
altar rails 1967 (adaption)

Ardsley, Yorkshire, WR
interior decoration 1950
fabric repairs 1963
flower stand 1964
stained glass (H. Harvey) 1966

Arksey, Yorkshire, WR
fabric repairs 1954, 72
cross, candlesticks, credence, decoration 1960
chapel north transept – altar and frontal

Armagh Cathedral, Co. Armagh, N. Ireland
RIF Chapel 1950: dossal, altar rail, priest's stall, altar, candlesticks, memorial casket, pews, Archbishop D'Arcy memorial screen 1950
RIF Gates 1955
Battle honours 1961

Armthorpe, Yorkshire, WR
reordering chancel 1957–58: altar rails, and servers' bench, with inscription, reredos decorated, altar

Arncliffe, Yorkshire, WR
west window 1959
tower arch screen 1964
fabric repairs 1964
restored coat of arms 1964
display case, west wall 1966

Askern, Yorkshire, WR
reordering chancel 1958: dossal, frontal, missal, altar rail
pulpit 1958
lighting installation 1958
fabric repairs 1970

Askham Richard, Yorkshire, WR
interior decoration 1962

Aston, Yorkshire, WR
fabric repairs 1958–9, 66
reordering interior 1962–4: acolyte candlesticks, altar rails, font cover, altar candlesticks, altar cross, standard flower vase, frontal, altar table, processional torch, adapt pulpit, hanging cross, choir kneeler, chancel south-wall monument decoration
re-glazing to west tower, and south-wall chancel windows 1962

Atherton, Lancashire
reordering chancel 1972: altar, with inscription, standard candlestick, bishop and server's seat, inscription

408

409

406 Existing seventeenth-century barn built from the stones of a medieval hospice[460]

407 After conversion in 1954

408 Interior showing the screen door to the 1963 extensions; and the later organ gallery

409 Interior facing east. The bank of windows drew inspiration from the woolworkers' houses of the West Riding

Auckland, Co. Durham (St Helens)
processional cross 1962

Aysgarth, Yorkshire, NR, School Chapel
light fittings 1971
internal decorations 1971

B

Badsworth, Yorkshire, WR
fabric repairs 1953

Bainton, Yorkshire, ER
memorial lych gate – abandoned 1946
priests' stalls/screen and inscription 1949

Balby (Doncaster) Yorkshire, WR
fabric repairs 1957, 64
leaded glazing west windows 1958
decoration 1962, 64–7
heating installation 1964
electrical installation 1964
north chapel 1966: reredos panels (Harry Harvey), aumbry, altar rail and screen, font candlesticks 1966, lectern platform 1966, altar candlesticks 1970

Baldersby, Yorkshire, NR
altar rail and inscription 1968
fabric repairs 1970

Barkston Ash, Yorkshire, WR
electric heating 1964
decoration 1973

Barlby, Yorkshire, WR
fabric repairs 1965, 67
heating installation 1970

Barnbrough, Yorkshire, WR
new organ in tower space
fabric repairs 1960

Barnbrough Rectory, Yorkshire, WR
alteration 1953

Barnby Dun, Yorkshire, WR
fabric repairs 1954, 59, 67, 72
lighting installation 1959

Barnoldswick, Yorkshire, WR
fabric repairs 1971
electric lighting

Barnsley, Yorkshire, WR (St Mary)
fabric repairs 1972

Barry, Glamorgan (St Paul's)
vestry screen
organ screen

Bassaleg, Newport, Monmouthshire
fabric repairs

Batley, Yorkshire, WR
south chapel furnishing: pews, altar cross, candlesticks, stalls 1953
electric lighting 1953
window glazing 1953
monument restoration 1954
parclose screens restoration 1954
high altar, choir stall, reredos 1958

Beeford, Yorkshire, ER
fabric repairs 1961
altar table, cross, candlestick
electrical installation

Bentley (Doncaster), Yorkshire, WR (St Peter)
heating system 1949
fabric repairs 1952
altar rails 1961
window tracery 1969
lighting scheme – abandoned

Bessacarr (Doncaster), Yorkshire, WR (St Wilfred)
new church centre 1956–9

Betwy, Penpont, Brecknockshire (Breconshire)
proposed reordering

Beverley, Yorkshire, ER (St Mary)
fabric repairs 1957, 61, 63–6, 71
window glazing 1959, 64–6, 68
decorations (including ceiling) 1961, 63, 70
light fittings to crossing 1961
reredos, St Michael Chapel, north and south aisles 1961
library display case 1961
Walker memorial porch and handrail 1962
altar frontal 1964
pulpit and lectern (repair and rail) 1964
flower-vase stand 1965
Canon Tardrew's memorial screen, north-east chapel 1968
pendant light fitting, south transept (originally at Luton 1961, and transferred in 1984)
layout of churchyard
handrail to north and south quire doorways 1974

Bilbrough, Yorkshire, WR
interior decoration 1956
fabric repairs 1965
reordering interior: chancel – adaption of reredos (from St Sampson's, York), hanging cross, aumbry, altar 1970
new nave ceiling – abandoned 1970

Bingley, Yorkshire, WR (All Saints)
reordering south chapel 1958–64: altar rail, cross, candlestick, frontal, priest stall windows, pews
organ and organ case 1959
Reordering chancel 1960–2: altar rails, choir stall, candlestick, frontal, flowerstand, cross
decoration north chapel 1960
fabric repairs 1960
memorial bookcase 1966
lectern 1967
hymn-book back
processional cross

Birdsall, Yorkshire, NR
light fittings 1954
sanctuary lamp 1971
Lord Middleton memorial 1972

Birdsall House, Yorks, NR
repairs to ruined chapel 1959

Birkenhead, Cheshire, St Aidan's College Chapel
reordering 1950s: altar, hanging cross, pulpit, lectern
chairs 1962
light fittings 1963

Birkin Church, Yorkshire, WR
light fitting 1954
fabric repairs 1955, 62

Birmingham, Warwickshire, (St Augustine, Edgbaston)
chandelier south chapel 1964
new baptistry west nave 1964
fabric repairs 1966
flowerstand 1966
font lid
candlestick for font
west window north aisle 1968
proposed north-east vestries – abandoned 1968
lenten array 1969

Birmingham, Warwickshire (Queen's College Chapel, Edgbaston)
silver altar cross and candlesticks 1960
processional candlesticks 1962

Birmingham, Warwickshire (St Martin in the Bull Ring)
    Chapel of the Holy Cross 1956: reredos, altar, altar rails, sanctuary lamp, light fitting, candlesticks, paving
    fabric repairs 1957–8, 60–1, 64
    window, south chantry 1958
    reordering chancel 1958: kneelers, frontal, processional candlesticks, flower troughs and restoration of sanctuary lamp
    organ screen 1958
    movable font
    prie-dieu 1959
    notice stands 1960
    bookcases, west screen 1964
    nave altar 1968
    light fittings 1969

Birtley Church, Co. Durham
    credence table 1952

Bishopthorpe, Yorkshire, ER
    light fittings 1949
    William Temple memorial, south aisle 1955
    standard candlesticks 1956
    priest's desk alteration 1957
    south chapel: altar cross and candlesticks, altar rails, paten, 1958
    Archbishop's Throne decorated 1960
    font cover 1960
    candlesticks and reredos 1960
    fabric repairs 1974
    litany desk

Bishopthorpe Palace Chapel, Yorkshire, ER
    decoration ceiling 1951
    standard lamp and bracket lights 1962

Bleddfa Church, Radnorshire
    reordering interior

Bolton Abbey, Yorkshire, WR
    gates to chancel 1974

Bolton on Dearne, Yorkshire, WR
    decoration 1951
    fabric repairs 1951, 62
    war memorial rood (Alan L. Durst) 1955

Bolton Percy, Yorkshire, WR
    fabric repairs 1962, 64
    light fittings 1965
    churchyard cross 1967
    heating installation 1968
    memorial to Bishop Knyvett 1971

Boston, Lincolnshire (St Bostople)
    fabric repairs 1962, 68–70
    restoration of reredos 1962
    windows: chancel, north aisle 1965, 68–9
    R. Willby memorial
    library cupboards
    boilerhouse door

Bradfield, Yorkshire, WR
    light fittings 1951
    heating installation 1951
    fabric repairs 1952, 54, 60, 63, 66–7, 69–70
    kneeling benches 1955
    standard candlesticks 1955
    reredos alterations 1957
    font cover 1959
    organ screen 1972

Bradford, Yorkshire, WR – Fairweather Green
    new church with fittings and furnishings 1966

Bradford, Yorkshire, WR (Holy Trinity)
    restoration of bells 1958

Bradford, Yorkshire, WR (St Barnabas, Heaton)
    adaption of organ screen

Bradley, Yorkshire, WR
    fabric repairs 1956, 66, 68

war memorial 1963

Brafferton School, Yorkshire, NR
    major alterations 1968

Braithwell, Yorkshire, WR
    fabric repairs 1960, 61, 64, 66
    bells 1964
    chalice and paten
    west screen 1969
    south porch door 1969

Bramhall, Cheshire (St Michael)
    alterations to organ-case, choir stalls, pulpit, reredos 1960
    major extension with new west tower 1961
    light fittings 1961
    windows 1961
    altar frontal, cross 1961

Bramham Park, Yorkshire, WR
    fabric repairs: Gothic temple, open temple 4 faces, jets column 1957–9, chapel 1959–63, obelisk pond, cascade and sunk garden 1962, third temple 1963, main house roof 1964–7

Brampton, Yorkshire, NR
    north chapel fabric repairs 1959–63

Brampton Bierlow, Yorkshire, WR
    decoration 1951
    fabric repairs 1957–60, 63
    adaption of altar rails 1959
    window glazing 1959
    churchyard scheme 1962
    lighting scheme 1966

Brancepeth, Co. Durham
    Bishop Cosin font-cover supports 1975
    south-east chapel reordering

Brandsby, Yorkshire, NR
    fabric repairs 1972

Bransholme (Hull) Yorkshire ER
    New church 1968–73

Branston, Lincolnshire
    fabric repairs (including new nave roof with new bosses) 1962–63
    rebuilding of chancel and major refurnishing 1964–6: altar, priest's stall, choir stalls, altar rail, standard candlesticks and cross, Bishop's seat, hymn board, pulpit array, south door, Mothers' Union Banner
    organ-case 1966–8

Brantingham, Yorkshire, ER
    electric lighting 1948

Braunston, Rutland
    fabric repairs 1962–3
    screen to tower arch 1965
    decoration
    memorial to H. E. Ruddy

Brayton, Yorkshire, WR
    fabric repairs 1962–3
    bells 1963

Brecon, Brecknockshire (Christ's College Chapel)
    reordering and extension scheme – abandoned 1966

Brecon, Brecknockshire (St David's)
    fabric repairs 1957

Brecon, Brecknockshire (Ely Tower Chapel)
    reordering 1956–7: crucifix, candlesticks, kneeler, lights, pews, reredos, windows

Bridgend, Glamorgan
    Bishop's chair (antique) 1953

Bridlington, Yorkshire, ER (Christ Church)
    fabric repairs 1951, 1959
    light fittings 1956

nave, aisle vaulting 1963
    decoration 1963
    chancel cross 1965
    altar rails
    draught screens, west end
    choir stall platform, with vaulting above

Bridlington, Yorkshire, ER (Dr Arthur's house)
    new house – scheme abandoned

Bridlington, Yorkshire, ER (48 Eight Avenue House)
    new entrance porch 1946

Brighouse, Yorkshire, WR
    electrical lighting 1956
    interior decoration 1956
    south chapel furnishings 1956

Brinsworth, Yorkshire, WR (St Andrew's)
    new church scheme – abandoned

Brisbane Cathedral, Australia
    advice on fabric

Bristol Cathedral, Gloucestershire
    advice only on: Newton Chapel reordering, Lady Chapel reordering, Berkeley Chapel reordering, North Chapel reordering, high altar, nave seating 1958

Brockfield Hall, Stockton on Forest, Yorkshire, NR
    exterior cornice repairs

Brodsworth, Yorkshire, WR
    interior decoration 1955
    churchyard memorial to Mr Bailey 1955
    electrical installation 1955
    font cover 1957
    fabric repairs 1957
    bell repairs 1960
    churchyard memorial cross 1964

Brompton, Yorkshire, NR
    fabric repairs – windows 1960, 67
    chancel reordering 1967: priest's desk and chair, altar rails, candlesticks, hymn-book shelves, reredos (F. Roper) 1967
    heating installation 1967
    chancel furnishings 1969
    prie-dieu
    inscriptions

Bronllys, Brecknockshire
    light fittings 1968
    west window glazing 1968
    repositioning of chancel screen 1968
    interior decorations 1969
    fabric repairs 1969
    standard candlestick/flower vase, cross, altar frontal 1970

Broughton, Yorkshire, WR
    interior decorations 1968
    reordering
    new organ screen

Burghwallis, Yorkshire, WR
    fabric repairs 1949, 65

Burghwallis Rectory, Yorkshire, WR
    subdivision of house 1956

Bubwith, Yorkshire, WR
    proposed chapel, south aisle – abandoned 1974

Burton Agnes, Yorkshire, ER
    fabric repairs 1949, 53–4, 63
    north chapel tomb repairs 1952
    windows, north aisle 1956
    bells/clock repairs 1966
    memorial Canon Twidle 1968
    south chapel – candlesticks, paving
    war memorial inscription

Burton Agnes Rectory, Yorkshire, ER
    new rectory 1951

Bushby, Staffordshire
proposed south porch abandoned 1961
chancel reordering 1963: altar rails, bookcases

C

Cadeby, Yorkshire, WR
electrical lighting 1951
fabric repairs 1955–6
leaded glazing to east and west windows 1956
new bellcote 1956

Caer Eithin, Swansea, Glamorgan (St Teilo, Cockett)
new church with all fittings and furnishings 1961–3

Caerphilly, Glamorgan
organ-case 1968
south chapel refurnishings 1969: hanging cross, altar rail, kneelers, glazing to screen, candlesticks, priest's seat, frontal, light fitting

Caerwent, Monmouthshire
chancel reordering 1965: altar rails, cross, candlesticks, altar table, priest's stall, desk

Cambridge, Cambridgeshire (Great St Mary's)
Majesty figure (A. Durst) 1959
aumbry 1960
inscription sanctuary floor 1960
fabric repairs 1960
organ-case alterations 1963
interior decorating/repairs 1963
nave altar 1964
light fittings 1968

Cambridge, Cambridgeshire (St Michael's)
major alterations to form hall at west end 1966
founders' chapel reordering 1966: altar and frontal, cross, candlesticks, flower vase

Cambridge, Cambridgeshire (Kings College Chapel)
side chapel reordered to form Dean Milner White Memorial Chapel 1970
Reordering of side chapels nos 1, 2, 8–17, abandoned 1970

Campsall, Yorkshire, WR
chancel screen repairs 1955
fabric repairs 1956–7, 61–2, 64, 69
nave pews 1959
wooden plaque, north arcade 1959
south transept, new chapel 1959: reset Pugin altar (from Ackworth), altar rail/kneeler
high altar and reredos repairs 1961
vestry screens 1961
light fittings 1968
memorial to Revd. W. A. Turner 1969

Campsall Vicarage, Yorkshire, WR
alterations 1953

Canterbury Cathedral, Kent
Lady Chapel reordering
memorial to L. and E. Meredita

Canterbury, Kent – King's School
memorial to Darcy Braddell in the Great Hall – 1970

Cantley, Yorkshire, WR
fabric repairs 1960, 61
memorial Jarratt 1961

Cardiff, Glamorgan
—St Alban's
altar frontal

—St Catherine's Canton
altar rails 1954

—St Dyfrig's
demolition supervised 1965

—St James
electric light fittings 1965
reordering south chapel 1965: altar table, screen, cross, altar rails, candlesticks
war memorial inscription

—St John's Canton
alterations to chancel
extensions/vestries 1959

—St John's
cross and candlesticks high altar 1965
decorations 1965
electric light fittings 1965
vicar's board 1965
inner west porch 1966
north chancel chapel altar, cross 1967
north aisle chapel altar, cross 1967
south aisle chapel refurnishing 1968
candlesticks
Herbert Chapel restoration and reordering 1969: tomb, reredos, candlesticks, cross, altar, housling benches
south chapel windows 1970
Chapel of St John 1970: paving, sword, processional cross, altar cross, banners, altar frontal, kneelers
acolyte for high altar 1971
fabric repairs 1973
vestries south aisle – abandoned
Duke of Windsor memorial

—St Luke's Canton
Screen for Lady Chapel – abandoned 1955

—St Mary's Bute Street
reordering 1973
electrical light fittings
screen modifications

—St Mary's Priory
reordering side chapel
candlesticks
cross
ceiling decoration
reredos
lighting installation/fittings

—St Samson's
demolition 1967
adapted rebuilding design scheme – abandoned 1969

—St Saviour's, Roath
electrical installation, pendants fittings 1961
reordering sanctuary
screen to north chapel – abandoned 1968

Carleton, Pontefract, Yorkshire, WR
Lady Chapel altar, south-east corner of nave 1953
chancel reordering 1954: choir stalls, housling benches 1957, altar rail, candlesticks
rood and BVM statue 1954
sanctuary lamp inscription 1954

Carlin How, Yorkshire, NR
advice on electric heating

Carlton Husthwaite, Yorkshire, NR
credence table 1954

Carlton in Cleveland, Yorks, NR
flowerstands 1969

Carlton Juxta Snaith, Yorks. WR
tower arch, screen and south porch gate 1948 – abandoned
fabric repairs 1951, 53, 62
interior decoration 1953
boilerhouse stair 1961

Carrington, Cheshire
proposals to reorder east end for Lord Stamford 1961

Cascob, Presteign, Radnorshire
repairs to roof and tower 1965
new leaded glazing 1967

Castle Bromwich, Staffordshire
electric lighting (adapting gas fittings) 1950

Castle Douglas, Kirkcudbrightshire, Scotland (St Ninian's)
spire – alteration and repairs (advice only) 1953

Castle Howard, Yorks. NR
The house and estate – repair works:
main house north-east corner 1957
Carrmire gate 1958
Temple of the Four Winds 1959
decoration music room 1959
south-west corner 1959–63
main house south front 1959–63
south-east wing new roof 1961
main house east side restoration 1961
total reconstruction of main dome (in association with Mr Trentwith-Wills) 1961–4
main dome drum 1961–4
the grass walk 1964
fountain 1964
south garden monuments 1964
west wing decoration 1965
Mr Howard's study, new design – abandoned
stable block
satyr gate
laundry block
chapel – credence table
Victoria gates
mausoleum: Phase I works 1968
memorial to Lady Cecilia
the dairies – alterations

Castleton, Yorkshire, NR
adaption of panelling 1961
fabric repairs 1963
heating installation 1968
electric installation 1971

Castleton Youth Hostel, Yorkshire, NR
additional sanitary accommodation 1950

Catcliffe, Yorkshire, WR
subsidence repairs

Cawood, Yorkshire, ER
statue west face tower (A. Durst) 1960
sanctuary lamp and aumbry 1964
addition to war memorial

Cayton, Yorkshire, NR
reglazing

Chadderton, Lancashire (St Mark's)
new church with all fittings and furnishings 1960–3

Chapeltown, Yorkshire, WR
pendant light fittings 1955
chancel reordering 1963: stone paving, altar frontal, altar rails, reredos gilded, W.I. flowerstands
altar frontal
south chapel reordering 1963
proposed reordering at west end
bookshelves, meeting rooms facilities – abandoned 1967
redecoration 1969
fabric repairs 1970
reglazing chancel windows

Chapeltown, Yorkshire, WR
new parsonage house 1958

Cheltenham, Gloucestershire, (St Paul's College Chapel)
advice 1958

Chepstow, Monmouthshire
decorative scheme 1951

Chester Cathedral, Cheshire
fabric repairs 1961–75
inscription, Gibbs, floor slab 1962
hymn trolleys 1963
north transept: oak table, oak screen 1964
choir – altar rails 1965
south transept – RAF aumbry 1965
Lady Chapel – pleated frontal 1965
Nave: credence table 1965, pulpit 1965, desk 1968, eastern choir stalls 1966
naval casket and inscription south transept 1965
floor ledger inscription – Canon Aubrey Baxter 1965
St Mary, St Oswald and St George's Chapels: stone credence shelves 1965, altar frontal 1966, memorial – Peter Jones 1966, floor ledger to Gamon 1966
St Erasmus Chapel: aumbry 1967, cobweb picture – frame and box 1968, bronze floor memorial – Sarah Hewitt 1968, high altar rails – adaption 1968, inscription on restoration of the pulpit 1968
St George's chapel: decoration 1968, altar cross 1971
Lady Chapel: altar, cross, candlesticks 1969
decoration of organ, north transept roof 1969–70
refectory heating underfloor 1971
west refectory porch 1972
high altar frontal 1973
painting of crossing ceiling 1973
memorial E. Jones in refectory 1973
freestanding bell tower 1975
doorway west wall of choir school
new entrance door to Cathedral
choir school keystone inscription
light fittings in choir school
wrought-iron panel on door to choir school
alterations to consistory court canopy table
frontal for St Erasmus choir
door in north wall chapter house
additional woodwork to organ case
doors south side of tower gallery
frontal chests
memorial quarry cloister window
hymn boards
stable door to Abbey gateway
Archdeacon Burne memorial
A. E. K. Pierce memorial
Canon Hardy memorial
Colonel Cooke memorial

Childwall (Liverpool), Lancashire
altar table 1971
adaption of choir stalls

Church Fenton, Yorkshire, WR
reordering south transept chapel 1950: altar, altar rails, repositioning of chancel screen in south chapel 1967
adaption and painting of organ case 1955
reglazing: east window 1958
reglazing: other windows 1959
electric heating 1959
fabric repairs 1966–8
altar rail, cross, candlesticks 1967

Claverton Tower, Henley in Arden, Warwickshire
conversion to house with extension 1967

Cleckheaton, Yorkshire, WR (Chapel, Whitechapel road)
electrical installation 1961

Clifford, Yorkshire, WR (St Luke)
fabric repairs 1967
reglazing: baptistry window 1971

Clifton Campville, Staffordshire (St Mary)
fabric repairs 1966–7, 69–70
vestry cupboards 1968
reglazing: north clerestory, north transept 1971
light fittings 1971
north chapel reordering 1972: kneelers, seating, priest's desk, altar, candlesticks, screen to north chapel

Clifton, Nottinghamshire, see Nottingham

Clumber Park Chapel, Nottinghamshire
offertory box 1959
fabric repairs 1955–6, 59–63, 66–7, 70
internal cleaning 1962
garden building repairs: lodges, gates, temples

Coatham, Yorkshire, NR
priest's stall, altar candlesticks 1953
fabric repairs 1953

Cockett (Swansea), Glamorgan
processional cross 1961

Coity, Glamorgan
kneeler/altar rails 1953

Collingham, Yorkshire, WR
fabric repairs 1960, 67–9
chancel reordering 1962–5
light fittings 1962–4
pews with inscriptions 1964–6, 68–70
decorations 1964
window reglazing 1969
notice board
many inscriptions, mainly in windows 1969

Colne, Lancashire
war memorial report 1948

Colston Bassett, Nottinghamshire (Market Cross)
fabric repairs 1968–9

Coneysthorpe, Yorkshire, NR
fabric repairs 1968–9
reordering and redecorating
monument in churchyard – abandoned

Conisbrough, Yorkshire, WR
north-east war memorial chapel 1957/58: altar rail, altar, light fittings, priest's stall, memorial plaque
fabric repairs 1963, 68

Conisbrough Vicarage, Yorkshire, WR
improvements 1954

Coolham, Sussex, (St Julian's)
reordering: altar, seat and screen to chancel, screen to north transept, bracket lights, altar cross and candlesticks

Cottingham, Yorkshire, ER
fabric repairs 1954, 69
light fittings – abandoned
inscriptions and window glazing 1969
movable font 1972
aumbry

Cowbridge, Glamorgan
altar rails 1966
fabric repairs
north porch doors
new porch

Cowick, Yorkshire, ER
decoration 1948
light fittings 1954

Coxwold, Yorkshire, NR
priest's stall – abandoned

Crambe, Yorkshire, NR
fabric repairs
heating installation 1971

Crayke, Yorkshire, NR
formation of north aisle chapel 1965: cross, aumbry, candlestick standard, flower-vase stand, altar kneeler, inscription, altar
fabric repairs 1966, 69
chancel reordering – abandoned
heating installation 1968

Cregina, Radnorshire,
fabric repairs 1958

Crickadarn, Brecknockshire
light fittings 1958

Crick, Northamptonshire
fabric repairs

Cudworth, Yorkshire, WR
interior decorations 1953
formation of Lady Chapel 1958: kneeling bench, screen, aumbry, altar, crucifix, candlesticks, sanctuary lamp
font cover 1961
candlestick standards 1961

Cudworth Hall, Yorkshire, WR
fabric report for National Trust

D

Dalby Hall, Terrington, Yorkshire, NR
new house 1961–3

Dalton Parva, Yorkshire, WR
processional cross 1958
electrical installation 1959
churchwardens' staves 1959
heating installation 1959
decoration 1959
fabric repairs 1963
organ-case and staircase 1965
priest's stall 1965
lectern 1965

Dalton Parva Church Hall, Yorkshire, WR
adaption of stable to form hall

Dalton Parva Rectory, Yorkshire, WR
alterations 1955–8

Danby in Cleveland, Yorkshire, NR
alterations to gallery front and organ case – abandoned 1955
fabric repairs 1962–4
heating installation 1969
electrical installation 1970

Darfield, Yorkshire, WR
fabric repairs 1953–4, 59, 63, 68
tower – additions to screen 1958
north aisle – screen, cupboard and memorial 1962

Darfield New Church Hall, Yorkshire WR
sketch scheme abandoned 1961

Darlington Town Centre, Co. Durham
conservation area scheme
proposals 1973

Darlington, Co. Durham
new church and church centre: sketch design – abandoned

Darlington, Co. Durham (St Cuthbert's)
window glazing 1969
fabric repairs 1971
crossing reordering 1975: altar, candlesticks, flowerstand, housling benches, president's chair, server's stool

Darnall, Yorkshire, WR (Holy Trinity)
fabric repairs 1952, 58

wooden cross to east window 1967

Darnall, Holy Trinity Church Vicarage, Yorkshire, WR
new vicarage 1958–9

Darrington, Yorkshire, WR
internal decorations 1954
fabric repairs 1954
heating installation 1960
south aisle stone cross repositioned

Darton, Yorkshire, WR
fabric repairs 1963, 67–70
conservation of monuments 1969
leaded glazing – clerestory lights 1967, 69

Deane, Bolton, Lancashire
stone credence
stone altar
hanging cross
flowerstand
standard candlesticks
organ-blower screen
altar rail
leaded glazing
chair
stained glass east window

Deepcar, Yorkshire, WR
advice on churchyard 1950s

Denaby Main, Yorkshire, WR
new church – sketch design – abandoned 1972

Denaby Main, Yorkshire, WR (All Saints)
light fittings 1962
reordering
altar table
hanging cross

Dent, Yorkshire, WR
notice board

Dewsbury, Yorkshire, WR (St Matthew's)
South chapel: war memorial screen 1953, kneeler 1953
inscription to tower screen 1958

Dinnington, Yorkshire, WR
memorial to rectors 1952
light fittings 1966
corbel stone and inscription for B.V.M. statue
adaption of piscina to form aumbry
seven-day candle holder

Dinnington, The Rectory, Yorkshire, WR
alterations 1956

Disserth, Radnorshire
fabric repairs 1954, 62, 64

Doncaster, Yorkshire, WR:
—*Christ Church*
chancel furniture – abandoned

—*Church House*
alterations 1956
garages 1957

—*Hexthorpe (St Jude)*
electrical scheme 1969
sanctuary lamp 1964
hanging lamp 1964
candlesticks 1964
font cover 1964

—*Intake Church (All Saints)*
new church with furnishings and fittings 1951–6
additional furnishings 1956–7, 59
mural east wall 1964

—*Intake Vicarage*
new vicarage 1958–9

—*New Bentley*
altar and reredos 1952
electrical installation, light fittings 1964

—*St Andrew's Church, Marshgate*
survey 1969

—*St Edmund's, Anchorage Lane*
formation of chapel and youth centre from existing barn 1954
extension room and vestry 1963
altar rails, altar cross, candlesticks, lectern, light fitting, gable cross 1964

—*St George's (Parish Church)*
fabric repairs 1954, 57–8, 63–6, 69
memorial – Rogers 1957
reordering – nave crossing 1970
restoration reredos to foreman chapel 1972

—*St James*
electrical installation 1966
reordering chancel and north aisle 1966
repairs to fabric 1966
decorations 1967
reordering to west end 1967
bookshelves and tract table
altar frontal
flowerstand
altar candlesticks

—*St Leonard and St Jude*
new church building 1957–60
furnishing 1961–3

—*Western Hospital Chapel*
cross, candlesticks 1963

—*Wheatley Hills (St Aidan's)*
electrical installation
proposed reordering

Dowlais, Glamorgan
fabric repairs – bellcote 1954

Drax, Yorkshire, ER
fabric repairs 1954–5, 64, 69
prayer desk 1965
memorial tablet (Adamsons) 1965

Dublin, Eire (Centenary Chapel, St Stephen's Green)
alterations and rebuilding – abandoned 1974

Dublin, Eire (Trinity College University Chapel)
reordering – abandoned 1974/75

Duncombe Park, Yorkshire, NR
chapel: lighting 1966, decoration 1966

Dunham Massey, Altrincham, Cheshire
pulpit and choir stalls 1963

Dunscroft, Yorkshire, WR
font and cover 1965/66

Durham – Co. Durham
—*Durham School – School House*
proposed alterations (abandoned)

—*Hallgarth House*
memorial to Sir R. H. Haslam 1964

—*Durham High School for Girls*
hymn board 1962

—*Durham Lightfoot House Chapel*
kneeling benches/altar rail 1959
light fittings 1959
altar frontal 1959

—*Nos 3 and 5 Owengate*
fabric report 1957

—*Sherburn Hospital Chapel*
repairs and decoration 1963–65
chalice 1968
font cover

Durham Cathedral
In 1971 George Pace drew up the following comprehensive list of those works carried out under his control between the years 1954–71, and this is repeated here in full, including, in this instance, details of the fabric repairs. Works completed in the period 1971–5 have been added.

—1954–56
Restoration of Prebends Bridge
experiment in repair technique on two bays of cloisters inscription stone recording completion of work on Prebends Bridge
conservation ironwork on monks' door
special bases for candlesticks flanking tomb of Venerable Bede
redesigning the surroundings of the war memorial, generally to precincts at the east end of the cathedral
conservation of roof timbers monks' dormitory
repairs to external stonework of Prior's kitchen phase 1
—1957
Reredos, altar and furnishing of St Gregory Chapel
—1957–8
Alington memorial ledger in the north transept floor
memorial credence table for high altar
chapel frontal, dossall, alterations to the riddles and new candlesticks and cross
special display for the south transept
—1959–60
M.U. banner
painting and gilding certain bosses and carvings in the cloisters including 'Fawcetts Angel'
conservation of the Neville screen
repairs to the south and east front of the Prior's Chapel (south-east corner of the deanery)
memorial silver chalice and paten

Over the years purchase of panels of medieval stained glass, the Knowles collection of medieval stained glass fragments and the Pugin stained glass from the Jesus chapel, Pontefract: also by gift stained glass by C. E. Kempe and from various churches in the diocese due to demolition. All this glass together with fragments of medieval stained glass from various windows in the cathedral set in specially designed lead cames and placed in the windows in the west and south walls of the Galilee Chapel to give colour and to reduce the glaring white light which previously ruined the aesthetic impact of the interior. Conservation of the wall paintings and medieval reredos on the Langley chantry.

cleaning and waxing the ledger stones
copes for the residentary canons
restoration of the sundial on the south wall of Prior's kitchen
memorial gates for choir-school arch (project abandoned)
purchase of the *Vision of St Gregory*: a fine fifteenth-century Nottingham alabaster temporarily placed in a case in the monks' dormitory
—1961–4
wrought-iron candlesticks for the font
over the years, a few bays at a time, phase 2 of the repairs to prior's kitchen
conservation of the wall paintings in the Galilee (work done by Mrs Baker)
full-scale repairs to the north-west turret spire of the nine altar (work by W. J. Furse of Nottingham)
full-scale internal structural repairs, new flooring and decorations, conservation of seventeenth-century bookcase and new specially designed leaded glazing

229

410

Caer Eithin – Swansea
New Church 1961–63:
this Church 'has a free-
standing altar for the
Celebrant to face the
people, and all the
lightness and simplicity
characteristic of this
Architect':[461]

410 Exterior west wall
faced in blue engineering
brick, looking north west

RIGHT
411 Interior, looking
north west

412 Plan

1. Nave
2. Choir and organ
3. Chancel
4. Vestries
5. Chapel with tower over (not built)

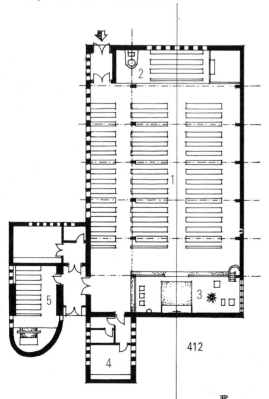

412

Fenwick St John's, Yorkshire, WR
heating and lighting installation 1967

Filey St Oswald's, Yorkshire, ER
proposed extension – abandoned

Finningley, Yorkshire, WR
fabric repairs – abandoned 1955

Firbeck, Yorkshire, WR
fabric repairs 1965–7
decoration
chancel – new paving

Firbeck/Letwell Vicarage, Yorkshire, WR
alterations 1954

Fishlake, Yorkshire, WR
fabric repairs 1956–8, 60
chalice and paten 1962
aumbry and light
south aisle west-window glazing 1972

Flaxton, Yorkshire, NR
chancel reordering – abandoned 1948

Foston, Yorkshire, NR
south doorway – report 1956

Frenchville, Sheffield (St Cyprian's), Yorkshire, WR
north chapel – pew and priest's stall 1961
vestry cupboards 1964
nave pews with inscriptions 1964–8, 70, 72
modification to chancel altar rails 1971

Frickley, Yorkshire, WR
fabric repairs 1965
stained glass 1962, 65
restoration of piscina and credence 1961

Friskney, Lincolnshire
nave rood 1969 (with Frank Roper)
fabric repairs – stained glass 1970

Fryup, Yorkshire, NR
decorations, heating and lighting installation
1963

Fulwood – see Sheffield

G

Glatton, Huntingdonshire
fabric repairs – south aisle and nave roof
1967

Goathland, Yorkshire, NR
churchyard memorial stone to Revd McLane
1965
bookcase/cupboard 1965
churchwardens' staves 1965
internal decorations 1966

Goldsborough, Yorkshire, WR
electrical installation 1968

Goldthorpe, Yorkshire, WR
fabric repairs – tower 1957
roof 1958

Goldthorpe Vicarage, Yorkshire, WR
repairs

Goole, Yorkshire, WR (St John)
fabric repairs – windows 1954, belfry
windows 1962, spire 1964, reredos gilding
and altar frontal 1956
crossing reordering – abandoned

Goole, Yorkshire, WR (St Paul's) (now demolished)
font cover 1958
altar frontal 1959
electrical installation and light fittings 1960
choir and priests' stalls 1961
heating installation 1967

Gordonstoun School, Morayshire
chapel font 1966

Gozo Cathedral, Malta
reordering – 1971

Grahamstown Cathedral, South Africa
dossal and altar frontal in Lady Chapel 1961
high altar lectern array 1961

Grainthorpe, Lincolnshire
fabric repairs

Grangetown, (Middlesbrough), Yorkshire, NR (St
Matthew's)
electrical installation and light fittings –
abandoned 1960
south porch reconstruction
extensions – abandoned 1970

Greasborough, Yorkshire, WR
frontal and missal cushion 1959
fabric repairs 1964
reglazing windows to new design 1964–6
heating installation 1966
internal decorations 1969

Great Ayton, Yorkshire, NR
club room link

Great Ayton, Captain Cook's School, Yorkshire, NR
proposed alterations

Great Budworth, Northwich, Cheshire
reordering chapel – abandoned 1965

Great Grimsby, Lincolnshire, (St James)
reordering sanctuary, chancel and crossing
standard candlestick
lectern array
priest's desk

Great Houghton, Yorkshire, WR
fabric repairs 1957–9
window glazing 1957–9
extension 1961
furnishings 1962
reordering 1964: choir stalls, box pew
modifications, altar frontal, lectern, fabric
repairs

Great Ouseburn, Yorkshire, NR
fabric reports

Grimston Park, Tadcaster, Yorkshire, WR
advice only 1956

Grosmont, Yorkshire, NR
churchyard entrance gates – abandoned 1946
war memorial 1950
alterations to chancel stage I: altar 1952
alterations to chancel stage II: altar rails,
standard candlesticks, desk, paving, brass
tablet 1955
W.I. banner

Guernesney, St Michael's, Monmouthshire
altar, aumbry, flowerstand, credence –
abandoned

Guisborough, Yorkshire, NR
reordering interior, cross and candlesticks for
high altar – 1967
window glazing – inscriptions north aisle
1952, south aisle 1962, 70

Guiseley, Yorkshire, WR (St Oswald's)
William Brooke Memorial and Headmaster's
Board 1966
inscriptions to S. Priest, R. Rawnsley,
Archdeacon Lower 1968

H

Hackness, Yorkshire, NR
proposed formation north chapel 1947, 70 -
abandoned
fabric repairs 1952, 59–60
reglazing east Window 1959
chancel floor new paving 1960

Hackness Hall, Yorkshire, NR
fabric repairs to gardener's cottage 1951

Haddlesey, Yorkshire, WR
priets's stall and desk 1963

Halifax, Yorkshire, WR (Holy Trinity)
survey report 1957

Halifax, Yorkshire, WR (St John)
electric lighting 1955

Halifax, Yorkshire, WR (St Mary's)
east end improvements – abandoned

Halton Gill, Yorkshire, WR
fabric repairs 1961–2

Halsall, Lancashire
light fittings (adaption of existing)
lectern frontal

Hambleton, Lancashire
memorial decoration 1967
window inscriptions 1967
pendant light fittings

Handley, Staffordshire (St John's)
pendant lights 1964
side chapel, choir vestry, cloakroom 1965
candlesticks
frontal
altar rail
flowerstand
lamp

Harpham, Yorkshire, ER
fabric repairs 1958

Harrow Weald, Middlesex
modifications to existing altar cross and
candlestick
new font cover

Harthill, Yorkshire, WR
fabric repairs 1959
south chapel kneeling bench 1971
Lady Osborne Monument restoration

Hatfield, Yorkshire, WR
altar rail (south chapel) 1957
windows north aisle 1961
fabric repairs 1965–9
windows south chapel 1966
RAF Memorial Window 1968
lighting fittings 1968
memorial to Welch 1971
windows south transept 1973

Hayton, Yorkshire, ER
war memorial – abandoned 1948

Haywood, Yorkshire, WR
light fittings 1957

Healaugh, Yorkshire, WR
fabric repairs 1962–3, 65
lectern candle-bracket

Healaugh Estate, Yorkshire, WR
improvements to cottages 1966–8

Healaugh Priory, Yorkshire, WR
alterations 1970

Heck, Yorkshire, WR
electrical installation – abandoned 1950

Helmsley, Yorkshire, NR
St Christopher Chapel reorder 1949–51:
candlesticks
font cover 1952
memorial inscription 1969
decorating 1972
light fittings – abandoned

Hemingbrough, Yorkshire, WR
south chapel – altar rails 1952
stalls and screen – abandoned 1953

Hemsworth, Yorkshire, WR
Archbishop Holgate's Hospital – fabric
repairs 1954

Hensall, Yorkshire, WR
decorations 1953
stained-glass window (Spear) 1969
fabric repairs
improvements to reredos and organ-case –
abandoned

Herringthorpe, Yorkshire, WR
decoration 1955

Heslington (York), Yorkshire, ER (University Church St Paul's)
fabric repairs and decoration 1969
reordering and extensions – abandoned 1969
(completed to new design by R.G. Sims
1971–3)

Heslington (York), Yorkshire, ER
Coach House adaption 1966

Hexthorpe – see Doncaster

High Hoyland, Yorkshire, WR
sundial restoration 1954
choir stalls 1959

High Kilburn, Yorkshire, NR
Overdale House: alterations 1944

High Melton, Yorkshire, WR
fabric repairs 1951, 54, 65–6
external light standard, interior bracket lights
1954
decorating 1957, 59
porch screen – abandoned 1966

High Melton Vicarage, Yorkshire, WR
improvements 1955

Hitchin Priory, Hertfordshire
J. Radcliff Memorial 1966

Hitchin, Hertfordshire
Delme Radcliffe Tombs repairs 1965
Aumbry Trinity Chapel 1965
sanctuary light 1965
light fittings 1965
decorations 1965
south chapel furnishings: pew kneelers, cross,
candlestick, altar rail, flowerstand 1965
fabric repairs 1965–7
reglazing windows 1966
heating installation 1966
west screen adaption 1966
reordering – altar (nave) 1966
altar candlesticks
bookstall 1967
church wardens' staves 1967
notice boards 1971
hymn boards 1971
book cupboard 1971
M.U. banner 1971

Hitchin Alsmhouse, Hertfordshire
conservation of memorials

Hitchin New Vicarage, Hertfordshire
abandoned

Hoar Cross, Staffordshire
New Church Centre – abandoned 1965–7

Hoar Cross, Staffordshire (Holy Angels)
fabric repairs

Holme on Spalding Moor, Yorkshire, ER
conservation north parclose screen 1947–66
inscription to lych-gate 1951
fabric repairs – tower including window
glazing 1960–2, 67

Holmpton, Yorkshire, ER
fabric repairs 1968

Holtby, Yorkshire, ER
decorations 1963
font cover – abandoned

Hook, Yorkshire, WR
high altar frontal 1946
fabric repairs 1956–7
light fittings 1958
choir vestry door 1971
heating and installation 1972
war memorial

Hooton Pagnell, Yorkshire, WR
fabric repairs – advice

Hooton Pagnell Vicarage, Yorkshire, WR
sub-division 1958–9, 61

Hooton Roberts, Yorkshire, WR
light fittings 1954
fabric repairs 1956

Hopetown, Yorkshire, WR
fabric repairs 1969

Hopwas, Staffordshire
stained glass window (Harvey) 1970

Hovingham Hall, Yorkshire, NR
decoration advice
Stammers window

Howsham, Yorkshire, ER
electrical scheme – abandoned 1949

Hoyland (Nether) Yorkshire, WR (St Peter)
fabric repairs 1963
pulpit 1968
proposed vestries – abandoned

Hoyland, Yorkshire, WR
New Parsonage House – abandoned 1956

Huddersfield, Yorkshire, WR (St John's)
decorations 1959

Huddersfield, Yorkshire, WR (St Peter and St Paul)
electrical installation – abandoned 1950
fabric repairs 1954–7

Hull, Yorkshire, ER
—Haworth Hall
advice on conversion to Theological College
1958

—*Holy Trinity 1973*
south porch draft lobby
nave roof decoration
memorial to police force
south boundary gates

—*St Aidan's*
bookcase and cupboards

—*St Augustine's*
reredos and Bishop's chair – abandoned 1946

—*St Mary's, Lowgate*
fabric repairs 1960–1
reorder chancel 1971: cross and candlesticks

—*St Mary's Convent, Anlaby Road*
advice on rebuilding school, chapel and
furniture 1953

—*St Martin's*
reordering chancel 1967: hanging cross,
candlestick, flowerstand
decoration 1970
vestments

—*St Paul's Soulcoates*
proposed new church – abandoned 1974

Husthwaite, Yorkshire, NR
stained-glass window (Harvey) 1969

Huttons Ambo, Yorkshire, ER
proposed vicarage – abandoned 1948

I

Ibadan, Nigeria, Africa
New University College Chapel
main building 1954
extended 1961

Ibadan Cathedral, Nigeria, Africa
new Cathedral
various schemes 1954–65 – abandoned

Igbobi, Lagos, Nigeria, Africa
New College Chapel
various schemes – abandoned 1954

Immingham, Lincolnshire (St Andrew's)
chancel reordering: altar, adaption of servers'
benches and priests' seats

Ingleby, Arncliffe, Yorkshire, NR
fabric repairs 1950
frontal 1955
hymn board alteration 1956
modifications to box pews 1960
inscription for bell restoration 1973
churchwardens' staves
Sir Hugh Bell Memorial
light fittings

Ingleby, Arncliffe School, Yorkshire, NR
new school 1974

Ingleby Greenhow, Yorkshire, NR
credence table 1960
inscription 1967
notice board 1970

Intake – see Doncaster

Ipswich, Suffolk (St John's)
light fittings 1958
processional cross 1967
frontal and cupboard 1968
organ chapel screen 1969
cupboards in priest's vestry 1969

J

Johannesburg, South Africa (St George's)
light fittings

K

Keele University Chapel, Staffordshire
new chapel 1965
organ 1966
memorial plaque – Sir Jones 1970

Keighley, Yorkshire, WR (St Andrew)
reordering schemes – abandoned 1961

Kellington, Yorkshire, WR
fabric repairs 1952, 60–5

Kenfig, Glamorgan
war memorial inscription 1955

Kepwick, Yorkshire, NR
lighting 1951

Keswick, Cumbria (St John)
headstone to S. B. Graham 1969

Kidderminster, Worcestershire
book trolley

Kidwell, Carmarthenshire
flower vase 1969
proposed boilerhouse 1970
light fittings

Kildale, Yorkshire, NR
dossal for high altar 1948
light fitting 1952
standard candlesticks 1953

413

St John's College, York:

413 New chapel, 1965–7

414 Plan

RIGHT
415 Interior looking east
(*see also* ILLUST 93)

1. Narthex
2. Chapel
3. Nave
4. Chancel
5. Transept

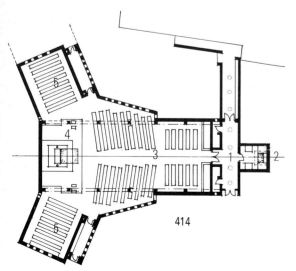

414

Llanbister, Radnorshire
decorations 1969
fabric repairs 1970
altar flower vase 1972
chancel screen – traceried panels added

Llanblethian, Glamorgan
proposed altar table

Llanbradach, Glamorgan
fabric repairs and heating report 1950

Llancarfan, Glamorgan
memorial to T. Evans
south chapel reordering 1960–4: stone altar
table, cloths, reredos (Harvey), kneelers,
pews, candlesticks, paving
processional cross
heating installation 1964–66
fabric repairs 1965
light fittings 1966
high altar reredos restoration 1969–70
south aisle paving and new western vestry

Llandaff Cathedral, Glamorgan
major reconstruction of war-damaged
Cathedral and fittings 1949–64:
chapter house roof reformed to new
conception 1954
Prichard's spire, nave and aisle roofs restored
1955 Welch Regimental Chapel and
processional way (including all fittings and
furnishings) 1956
lenten array 1956
frontal to lady chapel 1957
completion of the nave with pulpitum and
rood 1957
pendant light fitting in aisles 1957
presbytery tombs and sedilia reconstructed at
new floor level 1958
advent blue frontal 1958
two W.I. processional candlesticks 1958
dedication of the organ and organ-cases 1958
lady chapel restored and redecorated 1958
St Illtud's Chapel 1958
Lych-gates and lych-gate path 1959
Piper and Reyntiens glass 1959
flowerstands 1960
Bishop's Throne 1960
Archbishop Morgan's pulpit 1960
St Euddogwy's Chapel 1961
high altar and sanctuary furnishings 1961
St Teilo Chapel: altar cross, candlesticks and
furnishings 1961
St Euddogwy (Oedoceus) Chapel: altar rail
and furnishings 1961
St Dyfig Chapel: aumbry 1961
carving of Regimental Chapel Battle Honours
1962
font candlesticks, W.I. 1962
St David's Chapel flowerstand 1962
cope for penitential seasons 1963
nave choir stalls 1964
green vestments for sacred ministers at Sung
Eucharist 1964
three Passion gospel stands in aluminium
(with F. Roper) 1964
frontal chests with W.I. panel inscriptions, in
south aisle 1964
W.I. gateway to Dyfig Chapel 1964
choir verge (silver) 1965
Dyfig Chapel, flowerstand 1965
Lenten dossal to high altar 1965
lady chapel reredos panels (Roper) 1965
canopy to Archdeacon's stall 1965
St Teilo Chapel Lenten array 1966
glazed oak doors and mahogany gates to St
Teilo doorway to Regimental Chapel 1968
gateway to west doors widened 1968
nave altar cross and standard candlesticks
1968

west door handrail and west window
handrail 1974

Llandaff, Glamorgan
Bishop's House alterations 1964

Llandaff, Glamorgan
Bishop's Palace Chapel (Llys Esgob): pews,
desk, credence, frontal

Llandaff, St Michael's College Chapel
new chapel with furnishings and fittings
1957–9
Majestas (Stammers)

Llandaff, Llys Esgob Choir School
proposed development of flats and houses

Llanddew, Brecknockshire
fabric repairs

Llandefalle, Brecknockshire
fabric repairs 1959
south chapel window glazing 1959

Llandegley, Radnorshire
proposed reordering – abandoned 1970

Llanfihangel-Nant-Melan, Radnorshire
fabric repairs 1964
west window glazing 1964

Llanfrechfa, Monmouthshire
electrical installation 1971
external light fitting
reconstructed oak screen north aisle 1971

Llangattock, Monmouthshire
proposed reordering – abandoned

Llangorse, Brecknockshire
light fittings (adapted)

Llanilid, Glamorgan
new east window 1964
proposed pulpit – abandoned

Llantilio Crossenny, Monmouthshire
door to west porch – abandoned

Llantilio Pertholey, Monmouthshire
light fittings 1973
south east vestry screen and external door
aumbry and sacrament light
fabric repairs
west window (Stammers) 1972
decorating

Llantrisant, Glamorgan
war memorial 1952
standard candlesticks 1961
pulpit crucifix 1962
altar rails 1963
fabric repairs 1965
pulpit 1967

Llantrithyd, Glamorgan
fabric report

Llantwit Major, Glamorgan
rood (Alan Durst) 1954
monument inscriptions 1957
organ screen 1959
western chapel reordering 1959: candlesticks,
altar
chalice and paten 1960
south aisle chapel 1960: altar, cross, frontal,
kneelers
aisle and nave pews 1960
window glazing 1961
priets's cope 1961
chancel flowerstands 1961
chantry proposed gates
light fittings

Llanwenog, Cardiganshire
fabric repairs

Llyswen, Brecknockshire
reordering of chancel: light fitting, altar
candlestick – abandoned

Llywel, Brecknockshire
fabric repairs

London – see under district
i.e. East Sheen, Putney or Southwark, etc.

Long Riston, Yorkshire, ER
fabric repairs

Lotherton Hall Chapel, Yorkshire, WR
monument – abandoned

Loughborough, Leicestershire (All Saints)
decorations 1966
organ-case 1966
nave and crossing reordering 1967–9:
paving, new choir stalls (adapted), altar,
altar rails, priest's desk and seat, altar
screen, altar frontal, candlesticks, lectern
light fittings 1970
seven day candle
aumbry

Louth, Lincolnshire (St Michael's)
major fabric restoration 1957–62, 66–9, 71
processional torches 1960
north chapel – credence table and aumbry
1961
kneeler
restoration fifteenth-century seats
altar frontal – Angel Chapel
high altar rails adaption 1966
chancel ceiling panels
church porch notice boards

Loversall, Yorkshire, WR
fabric repairs

Loversall Vicarage, Yorkshire, WR
proposed new vicarage – abandoned 1952

Low Catton, Yorkshire, ER
monument – Mr Bush 1962

Lund, Yorkshire, ER
organ (from St Michael's, Spurriergate, York)

Luton Parish Church, Bedfordshire (St Mary)
chancel reordering 1959, 61: light fittings
(see St Mary's Beverley), repaving,
Bishop's chair, kneelers, silver candlesticks
silver cross 1962
Beckwith Memorial 1963
banner 1963
vicars' record board 1966
organ-case and console 1971
north porch notice boards
Barnard Chantry — cross, candlesticks

Luton Parish Church Hall, Bedfordshire
Church Hall extension 1966–9

M

Maesmynis, Brecknockshire
reredos (Harvey) 1963
altar candlesticks 1964
east window (Harvey) 1964
altar frontal 1964

Maltby, Yorkshire, WR
—*Church of the Ascension*
fabric repairs 1958–9
processional torches 1961
altar 1962
north aisle screen 1964
flowerstand 1970
churchyard gate 1970

—*Parish Church: St Bartholomew*
window glazing 1960

silver crucifix and candlesticks 1960
frontal 1960
internal vestry with screens 1962
churchwardens' staves 1967
proposed south porch gates – abandoned
1967
flowerstands 1969
rebuilding of roof after fire 1972
font cover additions
churchyard reordering
altar table
memorial to A. Trueman
new Parsonage House 1955

—Bede Church Centre, Manor Park
new dual-purpose building 1958–61
additional furnishings 1970

Margate, Kent (St James, Westgate)
east window (F. Spear) 1960

Market Weighton, Yorkshire, ER
heating installation 1964
reredos modified and decorated 1965
decoration 1965
fabric repairs 1965–6, 72
memorial plate Revd D. Evan 1967
light fittings 1969
reorder south aisle and baptistry 1972

Marr, Yorkshire, WR
fabric repairs 1953
light fittings 1957

Marrick Priory, Yorkshire NR
restoration of Priory, formation of chapel and
outdoor centre 1959–60, 68–72

Marshchapel, Lincolnshire
fabric repairs

Marske in Cleveland, Yorkshire, NR (St Germain's)
demolition supervision

Masborough – see Rotherham

Merthyr Dyfan, Glamorgan
fabric repairs 1972
reordering 1974: pendant lights,
reconstruction of floors, housling bench,
hymn-book shelves, gate to south porch,
churchwardens' staves, priests' stall, tower
screen

Merthyr Tydfil, Glamorgan
Lady Chapel 1965: priest's desks, kneeler,
stone altar, cross, candlestick, hanging
cross, flower-vase stand, credence

Mexborough, Yorkshire, WR
fabric repairs 1950, 60, 70, 71
decorations 1953
organ-case restoration 1954
inscription plate 1958
flower-vase stand 1960
new choir stalls 1964
north aisle window glazing 1965
processional cross 1970
cross and candlesticks, north chapel
lectern light fitting
choir hymn board
electrical installation

Mickleover, Derbyshire
reordering and south chapel – abandoned
1954

Middlesbrough, Yorkshire, NR
—St Cuthbert
handrail
new seats

—St John's
Lady Chapel 1955–6: altar rails, Piscina,
aumbry, cross, candlestick, sanctuary lamp

—St Martin's, 1953
adaption of altar
Majestas Rood (Alan Durst)
sanctuary decoration

—St Oswald's
inscription J. T. Long, bronze plate 1969
new window

Middleton, Lancashire
war memorial 1954
light fittings 1956–7
window glazing north aisle (repairs) 1955
new vestries extension 1957–60
flooring Assheton Chapel 1958
vestry and switch cupboard 1960
fabric repairs 1961–2, 64, 65
processional cross (Alan Durst)

Middleton, Lancashire
new rectory 1957

Midhope Chapel, Yorkshire, WR
fabric repairs 1959–60, 62, 65
light fittings 1960–1
memorial P. Bramhan 1965

Mirfield College Chapel, Yorkshire, WR
proposed alterations – abandoned 1964

Miskin, Glamorgan
pulpit crucifix (Frank Roper) 1964

Monk Bretton, Yorkshire, WR
lych-gate – abandoned
decorations 1959

Monk Fryston, Yorkshire, WR
fabric repairs 1959
south chapel: altar, hanging cross, credence
Church Hall 1969

Monk Hesleden, Co. Durham
fabric report 1955

Monkton Combe School, Somerset
chapel alterations 1964

Monmouth, Monmouthshire (St Mary's Priory)
reordering – reposition chancel screen at
west end
altar frontal (all seasons)
high altar lectern array
modification and decoration to hanging rood
handrails to chancel steps
fabric repairs

Moor Monkton, Yorkshire, WR
Red House School Chapel: fabric repairs
1971

Morriston, Swansea, Glamorgan
reordering

Mortlake (London)
new church – abandoned
churchyard landscaping 1969

Murton (York) Yorkshire, ER
entrance gates 1974

Mytholmroyd, Yorkshire, WR
barn conversion to house

Myton on Swale, Yorkshire, NR
light fittings 1970
fabric repairs 1970

N

Naburn (York) Yorkshire, ER
village hall – alterations: abandoned 1945

Nafferton, Yorkshire, ER
altar rails 1965
pulpit – abandoned 1965

Nawton Tower, Yorkshire, NR
minor fabric repairs to house 1961

Neath, Glamorgan
repairs to font 1960
font cover – abandoned 1960

Nether Poppleton, Yorkshire, WR
Lych-gate 1949
churchyard improvements
rood 1960 (with Harry Harvey)
reordering 1972: pews, priest's seat and desk,
chancel paving, altar frontal, west door,
hymn-book rack, restoration of
monuments, decoration to roof timbers
and balcony, adaption and liming of pulpit

New Bentley – see Doncaster

Newby (Scarborough), Yorkshire, NR (St Mark's)
proposed new church – abandoned 1955

Newcastle Cathedral, Northumberland
fabric repairs 1968
light fittings 1970
major internal decorating 1971
candlesticks, Chapel of Annunciation 1971
pyx – abandoned 1974
churchyard landscaping
memorial plaque

New Edlington, Yorkshire, WR
fabric repairs 1969

Newport, Christ Church, Monmouthshire (Holy
Trinity)
rebuilding and new furnishing and fittings
1955
additional fittings and furnishings 1958–9,
63, 66–7
memorial Revd King 1970
east window – Stammers

Newport, Monmouthshire (St Mark's)
fabric repairs
light fittings
decoration

New Radnor, Radnorshire
fabric repairs 1954, 64
altar frontal 1964
light fittings 1964
reordering 1964: standard cross, candlesticks,
flowerstand, reposition organ, tower
windows leaded glazing, alms dish, notice
board, Lenten array, standard candlestick,
adapted altar rails, decorating

New Rossington, Yorkshire, WR Parsonage House
fabric report 1955

Newquay, Cornwall (St Michael's)
fabric report 1971

Newton Kyme, Yorkshire, WR
churchyard memorial – D. Gront
alms dish

Nolton, Pembrokeshire (St Mary)
chancel furnishings – abandoned 1953

Normanby, Yorkshire, NR
doorway and door to priest's vestry 1960
handrail to pulpit 1961

Northallerton, Yorkshire, NR
litany desk 1959
standard candlesticks 1960
fabric repairs 1961–4
north transept chapel 1963: paving, altar rail,
credence, aumbry, pews, candlestick, cross,
altar frontal, window reglazing
south transept south window; south aisle
window 1964
light fittings 1964

north aisle – paving/pews 1964–5
decoration 1965
collection box/banner 1966
pew 1967
hymn boards 1969
re-use of fifteenth-century screens
pew kneelers
proposed north-east extensions

Northfield, Yorkshire, WR
fabric repairs 1952

Norton Lees (Sheffield), Yorkshire, WR (St Bartholomew)
altar cross
candlestick

Norton on Tees, Co. Durham
lych-gate design advice 1950
altar rails – abandoned 1952
fabric report 1955

Nottingham, Clifton, Nottinghamshire (St Mary's)
alteration to vicar's vestry and new rooms
chancel ceiling decoration 1969
vestry cupboards
nave roof and ceiling
south transept roof and ceiling
tower ceiling decoration
fabric repairs
kneeler (hassock)
flooring nave and aisles
window glazing
pendant lights adapted
memorials – Murden
flowerstand
organ-case

Nunburnholme, Yorkshire, ER
lighting installation 1963

Nunnington Hall, Yorkshire, NR
restoration report 1954

Nunthorpe, Yorkshire, NR
fabric repairs
porch door – abandoned
electrical installation

O

Old Edlington, Yorkshire, WR
fabric repairs 1955–6
chancel roof dormer
notice board

Old Fletton (Peterborough), Northamptonshire (St Margaret's)
fabric repairs 1966
window glazing 1966

Old Malton Priory, Yorkshire, NR
fabric repairs 1964, 71–2
war memorial 1971
memorial plate: H. Greenley 1971

Ormskirk, Lancashire (St Peter and St Paul)
clock and bells restoration 1972
proposed extensions: Schemes A–D 1972–3
– abandoned
proposed upper room in tower – abandoned
light fittings
font cover
light fitting – choir stall
churchyard reordering

Osmotherley, Yorkshire, NR
altar rails 1959
reredos
desk for Bishop's chair 1960
alterations to churchyard

Oswaldkirk, Yorkshire, NR
reordering churchyard

interior reordering
war memorial – 1947 – abandoned

Otley, Yorkshire, WR
proposed reordering – abandoned 1969

Oughtibridge, Yorkshire, WR
proposed alterations to chancel – abandoned 1962
fabric repairs 1967

Outwood, Yorkshire, WR
alterations to pews, pulpit, paving, 1954
electrical installation 1956
window glazing 1956
interior decoration 1956
standard candlestick 1956–8
pendant light 1956/58
war memorial 1963

Owston, Yorkshire, WR (also known as Skellow)
light fittings 1952
north door 1953
south chapel: frontal, candlestick 1955
heating installation 1962–70
fabric repairs 1972

Oxford, Oxfordshire:
—New College Chapel
new organ and organ-case with adaptations to gallery 1969–71
proposed lighting 1974
—Wycliffe Hall Chapel
reordering – 1962–3: altar, priest's seat, reading desk, alterations to pews, candlesticks, cross, light fittings, window glazing
—Cowley Fathers' Chapel
nave altar
altar rail
lectern
standard candlesticks
pave sanctuary floor
altar frontal
—St Giles
proposed reordering

P

Padgate, Lancashire (Christ Church)
notice board 1962
fabric repairs 1962–4, 69, 71
cope and hood (Mrs Ozanne) 1963
window glazing 1963–4
light fittings 1964
bookshelves 1964
hymn boards 1965
decorations 1965, 67
chancel reordering – 1966, 71: choir stalls, door to organ, Bishop's seat, vestry cupboard, altar cross, altar rail, flowerstand, moveable font
remembrance-book table
altar frontal
hassock
M.U. banner
reordering churchyard
processional candlestick
Colling Memorial Ledger stone

Parkgate, Yorkshire, WR
fabric report 1957
demolition supervision 1960

Patrington, Yorkshire, ER
electrical installation 1958
fabric repairs

Peakirk, Northamptonshire (St Pega's)
fabric repairs 1963–5
light fittings – abandoned 1966
nave north door 1967

Penarth, Glamorgan (All Saints)
new dual-purpose building with furnishing and fittings 1959–60
proposed organ screen
chalice and paten 1970
churchwardens' staves

Penarth, Glamorgan (St Augustine's)
alterations to churchyard cross 1970

Pencoed, Glamorgan
proposed extensions – abandoned 1973

Penistone, Yorkshire, WR
priest's stall 1959
fabric repairs 1959–60, 68, 69
priests' chairs 1963
prayer desk 1965
light fittings 1968
decoration chancel monuments 1969
organ-case 1975
reordering choir 1975
plaque 1975
window glazing – south-east chancel

Penshaw Monument, Co. Durham
repairs Stage I, 1960

Perlethorpe, Nottinghamshire
fabric repairs 1961, 70–1
door to spire

Pershore Abbey, Worcestershire
choir kneeling desk 1962
pulpit alterations 1962
benefactors' board 1967
processional candlesticks
new pulpit/pulpit desk
processional cross
Majestas (Harvey)
south transept chapel: aumbry, priest's desk/stall
east window glazing
lectern

Peterborough Cathedral, Northamptonshire
credence table 1959
west front pinnacle cross 1959
fabric repairs – west front
reglazing windows
St Oswald's Chapel reordering 1963–7: pews, altar kneeler, stair gate, lamp and light fittings
St Sprite's Chapel reordering 1966–7: credence table, kneeler, pews, back stalls
Inscription to L. Rowell, firewatchers' tablet 1968, cloakrooms south transept 1969, north transept memorial door to Consistory Court 1970
St Benedict's Chapel: aumbry, lamp
choir stalls light fitting
screen door to sacristy
hymn board
moveable nave altar
nave cross and candlesticks
information board
window glazing – south transept, nave and north aisle 1968
inscriptions: Dean Christopherson and Canon Millard
small organ-case
flowerstands
collecting box
St Kyneburgh altar frontal 1973
pulpit light and bookrest
memorial table and chair: Music Library
cleaning west front 1974
nave hanging rood (F. Roper) 1975

Peterborough Cathedral Close
Archdeaconry House: alterations
Canonry House: alterations
No. 19 The Precincts: alterations 1963

Peterborough – Table Hall
　　alterations
　　restoration – proposed 1959

Pickering, Yorkshire, NR
　　font cover 1948
　　light fittings 1954
　　fabric restoration 1954, 58, 63–6, 72
　　Bruce Chapel – altar cross 1956
　　silver cruets 1960
　　Bruce Chapel – sanctuary lamp 1964

Pocklington, Yorkshire, ER
　　organ-case 1950
　　Lady Chapel – reordering 1952, 54: altar,
　　　　altar rails, cross and candlesticks, credence
　　　　shelf, window glazing
　　reorder chancel 1954: choir stalls, priest's stall
　　nave west window 1953
　　chancel south side windows
　　fabric repairs 1954, 59
　　coke store 1954
　　organ console light bracket 1956
　　new vestries and heating chamber 1958
　　housling benches 1961
　　north transept – east window 1961, west
　　　　window
　　north chapel 1965: aumbry, sanctuary lamp
　　　　bracket
　　organ screen 1970

Pollington, Yorkshire, WR
　　pendant lights 1951
　　war memorial 1954
　　memorial window (F. Spear) 1954
　　interior decoration 1954
　　fabric repairs 1959, 68
　　priest's stall 1961
　　heating installation 1967
　　window glazing to aisles 1971–2
　　choir stalls – abandoned

Pontefract, Yorkshire, WR (All Saints)
　　fabric repairs to ruins 1953
　　major extension within ruined nave including
　　　　fittings and furnishings 1967

Pontefract Town Hall, Yorkshire, WR
　　fabric repairs – report 1969

Putney (London)
　—All Saints
　　proposed reordering – abandoned 1974

　—St John's
　　proposed reordering – abandoned 1974

　—St Mary's
　　feasibility study on rebuilding as church
　　　　centre 1974–5

R

Ravenfield, Yorkshire, WR
　　W.I. entrance gates
　　fabric repairs
　　reordering proposals – abandoned

Rawcliffe, Yorkshire, WR
　　fabric repairs 1958–9
　　alterations to gallery – abandoned

Rawmarsh, Yorkshire, WR (St Mary's)
　　reordering sanctuary 1959: reredos/dossal
　　　　curtain, altar rails, paving
　　war memorial plaque 1962
　　fabric repairs 1962–3
　　reposition font 1968
　　church banners 1968

Rawmarsh Rectory, Yorkshire, WR
　　alterations and subdivision 1954

Rawmarsh, Yorkshire, WR (St Nicholas)
　　proposed reordering and completion of
　　　　chancel – abandoned

Redcar, Yorkshire, NR
　　aumbry north chapel 1962
　　light fittings 1964
　　altar frontal 1966
　　rebuilding organ gallery 1966

Retford, Nottinghamshire
　　fabric repairs 1964–5, 67, 70
　　window glazing (stained glass – N. Allen)
　　　　1969–70
　　decorations 1970
　　electrical installation 1971
　　external notice board
　　hymn-book shelves
　　reredos

Riccall, Yorkshire, WR
　　fabric repairs 1953–4
　　stone water-chutes

Rievaulx, Yorkshire, NR
　　electrical heating – abandoned

Ripley, Yorkshire, NR
　　proposed shaft for ancient cross base

Ripponden, Yorkshire, WR
　　fabric repairs 1963–4

Roade, Northamptonshire
　　south porch doors 1970
　　light fittings
　　moveable altar

Romanby, Yorkshire, NR
　　candlesticks 1959
　　fabric repairs 1965
　　decoration (reredos and ceiling detailing)
　　　　1966
　　electrical installation 1968
　　apex gable cross 1969

Rossington, Yorkshire, WR (St Michael)
　　fabric repairs 1952, 64–5, 66
　　decorations 1952, 71
　　pews 1959
　　notice board 1959
　　rector's board 1965
　　light fittings 1965
　　tower stair door
　　organ screen

Rossington Rectory, Yorkshire, WR
　　sub-division 1954, 56

Rotherham, Yorkshire, WR
　—St Stephens' Eastwood
　　fabric repairs 1963

　—St John Masborough
　　altar rails 1949

　—St Paul's Masborough
　　fabric repairs 1962–3, 68, 70
　　leaded glazing 1971
　　decorate reredos cross and screen
　　reordering – abandoned

　—The Bridge Chapel
　　window glazing with Alan Younger

　—All Saints (Parish Church)
　　light fittings 1957–8, 67
　　fabric repairs 1957–9, 64, 66, 68
　　nave altar-table 1961
　　bookstand 1962
　　leaded glazing 1962–3
　　missal (reading) desk 1962
　　chancel stall screens 1963
　　south porch revolving doors 1965
　　flower vases 1966
　　heating installation 1968

Rudstone, Yorkshire, ER
　　proposed restoration – abandoned

Rumney (Cardiff), Glamorgan
　　extension to vestry 1983

Rushmere (Ipswich), Suffolk (St Andrew's)
　　paten and chalice 1966
　　major extensions with furnishings and
　　　　fittings 1967–8

Ryther, Yorkshire, WR
　　heating installation 1971

S

Saare Yesu, Africa
　　cross and candlesticks

St Alban's Cathedral, Hertfordshire
　　Watkin Memorial 1964
　　Abbot's board 1965
　　Saints' Chapel: pendant lights 1965
　　Ramryge Chapel: light fitting 1965
　　collecting box 1965–7
　　headstone Canon Cockbill 1966
　　Saints' Chapel: candlesticks, processional
　　　　cross, rails, altar, frontal, cross 1967
　　frontals and vestments 1967
　　High Mass set: priest's chasuble, deacon's
　　　　chasuble, sub-deacons' chasuble 1967
　　lighting – presbytery and Lady Chapel 1967
　　headstone Constable Moore 1969
　　inscription to cathedral watchers
　　proposed library to north transept
　　inscription to bell-ringers
　　notice stand
　　radiator covers
　　inscription to library screen panel
　　exterior notice board
　　improvements to the Close
　　reordering nave: moveable pulpit, moveable
　　　　choir stalls, kneelers, banner and pole
　　proposed vestries and cloakrooms: schemes
　　　　A–H
　　altar rail
　　Bishop's/minister's seat
　　adaption of crystal cross
　　bells restoration
　　ledger stone, Mr Perrycoate
　　north nave doorway
　　fabric repairs

St Bride's-Super-Ely, Glamorgan
　　reglazing east window 1957
　　tabernacle 1959

Salesbury, Lancashire
　　formation of vestry and chapel in south
　　　　transept – abandoned 1966

Salterhebble, Yorkshire, WR
　　ledger stone to Pickles 1972

Sandal Magna, Yorkshire, WR
　　war memorial chapel, north transept 1953
　　south chapel dossal frame 1953
　　altar cross and candlesticks gilding 1961
　　light fittings 1966
　　south chapel furnishings – abandoned 1968

Sandridge, Hertfordshire
　　font cover

Sawbridgeworth, Hertfordshire
　　alterations to organ 1963

Saxton Village, Yorkshire, WR
　　six cottages – improvements 1950

Scarborough, Yorkshire, NR
　—Christ Church
　　lights to nave 1946
　　south porch screen narthex 1950

416

St Sampson's, York:
conversion of redundant
church to old people's
centre, with enclosed
chapel at east end, 1974:

416 Statue in niche
gilded. Windows with
new leaded glazing

priest's vestry door 1951
flower-vase bracket 1952
fabric repairs 1952, 54, 66–7
heating installation 1965
proposals to reduce church 1967

—St Martin's
reordering Lady Chapel – abandoned 1951
electrical installation – abandoned 1951

—St Mary's
fabric repairs 1946, 51, 53, 58, 60–5, 67–8,
71
war memorial 1952
churchyard improvements 1954, 57, 61, 63,
70
vestry wall recesses 1957
reconstruction of east end 1957
reconstruction of south aisle window 1957
lighting fittings 1957, 70
font cover 1961
window glazing 1962
heating installation 1964
south-west porch screen doors 1965
memorial to Canon Parker 1969
internal priest's vestry and screen 1970
adaption of wall panelling 1970

—St Mary's Church Hall and Chapel
rebuilding work, furniture and fittings 1968

—St Saviour's
reordering chancel – abandoned 1954
light fittings 1965
fabric repairs 1965

—St Thomas
decorations 1963

—St Thomas and St Paul
new church with furnishing from St Thomas
and St Paul 1969

Scargill, Yorkshire, WR
alterations to main house 1958–9, 61–2, 64,
66–68
new chapel with fittings and furnishings 1961

Seaton Ross, Yorkshire, ER
altar cross 1948
reconstruct east end 1953
processional candlestick 1964
decorations 1966

Selby Abbey, Yorkshire, WR
organ grilles 1950
Lathom Chapel: vestry with re-used screen
1954
fabric repairs 1955–7, 59–61, 64–5, 67, 69,
73–75
war memorial chapel 1955, 60: altar frontal,
credence shelf, altar rails, pews and
kneeler, crucifix, candlesticks, casket, oak
door
processional torch
G. Mortimer memorial plate
Foster memorial plate
Richardson memorial window
desk and piano screen, mural
lighting installation 1960, 69
stained glass (N. Allen) 1961
processional cross 1962
alms table 1962
heating installation 1962
freestanding heating chamber 1962
proposed moveable choir stalls and screen
stained glass to High Steward's stall
display case, south transept
organ console, platform with W.I. railings
1966
audio system 1969
churchwardens' staves 1969
cope and stole 1969
light fittings (transepts, sacristy chapel) 1969

Selby, Museum Hall, Yorkshire, WR
proposed alterations to façade – abandoned

Settrington, Yorkshire, ER
alterations to war memorial 1949
reordering south chapel 1954: pews, kneeler,
paving, altar rail, credence shelf
fabric repairs 1954–5, 67
decorations 1955
window glazing 1969, 71

Sheffield, Yorkshire, WR
—Abbeydale St John's
aumbry 1967

—Abbeydale St Peter's
memorial inscription B.L. Forcitt 1970

—Arbourthorne St Paul
fabric repairs 1961–2

—Attercliffe Christ Church
fabric repairs 1961
alterations to chancel: altar, rail, cross, screen,
credence, pulpit, font

—Attercliffe Emmanuel Youth Centre
alterations and extensions 1954

—Basegreen Gleadless St Peter's
inscription plate J. Francis

—Bramhall Lane St Mary
north aisle chapel 1967–8: altar, fair linen
cloth, altar rails, hanging cross, credence,
candlesticks, standard candlesticks, flower
vase

—Bramhall Lane, St Mary's Parsonage
new parsonage house – abandoned 1955

—Brightside All Saints
fabric repairs 1957
decorating 1957

—Brightside, All Saints Vicarage
subdivision survey 1956

—Brightside St Margaret's
reordering 1970: candlestick, flowerstand,
pendant light, altar, W.I. gate, priest's stall
and kneeler, cross, canopy
fabric repairs 1957

—Brightside St Thomas
decorations 1957
reredos 1962
adapt altar 1962
candle sconces 1962
crucifix 1962
lectern 1963
stone credence
kneeling bench
alterations to gallery for new organ
proposed north chapel
revised chapel seats

—Brocco Bank St Augustine's, Endcliffe
light fittings 1966
hymn-book trolley
alterations at west end: dual-purpose rooms
within nave, new entrance narthex, kitchen
toilets 1971
decorations

—Broomhill St Mark's
demolition of ruins 1954
restoration of spire and tower 1955–6
new church erected 1963
all interior fittings and furnishing completed
by 1967

—Carbrooke St Bartholomew's
nave altar, vestry – abandoned 1951
supervision of demolition

—Carbrooke St Bartholomew's Vicarage
conversion 1951

—Sheffield Cathedral
openings to south choir aisle 1954
fabric repairs 1956
space under central tower 1957
organ console 1957
monument to Bishop Burrow (Kindersley)
1957
completion of Cathedral – several schemes
from 1955–61 – abandoned 1961
memorial to Bishop Heaslette 1958
layout of churchyard 1959
Yorks. and Lancs. (St George's) Chapel
1959–60: credence table, two parclose
screens, seats, desks, regimental badges
(Harvey)
tower completion 1961
organ restoration 1961
notice board
high altar cross and candlesticks

—Cathedral Vicarage
alterations 1954

—City General Hospital Chapel
formation of chapel 1957: credence shelf,
pendant light, altar table, altar rail, door,
altar cross, altar candlestick, aumbry,
priest's desk
kneeling rail 1961

OPPOSITE
417 Enclosed chapel
formed with new stone,
timber and glazed screen
across former nave. The
new reredos reuses old
panels

—*10 Claremont Place*
  alterations 1954

—*Crookes St Thomas*
  fabric report 1957
  altar table
  tract and notice board
  inscription
  reordering churchyard
  west door 1967
  inner south-west porch and tower cloakroom
    1967
  fabric repairs 1967
  north aisle ceiling 1967
  decorations 1967
  electrical installation 1967

—*Crookes St Timothy*
  formation of children's corner 1959: altar
    rails, baptismal roll table, flower vase

—*Fir Vale St Cuthbert's*
  altar rail 1951
  Chapel of Chivalry reordering 1955: altar
    rail, altar cross
  completion of west end – abandoned 1956
  flowerstand 1969
  hymn board 1969
  electrical installation 1969–71
  notice boards 1971
  reordering chancel – abandoned 1971
  aumbry

—*Fir Vale Infirmary Chapel*
  formation of Chapel 1965: vaulted ceiling,
    windows, entrance doors, organ screen,
    pendant light, altar table, lectern,
    candlestick, flowerstand, priest's stall
  Book of Remembrance table 1966

—*Fulwood Christ Church*
  major extensions 1954: chancel, south aisle,
    west porch including furnishings: altar,
    pendant lights, altar rails, kneeler, font
    cover, altar cross, altar vases, choir stalls,
    pews, hanging cross

—*Gleadless Christ Church*
  window glazing 1960–1
  crucifix 1964
  bookstand 1971
  priest's desk 1971
  fabric repairs 1971

—*Gleadless Christ Church Vicarage*
  alterations 1959–60

—*Gleadless Valley Holy Cross*
  alterations to organ screen

—*Handsworth Woodhouse St James*
  south aisle chapel
  cross, candlesticks, inscription, plate

—*Handsworth St Mary's*
  war memorial 1954
  chancel improvements 1956: gilding reredos
  decorations 1956
  fabric repairs 1962–3
  altar frontal
  entrance gates
  north-east chapel – altar rails and table
  priest's stall, nave

—*Handsworth St Mary's Vicarage*
  alterations 1952

—*Heeley Christ Church*
  south transept chapel 1958: altar rail, pews,
    altar table, candlesticks
  electrical installation

—*Heeley Christ Church Vicarage*
  alterations and improvements 1953

—*Malin Bridge St Polycarp*
  fabric repairs 1965
  decoration 1972
  electrical installation

—*Millhouses Holy Trinity*
  Lady Chapel altar rail alteration
  dossal curtain 1956

—*Millhouses St Oswald's*
  organ reconstruction 1954
  south chapel altar rail – abandoned 1954
  fabric repairs 1954–5
  Memorial plate Revd Japing 1971
  hanging rood alterations

—*Molescroft*
  feasibility study for Bishop's House

—*Neepsend St Michael's*
  demolition supervision 1955
  relocation of fittings (ref. Netherthorpe)

—*Netherthorpe Burgoyne Road St Bartholomew*
  proposed reordering – abandoned

—*Netherthorpe St Phillip and St Anne's*
  standard candlesticks 1952
  north chapel 1954: altar, altar rails
  reglazing east window, west window and
    north clerestory windows 1954
  altar cross 1956
  fabric repairs 1956, 62, 64
  chancel furnishings – re-used from St
    Michael's Neepsend

—*Netherthorpe St Phillip and St Anne's Vicarage*
  alterations and extension 1954

—*Newhall St Clement's*
  proposed reordering at west end

—*Owletton*
  altar candlesticks 1958

—*Park St John's*
  fabric repairs 1960, 63
  reordering – abandoned

—*Parsons Cross St Cecilia*
  new vaulted ceilings
  electrical installation
  organ-case – abandoned
  alterations to altar table

—*Pitsmoor Christ Church*
  decoration 1955
  heating installation 1966
  fabric repairs 1968
  reordering – abandoned

—*Royal Infirmary Chapel, 1955*
  stone inscription, screen, window, door,
    candle bracket, memorial bookcase

—*St Aidan's*
  font cover 1958
  proposed reordering – abandoned

—*St Barnabas*
  fabric repairs 1957

—*St Catherine's Hastelar Road*
  fabric repairs 1972

—*St George's*
  fabric repairs 1953, 61–3, 71
  window glazing 1963–4
  pulpit 1964
  gallery lights 1964
  reordering chancel 1964
  decorations 1966

—*St George's Vicarage*
  alterations 1957

—*St James*
  fabric repairs 1954
  decoration of organ-case

—*St Mathew's Carver Street*
  fabric repairs 1952, 57, 61–2
  heating installation 1954
  south chapel reordering 1957: altar, altar
    rails, piscina, credence, aumbry housing,
    frontal chest, cross, candlesticks
  west entrance doors 1958
  electrical installation 1958
  organ screen – abandoned 1963
  reredos gilding 1963
  decorations 1966
  bronze plaque 1967
  vestry screen modifications

—*St Nathaniel's*
  alteration to chancel 1956: standard
    candlestick, altar frontal, new base for
    pulpit

—*St Silas*
  decorations 1955

—*St Stephen's Community Centre, 1955*
  alterations and improvements
  chapel furnishings – altar cross, candlesticks,
    credence, adapted pews

—*Sharrow St Andrew's*
  fabric repairs 1952
  electrical installation 1955–7
  decorations 1956, 68
  porch doors and alterations to north porch
    1966
  notice boards 1966

—*Shiregreen Cemetery*
  Bishop Heaslett Memorial (Bishop of Tokyo)
    1958

—*Shiregreen St Christopher's Vicarage*
  alterations 1951

—*Shiregreen St Hilda's*
  south aisle chapel 1967: cross, candlesticks,
    altar rail, reredos, altar table
  decorations
  alterations to chancel screen and organ-case
    1952
  tombstone

—*Tapton Court Nurses' Home*
  formation of chapel 1958: screen, door, pews,
    light fittings, candlestick, altar, memorial
    plaque

—*Wadsley Bridge Chapel*
  fabric report
  east window reglazing (Stammers) 1957
  decorations 1969

—*Wadsley Christ Church*
  reordering – abandoned 1948, 52
  candlesticks 1955
  proposed lych-gate and standard light
  east window 1971

—*Walkley St Mary's*
  electrical installation 1949
  nave pendants
  font cover 1953
  war memorial 1953
  candlesticks 1955

—*Walkley St Mary's Vicarage*
  alterations 1953

—*Whirlow Grange*
  demolition of stable 1957
  new chapel with fittings and furnishings 1958
  priest's stall 1962
  lectern 1962

—*Wicker Holy Trinity Church Hall*
  fabric repairs 1958

—*Wincobank*
  decorations 1952
  electrical installations

altar rails 1952
standard candlesticks

—*Woodseats St Chad's*
North Chapel 1961: altar rail, kneeler,
credence table, altar table, candlesticks,
screen
fabric report 1957
decorations 1970
vestry and parish room

Sheldon, Derbyshire
electrical installation 1970
decorations 1971

Sherburn Hospital Chapel, Co. Durham
wafer box 1959
silver paten 1969

Sherburn in Elmet, Yorkshire, WR
electrical installation 1953
fabric repairs 1955–62
alterations to vestry – abandoned 1957

Sherburn, Yorkshire, ER
light fittings 1948
font ewer, inscription
table with inscription

Sheriff Hutton, Yorkshire, NR
alterations to north chapel proposed 1949 –
abandoned
Prince's tomb restoration 1950
alterations to north porch 1957
ledger memorial stone, Jackson 1962
alterations to chancel 1962
reredos brackets, inscription plate
fabric repairs 1962–3, 69
heating installation 1964, 69
war memorial 1966
light fittings
chimney flue

Shrewsbury, Shropshire (St Mary's)
alterations to north porch 1957
war memorial 1957
electrical installation 1957

Silkstone, Yorkshire, WR
fabric repairs 1964, 66
heating installation 1968
lighting fittings 1969
reorder aisle pews 1969

Silsden, Yorkshire, WR
candlesticks 1965
processional cross 1966
major reordering 1967–8: west gallery
modification, choir stalls, draught lobby,
altar rail, alteration to church warden's
seat, alteration to pulpit, alteration to
Bishop's seat, priest's stall, pendant light
fittings, new stand to cross, flower vase,
east-end paving, chancel ceiling, organ
spiral stair, organ screen (abandoned),
reredos, altar frontal, decoration

Skefling, Yorkshire, ER
Light fittings

Skelmersdale, Lancashire
Bishop's chair 1972
Liverpool diocesan arms

Skellow
see Owston

Skelton (near York), Yorkshire, NR (St Giles)
fabric repairs
Hotham Memorial restoration 1968
lighting fittings 1969
doors 1969
seven-day candle tray 1969
heating installation 1970
aumbry 1971

crucifix 1971
aumbry lamp
candelabrum
candlestick, south chapel
motifs for two chasuble clothes
south chapel: altar table, standard
candlesticks
oak base to pulpit
organ cupboards and screen
Lady Chapel cupboard
inscription base of pyx
wafer box

Skelton (near York), Yorkshire, NR, ('Woodlea')
alterations to architect's own house 1949, 61

Skipton, Yorkshire, WR (Holy Trinity)
decorations 1972
window glazing 1972
inner west porch
vestry

Skipton High Street, Yorkshire, WR
civic townscape improvement scheme: 1963,
68–9

Skipton Town Hall, Yorkshire, WR
main entrance doors 1966
annex entrance doors 1966

Skirlaugh, Yorkshire, ER
fabric repairs 1957–8, 67
light fittings 1967
nave ceiling vaulting 1967

Skipwith, Yorkshire, ER
proposed children's corner – abandoned
heating installation – abandoned

Sledmere, Yorkshire, ER
monument Dame Sykes – chancel
monument Lady Sykes – south aisle

Sleights, Yorkshire, NR
processional cross 1960
fabric repairs
notice board
collection boxes

Snaith Priory, Yorkshire, WR
fabric repairs
columbaria
window glazing, nave, south wall, tower
west window 1962
north-east chapel: furnishings – abandoned,
proposed font cover, altar rail with old
tracery, inscription to turret stair

Snaith Yew Lodge, Yorkshire, WR
alterations 1954

Snaith Vicarage, Yorkshire, WR
proposed vicarage – abandoned 1955

Somerton, Somerset
monument Revd Jackson

South Anston, Yorkshire, WR
high altar with painted panels 1963
fabric repairs 1963–6, 69–71
light fittings 1968
south aisle chapel 1969: altar, flower
container, altar rails, candlesticks, frontal
high altar rail adapted
window glazing

South Kilvington, Yorkshire, NR
fabric repairs – abandoned

South Kirby, Yorkshire, WR
fabric repairs 1960, 63
heating installation 1963
light fittings 1963 (chancel wall brackets)
decorations 1963

Southwark Cathedral, London
early schemes for vestry extensions

bookstall west end nave 1971
stand for the Friends
notice stand
collecting box
flower-vase stand
moveable lectern
crossing ceiling decoration
crossing nave altar – proposals 1974
(completed by R. G. Sims)
Harvard Chapel reordering 1974: screens,
bracket light, altar, kneeler, adapted Pugin
tabernacle, processional cross, oak stools
cope 1974
memorial G. G. Pace 1975

Sowerby Bridge, Yorkshire, WR
memorial, Stansfield 1968

Sowerby (Thirsk), Yorkshire, NR
lectern, altar rails and inscription 1957
cloakroom 1967
decorations including reredos 1967
window glazing 1968
fabric repairs 1971–2
reordering south transept
aumbry, south chapel

Spalding, Lincolnshire
reordering: 1971
organ-case and gallery, light fittings, gate to
gallery, 1972

Spotborough, Yorkshire, WR
fabric repairs 1951, 70
priest's stall 1955 (formed from medieval
panels)
lectern 1955
north porch doors 1961
south chapel altar 1963
heating installation 1965
formation of pews at west end (re-use of pew
ends from Old Edlington)
proposed reorder to chancel 1974

Spotborough Rectory, Yorkshire, WR
alterations 1951

Stainforth, Yorkshire, WR
electrical installation 1963
fabric repairs 1971–2
window glazing 1972
proposed extensions for vestries –
abandoned
formation of church hall with glazed screens
to north aisle and chancel arch, and
staircase to upper room

Stainforth Vicarage, Yorkshire, WR
new vicarage 1957

Stainton, Yorkshire, NR
window glazing (Harvey) 1972
inscription N. Dickins 1972
lighting installation – abandoned

Stainton, Yorkshire, WR
boiler flue 1952
light fittings 1955
inscription G. T. Skelton Cook

Standish, Lancashire
electrical installation with light fittings to
vestry 1962
reordering Standish Chapel 1962: light
pendants, credence, housling bench,
adaption of pews, altar table, guard rail,
frontal chest, flower vase, candlesticks,
frontal
east window glazing (Stammers) 1963
fabric repairs 1963, 66–7, 69
restoration monuments 1965–6
sanctuary memorial stalls and kneeling desk
1966
alms dish 1967

light fittings 1952 (adapted 1982)
decorations 1952
additions to war memorial 1952
font cover 1953
standard candlesticks 1957
new window south-west nave 1958
stained glass (Spear) chancel 1958
chancel walls stone lining 1958
brass plaque – Needham – 1960

Tinsley Vicarage, Yorkshire, WR
alterations 1955

Tintern, St Mary on the Hill, Monmouthshire
proposed controlled ruin 1973

Todwick, Yorkshire, WR
fabric repairs 1957, 63, 67–8, 74
window glazing east window 1963 – revised 1976
flagstaff 1967
reordering and extensions – abandoned 1970
tower cupboards 1972
porch roof dormer window 1974 – revised 1976
credence table
south porch doors
memorial plaques to Baker and to Sandford
pulpit light

Todwick Rectory, Yorkshire, WR
alterations 1955–6

Treeton, Yorkshire, WR
fabric repairs 1953, 64–6
electrical installation 1955
heating installation 1959
leaded glazing – clerestory windows, north aisle 1966
new vestries 1973

Trianglass, Brecknockshire
fabric repairs

U

Ugglebarnby, Yorkshire, NR
fabric repairs 1966
pulpit cross 1966

Upper Poppleton (York) Yorkshire, WR
candlesticks 1959, 61
chancel reordering 1960
altar cross 1961
decorations 1961, 72
light fittings 1962
flower-vase stand 1962
altar rails
frontal
credence
fabric repairs 1963, 65

V

Vaynor, Brecknockshire
alterations to tower roof

W

Wadworth, Yorkshire, WR
fabric repairs 1961–2, 65–6
south chapel reordering: priest's seat, credence shelf, altar rail, altar, flower vase, altar cross, altar candlesticks, altar frontal, chairs, reposition tombs
reordering of baptistry

Wainfleet, Lincolnshire
reglazing east window 1973

Wakefield Bridge Chapel, Yorkshire, WR
fabric repairs 1952, 54, 63, 69, 71–2

light fittings 1961

Wakefield Cathedral, Yorkshire, WR
bishop's throne 1974

Wakefield, Yorkshire, WR (Holy Trinity)
demolition advice 1955

Wales, Yorkshire, WR
entrance gates 1962
font cover 1962
processional candlestick 1968
alterations to porch – abandoned

Wallasey, Lancashire
reordering crossing

Walsden, Yorkshire, WR
major rebuilding after fire damage: Stage 1 1954–6; Stage 2 1956–9
furnishings and fittings 1956–8
crucifix (Roper figure) 1967

Walton, Yorkshire, WR
fabric repairs 1972
gospel candlestick

Walton-on-the-Hill, Lancashire
reordering chancel
light fittings

Warmsworth Rectory, Yorkshire, WR
alterations 1954

Warrington Church, Lancashire
fabric repairs
alterations to choir vestry
churchyard gate

Warter, Yorkshire, ER
mausoleum – fabric repairs

Wath upon Dearne, Yorkshire, WR
fabric repairs 1967–9
decoration to nave roof bosses 1969
churchyard gates
churchyard reordering

Welburn, Yorkshire, NR
proposed Lady Chapel – abandoned

Welbury, Yorkshire, NR
light fittings – abandoned 1953
fabric repairs 1965
decoration 1966

Wellingborough, Northamptonshire (All Hallows)
Bishop's chair 1969
hymn board 1969
bench 1971

Welwick, Yorkshire, ER
fabric repairs 1962
chancel reordering – abandoned

Wem, Shropshire
light fittings
lectern

Wentworth, Yorkshire, WR (Holy Trinity)
memorial window (Harvey) 1968
fabric repairs 1969
pulpit and lectern light 1970
new lectern

Wentworth Old Church, Yorkshire, WR
churchyard lantern 1969

Wentworth Vicarage, Yorkshire, WR
reconstruction 1952

West Norwood, London
reordering

West Melton, Yorkshire, WR
altar rails

West Melton Vicarage, Yorkshire, WR
proposed vicarage

West Rounton, Yorkshire, NR
electrical scheme – abandoned 1952
fabric repairs 1965–6, 68, 70
decoration 1966
leaded glazing: chancel south window, vestry window 1970

Westow, Yorkshire, ER
reconstruction and modification to south porch 1973

Whalley, Lancashire
war memorial 1950
fabric repairs 1955, 68

Whiston, Yorkshire, WR
fabric repairs 1956
reforming tower parapets 1956
light fittings 1956
tower arch screen – abandoned 1967
decorations 1972
churchyard reordering 1973
font cover – abandoned
frontal

Whitburn, Co. Durham
proposed font

Whitechapel, Yorkshire, WR
electrical installation

Whitgift, Yorkshire, ER
fabric repairs 1966–7
wafer box 1967
proposed reordering 1967
processional cross 1970
churchyard reordering 1973

Whitley Lower (Dewsbury), Yorkshire, WR
fabric repairs 1962
proposed new roof to aisles 1967
decorations 1968

Whittlesey, Northamptonshire
window glazing 1969
fabric repairs 1970–1

Whorton in Cleveland, Yorkshire, NR
alterations to chancel

Wickersley, Yorkshire, WR
fabric repairs 1957–9
decorations 1960, 67
west window 1967

Wickersley Vicarage, Yorkshire, WR
improvements 1950

Wilberfoss, Yorkshire, ER
pulpit 1965

Wilmslow, Cheshire (St Bartholomew)
alterations to churchyard
proposed extensions – Schemes A – F
reredos panels
memorial Jackson Family

Wilton in Cleveland, Yorkshire, NR
fabric repairs 1969
pendant lights – abandoned
flower vase
wafer box

Wilton le Wold, Lincolnshire
memorial – Smith 1966

Windermere, Westmorland
font cover 1958 (revised top 1962)
new vestry extensions 1961
standard candlesticks W.I. 1961

Windsor Castle, Berkshire, (St George's Chapel)
King George VI Memorial Chapel 1969
Canon's stalls to nave 1972
memorials – Major Clough, Brigadier Byrne Furze, Canon Armstrong
choir stalls and nave lights, nave altar and furnishings – abandoned

formation of vestries, western store –
  abandoned
reordering King Edward IV Chantry Chapel
  – abandoned
formation of new tourist entrance below
  ground level with bookshop and treasury
  – abandoned
memorials – Canon Ritchie, W. Harris, Sir
  Isaac Heard, Canon Verny (carved by
  G.G.P.)

Windsor Castle, Berkshire, St George's House
proposed lecture room and library

Wombwell, Yorkshire, WR
decorations 1955
standard candlesticks 1958
completion of west tower 1960–2
altar table
tract table
proposed reordering

Womersley, Yorkshire, WR
fabric repairs 1952, 68–71
decoration 1954
new base for antique cross 1966
new bracket sanctuary lamp 1967
tower window glazing 1968
churchyard notice board 1970

Woodlands (Doncaster), Yorkshire, WR
fabric repairs 1961, 63
light fittings 1962
decorations 1963
electrical installation 1963
memorial seat – abandoned

Woodsetts, Yorkshire, WR
light fittings 1970

Woolston, Lancashire
new church with fittings and furnishings
  1970

Worsborough, St Mary's, Yorkshire, WR
fabric repairs 1961, 65–7, 69
south porch doors 1966
war memorial 1967, 70
nave north door – abandoned 1968
Elmhirst memorial inscription
window glazing to nave and vestry

Worsborough Bridge, Yorkshire, WR
electrical installation 1952

Worsborough Common, Yorkshire, WR
vestry alterations 1955
window glazing 1955

Worsborough Dale, Yorkshire, WR
reordering chancel 1954: high altar, altar,
  kneelers, stone altar pace and stone
  paving, aumbry door, inscription, choir
  placed at west end of nave
south chapel furnishing 1954: kneelers, altar
  pace, aumbry, altar, cross, candlesticks,
  light fittings

Worsborough Dale Vicarage, Yorkshire, WR
alterations 1956

Wortley, Yorkshire, WR
altar table 1955
fabric repairs 1955–6
reglazing east window 1968
decorations 1968

Wortley Vicarage, Yorkshire, WR
new parsonage house 1953

Wrentham, Suffolk
reordering south aisle 1967: altar table,
  candlestick, fair linen cloth, missal cushion

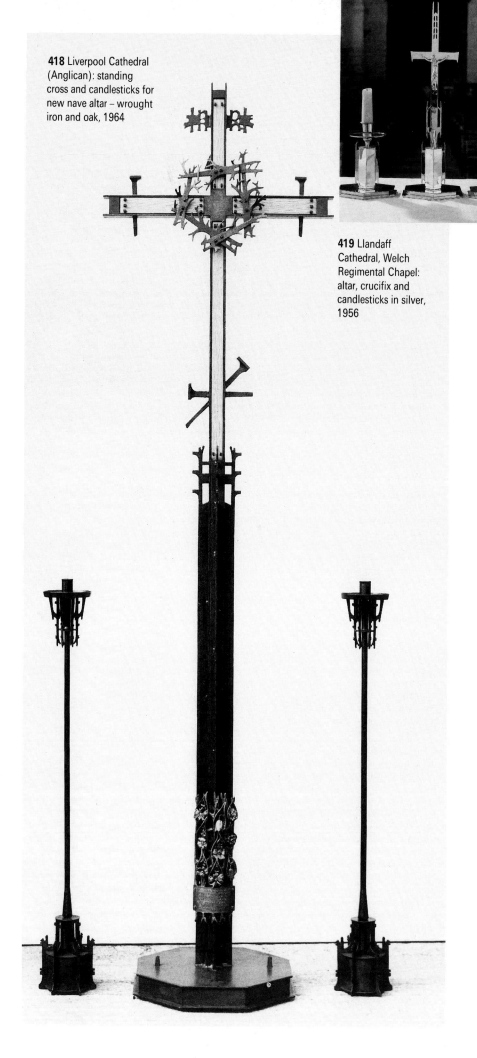

418 Liverpool Cathedral (Anglican): standing cross and candlesticks for new nave altar – wrought iron and oak, 1964

419 Llandaff Cathedral, Welch Regimental Chapel: altar, crucifix and candlesticks in silver, 1956

420 James the Deacon, Acomb, York: altar crucifix, and candlesticks in oak, 1955

421 Selby Abbey, War Memorial Chapel: altar crucifix, and candlesticks in silver, 1955

422 Intake, Doncaster: processional cross in hammered wrought-iron with silver centre-piece, and oak stave, 1959

423 Prototype processional cross in cast aluminium for unidentified church, undated (late 1960s)

Wyberton, Lincolnshire
reordering apse: hanging cross, window glazing, flower vase, altar frontal, fair linen cloth, Consecration cross, war memorial

Wydale Hall, Yorkshire, ER
formation of chapel 1967: seats, housling benches, altar table, light fittings, candlesticks, flower vase, hanging cross, pews, lectern

Wymering, Hampshire
proposed extensions

Wythenshawe (Manchester), Lancashire
new William Temple Memorial Church (and parsonage) with all furnishings and fittings 1965–6

Y

Yapham, Yorkshire, ER
font cover 1961

Yearsley, Yorkshire, NR
fabric repairs 1967, 68
decoration

York, Yorkshire:
—Acomb Holy Redeemer
new church incorporating parts of the medieval Bishophill Senior, with all furnishings and fittings 1962–5

—*Acomb Moor (James the Deacon) Moor Lane Estate, Dringhouses*
dual-purpose church/hall with furnishings and fittings 1956

—*Acomb (James the Deacon) Moor Lane*
Parsonage House 1960

—*Acomb (James the Deacon), Woodthorpe*
new church with furnishings and fittings 1970–1

—*All Saints, North Street*
fabric repairs 1968

—*Archbishop Holgate's School Chapel in the Dining Room*
furnishings 1966: cross, window glazing, altar, candlesticks, missal stand, dining tables and benches

—*Butchers Hall, Shambles*
entrance inscription 1952

—*Chase Hotel*
alterations 1946

—*Clifton Church (St Phillip and St James)*
fabric repairs 1958
decorations 1958

—*Clifton Lawn, Shipton Road*
alterations to drawing room and gardens

—*15 Clifton Green*
new house – abandoned 1973

—*18 Clifton Green (Architect's own house)*
alterations 1954, 60, 65

—*Derwent Plastics Factory, Hull Road*
new factory – sketch designs 1945–8 – abandoned

—*Holy Trinity, Heworth*
fabric repairs 1958–9
decorations 1959
churchyard gates – abandoned
proposed reordering

—*Holy Trinity, Micklegate*
fabric repairs 1951, 56–7, 61–2, 65, 68, 71
new font with existing cover revised 1951
altar rails
St Nicholas Chapel – frontal
war memorial
organ and organ screen 1965
electrical installation 1967
notice board 1967

—*Jacob's Well, Trinity Lane*
restoration – abandoned 1969

—*Kings Manor, University of York*
restoration of Royal coat of arms 1972

—*4 Minster Yard*
curtain pelmets 1949

—*Norman House, Stonegate*
fabric repair 1967
notice board 1969
landscaping – paving

—*Rawcliffe (St Mark's)*
dual-purpose building
new church and hall with furnishings and fittings 1967–9

—*St Aelred's*
reordering chancel: priest's seat, aumbry, seat and desk for weddings

—*St Clement's*
fabric repairs 1961, 64–5, 67
aumbry 1963
sanctuary lamp 1963
lighting installation

—*St Cuthbert's, Peasholme Green*
proposed alterations to chancel – abandoned

—*St Helen's*
window glazing 1958, 63–4
fabric repairs 1959, 61, 66
organ-case 1959
electrical installation 1960
reordering sanctuary 1960
decorations 1964
heating installation 1966, 71
memorial plate – Saville 1968
hanging crucifix 1968

—*St John's, Ousebridge*
fabric repairs 1952–3
window glazing 1953–4

—*St John's College (Old) Chapel*
refurnishing east end and creation of oratory 1954–6
ciborium high altar
candlesticks
priest's stall
cross
south screen
light fittings
extensions to chapel – abandoned 1955, 59
alterations to gallery 1962 with statues (Alan Durst)

—*St John's College Chapel*
new chapel with furnishings and fittings 1965–7, 69

—*St John's College boathouse*
new boathouse 1957

—*St Martin-cum-Gregory*
fabric repairs 1956–60
proposed office building in churchyard – abandoned
proposed centre for York Diocesan Youth Council – abandoned

—*St Martin le Grand*
major reconstruction and alterations to form chapel and memorial shrine with all furnishings and fittings 1956–68
fabric repairs 1961, 70
organ 1967
reredos (F. Roper) 1968

—*St Mary Bishophill the Elder*
supervision of demolition 1965

—*St Mary Bishophill Junior*
moving organ to tower area 1950
reredos south aisle chapel 1962
window glazing 1964

fabric repairs 1966, 68–9
reordering chancel 1969
furnishing north chapel

—*St Mary's Castlegate*
fabric repairs 1965–6, 68
conversion to Heritage Centre
1974–5 – unfinished (completed by R.
Sims 1976)

—*St Michael le Belfry*
fabric repairs 1963
restoration of reredos and monuments
roof panels decoration
portable font
tract units
hymn-book racks

—*St Michael, Spurriergate*
fabric repairs 1963, 67–9
reordering interior 1965: paving, formation
western entrance lobby, restoration of
reredos and monuments, altar frontal,
crucifix
proposed formation of offices in north aisle –
abandoned
new tower roof (tower lowered)
tower window glazing
conversion of chest into collecting box
organ (removed to Lund)
new ceiling to nave and aisles

—*St Olave's Church*
fabric repairs 1953, 55–8, 61
organ-case 1953
formation war memorial chapel 1953: altar
rail, altar
collecting box 1955
sanctuary lamp north-east chapel 1956
Thornton Memorial restoration 1957
B.V.M. statue setting 1959
hymn boards 1959
electrical installation 1963
decoration 1963
font cover 1963
candlesticks 1964
Stations of the Cross (Harvey) 1965
vicar's board 1968
memorial belt 1970
tract table 1970
chasuble and high mass vestments set – sub-
deacons dalmatic 1973 (Rosamund Angus)

—*St Peter's School Chapel*
war memorial 1950
decorations 1955
light fittings 1956
western gallery 1956
narthex 1956
Burgess memorial stall 1956
fabric repairs 1964
gable cross

—*St Sampsons*
fabric repairs 1956–8, 74
formation of old people's centre with small
chapel 1974

—*St William's College*
fabric repairs 1954–5, 60
decoration 1966
alterations to ground-floor office

—*Treasurer's House*
fabric repairs 1954–5, 60
cloakroom 1955
proposed second-floor flats – abandoned
fireplace to dining room
light fitting

—*Westminster Bank, Coney Street*
restoration of the Beckett Crest 1968

York Minster
W.I. gates to crypt – abandoned 1946
Dean Milner White Memorial: inscription –
camera cantorum (south transept) 1967
collecting boxes 1968

Ystradfellte, Brecknockshire
light fittings

PUBLICATIONS, ARTICLES, LECTURES, TALKS AND EXHIBITIONS 1938-75

Note: many of the smaller articles, lectures, and talks were not published in any form and remain either as typescript, or as more often, rough handwritten notes. These are placed together with unfinished major works in the records of George Pace retained by the author.

1938–46:

'East Anglian Niches, being some observations on their use during the Perpendicular period' – thesis for RIBA Finals, presented to the RIBA Library, 1938–39.

Report on a scheme for the regular *inspection of churches* (IC) in the diocese of Sheffield, January 1940 – (prepared before the introduction of the Statutory Measure and in some ways its precursor).

'Bed-heads in the Home Counties' – illustrated article in *Architect and Building News*, 17 January 1941. Also published in *Monumental and Architectural Stone Journal*, March 1941.

'The Great and little contrasts' – an article on the 'Contrasts' produced by William Twopenny and Pugin. Sent to N. Pevsner, Editor, *Architectural Review* (unpublished) 1942.

'Alfred Bartholomew – A pioneer of functional Gothic' – article on the research work of this early nineteenth-century architect who produced theories on the Gothic structural systems, published in the *Architectural Review*, 1 October 1942.

'A Critical Approach to Architectural History' – a lecture to York Georgian Society, 16 January 1943.

'Alia terranda via est' – illustrated article for new adjustable lamp (also designed by G. Pace) in *Architects' Journal*, 16 September 1943.

'The Public takes a Hand' – an article on the merits of re-building the bomb damaged church, St Michael le Grand, York. Submitted to N. Pevsner 21 February 1944 – for inclusion in *Architects' Journal* but not published.

'The Gothique Safes of York' – illustrated article in *Architectural Review*, April 1944.

'Prelude to Physical Reconstruction' – article about a new culture, submitted to the *Architects' Journal* (considered as a possible leader, but later refused as, 'an architectural weekly is not the place for political polemics', Ed.) 1945.

'Ecclesiology at Leeds' – article on the involvement of Pusey in the Gothic Revival church of St Saviour's, Leeds, published in *Architectural Review*, December 1945.

'Bedhead Embellishments' – illustrated article in *Architectural Review*, February 1946.

1947:

Review of *Modern Church Architecture* by Edward Maufe (Incorporated Church Building Society) in the *RIBA Journal*, 1947.

Review of *Fifty Modern Churches* by The Incorporated Church Building Society in the *RIBA Journal*, 1947.

Review of *Modern Church Design* by Richard Mellor in the *RIBA Journal*, 1947.

Review of *Post-War Church Building* edited by Ernest Short in *The Listener*, November 1947.

1948:

'Twentieth Century Church Architecture: 1890–1947' – contribution to *Chambers Encyclopaedia* 1948.

1949:

Llandaff Cathedral – 'Friends Annual Reports' 1949–75. (These and other Cathedral Reports contain many articles by G. Pace, mainly on the Cathedral works. Any articles of broader interest are recorded separately in this list as and when they occur.)

Lichfield Cathedral – 'Friends Annual Reports', 1949–75.

Review of *Old Churches and Modern Craftsmanship* by Alban Caroe in the *RIBA Journal*, 1949.

'St Mary's Church, Scarborough' – Notes prepared for article in the *Scarborough Evening News*, 29 June 1949.

1950:

Review of *The English Cathedrals* by Herbert Felton and John Harvey in *RIBA Journal*, 1950.

'First Impressions of Llandaff Cathedral' – a talk to the Friends, 1 July 1950.

1951:

'The Maintenance of Ancient Churches' – a memorandum submitted to the Church Assembly Commission on the Repair of Churches, sitting under the Chairmanship of Mr Ivor Bulmer Thomas, 28 September 1951.

1952:

'The New Church' – article in *St Mark's Church – An Appeal for its Rebuilding and Furnishing* – (outlining the context of building a modern church 'Today'). Undated (around 1952).

'The Planning of churches', 'The legal position', 'Town and Country Planning Act 1947 in relationship to church fabrics' – lectures in a course on Repair of Ancient Buildings, York Civic Trust Summer School 1952.

Lecture to course on 'Protection and Repair of Ancient Buildings', York Civic Trust Academic Development Committee. 8–20 September 1952.

1953:

Lecture to course on 'Protection and repair of Ancient Buildings', York Civic Trust Academic Development Committee, 23 March–4 April 1953.

'Church Arrangement and Layout', 'Practical Problems', and 'Organisation, Supervision and Costs of Repairs to Ancient Buildings' – lectures on the course 'Protection and Repair of Ancient Buildings', York Institute of Architectural Study, 23 March–4 April 1953.

'Church Administration', 'Church Planning' – lectures on the course on 'Protection and Repair of Ancient Buildings', York Civic Trust Academic Development Committee, 9–16 April 1953.

'Modern Tendencies in Church Building' – article in the *Church of England Newspaper*, 25 September 1953.

'Practical Problems' – lecture on 'Protection and Repair Course', York Civic Trust Academic Development Committee, 25 September 1953.

1954:

Durham Cathedral – 'Friends Annual Reports' 1954–75.

'Church Administration', 'Surveys, Church Planning costing' – lectures on the course 'Care of Churches', York Institute of Architectural Study, April 1954.

'Church arrangement and layout', 'costing and supervision', 'Practical Problems', – lectures on a course on 'Protection and Repair of Historic Buildings' at York Institute of Architectural Study, March and April 1954.

424 St Augustine's,
Birmingham: new vestries
from the north east and
plan, ink on tracing paper
(actual size)

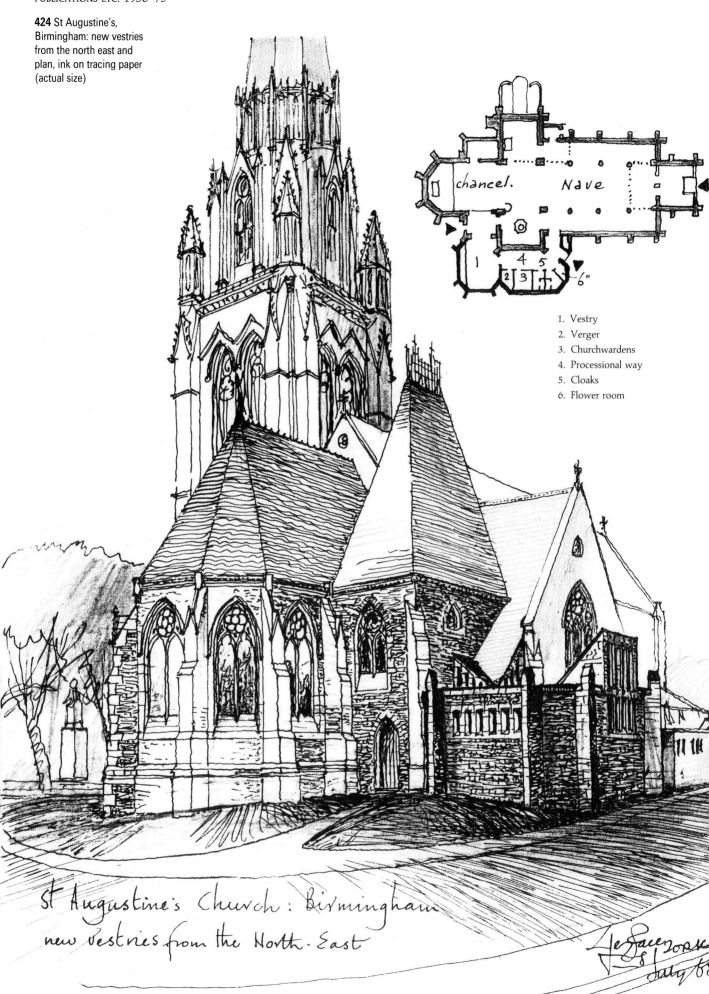

chancel. Nave

1. Vestry
2. Verger
3. Churchwardens
4. Processional way
5. Cloaks
6. Flower room

St Augustine's Church: Birmingham
new vestries from the North·East

'Repair of Timber Buildings' – lecture on the course on 'Protection and Repair of Historic Buildings' at the York Institute of Architectural Study, 13–18 September 1954.

1955:

Talk to the Friends of Lichfield Cathedral in the nave, 26 June 1955.

'Church Planning I – Fabric', 'Church Planning II – Fittings', 'costing and supervision of work'; discussion of practical problems for lectures in the course 'Care of Churches' at the York Institute of Architectural Study, 14–20 September 1955.

1956:

Peterborough Cathedral – 'Friends Annual Reports' 1956–75.

Review of *The Modern Church* by Edward D. Mills in the *RIBA Journal* 1956.

Conference on 'Architectural Office Management' – G. Pace, Chairman of York Institute of Architectural Study, 6–10 January 1956.

'Organisation, Supervision and Costing' and 'Practical Problems' – lectures on the course on 'Protection and Repair of Historic Buildings', York Institute of Architectural Study, 11–20 April 1956.

'The Restoration of Llandaff Cathedral' – talk to the Friends on 30 June 1956.

Review of *Studies in Architectural History Vol. II*, (York Institute of Architectural Study) in the *Yorkshire Evening Press*, 23 August 1956.

'On Designing New Churches' – an introduction (pp. 4–10) in the catalogue to an 'Exhibition of Post-war Church Buildings', arranged by the Central Council for the Care of Churches, 1956–57.

1957:

Review of '*Neue Kirchen in Erzbistum Köln – 1945–56*' by Willy Weyres, in the *RIBA Journal* 1957.

'Victorian Architecture in York' – a paper in the *York and East Yorkshire Architectural Society Year Book 1956–57* (pp. 20–35).

'Site Organization, supervision and costing': 'Practical Problems': lectures in the course on 'Protection and Repair of Historic Buildings', York Institute of Architectural Study 2–11 April 1957.

'Restoration' – a radio programme on Llandaff Cathedral broadcast on the West Home Service, BBC Radio with the Most Revd John Morgan, Rt Revd Glyn Simon, G. G. Pace, Revd Moelwyn Merchant, R. L. Charles, A. J. Chandler and the Very Revd Eryl Thomas, 10 April 1957.

'Church Surveys', 'Church Planning' and 'Practical Problems' – lectures in the course 'The Care of Churches', York Institute of Architectural Study, 11–16 April 1957.

'The Restoration of Llandaff Cathedral' – lecture delivered to the Ecclesiological Society in London, 7 December 1957 at The College of Preceptors in Bloomsbury.

1958:

'Yorkshire, North Riding' – a personal selection of churches published in *Collins Guide to English Parish Churches* edited by John Betjeman, 1958.

Article 'Landaff Cathedral Restoration 1946–57' in the *South Wales Institute of Architects' Journal*, Vol. 2, No. 1, January 1958 (pp. 2–6).

'Roof Coverings', 'Site Organization and Costings', 'Practical Problems' – lectures in course on 'Protection and Repair of Historic Buildings' at The York Institute of Architectural Study, 25–28 March 1958.

'Church Planning, Practical Problems' – lectures in the course 'Care of Churches' at The York Institute of Architectural Study, 30 March–2 April 1958.

Lecture to The Cardiff Civic Society on 'Work at Llandaff Cathedral' – Reardon Smith Lecture Theatre, 22 April 1958.

'New Approaches to Church Building' – article in *St Martin's* (in the Field, London) *Review*, May 1958, No. 806 (pp. 134–137).

'A new Approach to Church Building' – article in the Welsh *Province* Magazine, Vol. IX, 1958 (pp. 37–39).

'Townscape' – a series of illustrated articles which appeared in the *Yorkshire Evening Press* over a number of months in 1958: 'Minster Yard', 9 May; 'A River View', 16 May; 'Our Streets', 23 May; 'Museum Street', 30 May; 'River Canyon, 6 June; 'St Helen's Square', 13 June; 'Kings Staith', 20 June; 'The Seeing Eye', 27 June; 'The Stonebow', 4 July; 'Unit of Habitation', July; 'A New Town (Harlow)', 18 July; 'The Old and the New', 25 July.

Talk on restoration work at The Friends of St Mary's, Scarborough, Annual General Meeting, 25 July 1958.

Exhibition – Royal Academy Summer Exhibition, London, 1958, where the following was displayed: Sheffield, St Mark's – New Church (model)

The York Institute of Architectural Study 'Church Inspection Conference'; participant 23–26 September 1958.

Review of 'Architectural History' The Journal of the Society of Architectural Historians of Great Britain Volume I; in the *Yorkshire Evening Press*, 7 November 1958.

Exhibition of Parsonage House Plans held by the Church Commissioners at Millbank House, London, including Intake Vicarage, Doncaster, 10–14 November 1958.

1959:

Review of *Kirchen Handbuch fur den Kirchenban* by Willy Weyres and Otto Bartning in the *RIBA Journal* 1959.

'Roof Covering', 'Site organization and costings – Practical Problems'. Lectures in the course 'Protection and Repair of Historic Buildings', The Institute of Advanced Architectural Studies, York, 27 April–8 May 1959.

'Church Planning, Practical Problems' – lectures in the course 'Care of Churches' at The Institute of Advanced Architectural Studies, York 8–13 May 1959.

'The Seeing Eye' – a series of 12 photographs of York shown in the *Yorkshire Evening Press* to encourage the 'endless aesthetic delights of the City', between May and October 1959.

'Sir Jacob Epstein, 1880–1959' – obituary published in the *Architects' Journal*, August 1959.

1960:

Contributions to *The Buildings of England – Yorkshire, The West Riding* by Dr N. Pevsner, 1960.

'Steps towards Building a New Church: The Church of England' – a paper submitted to the Christian Teamwork Organization, 1960.

'A plea for the Box Pew – Modern Adaptions': an article for the Central Council for the Care of Churches, 14th Report 1960, entitled *Both Old and New – Churches: their care and furnishing* (pp. 26–36).

Contribution to Roofing Committee publications by Central Council for the Care of Churches, 1960.

'Building New Churches' – contribution to a statement of advice suitable for use in briefing architects to design churches published by the Central Council for the Care of Churches on the instructions of The Church Assembly, 1960.

'Modern Church Architecture' – an article in the book *The Church and the Arts* (pp. 55–69). Edited by Frank Glendenning, SCM Press Ltd, 1960.

'A good church building is normally the finished work of a single designer briefed by the congregation and not closely controlled by the committee' – talk at the conference 'The Architect and the Church' held in London by Christian Teamwork, 4–5 March 1960.

'Roof Coverings: Practical Problems' – lecture in the course 'Protection and Repair of Historic Buildings', 13–16 March 1960 at The Institute of Advanced Architectural Studies, York.

'The Quinquennial Inspection (Q I)', 'Church Planning', 'The Churchyard', 'Practical Problems' – lectures in the course 'Care of Churches' 16–20 March 1960, at The Institute of Advanced Architectural Studies, York,

'Welsh Churches and Chapels – a National Heritage' – article in the *Western Mail*, 4 April 1960.

'Roof Coverings' and 'Discussion on Practical Problems' – lectures in the course – 'Protection and Repair of Historic Buildings', at The Institute of Advanced Architectural Studies, York, 26 April–5 May 1960.

'Church Planning I: The Fabric'; 'Church Planning II: Fittings', 'The Quinquennial Inspection' and 'The Churchyard' – lectures in the course 'The Care of Churches' at The Institute of Advanced Architectural Studies, York, 5–9 May 1960.

'Status and Emoluments' – a talk to the Cathedral Architects' Conference, Gloucester, 14 May 1960.

'Nineteenth Century Buildings in York', 28 June 1960 – lecture at The Institute of Advanced Architectural Studies, York, 28 June 1960 – part of a series for the York Festival June/July.

1961:

Chester Cathedral – 'Friends Annual Reports' 1961–75.

'Roof Coverings – Practical Discussion' – lectures in the course 'Protection and Repair of Historic Buildings', The Institute of Advanced Architectural Studies, York, 9–16 March 1961.

'The Q I', 'Church Planning', 'The Churchyard', 'Practical Problems' – lectures in the course 'Care of Churches', The Institute of Advanced Architectural Studies, York, 16–20 March 1961.

'Towards the Modern Church' – an article in the *Church of England Newspaper*, 28 April 1961.

'The Architectural problems which may arise in a Liturgical. Re-ordering and ways of solving these problems without spoiling old churches' – a paper delivered during a course held by the Department of Extra-Mural Studies, The University of Birmingham entitled 'The Liturgical Re-ordering of Existing Churches' at Attingham Park, Nr Shewsbury, May–June 1961.

'The Cathedral Architect today' (also referred to in other notes as 'The Chapter and its Architect') – talk at the Deans' Conference, Christ Church, Oxford, 11 July 1961.

'Art and Worship' – a BBC television programme in the series *Seeing and Believing* with the Dean of Llandaff, George Pace and Robert Joyce. Transmitted Sunday, 27 August 1961 from Cardiff.

'Modern Churches' – a paper delivered at the Bradford Diocesan Conference, Church House, Bradford, 2 December 1961.

1962:

St Alban's Cathedral – 'Friends Annual Reports': 1962–73.

Liverpool Anglican Cathedral – 'Friends Annual Reports': 1962–75.

Contribution to *New Churches of Great Britain* edited by E. D. Mills, 1962.

Chambers Encyclopaedia – revision to 'Church Architecture – Modern Trends' 1962.

Review of *English Monasteries in the Middle Ages*, by G. H. Cook in the *RIBA Journal* 1962.

Peterborough Cathedral – guidelines for the Dean and Chapter when considering any proposed alterations to the environment around the Cathedral precincts 1962. (Revised 1963, 71).

'The York Aesthetic' – major article in the *York Civic Trust Annual Report*, 1961–62.

Contribution to *Building New Churches*, prepared by the Central Council for the Care of Churches, 1962; published by Church Information Office, London.

'Principles and Precepts – The Importance of not spoiling old churches by a scheme of Re-ordering' – article in a book *Making the Building serve the Liturgy* edited by Gilbert Cope, A. R. Mowbray & Co. 1962 (based on paper delivered at Attingham Park Conference May–June 1961).

Address to the Yorkshire W. R. Society of Architects, Bradford Chapter AGM, 4 April 1962.

'Church Architecture – A Practising Architect's Viewpoint' – a paper delivered at the Cambrian Archaeological Association Easter Conference – Church Architecture in Wales, 26 April 1962 at St David's College, Lampeter, Cardiganshire.

'Artists Serve the Church' – contribution to an exhibition of modern religious work organized by the Exhibition Committee of the Coventry Cathedral Festival 1962, held at the Herbert Art Gallery and Museum, Coventry, 2 June 1962.

'Church Architecture Today' – lecture at the Concord Club, Manchester University, 18 June 1962.

'Architecture and Craftsman' – lecture at The Art Workers' Guild, 6 Queen Square, Bloomsbury WC1, 4 July 1962; some of the craftsmen who worked for George Pace also spoke – Mr Crisp Jones (silversmith), Mr Patrick Reyntiens (stained glass artist), Mr Dowson (blacksmith) and Mr Dunstan Pruden (silversmith).

Exhibition – Royal Academy Summer Exhibition, London, 1962: The Completion of Sheffield Cathedral Drawing

Contribution to *Cathedrals of England* 3: 'Lichfield'. Broadcast by the BBC on the Home Service, 19 August 1962 (also broadcast in the BBC General Overseas Services 10 April).

'Architecture and Architect in the Service of the Church' – a major paper presented at a conference arranged by the Department of Extra-mural Studies, the University of Liverpool, in Rathbone Hall, entitled 'The Modern Architectural Setting of the Liturgy', 19 September 1962.

'Modern Churches' – Talk to the Clifton Young People's Club, York, 14 October 1962.

'The Modern Church' – lecture to the Harrogate Chapter: WR Yorkshire Society of Architects, Granby Hotel, Harrogate, 6 November 1962.

'Architecture and Religious Communication' – a lecture in a series entitled 'The Communication of Religious Knowledge and Religious Experience', held at the University of Leeds Institute of Education, 30 October 1962.

'William Butterfield 1814–1900' – extracts from a fuller article in the *Official Opening and Dedication* booklet for an extension to Pollington cum Balne Church of England School, 19 December 1962. (The full text is deposited in the School Library).

1963:

'Worship and Architecture' – a monumental work encompassing an earlier unfinished book, *New Churches* (1940–45), begun in 1963 and constantly being added to, typed out, but it remained uncompleted.

'Durham Cathedral Processional Cross' – article in

Friends of Durham Cathedral Thirteenth Annual Report describing Harry Wilson's work, 1962–63.

'The Work of a Cathedral Architect Today' – article in the Thirteenth Annual Report of the Fraternity of the Friends of St Alban's Abbey, 1963.

Judging of 1963 Design Competition for Bradford Branch West Yorkshire Society of Architects – Student Prizes Project set by G. Pace – a small crematorium: a private chapel: a memorial lychgate.

Review of *The Architectural Requirements of Protestant Worship*, by Victor Fiddes, in the *RIBA Journal* 1963.

Review of *The Architectural Setting of Baptism* by J. G. Davies in the *RIBA Journal* 1963.

'Modern Embroideries for Church, Home and Office' – contribution to an exhibition at Guildford House, Guildford. 1963.

'St Mark's Church' – article in the *New Guide to St Mark's Church, Sheffield* upon its completion and consecration 1963, (with articles by the vicar, Revd Michael Adie, Harry J. Stammers and John Piper).

'Skipton High Street Improvement Scheme' – an exhibition sponsored by the High Street Improvement Committee of the Skipton-in-Craven Civic Society, 11–15 January 1963, (photographs, drawings, reports and introduction speech).

'Ecclesiastical Architecture' – talk to Centre of Further Education, Marygate, York, 5 April 1963.

'Cost Control' – lecture at The Institute of Advanced Architectural Studies, York, in the series entitled 'Church Building: A Programme of Research', 16–18 April 1963.

Address to the Friends and Builders of Liverpool Cathedral Annual Festival, at the Cathedral, on the 'Life and Work of Sir Giles Scott', 25 May 1963.

'Roofing Materials for New Churches – Maintenance' – an article in *Maintenance and Equipment News for Churches*, June 1963.

'Church Restoration' – talk at the thirteenth AGM of the Friends of St Mary's, Scarborough. 30 June 1963.

'Modern Church Design' – lecture at the University College of Swansea, Department of Extra-mural Studies, Extension Course 'Architecture Today' at Berwick House, Swansea, 19 November 1963.

Exhibition – Royal Academy Summer Exhibition, London, 1963, where drawings of Durham University Library were displayed.

'The Re-ordering of Existing Churches' – a lecture in a series on 'Modern Church Architecture' held by the University of Sheffield, Department of Extra-mural Studies, 25 November 1963.

'The Problems presented by Victorian Churches'. Lecture to the Architecture Society, The University of Nottingham, 5 December 1963.

Lecture to Lichfield Theological College, 2–3 December 1963.

1964:

'Church Art and Architecture' – review of New Church, St Mary's Priory, Leyland, in the *Clergy Review* (The Tablet Publishing Co. Ltd, London) 1964.

'Architecture and Architect in the Service of the Church' – a major article in the book *The Modern Architectural Setting of the Liturgy* edited by William Lockett, SPCK, 1964. (Based on a paper delivered to the Liverpool Conference 19 September 1962).

Review of *Out of the Ashes* by Basil Spence and Henk Snoek in *Anglican World*, January 1964.

'The Keele Chapel' – an article in *Ichthus* (Keele University Christian Paper) February 1964.

'Modern Churches' – lecture to St Michael's Theological College, Llandaff, 6 February 1964.

'Building Repairs' – talk to the Nottingham Centre of the Institute of Builders' Discussion Club at the Midland Design and Building Centre, Nottingham, 21 February 1964.

'Rebirth of Llandaff Cathedral' – lecture to the Cardiff Naturalists' Society, 12 March 1964.

'The Re-ordering of Victorian Churches' – a lecture to the Faregate Society at Shire Hall, Worcester, 18 March 1964.

Review of *Churches and Public Buildings* by Helen Mary Petter in *Anglican World*, April 1964.

Review of *The Building of the Eighteenth Century Church* by Basil F. L. Clarke in the *Anglican World*, April 1964.

'The Church and the New Town' – lecture at the Annual Conference of the Society of Christian Artists, Willersely Castle, Cranford, Derbyshire, 7–10 April 1964.

Exhibition of 48 new parsonage houses commissioned by the Church Commissioners, held at Institute of Advanced Architectural Studies, University of York, Micklegate, 1–16 May 1964 (including the parsonage house at William Temple Memorial Church, Woodhouse, Wythenshawe, Manchester by G. Pace).

'Surveys and Reports: Grants' – lecture in the course 'Restoration of Georgian Buildings' at The Institute of Advanced Architectural Studies, 11 May 1964, with directed tour of Castle Howard in conjunction with G. Howard and Prof. Thompson, 13 May 1964.

Talk to the Society of the Friends of Chester Cathedral, 20 June 1964.

'St Mark's Church Sheffield' – a talk to Sheffield Society of Architects and Surveyors, 27 June 1964.

'The Chapel Complex at Keele and the New Cathedral at Ibadan' – talk on current work, at The Institute of Advanced Architectural Studies, York University, 12 July 1964. (Other speakers included David Crease, James Stirling, Colin St John Wilson, Cedric Price and William Whitfield.)

'Ecumenical Architecture' – article in *Llandaff Cathedral Magazine*, September 1964.

'Ecumenical Architecture' – a talk to York Round Table, October 1964.

Revised *History of the Church of Holy Trinity, Christchurch, Newport*, October 1964.

'The Church and the Arts today' – talk at the conference held at St Mary's Roman Catholic Church, Leyland, for senior pupils from Preston and District arranged by the Student Christian Movement in Schools, 27 November 1964.

'Modern Churches' – lecture to the Theological Society, St Peter's School, York, November 1964.

1965:

'Modern Churches' – lecture to Church Union, Bridlington, 3 February 1965.

Series of lectures to St Michael's Theological College, Llandaff, 11 February 1965.

'St Mary's Luton' – talk at the Inauguration of the Friends of Luton Parish Church, 19 February 1965.

'Modern Church Buildings' – talk to the Wesley Brotherhood, Wesley Chapel, Priory Street, York, 22 February 1965.

Review of *The New Churches of Europe* by Kidder Smith in *RIBA Journal* March 1965.

'The Architects Approach to Architecture' – talk to the Ecclesiastical Architects' and Surveyors' Association, 28 May 1965 at Skipton.

'The Architecture of Selby' – a Festival lecture at the Hawdon Institute, Selby, 12 June 1965.

'Modern Church Architecture with reference to an understanding of the Liturgy' – a talk for the Westcott House Refresher Course, Cambridge, 16 June 1965.

Exhibition – Royal Academy Summer Exhibition, London, 1965, where the following drawings were displayed: 'Llandaff Cathedral – The Restoration' and 'Ibadan Cathedral – (model)'.

Tour of redundant churches in York led by Dr E. A. Gee and G. Pace for members of the York Georgian Society, 7 July 1965.

'Building in Nigeria' – talk to York 41 Club, 13 July 1965.

'An Approach to Church Decoration and Furnishing, with reference to Elloughton Church, E. Yorkshire' – talk to the Reconstruction Committee.

Conference – 'Building a New Church' held by Society of Church Artists – an association of Methodists interested in the visual arts – at Penarth, S. Wales, 27–30 July 1965; when a tour of Llandaff Cathedral and College and the New Lutheran Church in Cardiff was led by G. Pace.

Notes on the history of All Saints' Parish Church, Branston, prepared for Mr Deverill for inclusion in the new *History and Guide to the Church*, 18 December 1965.

1966:

Newcastle Cathedral – 'Friends Annual Reports' 1966–75.

Contribution to *Collins Guide to English Parish Churches, Yorkshire: The West Riding* (with J. Hutchinson and R. G. Sims) 1966.

Contribution to second edition of *The Buildings of England*, Yorkshire, West Riding volume by Nikolaus Pevsner, 1964–66.

'Modern Churches' – talk to Copmanthorpe Wesleyan Church, York, 17 February 1966.

'Victorian Architecture in Yorkshire' – lecture to York Georgian Society, 18 February 1966.

'The Repair of Ancient Buildings' – a talk to the Chartered Auctioneers' and Estate Agents' Institute of Leeds at the Chase Hotel, York, 23 March, 1966.

'The Rise of Modern Architecture' – a lecture given at St John's College, York, 26 March, 1966.

'Modern Church Architecture' – a lecture to the Newman Association, York Circle, 26 April 1966 at the IAAS Micklegate, York.

'The Architect and the Church' – a BBC TV programme in the series *Viewpoint* where George Pace was questioned by The Ven. Hetley Price with The Ven. George Youell and Canon Philip Lamb, showing many of George Pace's works 'in which he describes the discipline required to raise or preserve a building which is a perpetual Act of Worship in its mere existence'. Transmitted on 27 April 1966 (details in Radio Times, 21 April 1966). (Film is destroyed but typed script remains.)

'Victorian Architecture in York' – a lecture in the series 'York as a City and its Place in National History', given to The Institute of Advanced Architectural Studies, University of York, in the Tempest Anderson Hall, 19 May 1966.

'Modern Churches' – talk to the Newman Society at The Institute of Advanced Architectural Studies, York, 24 May 1966.

'Within our Churches – Beauty or Utility?' – an article in *Church News* July 1966. Edited by Revd Canon Cecil Rhodes.

'Origins of Modern Architecture' – lecture to Nunthorpe Grammar School, York, 4 July, 1966.

Exhibition in West Berlin of model and drawings for Ibadan University College Chapel and Ibadan Cathedral, 1966.

Exhibition of work at Biennale Christlichur Künst Der Gegenwart, Salzburg, September 1966.

'The Architects of Peterborough Cathedral' – talk in the nave at the Annual Gathering of Friends, 24 September 1966, (also published in the *Friends of Peterborough Cathedral Annual Report* 1967).

'An Architect's View of Selby' – lecture in the Selby Abbey Stewardship Lecture series, 3 October 1966.

'An Architect's View of Selby' – lecture to Women's Institute at Brayton, near Selby, 4 October 1966.

'Origins of Modern Architecture' – talk to Bradford Grammar School, 12 October 1966.

'Liturgy and Architecture' – a talk to the Christian Education Movement, York Association at St John's College, York, 21 October 1966.

'Modern Church Architecture and Church Restorations' – lecture to the Kingston Ecclesiological Society, the University Catholic Chaplaincy, Hull, 25 October 1966.

'University of Keele: the chapel' – an article in the *University of Keele Chapel Guide* (pp. 9–11) November 1966.

'Modern Churches' – talk to West Riding Adult Education Centre, Wetherby, 3 November 1966.

'Principles of Design for the Teaching Church' – lecture at the Conference 'Design for the Teaching Church', Birmingham Diocesan Council for Religious Education, St Martin's Hall, Birmingham, 12 November 1966.

'Modern Church Architecture' – lecture to Bedfordshire Society of Architects, 18 November 1966.

'Wakefield Bridge Chapel' – talk to a Public Meeting, Wakefield, 23 November 1966.

'Modern Church Architecture', 'Church Architecture' and 'Maintenance and Repair' – a series of talks to Lichfield Theological College, 1/2 December 1966.

1967:

'Church Architecture' – a lecture at St Michael's College, Llandaff, 19 January 1967.

'The structure of Georgian Buildings' – a lecture in series entitled *Adaption and Restoration of Georgian Buildings* held on a one-day seminar, Department of Architecture, University of Bristol, 20 January 1967.

'Modern Churches' – a lecture to Clifton Men's Society, York, 6 February 1967.

'Christian Layman speaks to Layman' – a talk as part of a series at Leicester Cathedral, 14 February 1967 forming part of the Fortieth Anniversary Commemoration of the restored See of Leicester. Published in *Leicester Cathedral Quarterly* Vol. 6, No 3, July 1967.

York and East Yorkshire Architectural Society – York Chapter – talk by G. Pace with other architects David Brown and Tom Adams about their work, 16 February 1967.

'Modern Churches' – lecture to St Peter's School Art Society, York, 18 February 1967.

'Two Modern Christian Artists' – an exhibition of the work of John Piper and George Pace, Derwent College, University of York, 6–17 March 1967.

'The Seeing Eye in Selby' – talk to Selby Women's Conservative Supper Club, 12 April 1967.

'Future Plans for the Cathedral' – a talk to the Friends of St Nicholas Cathedral, Newcastle, at their AGM in the Cathedral Library, 20 April 1967.

'Cathedral – Maintenance, Restoration Appeals' – notes for the Cathedrals Advisory Committee read on behalf of G. Pace. Contribution to catalogue for exhibition of Lichfield Cathedral Choir Hangings, prepared by the Council for the Care of Churches, June 1967.

'Victorian Architecture – Yorkshire' – inaugural lecture to the Victorian Society: Anglo-American Tour at the Old Swan Hotel, Harrogate, 5 June 1967.

The Friends of Lichfield Cathedral Annual Festival Garden Party – address in the nave by the architect, 17 June 1967.

'The New Vestments' – article in the *St Alban's Abbey Magazine*, August 1967.

'University and School Chapels' – paper read to conference of chaplains of universities and schools entitled 'Planning for Student Worship', St John's College, York, 11–15 September 1967.

'Historic Churches and Repairs' – lecture at Whirlow Grange, Sheffield, 19 September 1967.

The Friends of St Mary's, Hitchin, AGM. Talk on the church restoration at Hitchin and at famous cathedrals and churches throughout the country, 29 September 1967.

'Modern Church Architecture' – a lecture to the Northamptonshire, Bedfordshire and Huntingdonshire Association of Architects, 12 October 1967.

1968:

'The Collegiate and Parish Church of St Edith, Tamworth – a walk-round guide, 1968.

Entry for 'Durham University Library' *Modern Architecture of Northern England* – edited by Bruce Allsop, Oriel Press. 1968.

'Modern Churches' – entry in *Chambers' Encyclopaedia* Church Architecture Section, revised 1968 (original 1948).

'Georgian Churches in Yorkshire' – a lecture to the York Georgian Society, 20 January 1968 (later published in *York and County* magazine March 1968).

'Georgian Churches of Yorkshire' – lecture to the Yorkshire Archaeological Society, Georgian Section, at Park Place, Bradford, 3 April 1968.

Fifteenth Annual Conference for the Secretaries of the Diocesan Advisory Committees (DAC) for the Care of Churches at St Edmund's Hall, Oxford, arranged by the Council for the Care of Churches. G. Pace, Chairman for morning session on 'churchyards', 25 April 1968.

'Rushmere 800 + ' – A commemorative brochure, 30 June 1968, with short article on the new works, contributed by G. Pace.

'Chester Cathedral – New Bellhouse' – article in *The Ringing World*, 1 July 1968.

'The Seeing Eye' – address to Roade Secondary School, Northamptonshire, Speech Day, 5 July 1968. (The school made wooden pendant light fittings designed by G. Pace for the Parish Church).

Exhibition – Royal Academy Summer Exhibition, London, 1968, where the following drawings were displayed: Kirk Sandall – rebuilding medieval church in enlarged form on a new site; Windsor Castle, St George's Chapel – King George VI Memorial Chapel and Luton, St Mary's Church – New Hall.

Annual Conference of the National Association of Master Monumental Stone Masons, St John's College, York. Exhibition of 100 pieces of work judged by G. Pace, 7–12 September 1968.

'The Restoration of Fishlake Church' (Yorkshire, WR) – talk to the village at a supper in the nave, 1 November 1968.

1969:

'Attitudes to Conservation (From Sixteenth Century to the Present Day)' – a monumental work started in 1969, but which remained uncompleted.

English High Gothic – a book begun in the late 1960s but which remained uncompleted.

St George's Chapel, Windsor Castle – 'Friends Annual Reports' 1969–75.

'Conservation Areas, North Riding of Yorkshire' – a report of 14 years detailing those villages worthy of inclusion, totalling 50 in all, prepared on behalf of the York Georgian Society and York Architectural and Archaeological Association, 1969.

Review of *Church Maintenance* by the Revd Vivian Symons in *Church Building*, January 1969.

'Modern Architecture' – lecture to Selby Grammar School, 14 January 1969.

'Problems of working with Old Buildings' – a lecture to the York Guild of Building, 4 February 1969, King's Manor, York.

'Modern Churches' – lecture to Ecclesiological Society, 27 February 1969.

'Repairing Ancient Churches' – talk to Helmsley and Area Group of Yorkshire Architectural Society, 28 March 1969.

'Shared Church Buildings' – article in *Church Building* No. 27, April 1969 (pp. 3–8).

Visit to Ancient Monuments in England by the Compagnie des Architectes en Chef des Monuments Historiques organized by the Franco-British Union of Architects. This included the city of Durham where G. Pace conducted a tour of the cathedral and other buildings, 23 April 1969.

'Durham and Other Examples' – a lecture in the series 'New Buildings in Historic Areas' held at The Institute of Advanced Architectural Studies, York, 5–8 May 1969.

'Working with Old Churches' – talk to Peterborough Rotary Club, 28 May 1969.

Talk to the Friends of St George's Chapel, Windsor Castle, in the nave, 31 May 1969.

Exhibition of Church Embroidery at York Minster, Chapter House, June 1969 included work designed by G. Pace.

RIBA Conference at IAAS, York University 'Preparing for the Eighties' – walk led by G. Pace to examine York churches, 2–5 July 1969.

Sixteenth Annual Conference of members of the Diocesan Advisory Committees for the Care of Churches at St John's College, York, July 1969:

visit to York churches conducted by G. Pace, 15 July 1969; lecture 'The Theory and Philosophy of Conservation' – a talk on attitudes and principles, 16 July 1969.

Exhibition – Royal Academy Summer Exhibition, London, 1969, where the following drawings were displayed: 'Chester Cathedral – The New Bell House' and Oxford – New College organ.

Talk to the Society of Friends, St Botolph's Church, Boston, AGM, 29 September 1969.

Church Assembly, Places of Worship Commission: evidence submitted in the form of a 125-page report, November 1969. (Copies lodged at the Council for the Care of Churches and the Royal Institute of British Architects Libraries).

'St George's Doncaster: The Lost Church – Scott's Church and Today' – a talk to the Friends of Doncaster Parish Church at the exhibition of the 'faire and large Paroch Chirche of St George' at the Museum and Art Gallery, Doncaster, 1 December 1969.

1970:

Southwark Cathedral – *Friends Annual Reports* 1970–75.

Shell Guide to ER Yorkshire – G. Pace compiled much of this book, under the guidance and editorship of John Piper in the 1970s, but it remained unfinished.

'St Mary's Priory' – guide to the church at Old Malton, N. Yorkshire, 1970.

'Development of Church Architecture' – talk to St Michael's College, Llandaff, 27 January 1970.

'Architecture in the 70s' – a lecture at Hatfield Parish Church, Yorkshire, 8 February 1970.

Lichfield Theological College – conference on church buildings. Tour of Birmingham Churches conducted by G. Pace, 19 February 1970.

'Reordering Churches' – talk in Hitchin Parish Church, 28 February 1970.

'Modern Churches' – a lecture to Carlisle Theological Society in Carlisle Cathedral, 20 March 1970.

'Working with Old Buildings' – lecture to the Guild of Freemen of the City of York, 7 April 1970.

Surveys and Reports on Historic Buildings – a paper read in the course 'Conservation and Repair of Historic Buildings', 13–17 April 1970 at The Institute of Advanced Architectural Studies, York.

'Modern Churches' – talk to the congregation of Centenary Church, Dublin, Eire, 20 April 1970.

Exhibition of wrought ironwork by the Council for Small Industries in Rural Areas, in collaboration with The Institute of Advanced Architectural Studies, King's Manor, York, including work by G. Pace, 30 April to 15 May 1970.

'Ironwork' – lecture to the Design Forum associated with the Wrought Ironwork Exhibition, sponsored by Yorkshire Small Industries

Committee of the Council for Small Industries in Rural Areas (Co Sira), King's Manor, York, 15 May 1970.

'The Churches of York' – a talk in a course 'Architecture in York and Neighbourhood' at Marygate Centre of Further Education, 18 May 1970.

Cathedral Architects' Conference at The Institute of Advanced Architectural Studies – paper 'Old Buildings and Vibrations' (previously published in *Architect's Journal*, 15 April 1970), circulated and discussed, 20 May 1970.

'The Work of a Diocesan Architect' – a lecture in the series 'The Care of Churches' at the Sheffield Diocesan Conference, Mexborough Grammar School, 4 June 1970.

Sermon at Sunday Evensong, Woolston Church, Warrington, 28 June 1970 on 'New Church Building Today'.

Exhibition – Royal Academy Summer Exhibition, London, 1970, where the following drawings were displayed: Durham Cathedral – The Alington Memorial; York, James the Deacon – New Church; and Cambridge, King's College – Dean Milner White Memorial Chapel.

'The Problem of Redundant Churches' – questions and answers. Chairman G. Pace at the Churches Inspection Conference 1970, Herringham Hall, Bedford College, University of London, 27 September 1970.

'Attitudes to the Repair and Reordering of Churches' – lecture to the Cambridge Ecclesiological Society, 30 October 1970.

'St George's Chapel, Windsor – Aesthetic and Place in English High Gothic' – talk to the Method Building Conference, 26 November 1970.

'Roods in Renaissance Churches' – article produced for St John's Cathedral Chapter, Providence, Rhode Island, USA, December 1970.

Obituary of Mr A. L. Durst, Sculptor in *The Times*, 30 December 1970.

1971:

'Southwark Cathedral – Historical and Architectural Notes' – pamphlet issued by the Friends, 1971.

Contribution to *History and Guide of Llancarfan Church* 1971.

Contribution on the cathedral in the *Lichfield Official Guide* prepared by the Lichfield Borough Council, 1971.

Contribution to *Louth Parish Church History and Guide* by Mr Hedley Warr, 1971.

The Three Tuns Hotel, Thirsk – evidence against the proposal to demolish the hotel submitted to Public Enquiry, 1971.

Talk based on evidence submitted to Places of Worship Commission (December 1969) given to Southwark Cathedral Council, 3 February 1971.

Talk on 'Attitudes to Conservation: Reordering and Decoration' after Evensong at Great Ayton Church, 7 February 1971.

Surveys and Reports on Historical Buildings, – a lecture to the Ulster Architectural Heritage Society, 2 April 1971 in their course on 'The Techniques of Building Conservation' 1–3 April 1971. Department of Architecture, Queen's University, Belfast.

'Antidote for Repairing Mania' – letter to *The Times*, 19 June 1971.

'The Inlaid Marble Ledgers at Victoria Cathedral', Gozo – a paper prepared for *L-Ghid Ta'L-Assunta*, July 1971, a magazine edited by Mgr. Carmelo Scicluna, Curate of Gozo Cathedral, Malta; published 15 August 1971.

Exhibition – Royal Academy Summer Exhibition, London, 1971, where the following drawings were displayed: Marrick Priory, Swaledale – adaption as young people's adventure centre; Thrybergh Church – the new vestries and Bransholme, Hull – new church centre.

'Talk to the Friends' of Tamworth Parish Church, 13 September 1971.

'Talk to the Friends' of Louth Parish Church, 17 September 1971.

'St Martin le Grand, and St Michael, Spurriergate, York' – talk at and about these churches to the Conference for Association for Studies in Conservation of Historic Buildings, 19 September 1971.

'Church Planning and Building Today' – a talk at a meeting celebrating the Patronal Festival at St Matthew's Church, Sheffield, 26 September 1971.

'Aims and Objectives of Recording and Documentation of Building' – paper read in the course 'Conservation: Analysis Recording and Documentation Techniques in Existing Buildings'. 27 September–1 October 1971 at The Institute of Advanced Architectural Studies, York.

'Conservation of Buildings' – talk at Elvington, 23 November 1971.

1972:

'York – Bishophill' – Interim Report on the Inner Core of Bishophill, commissioned on behalf of the York Civic Trust and the Joseph Rowntree Memorial Trust 1971–72.

Contribution to *Braunston Church Guide* by Mr Herlihy, 1972.

Contribution to *St Mary's, Scarborough Guide* by Maurice Harspill, 1972.

Southwark Cathedral – 'Historical and Architectural Notes' (pp. 1–8) drawn up for and issued by The Friends of Southwark Cathedral 1972.

Obituary for the Most Revd Glyn Simon, *The Times*, 22 June 1972.

Touring exhibition of 'Aspects of Conservation in Britain and Europe' intended to create interest in European Architectural Heritage Year 1975. This included a display of the Durham University Library and was held in York at the Guildhall, York, 3–13 January 1972, and in cities throughout the continent during the same year.

'Cleaning the Exterior of the Church' – article in *The Churches Outlook – Morning Telegraph* extra newspaper, Sheffield, 29 August 1972.

Lectures on conservation to the Travelling School for Restoration at The York Institute of Advanced Architectural Studies, University of York, August, September and October 1972.

Exhibition – Royal Academy Summer Exhibition, London, 1972, where the following drawings were displayed: Windsor Castle, St George's Chapel – Canon's Stalls and York, Archbishop Holgate's School – Interdenominational Chapel.

'Ecclesiastical Architecture' – a lecture to the York Guild of Building, St Antony's Hall, 24 October 1972.

'Sonic Boom, Traffic Vibration – a Plea for more Research' – article in *Focus* (Louth Church) October 1972.

'Conservation of Ancient Buildings – aesthetical considerations' – a talk to Selby Civic Society, 23 November 1972.

1973:

Contribution to a Berlin University Dissertation (1968) – 'Chorgestuhl und Orgelprospekt in England' (Relations of choir stalls with organ-cases in England from the sixteenth-century to the present day) by Joachim Uhlworm, published by Gebr. Mann Verlag, Berlin. 1973 (included illustrations of organs at Llandaff Cathedral, Chester Cathedral and New College Oxford).

Illustration – plan of Durham Cathedral and claustral buildings in *This Sumptuous Church* by Archdeacon Stranks, published by SPCK, 1973.

Review of Royal Commission on Historical Monuments (England) – City of York, Volume III, south-west of the Ouse – for the Society of Antiquaries, London, 1973.

'Attitudes to the Restoration of Buildings' – lecture to Architectural and Archaeological Society of Durham and Northumberland, 24 February 1973.

'Face-lift' – article in *Housing and Planning Review*, May–July 1973.

Darlington Town Centre Inquiry – 'Darlington Aesthetic'. Submission of Proof of Evidence to Public Enquiry 5–6 June 1973. (Parallels with York Aesthetic, Llandaff Aesthetic).

Harvest sermon at Holme-on-Spalding Moor Parish Church, September 1973.

'Face-lifts' – article in *York Civic Trust Report*, November 1973.

'Attitudes to Conservation' – talk at Annual Dinner for Provost and Greater Chapter, Newcastle Cathedral, 6 December 1973.

1974:

St John's Church, Masbrough – assessment of a William White church (unpublished), 1974.

'Bishophill: York. Appraisal and Renewal' – a study for the York Civic Trust published in association with William Sessions Ltd, 1974.

Coade Stone – notes (used by Peter Robb in compiling a book on the subject), 1974.

A review of *The Works in Architecture of John Carr* – a list prepared by the York Georgian Society – published in the first issue of the *Yorkshire Architectural and York Archaeological Society New Journal*, 1974.

Selby New Coal Mine – voluntary report on the churches likely to be at risk due to mining activities (57 churches) and measures for their protection, 1974.

'Surveys and Inspection Reports' – lectures to The Institute of Advanced Architectural Studies, University of York, 4 February 1974.

'Churches – Inspection Measures and Redundancy Procedures' – lecture to the Yorkshire Philosophical Society, Tempest Anderson Hall, York, 23 March 1974.

Address to the Friends of Lichfield Cathedral (to mark the Architect's Silver Jubilee) on 'The Work of the Cathedral Architect', 20 July 1974.

Exhibition – Royal Academy Summer Exhibition, London, 1974, where the following drawings were displayed: Durham Cathedral – New Vestry Complex; Brancepeth – New Setting for font cover and Wilmslow – New Vestries.

Improvements in Cathedrals – a talk to the Friends of Southwark Cathedral, AGM, 12 October 1974 in the Chapter House.

Talk on the Church at the launching of the Friends, St Mary the Virgin, Nottingham (notes only), 21 October 1974.

'An Architect reflects on the Central Theme' – (architects, church and culture) – lecture at the Clergy Week II: 'Christian Communication in the contemporary culture' at Whirlow Grange, Sheffield, 19 November 1974.

1975:

'The Architectural Perspective from the 1740s to Modern Times' – an article in the book *A skilful Master Builder – William Anelay, Ltd* by H. E. C. Stapleton, G. G. Pace and J. E. Day, published by The Ebor Press, York, 1975.

'Restoration and reordering of the Chapel' – talk to Trinity College Chapel, Dublin, Eire, 30 January 1975.

'Techniques for Surveying Cathedrals and the Preservation of Reports' – inaugural address to The Cathedral Architects' Conference, 10 April 1975. (Typescript copy 22 pages in length read to the Conference by Martin Caroe as G. Pace too ill to attend.)

'Report on the Sixteenth Century Stained Glass' by Galyon Houe at Preston Grammar School, March 1975.

OPPOSITE
425 Spalding: organ-case, ink on tracing paper, 9 × 7in (22.9 × 17.8cm), 1971

426 Cardiff, St Saviour's, Roath: proposal for wrought-iron screen. Pencil drawing, 12 × 16in (30.5 × 40.6cm), extract taken from office drawing no.22 drawn by J. Hutchinson, 1967

Spalding Parish Church.
organ case in
North.
Transept.

425

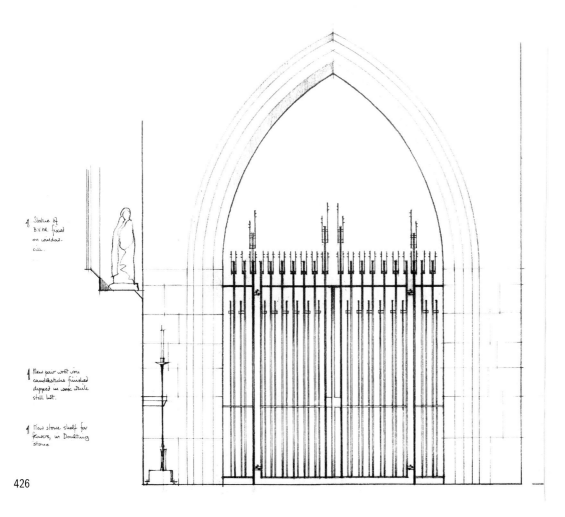

1 Statue of
B.V.M. fixed
on window-
cill.

1 New pair wrot iron
candlesticks finished
dipped in wax while
still hot.

1 New stone shelf for
flowers, in Doulting
stone

426

259

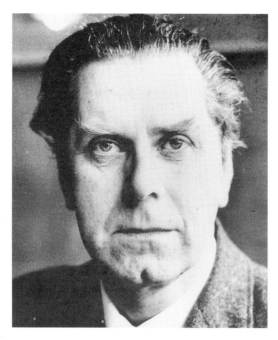

PACE, George Gaze, CVO 1971; FRIBA; Architect in private practice since 1949; b. 31 Dec. 1915; son of George Henry and Alice Barbara Pace, Croydon; married 1941, Ina Catherine, daughter of Harvey Sheridan Jones; three sons, two daughters. Educ: privately; articled James Ransome, FRIBA, London; School of Architecture, Polytechnic, London. Lecturer, School of Architecture, Polytechnic, London, 1939–41. Queen's Royal Regt, RE, 1941–42; Superintending Valuer, WO (Major, Gen. List), 1942–49. Surveyor to Dio. of Sheffield, 1949–56; Cons. Architect to cathedrals of: Lichfield, 1949; Llandaff, 1949; Sheffield, 1953–61; Durham, 1954; Peterborough, 1956; Chester, 1961; St Albans, 1962–72; Liverpool (Anglican), 1962; Newcastle, 1966; Southwark, 1971; Surveyor, St George's Chapel, Windsor Castle, 1969. Cons. Architect to dioceses of: Wakefield, 1948, Bradford, 1949, Sheffield, 1956, York, 1957, Llandaff, 1967, and Monmouth, 1969; Hon. Cons. Architect: Historic Churches Preservation Trust; Yorks Architectural and York Archaeological Society; Mem., Dio. Adv. Cttees, York, Sheffield and Liverpool; Vice-President: New Churches Research Group; Council York Civic Trust. RIBA Pugin Student, 1936; Robert Mitchell Gold Medallist, 1936; RIBA Ashpitel Prizeman, 1938; MA Lambeth, 1961. FRIBA 1949; FSA 1950. *Work includes:* rebuilding Llandaff Cathedral, 1949–63; Chapel of the Resurrection, University of Ibadan, 1951–62; completion schemes, Sheffield Cathedral, 1955–61; Holy Trinity, Newport, Mon, 1958; All Saints', Doncaster, 1958; Scargill Religious Centre, 1958; The Chapel, St Michael's Theological Coll., Llandaff, 1959; New Cathedral, Ibadan, 1960-; St Mark's, Sheffield, 1963; St Mark's, Chadderton, 1963; Caer Eirthin Church, Swansea, 1963; Chapel Complex, Keele Univ., 1965; William Temple Memorial Church, Wythenshawe, 1965; St John's Coll., York Chapel, 1966; Durham Univ. Library, 1966; St Andrew's, Rushmere, 1968; (in association with Paul Paget) King George VI Memorial Chapel and Tomb, Windsor Castle, 1969; Woolston Church, 1970; St Mark's Thornaby, 1970; James the Deacon, York, 1971; Bransholme Church Centre, 1973; *restorations include:* Castle Howard; Bramham Park; parish churches of Boston; Louth; St Mary's, Beverley; Selby Abbey; Doncaster; Branston; Holy Trinity, Hull; *alterations etc. to churches include:* Armagh Cathedral; Great St Mary's, Cambridge; Luton; Pershore Abbey; Wycliffe Hall, Oxford; St Martin's, Birmingham; Bramhall; St Aidan's Theological Coll. Chapel; St Michael's, Cambridge; St Martin le Grand, York, 1968; St Mary's Church, Luton, 1969; Organcase, New Coll., Oxford, 1969; King's Coll. Chapel, Cambridge; Treasury, Ely and Durham Cathedrals; The Chapel, Trinity Coll., Dublin. Townscape analysis: Skipton; Bishophill, York. *Publications:* contributions to: *Chamber's Encyclopaedia,* 1948 and 1963; *Collins' Guide to English Parish Churches,* 1958, 1968; *The Church and the Arts,* 1960; *Making the Building Fit the Liturgy,* 1962; *The York Aesthetic,* 1962; *The Modern Architectural Setting of the Liturgy,* 1964; *Bishophill: York, Appraisal and renewal,* 1974; contributions to technical, archaeological and ecclesiological journals. *Recreations:* walking, looking at old buildings. *Address:* 18 Clifton Green, York, *T:* York 55029. *Clubs:* Athenaeum, Art Workers' Guild. [Died 23 August 1975]

REFERENCES AND NOTES

1. 'Church Architecture – A Practising Architect's Viewpoint'; talk at The Cambrian Archaeological Association Conference, Lampeter, Wales, 1962.

2. Addiscombe New College School, followed by Oxford Local. His parents, particularly his mother, endured considerable personal sacrifice in order to fund his education, and private studies at home.

3. He became a Senior Lecturer in Art and Canon Theologian at the University of Liverpool.

4. William Lockett, *New Fire* (Quarterly Journal of the Society of St John the Evangelist) Vol. IV, no. 27, Summer 1976. Article: 'Modern Church Architecture and George Pace'.

5. His drawings from this period survive.

6. 'Architecture and Architect in the Service of the Church', by G. G. Pace in *The Modern Architectural Setting of the Liturgy*, edited by W. Lockett, SPCK, 1962.

7. The drawings were exhibited world-wide – but frustratingly they were trapped in India during the war!

8. George Pace bought a complete set of AA sketch books in the 1970s which he had indexed and displayed in his library.

9. Studies between 1935–7 included: Beddington Church, Surrey (fifteenth-century lych-gate and sixteenth-century chancel screen); Fotheringhay, Northamptonshire (fifteenth-century aisle roof, thirteenth-century porch); Stonechurch, Kent (thirteenth-century arcade and south aisle); Shoreham, Kent (fifteenth-century roof); Peterborough Cathedral, Northamptonshire (fifteenth-century 'New Building', south choir aisle); and Westminster Abbey London (fifteenth-century reredos to St Margaret's Chapel).

10. His mother was born in Peterborough.

11. *Church Assembly: Places of Worship Commission Evidence*, submitted by G. G. Pace, December 1969, (p. 73). This monumental work set forth much of George Pace's philosophy on conservation, the role of the church architect, the Dean and Chapter, committees, and of State control (see also ref. 193). Upon its publication the Right Revd Eryl Thomas, Bishop of Monmouth (formerly Dean of Llandaff Cathedral) wrote in a letter to George Pace, 15 December 1969: 'How you ever found time to do this sort of work on top of everything else, I really don't know, but I hope that what you have written will become known on a very wide field as there are some wonderful *obiter dicta* for all and sundry to digest. If this sort of thing could have been written years ago and indeed in parts of the last century what might we have been saved'.

12. Ibid., p. 71.

13. Ibid., p. 73.

14. This reference to Temple Lushington Moore (1856–1920) occurs in George Pace's article 'Power Houses of Faith – the New Cathedrals of Liverpool and Guildford,' *Anglican World* no. 6, 1961. Temple Moore's churches represented an important link between the churches of the Bodley School and the final phase of Gothic Revival as seen in the work of Giles Gilbert Scott (1880–1960), Temple Moore's own pupil. Temple Moore's son was drowned at sea, but his work was carried on by his niece's husband Leslie T. Moore (1883–1957).

George Pace held the work of both these architects in the greatest esteem.

15. Peterborough Cathedral Friends Report 1967.

16 One was at East Grinstead by Philip Webb. Darcy Braddell became a good mentor and friend. George Pace designed his memorial in King's School, Canterbury, 1970.

17. Parental pressure forced her to abandon this career, much against her will.

18. From George Pace's card index, ref. 'Office – Applications for Jobs'.

19. See *'Power Houses of Faith'* article (as 14). Construction of Guildford Cathedral began in 1936.

20. There is a description of his work in a newspaper article 'North East People' no. 256, in the *Yorkshire Evening Press*, 6 February 1959.

21. Used in 1963 as the basis for a new book *Worship and Architecture*. The first draft was constantly added to up until 1975 but the book remained uncompleted.

22. As 1.

23. As 20.

24. Competition for the redevelopment of Castle Hill site, Ilkley, Yorkshire, W.R.

25. Competition for the replanning of West Hartlepool, Co. Durham (in collaboration with architects Adhead and Needham).

26. Derwent Plastics Factory, York. Both detailed design drawings and a model were produced, but a change in the site led to the project being abandoned.

27. *Architectural Review*, December 1945: 'Ecclesiology at Leeds'. An account of the Gothic Revival church of St Saviour's, Leeds where Pusey became so involved. Later works were carried out by Bodley. George Pace looked after this church and carried out a complete redecoration which followed Bodley's earlier work where possible, but the crossing ceiling could not be deciphered and an early Pace traceried pattern took its place (1965). Ref. *The Builder*, 30 April 1965 (p. 941).

28. *Eric Milner White 1884–1964*. by Philip Pore and Donald Harris, SPCK 1965.

29. The Vicar of St Mary's and Christ Church Scarborough (1944–7), the Revd G. K. Townley (later to become a bishop) remembers, 'Those war years, when Dean Milner White introduced George Pace to me as this rising architect'. Letter to I. F. C. Pace 1975 from Earls Barton.

30. Letter from General Sir Gerald Templer 29 August 1975 to I. F. C. Pace. After Armagh he lost personal contact with G. G. Pace, though he acted as a trustee to the Historic Churches Preservation Trust and through them heard much of G. G. P.'s later career, and perhaps had some indirect influence.

31. Sir Charles Nicholson was architect to seven cathedrals – Belfast, Lincoln, Lichfield, Llandaff, Portsmouth, Sheffield and Wells. (Ref. *Edwardian Architecture*, by Stuart A. Gray, Wordsworth Editions, 1985). Of the many churches left without an architect, a typical example is Bainton on the Wolds, Yorkshire, E.R. Here George Pace added a

priest's stall and desk, 1950, to complement the Nicholson nave pews.

32. As 1.

33. Ibid.

34. Address to the Friends of Lichfield Cathedral by G. G. Pace in June 1974 to mark the Silver Jubilee of his work as Cathedral Architect.

35. An encounter remembered by R. C. Thompson, stonemason, when serving his apprenticeship. (*see* ILLUST. 207 *far left*).

36. As 34.

37. *Concrete Quarterly*, no. 48, March 1961. Other articles also appeared worldwide, for example, *Interiors*, December 1957, Whitney Publishers Inc., New York; *Bonytt* – Official Journal of the National Society of Norwegian Arts, nos 11–12, 1956; no. 135 of the *Revista Informes de la Construccion*, November 1961, Instituto Eduardo Torroja de la Construccion y del Cemento, Spain.

38. Dick Reid of York, Master Woodcarver, remembers an incident where George Pace found difficulty in describing what he wanted. His solution – to stand behind Dick holding his wrists and guiding his hands whilst the skill of the carver did the rest – was not particularly successful. 'I would never allow anyone to do that to me now' (conversation with the author 1989).

In another incident Frank Roper, sculptor, was asked by George Pace to conduct some first-hand research before commencing work on the Llandaff Cathedral Lady Chapel reredos panel reliefs, and he describes the outcome in an article in the *Llandaff Friends Report*, no. 32, 1964–5, p. 18:

My brief was to be 'as faithful to the subject as possible' – one letter from Mr Pace suggesting that I should seek inspiration by putting my head into a thorn bush! This painful operation was intended to prevent my formalizing or inflicting my conventions on the subject.

See also p. 90 on artists.

39. *Sir Ninian Comper* by Anthony Symondson, RIBA catalogue, Heinz Gallery, 1988.

40. *Brierley in Yorkshire* by Patrick Nuttgens, York Georgian Society, 1984. See also *A Skilful Master Builder* (the story of William Anelay by H. E. Stapleton; G. G. Pace, and J. E. Day, published by William Sessions Ltd, 1975).

41. Abstract from an article prepared by A. Gillam, of C. H. Gillam and Son of Sheffield, at the request of the author, January 1987.

42. *Richard Norman Shaw* by Andrew Saint, Yale University Press, 1983, (p. 162).

43. *William Butterfield* by Paul Thompson, Routledge and Kegan Paul, 1971, (pp. 70–1).

44. *The Work of a Cathedral Architect Today* by G. G. Pace, St Alban's Cathedral Report, 1963.

45. See pp. 181–3.

46. See p. 191.

47. As 27.

48. *The York and East Yorkshire Architectural Society Year Book – 1956–57*: 'Victorian Architecture in York'.

49. Ibid.

50. *Welsh Churches and Chapels – A National Heritage* by G. G. Pace, published in Western Mail, 4 April 1960.

51. *Shell Guides to the Counties of Wales*, edited by John Betjeman and John Piper, published by Faber and Faber, appeared in the 1960s and 1970s, and go a long way towards presenting this view of Wales and its churches. George Pace was working on a *Shell Guide to Yorkshire East Riding* with John Piper, and although much was written, his illness in 1974 prevented him from finishing the work.

52. Bishop Eric Wakefield – *Wakefield Diocesan News*, October 1975.

53. William Lockett, 'Modern Church Architecture and George Pace', *New Fire Magazine*, Vol. IV, no. 27, Summer 1976.

54. Between 1945–58 a total of 97 new churches and 137 hall churches were erected by the Church of England (figures taken from an article by the Very Revd Sewiol Evans, Dean of Gloucester – *Sunday Times* 20 April 1958).

55. *A New Approach to Church Building* – Province Vol. IX, Summer 1958. (A 'Church in Wales' quarterly publication).

56. Published in 1960 with other essays, edited by Frank Glendenning, under the common title *The Church and the Arts*.

57. See *Liturgy and Architecture* by Peter Hammond, published Barrie and Rockliff, 1960, p. 6.

58. *The Continuing Heritage: The Story of the Civic Trust Awards* by Lionel Esher published by Franey & Co. Ltd, 1982 re Durham University Library.

59. As 57.

60. As 6.

61. 'The Architectural problems which may arise in a Liturgical re-ordering and ways of solving these problems without spoiling old churches' – G. G. Pace, June 1961. A paper read at Attingham Park, later condensed and published as *Making the Building Serve the Liturgy*. (George Pace had an annoying habit of misquoting – in addition to ascribing incorrect dates! – and constantly referred to this article in his *Who's Who* entry as 'Making the Building Fit the Liturgy').

62. 'The York Aesthetic', *York Civic Trust Report*, 1961–2, G. G. Pace.

63. Conservation Areas were eventually created under the government legislation of The Civic Amenities Act 1968.

64. John Shannon, Chairman of the York Civic Trust, who sought George Pace's advice over many years acknowledged that, 'he grasped more fully than anyone we have ever met the special character and "feel" of York. He was a great friend and mentor to the Trust. Nothing was too much for him to do; his advice was at all times readily and freely given . . . Many, many times when we were in doubt as to how some work of restoration or reclamation should be done, we ended up saying 'Let's ask George Pace' . . . His memory will be enshrined in the many places and corners throughout the City, be it a chapel or a church, or the gilding of an old gas lamp . . .' *York Civic Trust Annual Report 1974/75*, p. 28.

65. *Craven Herald & Pioneer*, 1 January 1963.

66(i). *The Llandaff Aesthetic*: 'An analysis of the character and attributes of the Llandaff Aesthetic and recommendations for its preservation and enhancement by George G. Pace 1966' – prepared on behalf of the Representative Body of the Church in Wales and the Dean and Chapter of Llandaff Cathedral – produced as a typewritten report with dyeline print hand-coloured drawings, with very limited numbers of copies.

66(ii). *Bishophill: York Appraisal and Renewal – A Study for the York Civic Trust* by G. G. Pace, 1974, published by the York Civic Trust in association with William Sessions Ltd of York – which formed an extended study of 'York: Bishophill interim report on Inner Core of Bishophill' commissioned 1971/2 on behalf of the York Civic Trust and the Joseph Rowntree Memorial Trust.

67. As 57.

68. *Architects' Journal*, 10 March 1960: report on conference 'The Architect and the Church'.

69. As 4.

70. As 20.

71. 'The History of the Parish Church of All Saints, Branston'. Notes made by George Pace for Mr Devrill, 18 December 1965.

72. *The RIBA Journal*, May 1960.

73. Ibid.

74. Seminar: 'Current Trends and Personalities in Architecture', 1964, with Cedric Price, George Pace, William Whitfield, James Stirling, David Crease (for Oscar Niemeyer), and Colin St John Wilson, held at the Institute of Advanced Architectural Studies, University of York. Article in *Perspective East Yorkshire*, September/October, 1964, by G. H. Broadbent, of the University of Sheffield.

75. Ibid.

76. The Revd. John Kent – *The Bridge*, October 1975 (Journal of Selby Abbey Parish and others).

77. As 72.

78. Paper by G. G. Pace, 5 February 1962: *DAC Procedure in Theory and Practice*. Later embodied within the 'Church Assembly Places of Worship Commission Evidence', Section M (see 11).

79. Abstracted in November 1984 from *Memoirs*, written by Mrs B. Helps, his secretary for 28 years, at the request of the author. Generally George Pace would spend most of the morning dictating letters from his home before walking in to the office at St William's College.

80. Mary Harrison – daughter of the author's godfather, the Ven. Harrison, Archdeacon of Sheffield and later Dean of Bristol – letter to I. F. C. Pace, 19 September 1975.

81. Mr Yendal, Director of Furse of Nottingham told the author of various examples (July 1988).

82. The Revd John Norman used this piece in his address at George Pace's funeral at St Olave's Church, Marygate, York, forwarding a copy of the text in a letter to Mrs I. F. C. Pace, 30 August 1975.

83. As 72.

84. George Pace always sought to achieve a sense of floating in space with his pendant lights.

85. Benedicite – Judith Scott in *Anglican World*, Issue 22, Vol 4, no. 2, 1964.

86. The offices in a part of St William's College, York, had a rather Dickensian air about them, which a good coat of paint would have helped to dispel. The Senior Curate of Beverley Minster, The Revd G. Hinton, noted in an article in the local *Evening Press* (27 November 1963) – 'Close to the East end of the Minster the attractive St William's College is in a state of depressing decrepitude, even though a justly famous architect has his office in part of the building'!

87. Neil Burton, 'Parish Counsel', *Designers' Journal*, January 1986. R. G. Sims took over the practice after the death of George Pace in 1975, and continues working in the same field, developing the distinctive architectural style with David Hopkinson and John Hutchinson, both former architectural assistants to George Pace for many years.

88. The Very Revd Ken Matthews – letter to I. F. C. Pace 28 August 1975, from Thursely Vicarage, referring to the Dean's Conference at Christ Church, Oxford in July 1961.

89. For example, when assisting the Cathedrals Advisory Committee as their adviser to York Minster on the decorating of the pulpitum niches, he wrote to Bernard Feilden (Consultant Architect to York Minster), in a letter dated 1 December 1973 enclosing his detailed recommendations on the decoration, saying he would stand up and be counted against any public outcry: 'This is what I would do and which I would be prepared to defend against any living person' he wrote.

90. Letter from George Pace to the next Dean – the Very Revd Peter Moore, 14 December 1973.

91. 'Modern Church Architecture' by G. G. Pace, in *The Church and the Arts*, edited by F. Glendenning.

92. *The Building of the Eighteenth Century Church*, by Basil F. L. Clarke, SPCK, reviewed by G.G.P.

93. St Mark's, Sheffield, *Appeal Brochure* 1951.

94. Ibid.

95. G. W. O. Addleshaw and Frederick Etchells, *The Architectural Setting of Anglican Worship*, Faber and Faber, 1948. Other books include *The High Church Tradition* and *The Beginnings of the Parochial System*. Addleshaw was Curate-in-Charge at St Michael le Belfry, York in 1949.

96. The Very Revd F. W. Dillistone, former Dean of Liverpool Anglican Cathedral, letter to I. F. C. Pace 27 August 1975.

97. See also 14.

98. Letter from George Pace to the Dean, 2 August 1960.

99. Letter from George Howard to I. F. C. Pace, written from Lindos, Rhodes, 29 August 1975.

100. This phrase is used in his reference to the Mausoleum in his talk 'Georgian Churches in Yorkshire' given to the York Georgian Society, 20 January 1968. The author also remembers comments in a similar vein made when he took myself and my other brother Martin on one of our 'Days Out' with him to visit the Mausoleum to view repair works in hand. These 'Days Out' provided a good opportunity for us as children to clamber over scaffolding and scramble up towers, usually to the contractors' alarm, but to no apparent concern of our father!

101. Friends of St George's, Windsor – *Annual Report*, Vol. IV, no. 10, 1968–9.

102. Notes on 'The Design by' G. Pace, 1 September 1967.

103. Firbeck Church, Yorkshire, W.R.

104. Countries visited included: Italy 1963, 68, 69; France 1968–71; Spain 1971; Gozo (Malta) 1970, 73, 74; Greece 1972; Turkey 1972.

105. Address given at the Memorial Service for Mr George Gaze Pace at Southwark Cathedral,

Tuesday 4 November, 1975 by the Very Revd G. W. O. Addleshaw, Dean of Chester.

106. *Churches Outlook,* 29 February 1972.

107. *Ormskirk Advertiser,* 29 March 1973.

108. As **105.**

109. As defined by the Revd Peter Hammond – see *Liturgy and Architecture,* Barrie and Rockliff, 1960.

110. *Worship and Architecture* by G.G.P., an unpublished book (1963–75) based on a previous unpublished book, *The New Churches* written during the Second World War.

111. *The Modern Architectural Setting of the Liturgy – Architecture and Architect in the Service of the Church,* by G. G. Pace. A paper presented at the Liverpool Conference 1962, and edited by W. Lockett, and published with other papers by SPCK, 1964.

112. As **110.**

113. 'Modern Church Architecture', by G. G. Pace – a paper in *The Church and the Arts* – edited by F. Glendenning and published by SCM Press Ltd, 1960.

114. Ibid.

115. As **110.**

116. Peter A. Fawcett, – 'Sheffield and the RIBA Festival Year,' published in *Yorkshire Architect – Journal of the RIBA Yorkshire Region,* November/December 1985, issue no. 105.

117. As **1.**

118. See list of written and published works, pp. 251–8.

119. As **111.** This article forms the main source for those thoughts expressed on pp. 51–76. All quotations may then be assumed to come from this article unless indicated otherwise.

120. See *Liturgy and Architecture* by Peter Hammond, ref. **109.**

121. *The Buildings of England – Cheshire* by N. Pevsner, 1971.

122. Articles in *Doncaster Chronicle* 10 November 1960 and the *Daily Telegraph,* 1 November 1960.

123. Article quoting G. Pace in *The Times,* 10 February 1969.

124. As **11.**

125. *The Buildings of England, South Lancashire,* by N. Pevsner, Penguin Books 1969, p. 52. And on p. 102 he goes on to remark, 'The font has really too odd a shape, but once again Mr Pace is capable of convincing his clients that they should let him have his way'.

126. Also see **1.**

127. George Pace considered that Pugin's 'Architectural gifts were not sufficient to permit him to achieve to the full his architectural visions, and thus many of his buildings are a disappointment. But where he was not unduly harassed by clients incapable of entering his enthusiasms and a reasonble amount of money was available, he produced real churches. The interior of St Giles, Cheadle; the chancel at Winwick; both exterior and interior of St Augustine's Priory Chapel, Ramsgate; the nave arcade at Birmingham Cathedral; and the internal spatial relationships of Nottingham Cathedral are examples'. (From the Church Assembly: 'Places of Worship Commission Evidence', see ref. **11**).

127(a). *Church Builders of the Nineteenth Century*

by B. F. L. Clarke (1938) p. 149–50.

128. As **113.**

129. As **1.**

130. As **113.**

131. 'Toward the Modern Church', G. G. Pace, article in *Church of England Newspaper,* 28 April 1961.

132. George Pace proudly possessed Goodhart-Rendel's card index of 'Victorian Architects'.

132(a). As **131.**

133. As **131.**

134. 'New Approaches to Church Building – St Martin's (in the Field)', *London Review,* May 1958, no. 806.

135. *Architecture,* by Sir Thomas Jackson, (quoted in J. Betjeman's *Ghastly Good Taste* 1933/70).

136. As **131.**

137. Mr Wardman in the *Bradford Telegraph and Argus,* 14 September 1966.

138. Provost of Derby, The Very Revd R. A. Beddoes, *Bradford Telegraph and Argus,* 19 September 1966.

139. As **134.**

140. For example quoted in **6, 113, 131.**

141. As **113.**

142. As **44.**

143. As **1.**

144. Ibid.

145. *Edwardian Architecture,* Stuart A. Gray, Wordsworth Editions, 1985.

146. See **4** and *Chester Cathedral Newsletter,* December 1975, for example; which surmise of George Pace's place in the architectural tradition.

147. In his entry for *Chambers Encyclopaedia,* 'Twentieth Century Church Building', he says of Leonard Stokes at St Clare's, Sefton Park and Miles Platting, Stokes 'created churches with fine exteriors and noble interiors and which take the passage aisle and internal buttress conception a stage further. Other churches by this architect also exhibit plain wall surfaces used in juxtaposition with points of concentrated elaboration. Briefly this is the essence of twentieth century Gothic. It is seen in its sublimest form in Sir Giles Gilbert Scott's Liverpool Cathedral . . .'

148. See **14.**

149. A. P. Fawcett, lecturer in architecture, University of Sheffield – letter to author, October 1986, which went on to form the basis of the preface to this book (p. 9).

150. 'Some Principles and Practical Aspects (of New Church Building)', design paper by G. Pace, 3 March 1962 – intended for the use of building committees in consultation with their architect.

151. As **113** and 'Within our Churches – Beauty or Utility,' by G. G. Pace, 21 April 1966, published in *Church News,* July 1966.

152. Dr Patrick Nuttgens, CBE, MA, Ph.D.; ARIBA – *Society of Architectural Historians of Great Britain,* Newsletter, no. 13, November 1975, p. 5.

153. 'The Church and The New Town', by G. G. Pace, *SCA Journal,* November 1964. Annual Conference of Society of Christian Artists, Willersley Castle, 7–10 April 1964. G. Pace was also President of the New Churches Research Group.

154. As **113.**

155. As **6.**

156. As **113.** In another article, 'New Approaches to Church Building', *St Martin's Review* (ref. **134**) he goes further and suggests 'If the Church expects and demands the Architect to utterly efface himself, then Church Boards and Committees must be prepared to obliterate themselves'.

157. J. Hutchinson, and D. Palliser, *Bartholomew's City Guide to York,* 1980.

158. *Sheffield Telegraph,* 12 June 1959. As also detailed in: the *Church Times,* 15 November 1957; the *Yorkshire Post and Leeds Mercury,* 15 November 1957; the *Manchester Guardian,* 15 November 1957; *The Times,* 15 November 1957; the *Sheffield Star,* 15 November 1957; the *South Yorkshire Times,* 16 November 1957.

With reference to the window influences in addition to Nun Monkton, Drax Church is referred to in sketch notes, particularly the transoms of the clerestory windows.

Sledmere Church also exhibits double mullions in the chancel designed by Temple Moore in 1898 – and G. Pace saw these by 1941, witness his reference to the Church in his Patrington sketch (ILLUS. 436).

159. See Section II, *Selected Works,* pp. 145–222.

160. Ibid.

161. Art Workers' Guild – obituary in *Annual Report,* 1977.

162. Address given at the Memorial Service for George Pace at Southwark Cathedral, Tuesday, 4 November 1975, by The Very Revd G. W. O. Addleshaw, Dean of Chester.

In his *First Report* to the Friends, January 1971, George Pace admits: 'Southwark Cathedral has been of particular interest to me for over forty years and the architecture of the Transepts, the Quire and the Retroquire have played a part in the development of my "style"'. (Taken from handwritten notes).

163. Neil Burton, RIBA, architect with English Heritage – observation made in letter to author, 21 April 1987.

164. *Buildings of England – York,* N. Pevsner, reference Holy Trinity, Micklegate, organ-case.

165. As **150.**

166. Letter in the Readers' Forum Section of *The Student Movement Magazine,* October 1957.

167. *Building* Magazine, 5 September 1975.

168. As **4.**

169. As **150.**

170. As **131.**

171. As **6.**

172. Ibid.

173. 'Within our Churches – Beauty or Utility,' by G. G. Pace, 21 April 1966. published in *Church News,* July 1966.

174. The change came about at Holy Redeemer, Acomb, where the pattern was developed for straight-headed windows, and then continued into the large Victorian geometrical style window re-used at the west end of this new church, to retain a consistency in the glazing throughout the building (John Hutchinson – discussion with the author, June 1989).

175. There is no evidence to suggest a direct influence here, though George Pace must certainly have been aware of Mondrian. He did possess the book *De Stijl*, Prof. Hans L. C. Jaffe, but this was not published (by Thames and Hudson) until 1967.

176. *The Buildings of England – Yorkshire, West Riding*, Nikolaus Pevsner, 1967.

177. *The Buildings of England – Staffordshire*, Nikolaus Pevsner, 1974, pp. 42 and 325.

178. *The Buildings of England – Staffordshire*, Nikolaus Pevsner, 1974.

179. As **164**.

180. 'Music – Visual beauty too in church organs', Francis Jackson. *Yorkshire Evening Press*, 25 July 1966. Review of book *Organs of the World*, Walter Haacke.

181. Bruce Buchanan – Director of J. M. Walker and Son Ltd, Organ Builders. Letter to author 22 October 1986.

182. In the *Design Report*, by G. G. Pace, 16 May 1966, he explains in great detail the meaning of the symbols and their appropriateness in this situation: the sword found on many Yorkshire medieval stone monuments denotes the memorial is a man – the sword of the spirit being appropriate for a priest, and fitting reference to the Revd McLane's activities during the great snowstorm of 1963 in which he died. The chalice and host is also a symbol often used on monuments to priests. Above the St Chad cross the fish is an early Christian symbol, the Greek word for fish – *Ichthus* – being a kind of acronym of *Ieosus Christos Theou Vios Soter* (Jesus Christ, Son of God, Saviour).

183. Battle Honours in the Welch Regiment Memorial Chapel – *Llandaff Cathedral Friends Magazine*, 1963, Frank Roper.

184. As **182**.

185. *Lettering in Architecture* by Alan Bartram, published by Lund Humphries, 1975.

186. 'New Vestments', *St Alban's Abbey Magazine*, August 1967.

187. *Peterborough Standard*, 16 November 1973. Saxon ornament also inspired the design on the cope at Llantwit Major, which is based on the saxon cross at the west end of the church (conversation with vicar, Revd Canon Jenkins and author, 1989).

188. As **186**.

189. As **113**.

190. Statement by G. Pace in *York Evening Press*, 24 March 1971. An earlier article on the church in the same paper, 12 July 1966, makes an interesting observation on George Pace's character following the report of his description of the church:

There is also evidence of a piece of fifteenth century cribbing. The pews and arches under the tower are styled after the Norman fashion, built into the church in 1170. Here the stonemason has 'consciously repeated' the design of the Norman craftsmen – but gone to the trouble to leave an indication of the date of his work. Little stone flowers cut into the stone are his mark, which, says Mr Pace, is typical of 1450. He says it with so much authority that it begs no argument.

191. *The Buildings of England – Yorkshire, York and the East Riding*, Nikolaus Pevsner, 1972.

192. 'The Work of a Cathedral Architect Today', by G. G. Pace, published in the *Thirteenth Annual Report of St Albans Cathedral*, 1963.

193. *Church Assembly: Places of Worship Commission Evidence*. Submitted by G. G. Pace

December 1969 (see reference 11 for previous comments). This document forms an excellent summary of George Pace's attitudes and approach to the conservation of cathedrals and churches. The document is 125 pages long with 515 separate paragraph headings. Over the next 30 pages constant reference to this work is made. For reference purposes the title is abbreviated to *Evidence*, with the appropriate page number affixed.

194. In addition to large files full of handwritten notes, and articles abstracted and marked ready for inclusion, numerous books around the house contain marks such as AT (Attitudes) – for example, *Northanger Abbey* by Jane Austen, has pages marked to show where differences between the Romantic and the Gothic ruin are discussed.

195. See **193**.

196. *Evidence* p. 7 (see **193**).

197. A pale version of Pelligrini's 'Fall of Phaeton' was repainted in tempera by the Canadian painter Scott Medd – ref. *The Work of John Vanbrugh* by G. Beard, published by B. T. Batsford Ltd, 1986. (Interestingly George Pace does not refer to the decision to 'restore' the main house, possibly because this would have been taken by George Howard before his involvement.)

198. A detailed account of this work was published in the *Photogrammetric Record* Vol. IX, No. 20, October 1962, based upon a paper read at the Technical meeting of the Society, 10 January 1961, by E. H. Thompson, University College, London, entitled 'Photogrammetry in the Restoration of Castle Howard.'

199. *Evidence*, pp. 8–9.

200. Article in *Daily Mail*, 21 March 1959.

201. In contrast to ref. **197**.

202. Sheffield Cathedral proposed extensions, for example. See *The Appeal Brochure*.

203. *Evidence*, p. 15.

204. *Evidence*, p. 40. The quotation from Basil Champney is taken from his *A Quiet Corner of England*.

205. The two items in brackets in this quotation were deduced and inserted by the author.

206. *Peterborough Cathedral Friends Annual Report* 1967. Alan Durst also carved the statue in the niche on the west face of Cawood Church (Yorkshire, ER): 'Rather than make a bogus fifteenth century statue to replace the missing one we have made a twentieth century statue designed to dwell in, and go with, the niche', G. Pace told the newspapers. (The vicar was so moved to complete the work he sold his Johannes Pressenda (1777–1854) violin to pay for it) – *Daily Telegraph*, September 1961.

207. The cleaning of Peterborough Cathedral west front was carried out virtually by one man and a spray hose pipe adjusted regularly during the day over several months (see *Technical Aspects*, p. 139).

208. *Evidence*, p. 17.

209. *Evidence*, p. 19.

210. *Evidence*, p. 21.

211. *Evidence*, p. 44.

212. Ibid.

213. Ibid.

214. *Evidence*, p. 33.

215. George Pace often used the phrase 'the wars'

when referring to the First World War and Second World War (author).

216. *Evidence*, pp. 27–29.

217. *Evidence*, p. 29.

218. *Evidence*, p. 55.

219. Design Report on the *Reconstruction of Branston Church*, by G. G. Pace.

220. 'A Plea for Box Pews – Modern Adaptations', article by G. G. Pace, published in *Both New and Old* – the fourteenth report of the Central Council for the Care of Churches, 1960.

221. Such proposals were made in a report submitted by the Association for Studies in Conservation of Historic Buildings formed by the Institute of Archaeology, University of London.

222. *Evidence*, p. 93.

223. In his inaugural address to the Cathedral Architects' Conference, 10 April 1975, he cited the works and writings of Philip Webb, E. S. Prior, Mervyn Macartney, W. R. Lethaby, William Weir, Charles Winmill, John Macgregor. Two examples of works containing the distilled virtue and summation of the art and aesthetics of conservation were *The Repair of Ancient Buildings*, by A. R. Powys, 1929 (reprinted by SPAB 1987), and *Old Churches and Modern Craftsmanship*, by Alban Caroe, 1949.

Two examples of books which were technically mines of information, but where the reader supplies in use the aesthetic content: *The Conservation of Antiquities and Works of Art*, by H. J. Plenderleith, 1966 and *Conservation of Cultural Property*, UNESCO, 1968.

224. *Evidence*, p. 93–4.

225. As **191**.

226. *Evidence*, p. 95.

227. *Evidence*, p. 82.

228. As **162**.

229. *Friends of Durham Cathedral – 43rd Annual Report*, 1975–76. Obituary of G. G. Pace by Dean Wild.

230. Article by the vicar in *Sheffield Diocesan Review*, January 1957.

231. The Cathedrals of Peterborough, Chester, Llandaff and Lichfield all assigned a stall to the Cathedral Architect, acting upon this advice.

232. *Evidence*, p. 84.

233. *Brave Day Hideous Night*, Sir John Rothenstein.

235. *Evidence*, p. 83.

236. *Evidence*, p. 32.

237. *Evidence*, p. 37.

238. George Pace uses a quotation from Dr John Robinson, *The Times* newspaper, 27 September 1969, on p. 38 of *Evidence*.

239. *Evidence*, p. 39.

240. *Of the Atmosphere of a Church*, J. N. Comper, 1947, for example, of which G. Pace had several copies.

241. *Evidence*, p. 39 and see ref. **104**.

242. *Evidence*, p. 41.

243. *Evidence*, p. 111.

244. *Evidence*, p. 121.

245. *Evidence*, p. 104.

246. *Evidence*, p. 100.

247. *Evidence*, p. 125 (on the other hand tourism itself presents a danger to the Church. See ref. **242**).

248. *Evidence*, p. 63.

249. Royal Academy Architecture – article in *Building*, no. 5 by David Rock, May 1972.

250. *Worship and Architecture*, G. Pace (unfinished).

251. *Evidence*, p. 64.

252. *The Buildings of England – Yorkshire, York and the East Riding*, by N. Pevsner, 1972.

253. *Evidence*, p. 65.

254. As **220**.

255. *Daily Telegraph*, 14 December 1960, in an article discussing the Council for the Care of Churches fourteenth report.

256. Letter from Canon R. Jones to I. F. C. Pace, 12 September 1975.

257. *Evidence*, p. 67.

258. *Evidence*, p. 65.

259. *Daily Telegraph*, 23 December 1968.

260. As **252**.

261. *Evidence*, p. 58. Many of the examples used are from churches under his care.

262. As described in *Design Reports* submitted to the Friends. The only pieces of evidence found were the urns from the corners mounted on pedestals on the cornice (*see* ILLUST. 262) which are now at ground level, opposite the old Prebendal House (*see* ILLUST. p. 4 in *Llandaff Cathedral*, by The Very Revd Eryl Thomas, published by Pitkin, 1986).

263. Barn found by the author and not necessarily known to G. Pace but indicative of similar works in the area.

264. Phrase used by G. G. Pace and quoted in an article about Llandaff Cathedral Organ Arch in *Concrete Quarterly*, No. 35.

265. *Evidence*, pp. 60–61.

266. Ibid.

267. *Evidence*, p. 96.

268. *Friends of Durham Cathedral, 43rd Annual Report*, 1975–76.

269. Ibid.

270. *Lichfield Diocesan Magazine*, Vol. 98, No. 11, November 1975.

271. Ibid.

272. *Concrete Quarterly*, No. 35, October–December 1957.

273. *Evidence*, p. 97.

274. Ibid.

275. As **105**.

276. See various obituaries on G. Pace including *The Times*, 29 August 1975 and *Building Magazine*, 5 September 1975.

277. Quote used in **6**.

278. Extracts from draft notes on George Pace made in preparation for his sermon at Evensong in his new Church at Woolston, 28 June 1970; where in addition to the parishioners, the service was attended by those who had built the church. The various comments on art emanate from a paraphrasing G. Pace made of an article by Christopher Booker in the *Daily Telegraph*, 27

January 1967. Similar extracts are quoted in G. Pace's talk at Leicester Cathedral, 14 February 1967.

279. *Evidence*, p. 15.

280. See **1**. He is quoting from the review in *Punch*, by Lewis Munford, on 'The City in History'.

281. *Evidence*, p. 82.

282. With his encouragement, the Dean and Chapter of Lichfield responded well and agreed to the restoration of the Scott screen in the early 1950s. However, the work had to wait until 1973 when more urgent exterior fabric repairs had been completed.

The other Cathedrals of Salisbury and Hereford were not so lucky – see article in *Country Life*, September 1960.

283. Address to the Friends of Lichfield Cathedral by G. Pace, June 1974, on the occasion to mark the Silver Jubilee of their Cathedral Architect. (See **34**.)

284. *Evidence*.

285. Letter from the Revd Michael Wright Warmsworth to I. F. C. Pace, August 1975.

286. *Building* magazine, 6 September 1974.

287. As **1**.

288. Dr Pat Nuttgens, Society of Architectural Historians Great Britain *Newsletter*, No. 13, November 1975.

289. Letter from the Dean the Very Revd L. Fleming, St George's Chapel, Windsor Castle, to I. F. C. Pace, 29 August 1975.

290. *Sheffield Diocesan News*, No. 10, October 1975, The Ven. Hetley Price, Bishop of Doncaster.

291. Patrick Marsh, Warden, Scargill House, in letter to I. F. C. Pace, August 1975.

292. The Revd W. Field, Llancarfan. Letter to Mrs I. F. C. Pace, 26 August 1975. He also refers to George 'always enjoying our Welsh cakes on his visits'.

293. The Revd John Kent. *The Bridge* (Journal of Selby Abbey Parish).

294. The Revd H. Stapleton – letter to I. F. C. Pace from Hoveton, 31 August 1975.

295. W. E. A. Lockett, University of Liverpool Senior Lecturer on Art and Canon Theologian – letter to I. F. C. Pace, 30 August 1975.

296. Canon Cecil Rhodes, Abbey Precincts, Bury St Edmunds, letter to I. F. C. Pace, 30 August 1975.

297. Patrick Reyntiens, letter to I. F. C. Pace, 1 September 1975.

298. Many used this phrase in letters of condolence to his wife in 1975. For example, Revd W. S. Wilkinson of Clifton, Nottinghamshire, who knew George Pace through the building of Wythenshawe Church (*see p. 217*), and the later work at Clifton, Nottingham (*see p. 146*) where he was instrumental in naming a room in the new extension 'The Pace Room'. Others such as The Revd David Scott of St Botolph's, Boston, who were involved with restoration work, were of much the same opinion.

299. George Howard. Letter to I. F. C. Pace 29 August 1975.

300. John Piper. Letter written to I. F. C. Pace from Henley, 2 September 1975.

301. The Cathedral Church of St Patrick, Armagh

– Regimental Chapel of the Royal Irish Fusiliers: *Appeal Brochure*, 1947.

302. Article in *The Yorkshire Evening Press*, 1950.

303. Article by John Taylor, General Secretary, *CMS Newsletter*, January 1964, No. 267.

304. 'Recent British Church Design: An Agreement to be Radical', by Peter Hammond, in the *Architectural Review*, December 1961. Reviewed in *RIBA Journal* 19 December 1963 where the following extract is quoted:
As long ago as 1952 George Pace's design for a University Chapel at Ibadan marked a decisive departure from the conventions of High Victorian Church planning and several modern churches built by this Architect within the last five years stand out from the general run of recent building by virtue of their simplicity, the straightforward handling of natural materials, and their adaption to the exigencies of the Liturgy.'

305. *Liturgy and Architecture*, by Peter Hammond, 1960, published by Barrie and Rockliff, in which the author says 'it is a building of great simplicity which possesses something of the radiant Poverty that characterizes so many of the finest churches of the last thirty years'.

306. A sculptor admired by Epstein – see George Pace's obituary on Epstein in *Architects' Journal*, August 1959.

307. George Pace refers to this church in his statement on current architecture published in the *St Mark's, Sheffield Appeal Brochure* (undated, but early 1950s), though he made no specific reference to its influence, if any, on his Ibadan chapel design.

308. *New Architecture in Africa* by Udo Kultermann, published by Thames and Hudson.

309. 'Notes on the New Chapel' by G. Pace, 1959 (used as the basis for a press release).

310. Details on the work have been taken from 'A Report on the Rebuilding' issued by the architect in 1955 (published in full in *The Story of the Church* by A. G. Spink, in 1965), which *The Builder* used for the basis of an article, 5 June 1959.

311. See Biographical Introduction (p. 18).

312. *Report on Llandaff Cathedral Restoration, 1949–57* by G. Pace.

313. *Notes on the Restoration, 1949–60*, by G. Pace.

314. *First Impressions of Llandaff Cathedral* – a talk to the Friends of Llandaff Cathedral, July 1950, by G. Pace. Also published in *The Friends Annual Report*, 1950.

315. Architect's report published in *The Friends Annual Report 1954–55*.

316. As **314**.

317. *Western Mail*, 5 August 1960.

318. Ibid.

319. *Report on Llandaff Cathedral Restoration, 1949–57*, by G. Pace.

320. Ibid.

321. As **313**.

322. As **319**.

323. Ibid.

324. Ibid.

325. As **315**.

326. As **314**.

327. As **312**.

328. *History and Architecture of Llandaff Cathedral* June 1959, published by the Dean and Chapter.

329. *Province* magazine, Autumn 1956, Vol. VII, No. 3, p. 77.

330. See notes **313**, **314**.

331. The full list includes – Halberstadt, Etandal, Nuremberg, Manchester Cathedral, Bath Abbey, Chichester Cathedral, St David's Cathedral, St George's Windsor, King's College Cambridge, St Mary's, Wellingborough.

332. See notes **264**.

333. As **328**.

334. Extracts from an article in *British Weekly* newspaper no. 3677, 2 May 1957, by Glyn Simon.

335. Handwritten notes by G. Pace in preparation for his BBC radio broadcast 1957.

336. See **313**.

337. As **314**.

338. In 1988–89 the present Cathedral Consultant Architect, Donald Buttress, reset the panels to form a true triptych, and sensitively repainted the main framework a 'Pace'-type green (in place of the earlier light-blue colour). With a new stencil pattern background on the wall behind in green and black, the total effect is admirable.

Where other new works have been added by yet another architect (e.g. the screen in St Dyfig's Chapel) a sympathetic but misguided attempt to design in keeping with the 'Pace Style' has been made. However well intentioned, perhaps a Society for the Protection of Ancient Buildings approach would have been more appropriate, delineating the old from the new unequivocally, thus preserving absolute integrity to both architects' work.

339. Sermon by The Rt Revd Glyn Simon. An extract is published in *The Friends Annual Report*, no. 28, 1961.

340. *The Guardian*, 8 August 1960.

341. *Llandaff Parish Magazine*, February 1959.

342. *Architects' Journal* – 'A Church in Scotland and a Chapel in South Wales, by Robert Maguire, 21 May 1959.

343 The Cambrian Archaeological Association Conference, Lampeter, Wales 1962 – 'A Practising Architect's Viewpoint' (handwritten notes).

344. Notes on the 'New Chapel' by G. G. Pace, 1959 – (used as the basis for a press release).

345. *Church of England Newspaper*, February 1959.

346. As **344**.

347. *Western Mail*, 28 January 1959.

348. As **345**.

349. *Church Times*, 6 February 1959.

350. Quotation used by G. G. Pace in the introduction to his 'Report by the Architect on the Completion of Sheffield Cathedral' published in the *Official Appeal Brochure*, 1957.

351. Letter from G. G. Pace to Leslie Hunter (Bishop of Sheffield), 3 October 1961 (the commissions referred to were three from the National Trust including a complete restoration of a model estate village, and a £700,000 commission from the North Eastern Electricity Board).

352. Report by the architect on the 'Completion of Sheffield Cathedral' – published in the *Official Appeal Brochure*, 1957.

353. Ibid.

354. G. Pace issued a statement to the Press and spoke individually to several newspapers on these matters – see ref. **158**.

355. *Sheffield Diocesan Review Magazine*, 1960.

356. As reported by G. G. Pace in a statement to Provost intended for public release.

357. Reported in *Church Times*, 23 March 1962 and *Sheffield Telegraph*, 17 March 1962.

358. Mr Arthur Bailey, architect, senior partner of Ansell and Bailey of London.

359. Press release by the architect, 1961.

360. *Yorkshire Post*, 30 March 1961.

361. *Yorkshire Post*, April 1961.

362. 'St Mark's Church', notes by the architect, 1963.

363. 'St Mark's Church, Sheffield.' An appeal for its rebuilding and furnishing (with article by G. G. Pace – 'The New Church' – undated, but evidently around the early 1950s as this is the first scheme).

364. As **362**.

365. Ibid.

366. *Yorkshire Evening Press*, 2 May 1958 on 'York Works at Royal Academy.'

367. As **362**.

368. Ibid.

369. *Sheffield Diocesan Review*, October 1961.

370. As **362**.

371. Ibid.

372. Austin Peter Fawcett, 'Sheffield and the RIBA Festival Year', *Yorkshire Architect*, November 1985. Pevsner describes the tracery to the east and west windows as 'wild' (*The Buildings of England, Yorkshire West Riding*, 1967).

373. As **85**.

374. *The Buildings of England – Staffordshire*, by Nikolaus Pevsner, 1974.

375. 'Shared Church Buildings,' G. G. Pace, published in *Church Building Magazine*, April 1969, No. 27.

376. Ibid.

377. *University of Keele: The Chapel* – report by G. G. Pace, January 1964.

378. Ibid.

379. *University of Keele: Chapel Guide* by G. G. Pace, November 1966.

380. Ibid.

381. In 1943 G. G. Pace prepared a scheme for a layout of the churchyard of St Mary Bishophill Senior including the church itself made into a designed ruin (ref. Bishophill York, see **66** [ii]).

382. *Yorkshire Evening Press*, 9 February 1959.

383. *Yorkshire Evening Press*, 11 May 1959 (letter from the Vicar, Revd. K. C. J. Wilkins).

384. Ibid.

385. *Yorkshire Evening Press* article, 28 November 1959.

386. Since the Sheffield Cathedral extension cancellation due to the costs (*see pp. 173–7*) George Pace appears to be at pains to emphasize that in all his new works the cost is generally significantly lower than works by his contemporaries – without sacrificing the quality of architecture.

387. *The Church of the Holy Redeemer, Acomb, York*. Report by the architect G. G. Pace for the Consecration Service, 12 December 1964.

388. As **252**.

389. *The English Parish Church* by Gerald Randall. Published by Batsford 1982.

390. *Can these Stone Live – Guide to the Church of the Holy Redeemer and History of St Mary Bishophill Senior, York* by K. C. J. Wilkins, (vicar 1939–64). Printed by F. Duffield of Leeds. Undated, but probably written around 1970 judging by the review in *Yorkshire Evening Press*, 13 November 1970.

391. See **328** and p. 158 where quality of light in the Welch Regimental Chapel is so described as necessary for atmosphere, a pre-occupation with G. G. Pace.

392. A review by G. G. Pace of the book *Out of the Ashes* by Basil Spence and Henk Snoek, which was published in *Anglican World* magazine, Issue 21, Vol. 4, No. 1.

393. 'Modern Powerhouses of Faith' by G. G. Pace, published in *Anglican World* magazine, Vol. 1, No. 6. 1961.

394. Ibid.

395. 'Ibadan Cathedral' – report by G. G. Pace, for use as a Press Release, March 1965.

396. *New Architecture in Africa*, by Udo Kultermann, published by Thames and Hudson.

397. Dr Patrick Nuttgens. Society of Architectural Historians of Great Britain. *Newsletter* No. 13. November 1975.

398. Dr Patrick Nuttgens in letter to author, 29 December 1987.

399. As **395**.

400. Interview with G. G. Pace, reported by *The Yorkshire Evening Press* newspaper, 9 January 1965.

401. As **395**.

402. *The Buildings of England – Durham* by Nikolaus Pevsner, 1953.

403. Notes prepared by G. G. Pace for a talk to the Friends of Durham Cathedral.

404. University of Durham Palace Green Library Report, G. G. Pace, 1964.

405. 'Architecture at the Royal Academy' reviewed by R. W. Paine, in *The Builder*, 10 May 1963.

406. Ibid.

407. As **404** – also it is worth noting the layout of the skylight is reminiscent of Corbusier's work at Atelier Ozenfant, Paris (1922–3) or particularly the Salvation Hostel in Paris (1929–33) – but is this pure coincidence? Also there is something of the spirit of the new extensions to Brasenose College, Oxford by Powell and Moya which G. G. Pace considered to be 'one of the most distinguished instances in this country of the placing of a real twentieth century building in the midst of other buildings of all dates, styles and uses, with the twentieth century building taking its place quite naturally and unaffectedly'. (Quotation taken from an extract from the 'York Aesthetic' by G. G. Pace, in the *Yorkshire Evening Press*, 23 November 1962).

408. Society of Architectural Historians of Great

Britain *Newsletter* No. 13, November 1975, obituary of G. G. Pace by Dr Nuttgens.

409. 'New Library at Durham' by Lucien Myers, in *Stone Industries*, July 1969.

410. IAAS Conference 'New Buildings in Historic Areas' report in *Yorkshire Evening Press*, 2 May 1969.

411. Civic Trust Awards, *Yorkshire Evening Press*. 28 April 1972.

412. 'Off with his head' by Roy Gazzard, in *The Architect*, September 1968.

413. Ibid. – quite how this mix-up over planning permission occurred is a mystery: changes required by the engineers to lift and ventilating shafts resulted in an increase in height, and presumably it was the bureaucratic importance of submitting a revised application which was misjudged.

414. Peter Tong, Secretary of City of Durham Trust – *Sunday Times*, 19 March 1972.

415. As **412**.

416. Ibid.

417. As **409**.

419. *Evening Chronicle* (Manchester), 19 September 1961. The vicar was the Revd Wilf Wilkinson who also commissioned later work at Clifton, Nottinghamshire (*see* **298**).

420. *William Temple Memorial Church* – report by the architect, G. G. Pace, 25 October 1965.

421. Ibid.

422. As **419**.

423. As **420**.

424. *Daily Telegraph*, 22 November 1965 and *Architect's Report*, 25 October 1965.

425. *The Builder*, 15 March 1963.

426. *Manchester Buildings*, an Architecture North West publication, Corinthian Press, 1966.

427. *The Buildings of England – South Lancashire* by Nikolaus Pevsner, 1969.

428. *The English Parish Church* by Gerald Randall, Batsford 1982.

429. Recollection by the author of conversation with his father 1965.

430. *Bartholomew City Guides – York*, J. Hutchinson and D. M. Palliser, 1980.

431. *The Buildings of England – Yorkshire, York and the East Riding* by Nikolaus Pevsner, 1972.

432. Ibid.

433. *Northern Echo*, 5 November 1957.

434. In his notes for the Press, 4 November 1957, he says, 'The over-large and ruined clerestory is to be removed together with the gable of the west wall. This immediately faces the tower, and immensely improves its proportions. In future it will take its place as one of the finest medieval towers in the country'.

435. In addition to war damage claim, money was provided by the West German Government.

436. *Yorkshire Evening Press*, 27 April 1968.

437. As **430**.

438. *Yorkshire Evening Press* – Dean Milner White, 5 November 1957.

439. From an article entitled 'The casework of the New Organ' by G. G. Pace, which appeared in the New College Oxford brochure, *The Inauguration of the New Chapel Organ*, May 1969. Also included is an article by Maurice Forsyth-Grant, providing 'An account of the New Organ.'

440. The organ is a mechanical action instrument and represents a radical departure from English organ building as practised in the last hundred years.

441. The casework was designed by G. G. Pace in consultation with the design department of Grant, Diegens and Bradbeer Ltd, who were responsible for the specification and building of the instrument.

442. As **439**.

443. Article in the *Chester Chronicle* by The Very Revd G. Addleshaw, 5 July 1968.

444. Article in *The Ringing World* by G. G. Pace, 12 July 1965.

445. As **443**.

446. Article in the *Chester Observer* by G. G. Pace, 20 November 1970.

447. As **443**.

448. *The Times*, July 1968.

449. *Daily Telegraph*, 30 November 1972.

450. As **444**.

451. Ibid.

452. Article in the *Chester Observer*, 5 July 1968.

453. *Chester Observer*, 14 February 1969.

454. *Chester Chronicle*, 14 February 1969.

455. *Chester Chronicle*, 20 November 1970.

456. *Building*, 9 May 1969.

457. The model is sold commercially as a card cut-out, and was made up by the author in 1979–80.

458 (i). See *'Report of the Society of the Friends of St George's and the Descendants of the Knights of the Garter'*, Vol. IV, No. 10, 1968–69, where an article by G. G. Pace on *'The King George VI Memorial Chapel'* is published p. 421.

(ii). Some additional points were taken from an unpublished report which accompanied the early design schemes in the form of an architect's report entitled *'Notes on the Design'*, 1 September 1967.

(iii). See also articles in the following newspapers and magazines: *The Times, The Guardian, Yorkshire Evening Press, Yorkshire Post* appearing 22 March 1968 and *Building* magazine, 29 March 1969 and 12 September 1969.

459. As **458 (i)**.

460. See *Guide to St Edmund's Church Centre, Sprotborough* by M. J. Jackson, (vicar) and Anthony Stratford, (curate-in-charge), 1969.

461. *Llandaff Parish Magazine*, February 1964.

462. His first entry in *Who's Who* was in 1964. The list was not revised in 1975 and important more recent works not included in this list were: (alterations to churches, etc.) St Sampson's Old Persons Centre and Chapel, York, 1974; (new works) Chester Cathedral, Bell Tower, 1975 (a tape of the new bells rung in the architect's honour was sent by the Dean and played to George Pace in hospital; though he never saw his building finished, and he gratefully relied upon his partner, R. G. Sims to solve difficult problems which arose during its construction) (Hon. Consultant Architect) – to the York Diocesan Redundant Churches Uses Committee, 1969. Hon. member of The Cambridge Ecclesiological Society.

PHOTOGRAPHIC ACKNOWLEDGEMENTS

OPPOSITE
429 Merthyr Dyfan: reordering 1974: new paving and altar table, president's chair, priest's stall, housling bench, churchwardens' staves and light fittings

The following took photographs in the book, or kindly gave permission for photographs to be used:
(*Figures indicate illustration numbers*)

A. & C. Photography (Belfast) – *274–8*
Bridgeman (Lichfield) – *179*
British Rail (York) and Castle Howard Estates – *204*
Building Images (Cambridge) – *134*
Catcheside (York) – *32, 133*
C. M. Cooper (Sheffield) – *223*
Cousans (Organ Builders) – *340*
Cosira (Rural Development Commission) – *58*
S. Dale (Liverpool) – for Rushworth & Dreaper Ltd – *224*
The Vicar and Wardens of St Edmund's Church, Doncaster – *406–9*
Elsam Mann and Cooper Ltd (Manchester) – *71, 94, 99, 248*
Elsam Mann and Cooper (EMC) (Liverpool) – *3, 5, 69, 96, 140, 226, 357–9, 376, 379–80, 392*
Furse & Co. – *201*
C. H. Gillam Ltd – *213–6*
D. Jenkins (Cardiff) – *31, 33, 148*
Keele University Library Photographic Department – *350*
Jim Kershaw (York) – Half-title, title page, *6, 8–10, 26, 30, 65, 87, 100, 117, 126–7, 130–1, 144, 235, 257, 263, 279–80, 292, 324, 327, 330, 334–5, 339, 368, 385, 390, 416, 417a*
A. F. Kersting (London) – *401*
P. E. Knight (Wellingborough) – *51*
Manchester City Council – *107*
Marshall & Co. (Nottingham) Ltd – for Furse & Co. – *27*
E. Meadows (Luton) – *82*
Millar and Harris (London) – for Mowlem & Co. Ltd – *405*
S. Newbery (London) – *306, 325, 328, 337–8, 393*
George G. Pace – *119–20, 122, 166, 211, 219, 234, 242, 261–2, 266–7, 404, 410*
Mrs Norman Pace – *425*
Peter G. Pace – *15, 23, 25, 35–7, 40–1, 44–7, 68, 116, 132, 135–6, 142–3, 150, 154, 161, 162b, 167, 174, 176–7, 181–2, 202, 212, 215, 227a, 236–7, 240, 264–5, 268, 375, 383, 394, 431*
Pitkin Pictorials Ltd (Andover) – *59, 306, 309, 310–11*
E. Parker (Manchester) – *222*
B. Pring – for G. R. Orrin – *429*
The Royal Commission on Historic Monuments (York) – *384*
Walter Scott (Bradford) – *206*
Ronald G. Sims – *54–5, 70, 74–7, 79, 81, 83–6, 95, 97, 102–3, 113–4, 145, 147, 156, 159, 162a, 170–1, 187, 205, 217–8, 227–8, 285–90, 341–7, 349, 351–3, 356, 360, 378, 411, 413, 415, 421, 432*
Henk Snoek (London) – *42, 101, 105, 247, 361, 363–4, 366–7, 369–73*
Fred Spencer (York) – *Front Cover, 19, 21–2, 24, 34, 38–9, 43, 56, 60–3, 66, 78b–c, 115, 121, 123, 125, 137–9, 141, 153, 164–5, 168, 172–3, 175, 178, 180, 183–4, 186, 191–3, 196, 197a–b, 198, 231, 238, 241, 245–6, 249, 258–9, 422, 434–5*
Spooner Group – *331–2*
S. T. P. Photography (Cardiff) – *316*
Thomas Photos (Oxford) – *194–5, 386–8, Back Cover*
Stanley Travers (Cardiff) – for the Dean and Chapter, Llandaff Cathedral – *Frontispiece, 12, 169, 190, 203, 232, 233, 269, 272, 291, 298–303, 307–9, 312–5, 419, 433*
Stanley Travers (Cardiff) – *57, 317–9, 321–3*
Tunbridge Ltd (London) – *67*
Tunbridge Ltd (London) – for John Mowlem & Co. Ltd (London) – *399–400*
Watts and Co (London) – *188a–b*
Western Mail – *295, 297*
G. B. Wood (York) – *13*
F. E. Wrightson (Kirbymoorside) – *418*
Yorkshire Post – *207*
Yorkshire Evening Press – *48, 64, 199, 427*
York Minster Library – *355*
Yorkshire Television – *4*

430 Selby Abbey: sketch design for church-wardens' stave, 1968. Ink on paper 5 × 1½in (12.7 × 3.7cm)

431 Llantilio Pertholey: Wrought-iron pendant light fitting to nave, 1973

432 Caerwent: chancel
reordering, 1965: altar,
altar rail, candlesticks,
hanging cross

INDEX

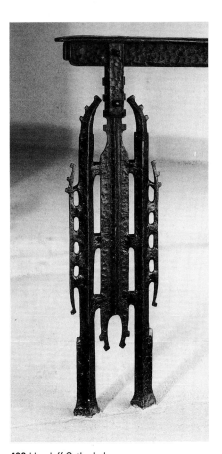

433 Llandaff Cathedral, Welch Regimental Chapel, altar rail support in wrought iron, 1956 (*see also* ILLUST. 303)

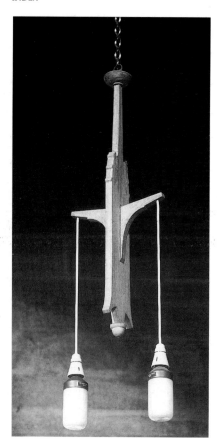

434 Lastingham: oak light fitting, 1951

435 Lastingham: organ
screen: lower section in
oak, 1959. Upper section
in softwood, 1963

APPENDIX I

Typical working drawings

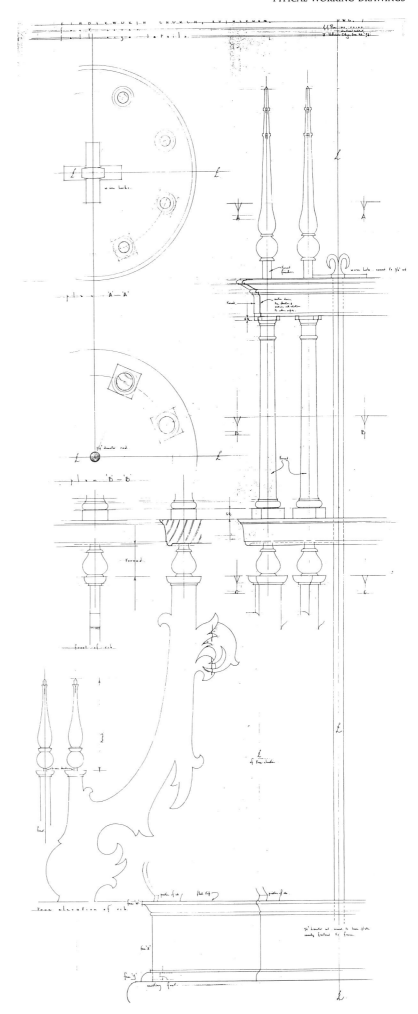

436 Kimberworth: font cover. Full-sized working drawing by G.G. Pace, 1956, pencil on detail paper – 29 × 72in (74 × 183cm). Compare with photograph of completed work (*p.84*)

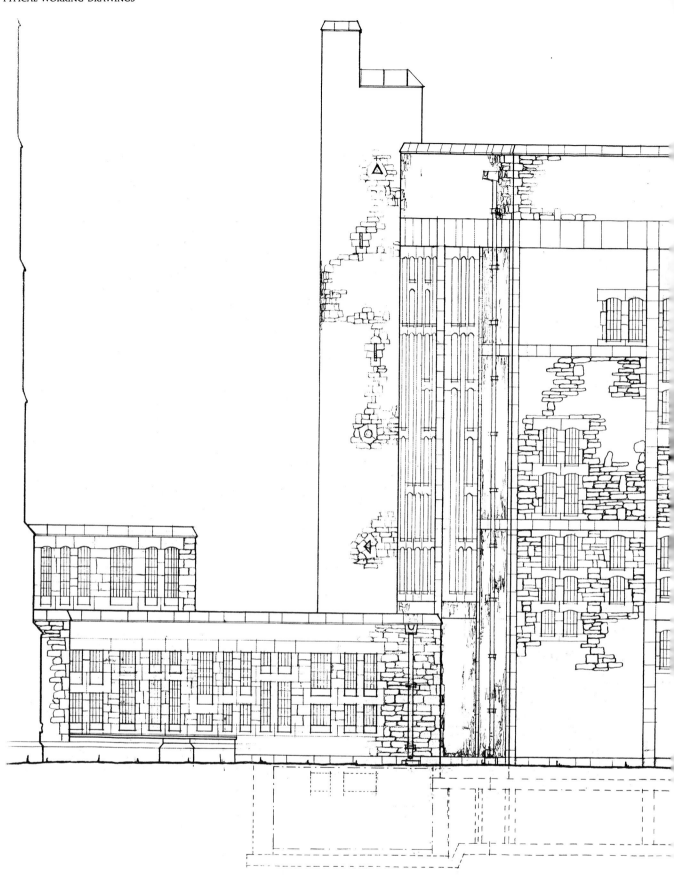

437 St Mark's, Sheffield; proposed rebuilding Scheme II, 1956. Extract from office working drawing no. 51 (ink on tracing paper – actual size) showing the south elevation. Materials are reinforced concrete frame clad in fairfaced ashlar stone, with infil panels built up in random rubble stone. (Compare with model, exterior view, illustrated on *p.182*)

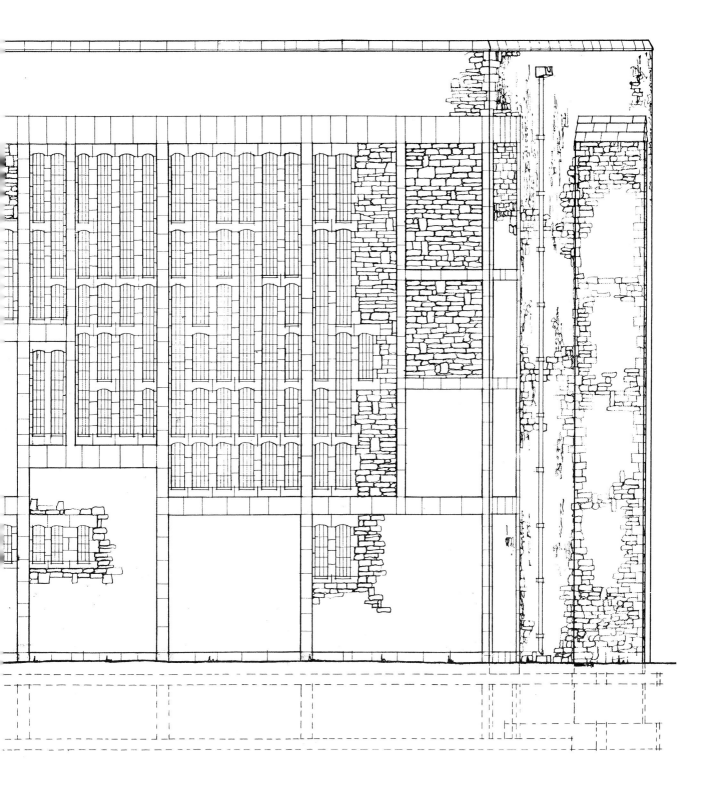

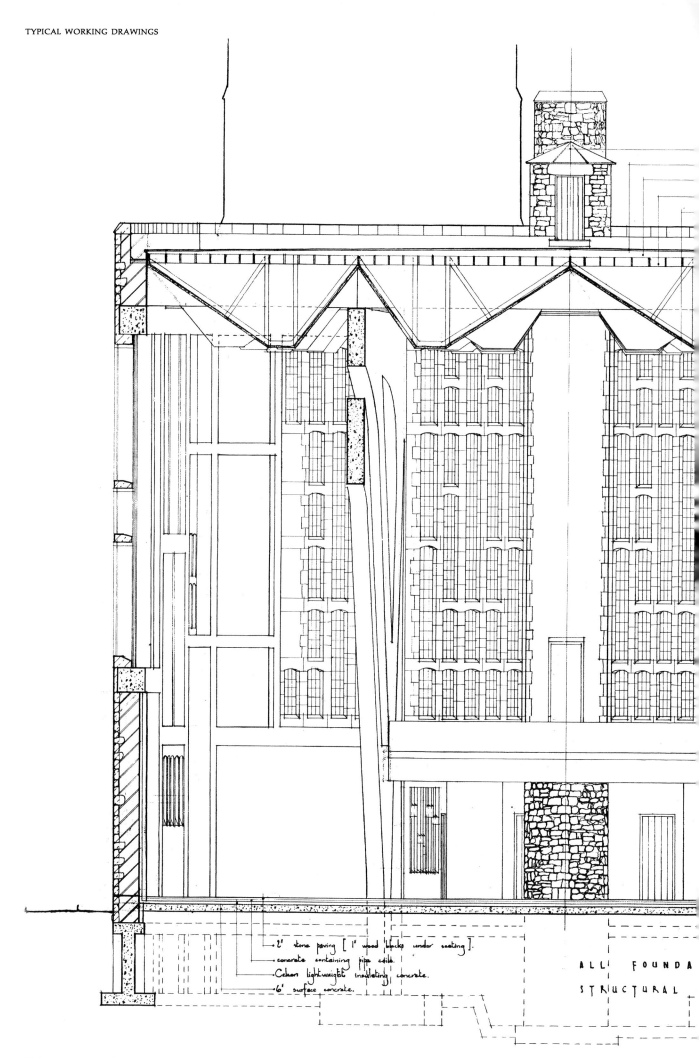

2' stone paving [1' wood blocks under seating].
concrete containing pipe coils.
Celcon lightweight insulating concrete.
6' surface concrete.

ALL FOUNDA
STRUCTURAL

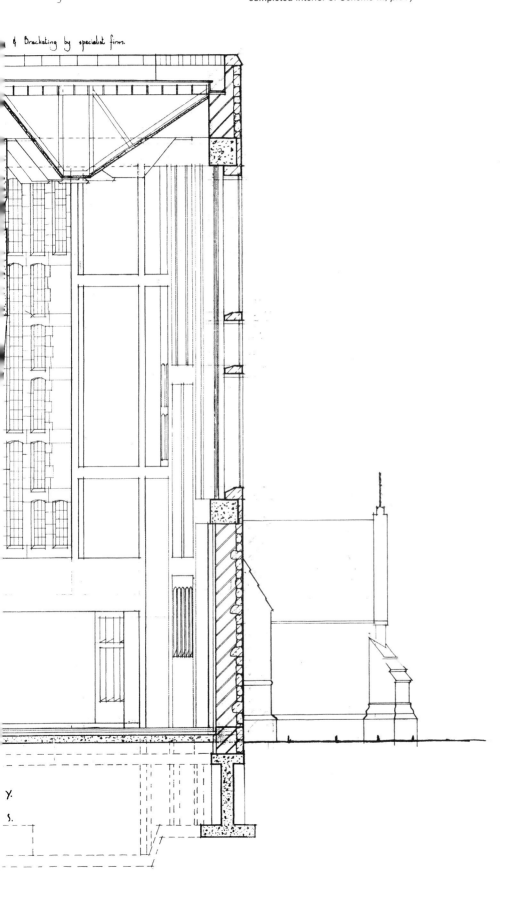

438 St Mark's, Sheffield; proposed rebuilding Scheme II, 1956: extract from office working drawing no. 52 (ink on tracing paper – actual size) showing an interior section through the building looking west. Concrete frame exposed internally with smooth plaster finish and panels between with rough-faced plaster. (Compare with model, interior view *p.180* and the completed interior of Scheme III, *p.61*)

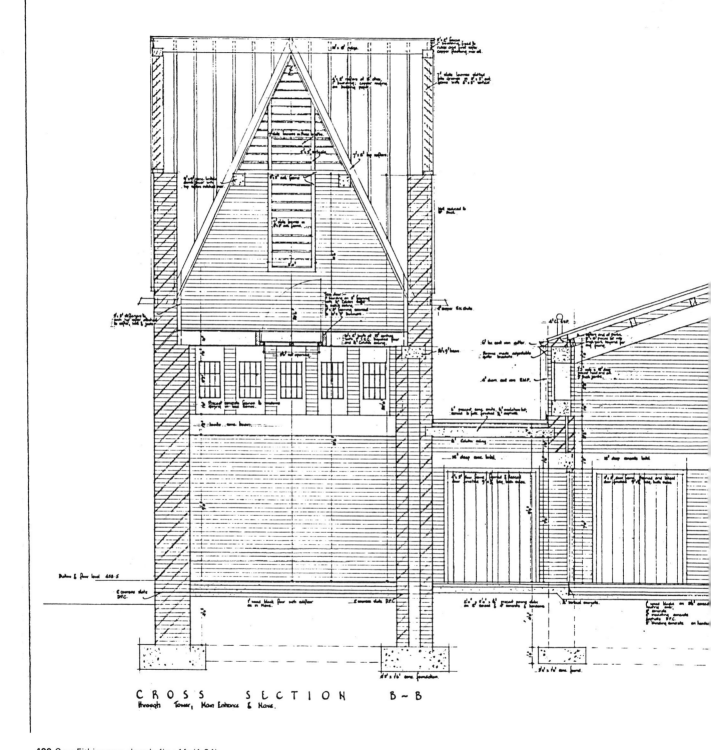

CAER EITHIN CHURCH SWANSEA.
half inch details.

CROSS SECTION B~B
through Tower, Main Entrance & Nave.

439 Caer Eithin: new church. ½in : 1ft (1:24)
scale office working drawing no, 15, showing a
cross section through the tower, main entrance
and nave. Pencil on tracing paper, 47 × 29in
(120 × 74cm) November 1960. Compare with
photograph of completed building (*p.230*)

DWG. No.~ 15

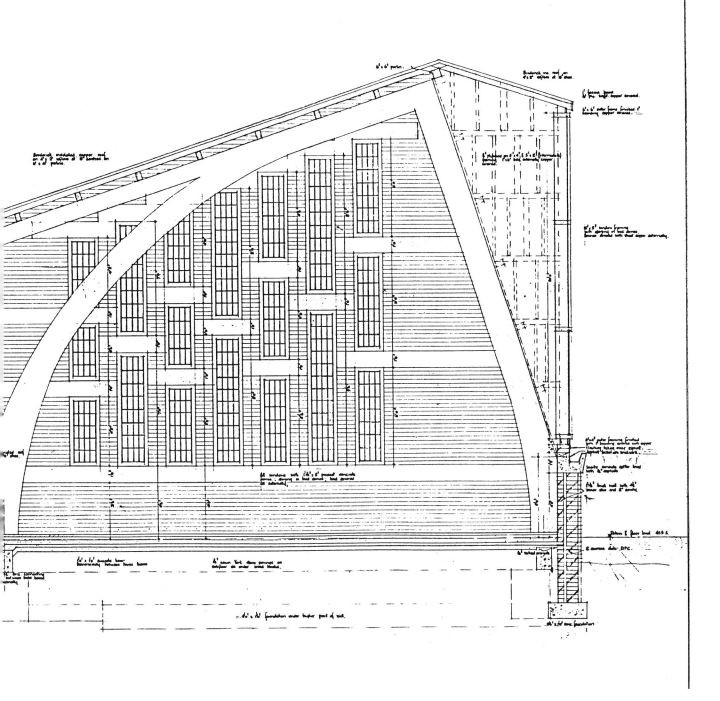

S T.   M A R K'S   C H U R C H . C H A D D E R T O N

Half Inch Details – Section B-B

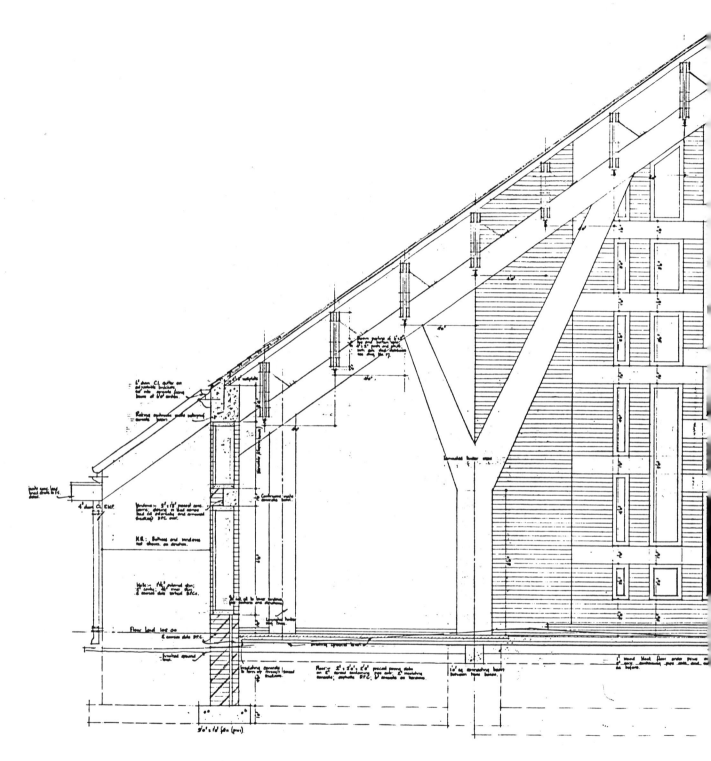

S E C T I O N   B - B . looking towards the altar.

440 St Mark's Chadderton, New Church: ½in :
1ft scale office working drawing no. 25,
showing a cross section looking east towards
the altar platform. Pencil on tracing paper
44 × 27in (112 × 69cm), 25 March 1961.
Compare with illustration of completed building
(*p.62*)

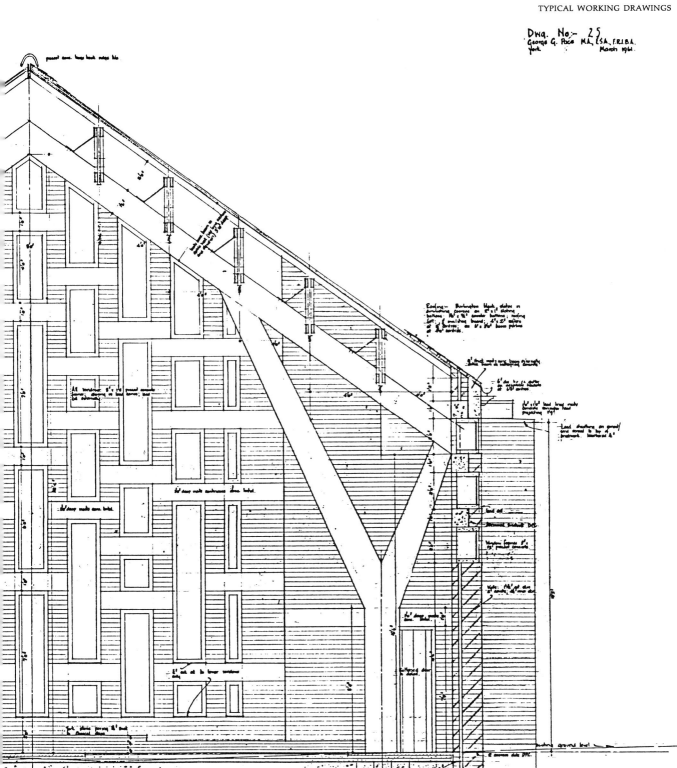

In the sketch (handwritten notes):

Patrington York[63]
steps. over tower
arch. S. Transept.

font △

The nave arcade
& aisle vaulting
appear to have furnished
Temple Moore with a model
for Sledmere Ch.
(S. porch & chamber over too).

7.10.43

441 Leaf from a sketch book: Patrington, Yorkshire, October 1943, pencil, 5 × 7in (12.7 × 17.8cm), published in *The Builder*, 1944

Back cover illustration: St George's Chapel, Windsor: King George VI Memorial Chapel: wrought-iron entrance screen gates from north quire aisle, 1969